D1453399

Saint Paul

Emil Bock

Saint Paul

Life, Epistles and Teaching

Floris Books

BS
2506
.B6213
1993

Translated by Maria St Goar

First published in German in 1954 as *Paulus*
by Verlag Urachhaus. Fourth edition 1981.
First published in English in 1993 by Floris Books

© 1981 Verlag Urachhaus Johannes M. Mayer
GmbH & Co KG Stuttgart
This translation © Floris Books, Edinburgh 1993

All rights reserved. No part of this publication may be
reproduced in any form without the prior permission of
Floris Books, 15 Harrison Gardens, Edinburgh EH11 1SH

British Library CIP Data available

ISBN 0-86315-130-2

Printed in Great Britain
by Cromwell Press Ltd. Wilts.

Contents

Acknowledgments

Unless otherwise stated, all quotations from the Bible are from the Revised Standard Version with kind permission of the Division of Christian Education of the National Council of the Churches of Christ (New Testament © 1946, 1971; Old Testament © 1952).
Where the context required it, Bock's own translation has been translated into English. These are marked *B* after the reference.

Preface

It is not the intention of this book to add yet another volume to the great number of books on Paul already existing in academic and theological literature. Nor does it wish to focus on the Apostle of nations as a 'theologian.' More than the great rulers and successful figures of the past, Paul belongs to the history of humanity in its totality. Paul does not merely represent one important stage in the history of human *consciousness;* he is one of its greatest creative catalysts and innovators.

In so far as this is true, he is of the same rank as Moses. Moses was more than a lawgiver and Paul was more than an Apostle. Filled with the Spirit of God, both were divinely appointed pioneers of a new consciousness. Out of the dreamlike, visionary consciousness preceding egohood, Moses had to pioneer the development of wide-awake thinking. His mission of consciousness was symbolized in the journey through the wilderness undertaken by him as the leader of his people since the new stage could only be reached by means of a temporary impoverishment. Paul's mission was an opposite one. With the fire of the heart, he was supposed to enkindle the light of a new vision in the darkened, impoverished thoughts of the head. His apostolic journeys were an image of this task. He did not lead a nation already in existence by virtue of blood ties; instead, by carrying the word and power of Christ to all the nations, he created a new community based on spiritual kinship.

With this seventh volume of the 'Contributions to the Spiritual History of Humanity,'* a certain correspondence to the second volume, *Moses,* has been attained. As in the description of Moses, here too, in at least a number of important examples, it was the author's concern to lend expression to the wealth of characterizations given by Rudolf Steiner in order to place before our age the secrets of human consciousness and human evolution which

* For English editions available, see *Bibliography.*

proceed in mighty phases.* The topical, heuristic significance of what he said pertaining specifically to Paul and the Damascus event will probably be fully understood and valued only in the future.

In a deeper sense, it is a current concern to occupy oneself with Paul. During the first 1500 years of Christian history, the figure of Paul stood waiting in the dark background. Today his time has come. The message of his destiny and mission are directed to our age. It is a matter of the greatest spiritual import to listen to it.

When the so-called 'modern age' dawned — anthroposophy speaks of the beginning epoch of the consciousness soul — a bright ray of light from the spirit of the age fell on the figure of the Apostle of nations. It is fraught with significance that this happened simultaneously at several focal points of humanity's life. Luther, the representative of Central Europe's Reformation, was not the only one who orientated himself in his religious experience and perception towards Paul. Born in the same year as Luther, Raphael along with other important figures of the Renaissance culture that flourished in southern Europe, looked upon Paul as the brightest star of the new age. Rudolf Steiner impressively pointed this out.[1]

Tragically, only Luther's point of contact with Paul has found a continuation, and moreover in an extremely one-sided manner. In his will nature, Luther did allow the moving spirit of the age to take hold of him; hence, he held up the torch of a more liberated future. In his thinking and feeling, however, he was more a man of the intellectual and mind soul whose unfolding in the Middle Ages had preceded the age of the consciousness soul. As if it were the devil in person, he recoiled violently from the new thinking which was to turn the epoch then beginning into the era of natural science and technology. His religious sentiments adhered to a few verses of the Letter to the Romans which

* Concerning the verbatim quotes from lectures by Rudolf Steiner, it must be pointed out that one is dealing with texts that were taken down in shorthand. They were neither checked nor stylistically altered prior to publication by the lecturer. The formulations were left the way they originated orally, borne of a specific human constellation in each case. Slight inaccuracies in the transcript must also be taken into account.

Luther, however, interpreted solely on the basis of his personal experience. Thus, instead of discovering in Paul the sounds of the broadly based, impersonal word, Luther placed his own image into Paul. A Paulinism arose that became reduced to a personal striving for redemption. Eventually many voices made themselves heard in modern Protestantism that protested against this distortion. Thus, William Wrede wrote in his book on Paul in 1905:

> Luther's soul struggles were the model for his conception of Paul ... Luther asks: How does individual man surmount the tortuous uncertainty of whether redemption, the forgiving of sins, applies to him personally as well? Paul does not have the individual person in mind at all; the question of the personal certainty of redemption therefore has no significance for him. In his teachings, he is not considering the individual and his inner psychological processes; he always ... refers to all mankind.[2]

And Otto Etzold observed:

> The question in those days was: How do I find a merciful God? Luther found the answer to that. Today, however, that answer is no longer timely. The cosmic clock has advanced. Today, everybody is hungering after an answer to the social question.[3]

The voices of those theologians who are calling for a more complete and true picture of Paul, surpassing that of Luther, are lost in the wind. Generally, the basic attitude of Protestant church life remains determined by the one-sided and partly erroneous relationship of Luther to Paul. This misconception, born of medievalism and a lack of joy for thinking, which Luther brought to bear on Paul, the great liberator of thinking, had particularly tragic consequences.

The southern Paulinism which lived in the great artists of the Renaissance and, in a certain manner, in Pope Julius II as well, was not expressed in the form of thoughts, but through artistic creativity. Raphael, who was a truly modern person, a representative of the dawning consciousness soul — and he was not alone in this — considered Paul the new seer; the one who, through the Damascus experience, has broken through to new vision. If one considers the fact that such an ideal image played its part in the origin of great works of art, the figure of Paul impresses us quite differently when seen in the cartoons which Raphael drew as the patterns for the carpets of the Vatican,* in the painting, *Saint Caecilia,* and finally in the central figures of *The School of Athens,* one of whom represents Aristotle but at the same time *Paul in Athens.* Standing in front of the majestic statue of Moses by Michelangelo,† we can imagine how Moses and Paul were supposed to have confronted each other as the two dominant figures in the unfinished monument for the tomb of Julius II; we shall thus behold vast perspectives of humanity in this image.

The Paulinism of the Reformation which arose in Central Europe has fallen victim to a tragic one-sidedness and constriction. The southern Paulinism of the Renaissance remained without a continuation. When will our age of the consciousness soul in its advanced state of apocalyptic drama — which, in its hour of birth, already reached out once towards Paul — utilize the help that can come to it from the Damascus light of the Pauline impulse? One can say that Rudolf Steiner placed his whole life and activity into the service of this concern for the future. The present book is meant to be a humble contribution towards the same goal.

Emil Bock

* London, Victoria and Albert Museum.

† Rome, San Pietro in Vincoli.

Background

1. Conversion and Initiation

The trinity of the great apostolic figures, Peter, Paul and John, has always been seen as a cosmic calendar representing the major stages through which Christianity has to go in its historical development. Christianity is successively Petrine, Pauline and Johannine, in the classic description of Schelling, for instance, at the end of his *Philosophie der Offenbarung*.

It is not fitting, however, simply to equate the eras of Peter and Paul with the epochs of Catholicism and Protestantism, no more so than to take for granted the existence of Johannine Christendom when it increasingly seems that Protestantism has concluded its historically progressive task. Certainly, the three great Christian streams, the Catholic, the Protestant, and the third which is at its inception, may well have a special affinity with one of these apostolic figures as patron saint and inspiring genius. However, the Christian mysteries and realities always have an infinitely broader scope than appears at any given time on earth. This is why we cannot by any means conclude that the specific developments of Christianity personified in Peter and Paul, are completely fulfilled today and exhausted in their potential.

The Petrine element may be thought of as having become manifest through the ecclesiasticism of the first two Christian millennia. Despite the role which the Letter to the Romans, for example, played for Luther and the Protestant development, hardly more than a first hint of the Christ mysteries concentrated in the figure, destiny and work of Paul has begun to be realized historically. And although, in our own time, the Johannine ideal must be consciously seized as the essential one, its illumination will remain above us for a long while yet, barely penetrated, an element of the future.

It could be one of the most timely and elevated tasks for our age to comprehend Paul anew in the dawning rays of the Johannine epoch, to understand him more correctly and comprehensively and to make him fruitful for Christian life.

Strictly speaking, the Protestant era leaves behind an open question, the clarification of which can represent only a first step towards a fresh understanding of Paul in the modern age. This question is contained in the striking contrast between Luther and one who may well be seen as the most prominent and noble embodiment of Protestantism in our time, namely Albert Schweitzer, the great theologian, medical doctor and musician. Luther believed that he was justified in appealing to Paul in all matters, although he passionately drew a dividing line between faith and knowledge, and designated thinking as the 'Whore Intellect.' Albert Schweitzer, on the other hand, concluded his book on Paul with the splendid thesis: 'Paul is the *patron saint of thinking* in Christendom.'*

One of the main reasons why the era of Protestantism could be no more than a first start towards Paulinism is that the four to five centuries that lie behind us were simultaneously the time of emerging materialism in humanity's world view, in science and all cultural endeavours, and of the slow extinction of all insights into the supersensory realm. With the Damascus event, on the other hand, a *supersensory event* of the first order stands not only at the beginning of the Christian part of Paul's life, but at the beginning of the spread of Christianity and, thereby, at the inception of world-encompassing Christendom as a whole.

Today, humankind has arrived at its Damascus. The confusion and agitation of our age drive human beings to the threshold of a great inner decision. Will humankind simply continue to harden itself more and more in the materialism of the earthly senses? Or will a small pioneering few at least open their eyes to the world of the supersensory, which, like the roaring surge of the sea, has

* 'Paul has safeguarded for all time the right of thinking in Christendom ... The result of this first appearance of thinking in Christianity makes it possible to establish for all time the certainty that faith has nothing to fear from thinking ... Paul is the patron saint of thinking in Christianity. All those who believe that they are serving the Gospel by the destruction of free thinking in the faith of Jesus must hide before Paul.' *(Die Mystik des Apostels Paulus,* pp. 365f).

long been breaking over us, and where the majestic light-form of Christ appears in a new apocalyptic proximity? In the flashes of revelation issuing forth from the storm-clouds of our times, those who yearn to experience a Christ who is present and timely can find their Damascus. Thereby, they can also rediscover the Damascus event of Paul and the full nature of his apostolic work for the nations.

It has been customary to designate the Damascus experience as the 'conversion of Paul.' If this expression were accurate, the development of Protestantism, particularly since the appearance of Pietism that considered 'conversion' its basic religious element, would indeed have led close to Paul. But even a quite superficial comparison between what happened in Paul's case and the conversion experiences of Pietism can show us that it could only be a semblance of Paulinism which lifted the Protestant era beyond the Petrine element of the medieval church.

The 'conversion of Paul' was above all a new 'enlightenment,' an expanding and elevating transformation of his consciousness. The light that opened his inner eyes was never again extinguished. The great glory became for him an inexhaustible source of enlightened insight and inspiration. It is clear that the hour of Damascus not only changed Paul's *consciousness* but also his *being*. He was a different man from then on. Yet, the new nature was the consequence and fruit of the new consciousness.

In contrast to this, the concept of conversion, as seen later on especially in Pietism, actually refers only to a certain change in the *nature* of man. For the kind of thinking prevalent today, it would even signify a weakening and devaluation if the emphasis were placed more on the side of consciousness than on that of human nature. It was in this way that Pietism arose in the seventeenth century as a reaction of human emotion and will against the predominance of the head-element which ruled in contemporary rationalism. One can decipher from the pietistic concept of conversion how the notion of 'personal piety' — the 'religious individualism' justifiably necessary for that age — emerging more and more strongly towards the end of the Middle Ages, faced the danger of ending up in religious subjectivism. Combined with fear of death and judgment, hope for the heaven of eternal bliss was the chief motivation for the almost methodical intensification of the mood of sinfulness, atonement and renewal that was characteristic of Pietism. A variety of ecstatic conditions of bliss were attained through these disciplines, occasionally even linked to a feeling of enlightenment, which were then taken to be fruits of 'conversion.' We must not fail to acknowledge that by virtue of the earnest longing for Christ that always prevailed, this Pietism of conversion created many lasting values. This holds true, for example, in the lyric and artistic character of the religious songs of the Moravians, or the moral and social nature of the charitable institutions set up by August Hermann Franke. Still, the Luciferic, egotistic striving for bliss, pervading proselytism almost everywhere, made itself clearly felt. It did so in the sectarian arrogance of the 'saved' as opposed to the 'unconverted,' in the inflexible proselytism with which the converted individuals believed they had to save others from eternal damnation. *Prior* to his Damascus experience, Paul had indeed been the prototype of fanatical proselytism, eager to persecute heretics. Later on, when he journeyed as an apostle, his message was as generous and liberal as possible.

Nevertheless, it is not impossible to find a connection between the Damascus experience of Paul and the conversion experiences of Pietists in a spiritual-historical sense. In Pietism, we are dealing with a last dilution and distortion of an inner stream which, in the final analysis, goes back to initiation practices of the mysteries of pre-Christian humanity. It is from this stream that the miracle of Damascus has to be comprehended as well. It is one of those primordial experiences through which the Christ event struck like lightning into the stream emerging from the mysteries of antiquity. Since the extinction of early Christianity, ecclesiastical theology chose to ignore the mystery practices of former times despite the Messianic anticipation which must be attributed to them in all instances where they had not already fallen into decadence. In the end, people no longer even knew that genuine initiation practices had ever existed. So it came about that instead of evaluating the Damascus event by understanding its religious-historical roots and source, it was measured against the last remaining phenomena (of former religious experiences) which had turned narrowly and selfishly human.

The Damascus experience of Paul represents a most significant halfway stage on the path leading from pre-Christian mystery practices to Pietism, between initiation and conversion. It is therefore useful to make clear that even Pietism cannot be fully understood if we do not recognize in it a distant reverberation and tentative re-emergence of ancient mystery beliefs, even though the Pietists themselves would not have wished to be interpreted in this way. We find a telling sign of this connection wherever the idea of a 'path,' a systematic inner discipline, leading through certain steps, dominates the religious life. In this category belongs the English Methodist tradition in all its different versions, which, through intensive communal Bible reading, praying and the singing of hymns, intends to lead to 'revival.' Here, particularly, the systematically practised moods of repentance and remorse evoke conditions of group ecstasy. We note the same features, for instance, in the booklet, *Die Ordnung der christlichen Wiedergeburt,* by the Swabian theosophist and church father, Friedrich Christoph Ötinger, where the stages passed through by the striving soul, rising up step by step to the attainment of grace, are described in pictorial manner. Doubtless, in some places, there still existed pure and genuine traditions of the 'mystic path,' free of religious egoism and suggestiveness. One can recognize these where the impatient urge for a change of attitude is replaced by a thoughtful, impersonal striving for a transformation of consciousness. Here, the ideal is not ecstatic bliss but grace-filled enlightenment, and the path to it does not lead through forcefully induced moods of repentance but through purification and meditation. The movement of the *Gottesfreunde* (Friends of God) or the Rosicrucians, accused of heresy by the church, were the final descendants of an ancient, genuinely esoteric Christianity, which had transmitted the courage and patience to embark on those paths which had as their goal the spiritual service of humankind, not the soul's personal deliverance. The enlightened, visionary consciousness from which, for example, Jakob Böhme, the shoemaker from Görlitz, or Johann Georg Hamann, the 'magus of the north,' derived their theology and wisdom of life, had also arisen from certain moments of 'conversion,' but these moments were experienced more like a mission to go out among the people, less like a personal redemption and rapture.

The true ancient initiation practices existed until the beginnings of the last pre-Christian millennium, particularly in Egypt and Asia Minor. At that time, the era of humanity's awakening to I-consciousness was still distant. Through the initiations, carried out in the mystery temples, specially chosen individuals were made capable of being active among their people as teachers and leaders. In reality, through such initiated individuals, the gods themselves guided the still immature human beings. The initiates were lifted so far above the human level that they could recognize the thoughts and aims of the gods and could act as tools of the divine will.

The neophytes who had been selected for initiation had to undergo a long, strictly prescribed sequence of instructions and soul trials through which their consciousness and whole existence became completely transformed. After a long preparation, designated as *catharsis,* meaning cleansing or purgation, there finally arrived the real act of initiation that was connected with 'enlightenment' *(photismos).* The traditional manner in which this act was carried out consisted of the following steps. Laid into a grave, the neophyte was placed into a deathlike sleep for three days by the hierophant. When this time was over, he was called back into life as a changed person. The temple sleep was a condition between sleep and death. Although, in principle, it was something quite different, it can be compared with the hypnotic deep sleep which to this day can be imposed by hypnotists on their mediums. We must realize that the inner possibility and justification for such procedures has not existed for a very long time, since the conditions of the ego in the human being have changed fundamentally. For centuries before the turn of time, this was the reason why the initiation mysteries were becoming progressively more invalid and decadent: humanity was developing from the pre-ego state towards a slowly budding egoity and maturity which turned all hypnotic practices into unjustified encroachments on the individual.

During the three days, the soul and spirit of the disciple were lifted out of the body and placed among the entities of the spiritual world. Due to the preparation which had preceded this, the soul did not remain enveloped by sleep in the sphere to which it had been translated. Rather, it attained to the blessed state of moving in full consciousness amongst the gods for whom it had been chosen as an instrument. Moreover, after its 'rebirth,' the thread of divine consciousness was not lost for such a soul. The awakened one rose from the grave as a bearer of a higher consciousness, consecrated by 'awakening' and 'enlightenment.'

A twilight of the gods came over the ancient mysteries during the last pre-Christian millennium. This, together with the depressing mood issuing from it, was the reason for the longing anticipation of a Messiah which suddenly arose among all the nations. If the gods ceased to send those individuals to men who were capable of functioning in their place as leaders among humanity, would not eventually the 'sheep be without a shepherd'?

Where they continued to exist at all, the initiation practices fell into decadence owing to misuse of the magic powers which formerly had been exercised properly and justifiably. In the place of initiated messengers of the gods, demon-possessed despots and megalomaniac Caesars emerged who demanded divine homage. Only in obscure channels, without any further striving towards public influence or power, the genuine mystery stream flowed on; for example in Eleusis, where spiritually justifiable initiations were carried out as late as the beginnings of the Christian era. What had existed until then as a mystery, as a carefully guarded secret, now had to be transformed into artistic creativity and philosophic-scientific knowledge in order to be conveyed publicly to humankind. Hence, the dramas created by Aeschylus, and the philosophies of Pythagoras, Heraclitus and even Plato, were transformed mystery-knowledge and mystery-powers.[4]

A submerged, indirect continuation of the genuine ancient mysteries did exist, however, and wondrous treasures of human spiritual life have blossomed forth from it. We can ask ourselves what passed through the souls and minds of formerly great initiates when they were reincarnated during periods when the twilight of the gods had already darkened over the mystery centres and the miracle of initiation was about to be extinguished. Did the fruit of earlier initiations not have to mature again and become visible at some time in present destiny? Rudolf Steiner once described how although they were not initiates in that particular incarnation, the figures of the great prophets of the Old Testament were still personalities in whom soul and spirit maturity, acquired in former lives, did come through again at certain turning points of destiny.[5] If a blow of fate struck them, the former initiation experience emerged as if from unfathomable depths, and on occasions, like a mysterious symbolism, situations arose that resembled those undergone previously within the precincts of a mystery temple. It is possible to recognize from the descriptions of the Old Testament or the Apocrypha how King Hezekiah, the prophet Jonah, even Jeremiah, for example, succumbed to a condition resembling the temple sleep without any apparent cause. This condition, however, resulted in the beginning or intensification of prophetic activity. In Hezekiah's case, it was an illness, the nature of which Isaiah recognized. In Jonah's case, the deathlike three-day period was concealed behind the mythical image of the large fish which swallowed the prophet and then let him go again. Thus, in the lives of the prophets, there could occur inner calls, sudden changes expressed in awakenings and conversions not expressly caused by an initiation as such. Nevertheless, such events belonged to the most wonderful fruits and gifts of which humanity could still partake in later ages as an inheritance of the former mystery centres.

The paramount and, at the same time, in regard to humankind's evolution, the most significant example of an initiation by destiny, in which the mystery experiences of ancient times bore fruit for the present, took place in the immediate surroundings of Jesus. The Gospel of John tells us of Lazarus' sickness and death and his resurrection by Christ from the tomb at Bethany.* Lazarus'

* In *Christianity as Mystical Fact,* published in 1902, Rudolf Steiner already gave the key to the 'Resurrection of Lazarus' by indicating its connection with the ancient initiation mysteries.

illness was not of an ordinary kind; it was certainly not brought about by normal causes. The powerful impressions and shocks that Lazarus, who was none other than 'the disciple whom Jesus loved,' experienced as a witness of the deeds and destiny of Christ, made it possible for the spirit transformation, undergone in former times and cultures, to arise again in the soul as if centuries and millennia had all at once been erased. The mystery of death and resurrection, which, long ago, turned a human being into a messenger of God, suddenly appeared again. And it was not only present because it arose out of the past; now, its most sacred culmination cast its mighty shadow out of the immediate future, for, in only a little while, Christ himself would die and rise again. Lazarus was not placed into the deathlike temple sleep by a hierophant who appeared before him in human form. The destiny which made him a disciple of Christ and a witness to his power, was his true hierophant. He died through the unprecedented enhancement of the Christ will, which, as the 'three years' drew to a close, became manifest as if in spiritual light and flame. Then it was Christ himself who took charge of the last act of the initiation drama. Like a hierophant, he stepped up to the tomb at Bethany and brought Lazarus to life again. With this deed, Christ affirmed this special joining of the ancient stream of initiation with what was to be inaugurated through his own dying and resurrection: Lazarus, transformed and having become 'John,' would bestow on humankind as the fruit of his most sublime awakening and enlightenment the Gospel of John and the Patmos Apocalypse.

So the ancient secrets of the initiation mysteries, arising anew, were passed down through the centuries. However, the possibilities for this to happen increasingly diminished as humankind hardened into its bodily existence, and human minds, filled almost exclusively with earthly things, became more and more impermeable. Weak and often distorted vestiges of the traditions may have played a part when, in Protestant Pietism and related movements, the methodical 'path of salvation' was invoked and the experience of a 'conversion,' a 'rebirth' or 'revival' was striven for. It may be that in a few individuals distant emotional after-effects of their experiences in former lives lingered on, or it could be that more general subconscious reminiscences of past ages when initiations took place now came into play.

Paul's Damascus experience belongs in the general line of development outlined above. To see this event as a kind of 'conversion' assumes that everything preceding this moment in Paul's life was wrong and evil. In that case, not only could he not have responded to this revelation and illumination, which struck him like lightning, in any receptive mood of self-knowledge and remorse, but there would have been nothing present in his nature to make him worthy of the favour of this revelation. The lightning flash would have struck him at random through a divine act utterly beyond our powers of conception. In that event, Paul could only have experienced an inner reversal, a 'conversion,' *after* the decisive occurrence.

It was, however, not by chance that the heavens tore open before Paul in the hour of Damascus. *Everything* in his life up to then had been a preparation for this moment. Had he not obeyed his innermost convictions with radical consistency, dedicating to them all his abilities? We shall see later that Paul was even led to believe he was serving the Christ, the Messiah as he pictured him, though his activities. It was not his fault that his early striving for insight had brought him to views which history had already made obsolete through the incarnation of Christ and everything ensuing from it. As we gradually come to answer the question of who Saul of Tarsus actually was, we shall realize that the lightning flash at Damascus did not strike blindly. As the result of all his destinies and activities in former lives, he brought along in his nature the prerequisites for receiving the grace-filled call of illumination granted him in the hour of Damascus. It is not true that he only now turned into one of the leading lights of humanity; he had already been one since time immemorial. In the light of the Christ sun now united with the earth, a flower of humankind blossomed in him which had already been bud, blossom and fruit many, many times for the sake of humanity. Like the miracle of Bethany, the miracle of Damascus, albeit in a quite different manner, represents the culmination into the earthly Christ sphere of pre-Christian mystery practices and contents. In so far as this is true, the great illumination which happened to Paul can be designated as an 'initiation,' the only difference being that the preparation immediately beforehand had not taken place within the confines of a mystery centre. Destiny itself had seen to this preparation, and indeed not only in Paul's present incarnation.

In the religious-historical interpretation of the Damascus event, we take another important step if, aside from the *transformation of consciousness,* we focus also on the *change in being* which this event called forth in Paul.

In an all-inclusive sense, Paul was a 'different human being' after Damascus. People often employ the quite pretentious phrase that someone or other, even the one who is speaking, has become 'a different person' — in a positive sense — through this or that experience. The great majority of such soul transformations are of brief duration and quickly give way again to former habits. There is absolutely no doubt, however, that, even in the hardened humans of today who have become almost incapable of true receptivity, inward transformations are possible; transformations through which eternal values are wrung from destiny — human encounters and blows of fate, artistic experiences and especially genuine religious experiences. But wherever somebody states with justification that he has become 'a different person,' one could just as well describe the change that has occurred in him by saying that he has become *more himself.* For we are not necessarily identical with our true being. We are fragments. What is visible as our physical form represents only our sheath. Only a fraction of our real being, which is of a supersensory nature, has actually entered into incarnation such that we can say: It is *here.* In particular, we are still overshadowed by those higher members of our being which are yet to be cultivated and unfolded in future rounds of earth's and humanity's evolution. We therefore indicate something absolutely real when we speak of our higher ego, our true self. Like a genius, this, our higher being, makes itself felt above and in us at high points of our life. Above all, when the soul is permeated by a mood of profound devotion and piety due to having felt something elevated, holy and divine, it is as if an angel were approaching us. Our own higher being is, after all, still 'in heaven' where the hierarchies dwell who bear it protectively in their midst. What we can say of a child's whole nature — namely, that it is still under the protection of its guardian angel — can also be said of the adult human being regarding the higher members of being. In this sense, a genuinely religious life always brings about a transformation of one's being, and we need not even speak here of the specifically Christian element. The human being makes room in his soul for his higher and true self, for his angel. It is in this direction that we must seek for the reality that underlies the experiences of revival and conversion that occur in Pietistic and related movements. It is easy, however, for an illusory element to interfere. First of all, this can happen because of religious egotism. Secondly, it can occur through the ideas suggested by traditional religion which have become unclear and impoverished, namely, in talking of experiences of God or Christ when, initially, it is merely a matter of experiencing the angel accompanying one's own soul. Where this illusory element enters in, it not only deprives the religious experience of its truth but of its power of transformation. People today, however, are not so easily fooled by the religious claim to be a reborn and 'new person.'

The initiations of former times accomplished more than an incorporation of a person's own higher self. They brought about transformations of an individual's nature that permitted higher hierarchical entities to speak and act through that man. This is the reason why the higher initiates also called themselves *theophoros,* or 'bearer of God.' For great leaders of humanity, however, the secret of incorporations by higher beings still existed well into the Christian era even after the ancient initiation mysteries had come to an end. Such incorporations enabled these individuals to act out of higher inspirations and faculties. Here, we touch upon a special secret of history and human guidance. For certain individuals transcending the general human level, it is not only possible to work together with angels, archangels and other hierarchical beings; there also exists a law of a certain union and cooperation among the geniuses of humankind themselves. This is an enhanced level of something like the case of a person who actualizes the inner connection to a revered dead person to such an extent that, finally, helpful thoughts and forces flow from the latter.

Rudolf Steiner indicated something of these mysterious spiritual laws which can be observed during such transformations of being. He spoke of the personalities whose task is to implant certain new faculties into the nature of man, but who accomplish this not in a doctrinal manner but by means of their own life and example. These individuals — usually referred to by the Oriental term *Bodhisattva* — are:

> the leaders of humanity who attempt to bring about this development to a high degree upon themselves, for only through the most sublime faculties the most sublime heights can be attained.

Such individuals can be recognized by the fact that they undergo a great inner transformation around the middle of life :

> It can be seen that, especially in the period between the age of thirty and thirty-three, a mighty change occurs in such a person's life ... that one cannot recognize in him prior to this point in time, prior to this transformation ... The earliest period of his youth is always totally different from the condition into which he has changed between age thirty and thirty-three. Thus he prepares himself for a lofty experience that will consist of the following: the old ego departs and a different ego enters. It can be an individuality like that of Moses, of Abraham, of Elijah. This new individuality will then be active in this body for a time ...[6]

Here we draw close to special destinies, ordained by Providence, wherein there come about transformation experiences of which it can be said in a very special sense that, here indeed, somebody has become 'a different person.' As a protective patron and spiritual helper, a great person allows a still greater one to enter into his being in order to carry out even more perfectly the service which he is supposed to accomplish for humankind.

This law of the transformation and elevation of being is exemplified by the destiny of Lazarus. When Christ called Lazarus, resting in the grave of Bethany, back to earthly life, the dead man did not only turn into a different person in the sense of a great enlightenment transforming his consciousness. Henceforth, a different genius dwelled in him: the superhuman, almost angelic ego of John the Baptist that also represented the individuality once incarnate in Elijah. After John's decapitation by Herodias, his genius-like ego had accompanied and overshadowed the paths and deeds of the twelve Apostles as their protective group spirit. During the mystery event of Bethany, this ego descended and united itself in a special manner with Lazarus when the latter returned to his bodily sheaths following the call by Christ. It was then that Lazarus turned into John, for, henceforth, like a higher angelic ego, the Elijah-John genius dwelt in him together with his own 'I.'[7]

From this direction, a light can even be thrown on an event which, as the pivotal point of all human history, introduced not only the transformation of being in a great human individual but that of all humankind and, beyond that, the transformation of the whole Earth. Notwithstanding the monumental uniqueness of this event, it is the sublime archetype of all future occurrences of 'conversion,' awakening and enlightenment. It is the event of the baptism in the Jordan through which the human being, Jesus of Nazareth, became the bearer of the divine Christ-being. The most mature individuality at the disposal of humanity received through John the Baptist, who baptized him in the Jordan, a form of initiation in which, as in a focal point, were contained all the initiations of earlier times. As a 'different man,' he emerged from the waters of the stream. Now, he was worthy of becoming the *Christophoros,* the Christ-bearer. He was allowed to receive into himself as a supportive, contributing force not only an angel, an archangel or another hierarchical being, or one of the individualities of genius who are leaders of humankind; he could exemplify in his life what Paul would later express as: 'Not I but Christ in me.' It was, after all, not an alien being whose bearer he became. Christ is the most sublime genius of humanity itself, the 'god of men.' His 'I' is the sum of all true human egos, the higher 'I' of all human beings. In a sense that surpasses all dimensions, it applies to Jesus of Nazareth also that through the baptism in the Jordan he had became both 'a different person' and, to the very highest, most divine extent, himself.

In this manner, we have found our way towards understanding the transformation of being which occurred in Paul through the Damascus event above and beyond the transformation of consciousness. As in the cases of Jesus of Nazareth and Lazarus, in Paul's case too, the event occurred between the ages of thirty and thirty-three. Through the lightning flash of illumination that fell on him, Paul, too, not only became a 'different man' in the sense of becoming 'more himself.' He also became the bearer and vessel of a higher being. We shall leave open the question as to whether one of the higher geniuses of humanity became the helping spirit pervading him as was the case with Lazarus. It is certain that in him too, though not in the unique manner of Jesus' baptism in the Jordan, the process took place that he later expressed in the words: 'Not I but Christ in me.' For the only place in the New Testament where Paul himself described the Damascus event — the descriptions of the Acts of the Apostles are stylized, after all, by Luke even where the text is purported to be the direct speech of Paul — refers to the fact that in the hour of Damascus the secret of a permanent, illuminating and strength-bestowing presence had begun in Paul: 'When it pleased God to reveal his son in me ...' (Gal.1:15*B*).

On the question of conversion and initiation in Paul, Steiner has this to say in one of his lectures:

> Paul had had abundant opportunity to inform himself, by observation, of the events in Palestine that were associated with the personality of Jesus ... Paul was a man who could not be persuaded of the meaning of the Christ impulse by evidence of the physical senses, but who could be convinced only by a supersensory experience. And the supersensible experience that came to him cut deeply into his life — so deeply that from that moment he became another man. It is indeed possible to say that Paul had become an initiate ... The very fact that the figure of Paul stands at the summit of Christian tradition ... is like a challenge to man to resort to supersensory knowledge. In a sense, this is the assertion that

Christianity cannot possibly be comprehended without having recourse to knowledge that has its source in the supersensible. It is essential that we should see in Paul a man who had been initiated into supersensory, cosmic relationships ...[8]

2. The Framework of the Acts of the Apostles

In the structure of the New Testament, the texts which prominently feature Paul, namely Acts and the Pauline Letters, or Epistles, occupy a humble position. The summits of revelation, elevating us beyond the normal human level, tower up at the beginning and end of the New Testament scriptures: the Gospels — a whole mountain range of light-inundated heights — and the Revelation of John. Between these, the Acts of the Apostles and the Letters appear like a low-lying valley in which only human experiences, thoughts and actions seem to be present. In particular, Acts relates what took place in the human surroundings of those who, after Golgotha, felt that they were again completely on their own. In the Letters, we hear the voices of those now fulfilling the task of gathering and leading the Christian congregations as best they could. It goes without saying that in Paul's Letters, too, only a human being was speaking. After all, how was it possible to sustain the lofty level on which each word of the Gospels proclaims the human incarnation of a supreme divine being? And how could the spiritual force, which revealed itself from the open heavens when the seer John became witness to the speech of the angelic trumpets, be already effective here?

The Acts of the Apostles appear as both an end and sequel to the Gospels, and the divine actions of the three years culminate here in the human story of early Christianity. The Letters of the Apostles follow — in their most far-reaching moments, a prelude to the Apocalypse, a striking of the spark which is to produce in time a mighty conflagration.

These middle texts of the New Testament focus on the consequences and handing on of the three years' divine work, in so far as they transmit the destinies and words of the principal witnesses to those years, especially those of Peter and John. In a modest way, the scenes concerning John at the beginning of Acts supplement the Gospel of John. The Letters by John are the most beautiful and intimate anteroom to the temple of the great trials revealed to us in Revelation. On the other hand, those belonging to the actual circle of the twelve Apostles have a minimal share in Acts as well as in the Letters. Paul, the stranger and opponent who did not share in the great events of the three years, stands right in the foreground. Those who had seen and heard the Lord, who had lived with him and accompanied him on his unassuming journeys, reach beyond the human level through their nature as witnesses.

But how does that stranger attain the prominence that he has in the middle section of the New Testament, even compared to Peter and John? Does not Paul's pre-eminence attach even more of a purely human character to the biblical scriptures between the Gospels and Revelation? We certainly do not deny the higher spiritual source of the holy scriptures if we open our hearts to the unassuming human character of its middle part: namely, the simple novelistic telling of the apostolic destinies, especially Paul's, together with the human style and temperament of the Epistles, again particularly those that Paul addressed to the congregations. The stream proceeding from the event of Golgotha pours into the human realm, seeking universal humanity.

The question posed by the New Testament's twofold middle section, however, does finally lead to the following insight. The framework of the 'holy scriptures' would not include Acts and Paul's Letters if the Christ event itself were not taking an important *new* step beyond the Gospels. The fundamental revelation of Christianity is not concluded with the death and resurrection of Christ. The witnesses to the first Christ events, proclaimed to us by the Gospels, were the twelve Apostles. Paul, who earlier had been a hostile persecutor, becomes the *first witness of a new Christ event* which has its start as the Christ impulse begins to take hold of and penetrate humankind.

A transition between the two stages, a prophetic preview of the impending future, was represented in what the restored circle of the twelve lived through and experienced on the morn of Pentecost.

The Christ had died and risen again for all human beings, indeed, for the future of the whole earth. Henceforth, whether or not fate brought a person into conscious connection with the

Christian stream, no living human being would remain untouched by the consequences proceeding from Golgotha. But the more human souls grow into a waking consciousness supported by thoughts, hence, into egoity, the more they are dependent on consciously grasping the mysteries of Christianity. The reason for this is that the present-day development of consciousness, if left uncontrolled to its own devices, increasingly separates and isolates man from everything supersensory, therefore particularly from all divine aspects. For many centuries now, human consciousness has been subject to the destructive allure and suggestion of matter, the purely earthly element. Not willing to admit the darkening of their consciousness, because of pride in the progressive technological and scientific mastery of the material world, modern society is only gradually becoming aware of having fallen from childlike innocence and closeness to God and realizing that it is only with the greatest difficulty that a religious life can be maintained *side by side* with the brainpower of modern civilization. The consciousness of modern man is turning unchristian, if not anti-Christian, and therefore Christianity must begin to influence the continuous development of consciousness itself. An attitude of perception and consciousness must be attained that does not limit itself to the sense world — either denying the world of the supersensory or assigning it to a realm of pious belief *aside* from knowledge — but which strives vigorously for a comprehensive and, at the same time, truly Christian world view. 'Christ' is then no longer merely a dogmatic article of faith, but instead the central content of an insight in which thinking and will, head and heart, are active in equal measure.

Humanity is not abandoned to the fulfilment of this task. Not only for his *existence,* but for his *consciousness* as well, a seed of redemption is mercifully available. It is the secret of the second Christ event, the *parousia,* the full unfolding of which runs its course through the first three millennia of Christian history, especially from our present age onward. The formulation, 'the Second Coming of Christ,' which does not occur at all in the New Testament scriptures, widely led people to expect an instantaneous future event, perhaps even one appearing physically. What it really refers to is a process of growth that experienced its germination soon after the resurrection and ascension of Christ but which has to mature into a major force when humanity faces the crises brought about by the evolution of its own consciousness.

The first Coming of Christ, bearing on the *existence* of man, took place on the level of earthly physical reality, a profound concession by the deity in response to human beings whose power to see the supersensory had already dimmed. The new Coming of Christ, on the other hand, takes place in the supersensory realms. Humanity will sleep through this event; it will be misunderstood in its effects, perhaps even turned into its opposite, if, by then, the breakthrough to a new *consciousness,* a consciousness which also encompasses the world of the supersensory, is not attained. When our materialistic, earth-bound consciousness reaches its fulfilment, an event that applies to our present age, the new proximity of Christ will be present so powerfully in the spiritual realm that through the Sun nature of his being the blind spiritual eyes of men can once again be endowed with sight. In the midst of the darkness of human consciousness, the miracle of light can come about, namely, that humanity experiences the new Coming of Christ. This is humanity's Damascus hour.

In the days of early Christianity, a number of ecstatic groups, particularly the Montanists, awaited the imminent physical return of Christ who, they believed, would then subject humankind to the Last Judgment. But hidden from human eyes, the new Coming of Christ had already taken place in its first germinal state. Before the gates of Damascus, Paul became its first witness. The Pentecost experience of the Apostles was already a fulfilment but it was still more a prophecy and promise. For inasmuch as the Resurrected One began to send out the Holy Spirit, he brought about the possibility of Christianization and redemption for humanity's spirit, consciousness and thirst for knowledge. Damascus was a new beginning and yet also a first unfolding and fulfilment of what had arisen amongst the disciples at Pentecost as an overwhelming vision of the future. Accordingly, Paul was the leader and guiding spirit on the path to renewal. His figure and proclamation will attain its full significance only when, in passing through its crisis of consciousness, humankind begins to share in the Second Coming of Christ. Paul is not the first Christian theologian and creator of a Christian system of teaching as is often assumed, but the first to bear and radiate the redeemed and illuminated consciousness. No matter, then, that the scriptures in the middle of the New Testament seem human by comparison with the Gospels and the Apocalypse. Through the light of Damascus, man tears himself away here from the cogencies of matter; he becomes master of his consciousness and, only thereby, truly Man. The secret of human freedom arises radiantly as a gift of the Resurrected One who reveals himself anew to humanity.

Since the third Gospel and the Acts of the Apostles are written by the same author, an intimate tie exists between the Gospels and the scriptures in the middle of the New Testament. A most astounding overlapping of causes is connected with this. Luke, a Greek doctor, of whom legend relates that he was also a painter, was a disciple of Paul. As is discernible in Acts, Luke in many instances accompanied Paul on his apostolic journeys and also stood by his side during the latter part of his life in Rome. Luke did not belong to the twelve disciples. It is possible that he was one of the group of seventy followers, of whom the Gospel speaks as a wider circle of disciples, but in any case, unlike Matthew and John, he did not have so close a share in the 'three years' that this participation could have induced him to become an evangelist. Mark, too, did not enjoy such a close participation but during the time when he was a disciple and aide to Peter, the spark of the Pentecost experience infected him so that he, too, was drawn into the bright awakening that made it possible for Peter, after the event, to survey the miracles of the 'three years' finally with understanding. Luke became the pupil of Paul, one who had participated even less in the 'three years,' who indeed had passionately rejected any share in it. Nevertheless, Luke's discipleship must have turned him into an evangelist. The Damascus flame of enlightenment gripped his soul and — paradoxical as it might at first seem — shed light not only on the 'three years' but also on the birth at Christmas, the childhood and youth of Jesus. Does this not lead us to conclude that through the

Damascus glory, Paul, who had so vehemently objected to the recognition of the incarnated Messiah in Jesus, learned to acknowledge the secret of the Incarnation itself and to understand, in retrospect, the events of the life of Jesus and the 'three years'? Thus, the unassumingly human middle part of the New Testament proves to be the fountainhead of the superhuman Gospel word.

When we take this into consideration, it becomes more revealing to follow the step from the Gospels to the Acts of the Apostles in the composition of the New Testament. In the introductory sentences that are like a prologue, the author of Acts presents his text as the continuation of what he had been able to describe in his Gospel. Notwithstanding all the similarities which, like golden threads or motifs, run from one book to the other, a clearly discernible difference of substance and style does exist between Luke's two books. In contrast to the hymnlike solemnity, which manifests the Gospel's revelatory character, the style of Acts possesses the humblest proximity to man. Here we are dealing with a text that can certainly be numbered among the classic reports of history in ancient literature. The purpose is not so much to reveal as to narrate. In simply enumerating the things that happened one after the other, narration is the life element of Acts. The regular recurrence of the same phrases in reports of departures from one place and arrivals in another could even be experienced as monotonous if it were not a device for expressing the basic mood of the forward flow, inherent in historical evolution like a river with many turns and rapids.

In the transition from the Gospel to Acts, what appears at first to be a descent from the superhuman level to the plane of mere human events is in reality an enhancement. The Gospels describe the incarnation of a supreme divine being entering into the world of humanity, ever more deeply and completely taking upon itself the physical destiny that has to be borne by the human being. Easter, then, was by no means the solemn final act in the life of Jesus; the Ascension did not signify a return into a world beyond. Christ's incarnation-will, directed towards the earth, did not cease. The Acts of the Apostles follows the same incarnation process and describes how it now continued and expanded beyond a single human entity and into the whole of humankind.

History is a profound mystery. In man, the experience of history presupposes a certain maturity and strengthening of inward independence and egohood. The young child is as yet unable to experience history. It lives in the dimension of fairy tales and myths which hover above the earth as does the soul of the child itself. In order to experience history, humankind must first discover itself, having fully arrived on the earth. Likewise, humanity could only develop a true awareness of history after it had completed the transition from the Orient, the realm of its childhood and nearness to God, into the Occident, hence into individual egoity. In the past few centuries, it was an error fraught with danger to consider the Gospels as historical descriptions in the customary sense. The more people interpreted them biographically and historically, the more the Gospels were lost to them. Owing to their nature, they reach above the level of history, they are 'meta-historical.' This does not imply that they do not contain true history. They picture what actually took place, but in most cases they describe the point at which the occurrences still hover between heaven and earth, where they are only on the verge of penetrating fully into the physical plane. It is not until the scenes of the Passion and Golgotha that the Gospels unequivocally flow from the super-historical on to the historical level. This applies particularly to the first three Gospels; in the Gospel of John, contrary to the views prevalent in Protestant theology, everything does possess significant biographical and historical concreteness. Thus, in a variety of ways, a process of enhancement runs its course from the Gospel of Matthew to that of John, leading ever more powerfully into the sphere of history and the level of incarnation.

This process continues in the transition from the Gospel of John to Acts. It only seems that an impoverishment takes place as the sublime heights recede. In reality, the mystery secret of history now begins to exert its full effect. The Gospels descend from heaven to earth. The Apocalypse breaks through again from earth to the heavens. The Acts of the Apostles along with the Letters allow us to perceive how heaven fully permeates earth. Henceforth, the divine flows along in the stream of earthly history.

In the Bible as a whole, we observe the emergence of three great circles, arising as if out of a spiral. The life of the people with their twelve tribes is followed by the life of Jesus in the circle of the twelve disciples. This in turn is followed by the life of the 'church,' that part of humanity which is Christianizing itself and which, according to John's Revelation, consists in the archetypal phenomenon of twelve times twelve thousand; meaning, partial communities of a cosmic wholeness that merge into a cosmically complete community. Three biographies follow one upon the other none of which is merely human. They are connected to each other by a variety of correspondences and mirror effects thereby allowing us to recognize the same canon of conforming images. Thus, each time, the contrasting drama of an infanticide stands at the beginning. At the point when the life of the people begins fully to unfold, the Pharaonic infanticide takes place in Egypt, the one from which the child Moses is saved. At the outset of the Gospel stands the Herodian infanticide which fails to strike down the child born in Bethlehem. On the third level, the corresponding attack of the opposing powers is revealed in the persecution of the Christians, beginning with the stoning of Stephen and the Herodian-Caesarian deeds of hate to which, first, the oldest apostle, James, and later the great numbers of Christian martyrs fall victim. Who represents the newborn child that escapes from this infanticide?

The Acts of the Apostles describe a biography of a higher kind, not that of a single person but one of a community. Unlike that in the Old Testament, however, it is not a community of blood ties but one inaugurated by the spirit. Thus, the biography depicted by Acts is the correspondence in humankind to the folk element of the Old Testament. We watch the nations of the world develop into members of a being whose course of life takes place before our eyes.

In two Gospels, the Christmas stories stand at the beginning, unfolding their magic all the way to the description of the Baptism in the Jordan. In Luke, the scenes of the birth and childhood, irradiated by heavenly glory above all in his Gospel, correspond exactly to the stories in Acts of the Ascension and Pentecost. Pentecost is the natal hour of the being whose life is to be narrated. It is clear that a fundamental difference of mood characterizes the two pictures painted by the same artist: side by side stand the world of the child and that of the grown man tested by the trials of fate. Furthermore, what the Baptism in the Jordan represents in the Gospel, in Acts is the Christ-encounter of Paul before the gates of Damascus.

In the new Christ development which embraces all humankind, three wellspring events stand out in the first half of Acts, — Pentecost, Damascus and, between them, the stoning of Stephen.

The polarity between Pentecost and Damascus is at the same time that between Peter and Paul. The Pentecost experience of the disciples occurs at early dawn in an enclosed room. What is experienced individually by the Apostles remains embedded in the community. The Damascus event of Paul is directed to an individual and occurs at noon under the open sky. The contrast of within and without, which dominates the scenery of both settings — the landscape of the sacred Cenacle on Mount Zion and that of the border zone between the hot mountainous desert and the fresh garden-like Oasis of Damascus — also characterizes the content of the experiences. A miracle of the inner soul dawns in the Apostles; an irradiation of the Resurrected One, taking hold of the cosmic circumference of the earth, opens the inner eye for Paul. In both instances, even the external position of the sun reflects the content of the experiences. At sunrise, something like an awakening comes to Peter and the other disciples. An intensified memory shows them what they have actually experienced during the three years and what sort of future message and view towards a coming spiritual community will result from it. Paul suddenly looks into the etheric world, which, as the spiritual Sun sphere, weaves and shines behind the light of the fully risen sun of daytime. The Pentecostal event allows ancient spiritual forces to come alive one more time in these souls, especially in Peter: the speaking in tongues that overcomes them restores ecstatic possibilities, which have already died down in humanity, in the service of a new beginning. The vision, on the other hand, that is born in Paul is a future faculty of soul that will awaken as a quite personal force in many individuals once the new coming of Christ is one day accepted by humanity. Sent far ahead of his time, Paul is the firstborn herald of a future humankind that will be awakening to vision.

The martyrdom of Stephen lies between Pentecost and Damascus as the third wellspring event of early Christian life. In Stephen, made visible as if by an inner sun, the higher being of man lights up; presence founded completely on itself. His opponents behold his countenance shining 'like the face of an angel' (Acts 6:15). The human ideal, revealed to them in utter harmony, arouses rage in the hate-filled persecutors. What had been the innermost purport of Greek culture, namely, the development of the true harmonious humanness, was fulfilled here through devotion to the Resurrected One. Stephen had been born a Jew but his homeland and mother tongue were Greek, as was his name which means 'wreath.' What the Greeks wished to express when, in their athletic contests, they placed a wreath to mark the elevated humanness of the winner, became reality in Stephen.

In Stephen's great speech as well as in the words with which he dies, the whole past is concentrated into the present. With his address (Acts 7), the quintessence of the whole Old Testament is incorporated into the New Testament. And those sublime contents of the New Testament that belong to the past are even now made a part of this moment through the words that Stephen utters as he is being stoned. It is as if the words of Jesus, spoken on the Cross and reported by the Gospel of Luke, were resounding once again from his lips: 'Lord Jesus, receive my spirit' and 'Lord, do not hold this sin against them.' (Acts 7:59f).

In the triad of Pentecost, the death of Stephen, and Damascus, the basic configuration of Acts becomes visible. The first three of four great acts find their high point in these. The same structural order that underlies the main Christian sacrament as the Reading of the Gospel, the Offertory, Consecration (or Transubstantiation) and Communion is followed in its structure by Acts.

The first part, corresponding to the reading of the Gospel, contains the events of Ascension and Pentecost. At that point, above all, a message and call went out to the Apostles. First, a riddle was posed to them which they confronted helplessly. In the first instance, the event of the Ascension, through which they were meant to become witnesses of how the Resurrected One poured himself into the earth's circumference as the 'Lord of the heavenly forces upon earth,' filled their souls with the feeling of having been completely abandoned. This marked the cessation of the blessed gifts that they had experienced for forty days in their association with the risen Christ. At Pentecost, they could begin to comprehend Christ's expansion into earth as the issuing forth of his being. In a jointly shared vision of the future they beheld the human beings who, through their apostolic service, would find the way to Christ through the coming ages. This promising spiritual perspective penetrated their hearts like the *reading of a gospel.*

The following passage from Rudolf Steiner's lecture, 'Whitsun: the Festival of the Free Individuality,' throws light on the visionary and prophetic character of the Pentecost experience:

> On this day of the Pentecost festival, time-honoured in their region, they who were first to confess to and understand the Christ impulse were gathered together. And their souls were lifted up to higher vision, they were summoned, as it were, by what is presented to us in the picture of the 'rushing mighty wind,' to turn their gaze on what was yet to happen, on what would await them when, with the fire-impulse they had received into their hearts, they should be living on this earth ... in future incarnations.
>
> And there is portrayed before our soul the picture of the 'tongues of fire' which descended upon the head of each of those who participated and confessed to Christ, and another tremendous vision revealed to them what the future of this Christ impulse is to be. For gathered together and beholding in spirit the spiritual world, these men, who were the first to understand the Christ, felt as if they were not speaking to people near to them in space or time: they felt their hearts borne far, far away, among the different peoples of the earth-sphere, and they felt as if something lived in their hearts which was translatable into

> all languages and which could be brought to the understanding of the hearts of all men. In this mighty vision of the future of Christianity which rose before them ... they felt as though surrounded by those who, out of all the peoples of the earth, would understand the Christ in future times. And they sensed this as if they would, one day, have the power to proclaim Christianity in words that would be understandable, not only to those directly near them in time and space, but to all men on the earth who, in the future, would encounter them.[9]

The second part of Acts stands in a twofold sense under the sign of the *Offertory*. It is only now that the text fully assumes the historical character that is its own. History commences but it does so as a sacrifice, an offering. The first developments of congregations, in what were certainly quite small circles, were supported by *voluntary* offerings which, extending even to the external ownership of property, made possible a communal life. From the Essene practices, followed by people in many matters of life style and ritual, the budding community adopted the principle of joint ownership. Aside from their conviction that the Messianic expectation of the prophets had now been fulfilled, the Christian group's ritual and social life-styles in particular evoked the hatred of the sternly orthodox Jews. The persecution that thus broke out demanded its *involuntary* offerings: the first martyrs paid with their lives. Stephen's death was the first offering of such an order required of the Christian community.

Developments ensued that partly followed the path of sacrifice, and partly allowed the fruits of that sacrifice to mature, thus preparing for the *Transubstantiation.* The stoning of Stephen was the signal for the outbreak of fanatical persecution, systematically orchestrated by the Jews. And it cannot be overlooked that the Pharisee, Saul, who was present at the slaying of Stephen, played a dominant and inciting role in these persecutions. Within the circle of the Christians, however, an important impulse resulted from the blows of Stephen's death and other martyrs of the persecution. Even ahead of the actual Apostles, a number of Christians took an apostolic initiative and ventured forth to spread the message of Christ in the adjoining regions. It is noteworthy that they also turned to non-Jews. Thus, even before the Apostles themselves set out on their apostolic task, centres of Christian life originated from the suffering experienced, for example, in Antioch of Syria and probably, even at that stage, in Rome.

The level of transubstantiation, the third act of the drama, was touched off by the lightning flash of Damascus. The transformation which took place in the persecutor, Saul, resulted in the most manifold, astounding events. Henceforth, new activities, both inner and outer, were set in motion even within the circle of the original Apostles. One wing of the developing congregations under the leadership of the younger James persevered in retaining the strict link with the Mosaic Law. But after Peter had even been directed beyond these ties by a puzzling divine ordinance in the house of the Roman captain, Cornelius, Paul was able to break the spell of the Old Testament and at last receive approval for his work from Peter, James and the other original Apostles. Imbued with the sovereign power of change, the great apostolic journeys of Paul carried the word and the power of the Resurrected One into the whole world, thereby leaving behind the horizons of the Orient and turning Europe into the first major arena of Christian history.

The so-called 'trial of Paul' makes up the fourth part of Acts. Taken as a prisoner from one court to another, Paul was ultimately brought to Rome in an eventful winter voyage because, as a Roman citizen, he had appealed to Caesar as the ultimate arbiter. Paul's apostolic role which, up to then, he had mainly carried out through force of words, thus came to be proclaimed through his whole destiny and being. It became clear that Christianity was not only to spread by means of sermons but, above all, through being drawn into what Paul called 'suffering with Christ, dying with Christ.' This is the stage of transubstantiation on the level of destiny and history: here Christ enters into individual human destinies. In man's fate, the Christ fate finds its metamorphosis and continuation. And hereby, the destiny of the human community that was becoming Christianized represented a further phase of the course of Christ's own life. The character of communion in Paul's fate during imprisonment came into focus quite clearly on one occasion when, in the midst of the shipwreck, he filled his terrified fellow passengers with peace and strength by distributing *Communion.*

It is inherent in the secrets of style and composition in Acts that all the main figures, one after the other, disappear silently from the scene. Acts mentions nothing about the last period of Paul's life and his death. Like John, James and Peter before him, Paul, too, leaves the stage in silence; we trace his path only to the point where he arrives in Rome. Had it been the writer's intent and purpose in Acts to give a biographical report, he would surely mention what happened subsequently to those described as the chief protagonists. He would add something about the martyrdom of Paul in Rome. Obviously, something mattered more than individual biography, even if it was that of Paul. The course of life and the development of a suprapersonal entity, an individuality of a loftier kind, was to become visible. After all, it was Christ himself who had now begun a new phase of his life in his body of humanity's history, a 'body' which we can call 'the Church.' It is therefore not really a disappearance when first John, then Peter, and finally Paul are no longer mentioned. Rather, in each case, it is a matter of a new beginning. When a nuance and direction of Christian life, which had embodied itself in a certain human figure, was incorporated in the Christian body as a whole and its course of life ran like a new vein, so to speak, the individual figure then disappeared. The person was replaced by the accomplishment of his being. With the arrival of Paul in Rome, the seed of Paulinism had been placed into the ground of humankind in such a way that its future growth, blossoming and fruition could be counted upon.

Nothing emphasises the world-transforming character of these quiet yet fundamental events in the Gospel and Acts more than the attempt to establish a calendar for them. Although such an attempt can have only a hypothetical character, it will be made here. It will be seen how everything condenses into an extraordinarily brief span of time.

If we follow tradition, which is much more trustworthy than

Bible criticism has been willing to admit, the 'three years' do not amount quantitatively to three full years. The Baptism in the Jordan comes soon after Jesus' thirtieth birthday, hence on January 6 of the year 31. April 3, 33, is Good Friday. Although the time between the Jordan baptism and Golgotha does fall over three distinct years, a more exact calculation shows that the Gospel events were concentrated in the short span of two and a quarter years. The event of Pentecost takes place some time before the middle of the year 33. Most likely, the stoning of Stephen, for which tradition sets the date of December 26, occurred at the end of the same year. Hence, the birth of the first congregations and the time of persecution, as described in the early chapters of Acts, would have filled the second part of the following year. From early times, January 25 is mentioned as the date of Paul's Damascus experience. So if Saul's acts of persecution following the martyrdom of Stephen lasted for about a year, the date of January 25 in the year 35, not quite two years after Golgotha, would appear probable for the Damascus event. At that time, Paul may have been about the same age as Jesus of Nazareth was at the time of the Crucifixion; here it is assumed that he was not only a contemporary of Jesus but about two years younger. If Paul was then killed during Nero's persecutions in about the year 67 or 68, he would have lived for about sixty-six years, that is, twice thirty-three years, the life-span of Jesus of Nazareth. A possible calendar would therefore be as follows:

AD 31	Baptism in Jordan	January 6
AD 33	Good Friday	April 3
AD 33	Easter	April 5
AD 33	Ascension	May 14
AD 33	Pentecost	May 24
AD 33	Death of Stephen	December 26
AD 35	Damascus	January 25

In the first of the two lectures, 'Easter, the Festival of Warning,' Rudolf Steiner spoke about Paul's life span and age. He indicated that the Damascus experience fell approximately in the thirty-third year of Paul's life and then went on to say:

> As physical man, Paul was of about the same age as Christ Jesus himself ... In this second half of his life he

experienced supersensibly what a man of that time could no longer ... experience through sense experience.

For about the same length of time that Christ had walked the earth, did Paul continue to live upon earth — that is, until about his sixty-seventh or sixty-eighth year, in order to spend this time carrying the teaching of Christianity into earth evolution. The parallelism between the life of Christ Jesus and the life of Paul is a remarkable one. The only difference was that the life of Christ Jesus was completely filled with the presence and Being of the Christ. Paul, on the other hand, had such a strong after-experience of this event acquired through initiation, that he was able to be the first one to bring to humankind true and fitting ideas about Christianity — and to do so for a period of time corresponding very nearly to that of the life of Christ Jesus on earth.[10]

Life

3. From Tarsus to Jerusalem

Paul is the Apostle of the world. He carried the seed of the Christ impulse, implanted by heaven in the soil of the earth, into all that was then 'world.' The expansion of Christendom that occurred through him was not merely geographical and spatial. First and foremost, its aim was the introduction of the Christian impulse into the course of time, into the evolution of humankind. Therefore, above all, Paul had to be in touch with the centres of cultural progress, the focal points of the 'modern' life of that age. He made Christianity fit for the world; he allowed it to become the most modern impulse in the world at any point in time; indeed, he made it the leaven of progress itself. He accomplished this by receiving the Christ impulse and integrating it into the evolving element in our history, namely, human consciousness. Paul did not turn Christianity into human thought content by placing it within a system of ready-made theological concepts. By means of grace-filled enlightenment, he could approach the Christ mysteries with living perceptions which, like seeds, are capable of opening, growing and blossoming throughout future history and which, at the same time, can become a leaven for the vitalization and spiritualization of thinking in general.

Three decades prior to Golgotha and Damascus, two contemporary images which could not be more different emerged in the stream of human history: Jesus' secluded and tranquil childhood in Nazareth, and Paul's early years in the cosmopolitan capital of Tarsus.

Nazareth, located on the heights of Galilee, was no city. It could not even be counted among the smaller settlements, the market centres and villages through which, on a small scale, there flowed something of the bustle of the world. As the centre of the Order of the Essenes, it was an enlarged site of a monastery.[11] The full members of the order, dedicated to an ascetic and meditative life, represented the guiding core of the community. The lay brothers and sisters, though they were permitted to carry on a trade and could marry, also followed a rule that limited their contact with the world to a minimum. The setting of Jesus' youth was a place where, away from the noise and bustle of normal life, eternal life was strictly guarded and cultivated as a light upon human existence. It was as if earthly nature was here trying to reflect the sphere of the eternal archetypes. For the *mountain of mountains* and *lake of lakes* belonged within the periphery of Nazareth: Mount Tabor with its rounded, heaven-reflecting form; and the Sea of Galilee through which the fountains of a higher life seemed to stream into human existence. The distance was filled with other symbols of greatness. In the west, the Mediterranean Sea, like liquid gold in the sun; in the north, the snowy summit of Mount Hermon, extending across Lebanon and the range of Anti-Lebanon, emphasised the duality of lake and mountain.

By contrast, *Tarsus* was both metropolis and port. Here, in the most colourful welter of nations, the world streamed through as nowhere else. Orient and Occident, Asia and Europe, came together, not only exchanging their goods but also their spiritual life. Above the teeming city, mountains and sea conducted a grandiose dialogue. In the majestic chain of Taurus' snowy summits in the north, rising to almost 4000 metres (12,000 feet), were the Cilician Gates, the mountain pass which led from middle and northern Asia to the European orbit of the Mediterranean Sea. Similarly, the lower Syrian mountains in the east formed another pass, the 'Syrian Gate,' that linked up with Babylonia, Persia and the more southern Orient. Coming from the Taurus mountains and pouring into the sea near the city, the roaring Kydnos river carried timber from the high forests for the construction of ships and dwellings. Here, the sea was not the archetypal reflection of celestial spheres of life; it was the setting for busy seafaring. Merchant vessels crowded the port of Tarsus. Together with

Antioch — the other world metropolis located on the other side of the Cilician-Syrian corner of the Mediterranean, which later on would also become an important city for Paul — Tarsus represented one of the focal points in the cultural development of that period. Here, in this key point of progress in the civilized world, Paul was born; here he spent his childhood and a large part of his early years.

There are three types of city that have contributed to the onward movement of culture and civilization.

The *ancient cities* were imbued with the mythical character of the sacred mysteries at the beginning of the turn of time and to some extent remained like this until almost up to our present age. Among them, Jerusalem stands in prime place. Its origins go back far beyond the historical times described in the Old Testament. Jerusalem enters recorded history from a very remote time; it is possibly the oldest city on earth. Rome, too, is one of the ancient cities, though one of the youngest. Its original mythical character was hidden only because, in later times, it absorbed each new phase of urban development. The ruins of some of the ancient cities of Asia, such as Babylonia and Nineveh, had already become obliterated by the desert during the Apostles' time; but in the European arena, aside from Rome, cities such as Ephesus and Athens still possessed their ancient vigour and, aside from their contemporary importance, were living evidence of a mythological age of proximity to the gods.

The second type of city, the *metropolis* of antiquity, owed its origin to the mighty awakening of humanity during and after the days of Alexander the Great. In Greece, the birth of human thought had occurred between the age of Thales and Plato, Pythagoras and Aristotle. Alexander, the young Macedonian king and Aristotle's pupil, had carried the culture of thought into the wider world. He penetrated deeply into the Orient where the ancient spirituality of the gods still reverberated. The enthusiasm of awakening thinking spread through the world like wildfire. At the Nile estuary in Alexandria, the first of the new metropoles, a seedbed, and at the same time symbol of the new spirituality, came into being and was renowned far and wide. Soon, the new cultural life here attracted expanding commerce and industry. Under Alexander's successors, the mighty first rulers of the Diadochi dynasties, an unprecedented fever of activity erupted. A wave of urban development caused countless modern cities to spring up as replicas in imitation of Alexandria. It cannot really be understood rationally how in so many locations, in such a short time, such huge masses of people drew together as populations of these cities. Only a new consciousness in humankind, emerging out of unconscious depths, could have led to this strange movement and new grouping. On the one hand, in these new cities, a clear organizing principle was at work, wherever the Apollonian element in the new culture of thought held sway. On the other hand, as an ecstatic legacy of the maternal Asian continent, a Dionysian excitement was evident both in the new cultural ferment and in the undying fervour nurtured by ancient cultures. The three most important cities of this type touched the life of Paul to a major degree: Tarsus, the city of his birth; Antioch, the place of his first apostolic activity; and Corinth, the site of one of the most important among Paul's congregations, to which the apostolic letters are addressed that are included in the New Testament.

In the twelfth and thirteenth centuries AD, a similar expression of a universal awakening of human consciousness gave rise to a third type of city, decisive in the development of modern Europe. A wave of urban establishments, from which arose the 'middle class town' and finally the *modern industrial metropolis,* moved across Central Europe. In our present age, the crisis of life in the big cities, symbolized particularly in the devastation of towns by bombs in the war, signals the end of the 'civil' era as well as the necessity and approach of a new transformation of consciousness.

Thus, if we wish to observe Paul's development in childhood and youth, we are transported to one of the most modern world capitals of that age, one among those that represented the dawn of a new consciousness of humankind between the eras of the ancient city and the modern industrial conglomeration.

The two youths, one in Nazareth, the other in Tarsus, were apprentices from early on in their fathers' trade. Young Jesus helped his father, who was a carpenter, continuing to work in this humble activity after Joseph's death. Paul grew up into the profession of carpet and tent weaving, working as his father's assistant from childhood onward. Until the time of his apostolic journeys, this trade allowed him to offer his services as a completely free gift to the congregations.

This quiet background of simple manual labour which we can envisage shows that neither of the two youngsters came from a wealthy family. The rich, whether they wish to or not, cling at all times to past conditions; after all, their wealth derives from past labours, not from work done in the present. Those without property stand more clearly within the direct present, and therefore can extend a more matter-of-fact openness and readiness towards anything new that is struggling to come to the surface.

There was, however, a fundamental difference between the carpenter's life of Jesus of Nazareth and the tent-weavers' milieu of Paul in Tarsus. There were no wealthy people at all in Nazareth, the quiet Essene colony in Galilee. In the environment of the Essenes, the law of common property prevailed. Everything belonged to the Order, the individual owned nothing. With its lack of contrast between poor and rich, the life of the community was quite different from that of normal society elsewhere. The skilled labour of the young Jesus took place in an atmosphere of fundamental poetic harmony.

Things were different in Tarsus. Here, there was a marked contrast between rich and poor for the very reason that riches abounded. Even nature lavishly bestowed her gifts here! The plain between the foot of the slopes of Taurus and the Mediterranean Sea, which today has become desolate steppe, was a huge garden of inexhaustible fertility through which flowed the Kydnos river. The city, which did not extend right to the coast, lay in the brilliant light of the sun like jewels embedded in green. Borne by innumerable ships, what riches flowed into the port at the mouth of the Kydnos, only to stream out again to many countries, enriched by the treasures of Asia Minor and the Orient, carried through the mountain passes. In Tarsus, opulence and luxury coexisted with the poverty and misery of those destined to toil and wearisome labour, the craftsmen and other humble people.

An early intimation of those social contrasts which in modern times have brought about a self-aware industrial proletariat, may well have existed already in Tarsus. Thus, young Paul grew up in a cultural background in which, as in the vanguard of an advancing army, could be traced all the tensions of the progress engulfing humanity as it struggled to escape the spell of the past.

Like other metropoles of that time, Tarsus was a gathering place for people from all over the known world. In the surging diversity of colours and voices one important thing was concealed. Like Alexandria, Tarsus was a centre of the newly awakened culture of thought. Here, within a culture founded on the Asian soul, saturated with suppressed ecstasy, the philosophers and scholars of this age pursued their ideas and research. And here, seeking the distinguished teachers active in their schools of wisdom, there gathered from all over the world those who wished to find fulfilment of their thirst for knowledge. It is quite likely that circles could be encountered here, more so than in Alexandria, among whom there persisted ancient orgiastic and ecstatic cults, emanating either from Babylonian cultural influences or from those of Asia Minor. Nevertheless, here too the modern life of the spirit basing itself on conscious thought set the tone. In many different ways, people gave themselves up to thinking, the youngest gift of heaven; for this thinking had the power to tame dark ecstasy and turbulent chaos. As time went on, Greek philosophy, which initially had been primarily concerned with the permeation of nature, increasingly made the ethical and moral life of human society and the individual its subject matter. In this, it approached the form that the new spiritual life had assumed in Rome where, early on, ancient mythology had been transposed into a philosophy of morals. An ally of Graeco-Roman thought, Hellenistic Judaism came to the fore, then spread far beyond the people belonging to it by ties of blood; for there were those who knew how to make the scriptures of the Old Testament effective as a textbook of a elevated moral teaching.

Fatefully, young Paul was placed in the midst of the modern cosmopolitan life of culture inasmuch as it had one of its most important centres in Tarsus. In him, the *Jewish, Greek* and *Roman* elements combined in a significant union. He was the son of Jewish parents. The fact that his father maintained a close connection to the order of the Pharisees and, from early on, was at pains to raise his son according to the order's rules, educating him to become a member, shows that in his family the Jewish religion was more than a mere matter of descent. In the Diaspora, that is, in the non-Jewish countries outside Palestine, the Pharisees and the body of Jewish Scribes under their authority considered it their responsibility for the spirit of the Old Testament to contribute to the moral and spiritual development of humanity. The latter thus became the subject of widespread Jewish propaganda.

Nevertheless, the language in which Paul grew up was Greek. Since the days of Alexander the Great, Greek had become the universal language. It united the diverse countries and languages that were gathered up politically in the powerful Roman Empire. World Jewry, also spiritually directed by the Pharisees, had purposely changed over to the Greek language, indeed, even in its ritual life. This had by no means been a matter of course, for long ago, during the era of the Babylonian exile, the order of the Pharisees had been founded with the explicit aim of ensuring the most radical segregation of Judaism from all pagan elements.[12] The *Septuagint,* the light-filled Greek version of the Old Testament scriptures, appeared alongside the darkly sacramental text of the original Hebrew. It was a fitting means for the dissemination of the Mosaic impulse of morality within a world awakening to thinking.

However, it was doubtless not only through the Greek language that Greek cultural life, still supported to a certain extent by the mysteries, contributed to the educational development of young Paul. We have only meagre reports about his youthful period. But his whole character and demeanour suggest that, in addition to his Jewish education, he might have attended Greek schools of learning.

Aside from Jewish and Greek culture, the fact that Paul had a full share in the Roman life of his time was to be decisive at a future date. Because he had Roman citizenship, he appealed to the Caesar in Rome as the highest authority in the heresy trial conducted against him, and was then taken there. Like all the peoples of Cilicia who belonged to the Roman Empire, the Jews of Tarsus had special privileges. They were not required to dwell in a ghetto segregated from the other inhabitants of the city; instead, they lived freely among others. Nonetheless, they were able to form not only a religious congregation but an independent social community as well. They were even free to acquire Roman citizenship for their families, thus attaining equal rights in all matters. Since Paul's father possessed Roman citizenship, it also passed on to Paul.

Just as the majesty of the mountains and sea dominated the city and implanted a breadth of vision into the hearts of its young people, equally great historical sites also surrounded the city's borders. There, one was reminded especially of those events in which the new world of Europe struggled free from the dreamlike grip of ancient Asian grandeur. Near Tarsus, Alexander the Great had vanquished at the battle of Issus the Persian armies across his path when he had set out to carry the banner of the newly awakened consciousness from Europe to Asia. In the same region, however, the energetic campaigns of Aristotle's young pupil almost met with a sudden and premature end. Between the city and the cataracts to the north, where the Kydnos river descended from the sanctuary of the mountains to the fertile plains, Alexander ventured into the waters of the stream to refresh himself. Despite the fiercely burning heat of the sun, the river waters, coming from the icy summits of the Taurus, were so cold that the King lost consciousness and almost drowned, and only with great difficulty did his followers bring him back to life. It is possible that this incident resulted in the recurrent fever to which he finally succumbed, having penetrated deep into the heart of Asia. Here, near Tarsus, were the spirits of the Old World attempting to repulse the onward march of the new consciousness?

In Tarsus, a scene also took place from which one can decipher how not only the culture of Greece, but even that of Rome had to tear itself loose from the spell of the Orient. When, after Caesar's death, Octavian, the later Caesar Augustus, and Mark Antony divided the rule of the Roman empire between them, Anthony, to whom the eastern part was allotted, made Tarsus his capital. Through this very fact, Tarsus became for a time a counterpole to Rome. Antony himself showed such an affinity to the Orient and was so susceptible that before long the alluring demons of Asian ecstasy, though apparently already dispelled, had recaptured Tarsus, filling it with a life of unbridled indulgence and passion. Cleopatra, the enchantress on the throne of the Egyptian Pharaohs, believed that her hour had once again come. On a fantastically decorated vessel, she sailed for Tarsus, clad in the costume of Venus, in order to wed herself to Antony, thereby to unite Egypt with the eastern part of the Roman empire. It was this theatrical intrigue, above all, behind which, nevertheless, stood so much decisive earnestness, that induced Octavian to move in battle against his co-regent. His victory over Mark Antony and the re-absorption of the Eastern empire into the Roman imperium, was at the same time a consolidation of European life in the face of the threat by the demons of the past. Tarsus, on the border between Asian and European culture, now turned with greater determination than ever before into a centre of modern learning. Four decades after Cleopatra's colourful entry, thirty years after Octavian's victory over Mark Antony, Paul was born in Tarsus.

In the decades prior to and after the beginning of the Christian era, the schools in Tarsus were so famous that the most illustrious houses of Rome, first and foremost the Consuls and Caesars, had sought teachers and instructors for their sons from there. This choice was primarily due to that form of Greek philosophy which appeared almost predestined to flow together with the most mature achievements of Roman spiritual life, namely, the Stoa. The Greek Stoics transformed both the traditions of the gradually declining mystery centres as well as the thought of the philosophers' schools into a kind of philosophy and wisdom of life. They sought for the concepts pertaining to self-awareness, newly arising in the human being, for concepts of individual ego consciousness and consciousness of freedom. Representative of the self-awakening all over the world, they strove to bring under the light of consciousness the miracle of the ego kernel through which the human being becomes the free master of his own decisions and morality. It must have given rise to a feeling of elevation, a restrained enthusiasm in teachers and pupils, to encounter that still point in the flow of phenomena, lifting the human being beyond all misfortunes and suffering and allowing him to triumph. What later ages, in a sort of catchword, termed 'stoic equanimity' was a condition of soul, the realization of which was considered by those early Stoic philosophers to be the most sacred fruit of all philosophizing, indeed, the discovery and dis-enchantment of the essential being of man.

It can certainly lead to a deeper understanding to observe how Stoic philosophy and Christianity emerge simultaneously, as it were, in the course of time. The Stoa lent expression to the birth of the ego towards which humankind evolved naturally as the Christian era approached. Yet it was merely an ego form, an element of self closing itself off from and becoming independent of its surroundings, which now made itself felt in man. Would it encapsulate itself, become pure egoism and degenerate? Or would it be capable of opening itself to a higher impulse? Christianity anticipated the ego impulse awakening in humanity, but it bore into the developing ego form the ego content, the higher I. Stoic philosophy was a more significant herald of Christianity than Christian theologians have been willing to admit. The ego that was becoming aware of itself was still sacred to the Stoa. It considered the ego a divine gift, indeed, the incarnation of a divine element in the human being. Where the Stoa was experienced genuinely and purely, however, the feeling of the 'divine in man' did not arise as a claim, but as a longing and inner readiness. Many who had passed through the school of the Stoa in the true sense became Christians, because in Christianity they recognized the fulfilment of what could not have been anything but presentiment and longing in the Stoa. We shall see that it was not without significance for Paul, when he had found his direction at Damascus, that he had already encountered the Stoa among other streams and learned from it during his early years in Tarsus.

When Paul was still a child, an awe-inspiring man lived and worked in Tarsus. About eighty years old, revered the world over, this man was seen as one of the fathers and noblest representatives of the Stoa: Athenodorus, the teacher and friend of Augustus.

His father had been a farmer in the vicinity of Tarsus. In his youth, he was a disciple of the last genuine mystery centre, or at least the pupil of teachers who could still transmit to him the initiation knowledge received there. Above all, on the island of Rhodes, he had been the pupil of Posidonius, one of the last great sages of the old world, who was still capable of proclaiming something of the Logos mysteries. When Roman governor of the province of Cilicia, even Cicero, who resided for some time in Tarsus, had once had Posidonius as his teacher. Athenodorus was one of those who, gripped by the new consciousness of personality and self arising in humankind, had transformed the ancient wisdom into the Stoa's body of knowledge. To him came seekers after truth from all over the world, just as he once had gone to Posidonius. When news of Julius Caesar's assassination reverberated through the world, Octavian, later Caesar Augustus, who as Caesar's adopted son was in the line of succession and now had to hasten to Rome, was studying at the feet of Athenodorus at Epirus in Apollonia. Later on, Athenodorus, as his advisor, spent a long time in Rome at the side of his imperial pupil. He spent the final two decades of his long life in his home town of Tarsus, helping to provide a communal constitution founded on the best ethical principles, while still exercising his role as the promulgator of Stoic wisdom. After his death, the citizens of Tarsus erected a hero's temple to him as one who had grown beyond normal human stature.

It was Athenodorus who was the first to introduce the concept of 'conscience' into ethics. It is one of the most indispensable keys for understanding the history of human consciousness to recognize that this term, which did not occur in the Old Testament, could and did appear in human language only with the emergence of the ego impulse, the awareness of a centre of being in man capable of inner decisions. Since this key is also of significance for the Pauline Letters, because there, above all, the word 'conscience' enters the language of the New Testament, we need to return later in more detail to this aspect.

One of the classic aphorisms of Athenodorus concerning conscience is the following: 'For every human being, his conscience is his God.' Around this basic thesis revolve all his guiding principles, his thoughts concerning his wisdom of life: 'Live with men as if God could see it; speak with God as if men listened to it.'

Statements such as these by the great Greek Stoic have been handed down to us through the Roman Stoic, Seneca, who, for his part, spins the thread of the philosophy of conscience even further:

> A holy spirit is within us as the observer and guard over our good and bad thoughts. When you perform honourable actions, all may know of it; when you do shameful things, however, what good does it do if nobody knows about it since you yourself are aware of them?

Even if young Paul received impressions of Athenodorus' character and activity only from afar or from hearsay, he would still have had to become familiar with the thoughts and doings of the Stoic philosophers. In Tarsus, there were a particularly large number of itinerant Stoic preachers who addressed the populace in the city's streets and marketplaces. It is easy to imagine that, on his later apostolic journeys, Paul made great use of the style of public speaking with which he was acquainted from the Stoics. Also, some historians have pointed to the similarity of literary style between the Letters of Paul and the *Diatribe,* the written summary in which the itinerant Stoics recorded what they had set forth orally.

At important junctures of his later life as well, Paul crossed the path of renowned Stoics. Here, we shall only mention the two brothers, Gallio and Seneca. Seneca was Nero's teacher in Rome and subsequently his court philosopher and advisor. A number of his texts have been preserved, and they stand among the most mature fruits of the Roman Stoa. No writings by Gallio have come down to us, but we can tell from the great reverence in which he was held, especially by his brother Seneca, that in his own day he was held as the shining embodiment of Stoic wisdom and its human ideals. Seneca expressed his admiration for Gallio by dedicating to him his most important book, *Concerning the Blessed Life (De vita beata.)* Gallio had just become Roman proconsul in Corinth when, after one and one-half years of activity, Paul was subjected there (in the year 52) to the most vehement defamations and persecutions by the Jews. Gallio placed Paul under his protection and strongly rebuffed the denouncers who demanded Paul's deportation. During the time that he spent in Rome prior to his martyrdom, Paul, having himself demanded to be brought before Caesar and living therefore in the vicinity of Nero's court, doubtless also came into contact with Seneca. It is often assumed, with some credibility, that in the legal proceedings against him Seneca is reputed to have interceded for Paul and therefore prolonged his period of grace. When, however, along with Peter and many other Christians, Paul fell victim to the mania of Nero's major persecutions, Gallio and Seneca, and with them a number of other philosophers serving humanitarian ideals, had already become martyrs. On Nero's orders, both brothers were forced to commit suicide.

We shall now attempt to probe more deeply into the soul of the growing boy, Paul. Alert in mind and spirit, he found himself surrounded both by a natural landscape at its most majestic, and an almost overwhelming profusion of human life at its most colourful and energetic. Which of the three great strands of culture was it — the Jewish, the Greek or the Roman — that dominated his consciousness? From the wealth of impressions immediately around him, his family background and religious ties to the Old Testament must have determined his fundamental attitudes to life. This background was supplemented, though, by the proud awareness of being a *civis romanus,* a citizen of the Roman empire with full rights. On the other hand, being brought up within the Greek language — a language as bright, light and colourful as the sun-filled air — opened his mind to the mood and refined spirit of Hellenistic culture. Here Paul was offered a wide range of choices. The orgiastic-ecstatic element found in Hellenized oriental culture repelled rather than attracted his curiosity. On the other hand, the philosophy and ethics of the Stoics, in which the Greek spirit had attained its most modern development, assuming at the same time a formality suitable to the Roman mind, powerfully addressed the ideals that Paul felt as a young man. And it could not be otherwise but that he absorbed a good deal of his knowledge from that direction. All kinds of things that were, so to speak, in between ecstasy and Stoicism, aroused questions and intimations in him of past mysteries and their exalted initiates. It is possible that, in his quite early years, Paul may have had knowledge of a contemporary who also grew up in Tarsus — perhaps even had some sort of contact with him — namely, Apollonius of Tyana. Even as a youth, Apollonius was reputed to be a reincarnated great initiate, particularly when, in a sanctuary dedicated to Asklepios (Aesculapius), he acquired the art of medicine, and forthwith, the sick gathered there from all over the world to be cured by the young miracle healer. Apollonius, however, owed his magic faculties to Luciferic forces. It is providential that, in the very beginnings of the Christian era, the last great pre-Christian adept passed his youth in Tarsus at the same time as Paul; while, in his old age, he dwelled in Ephesus along with the aged presbyter, John.[13] There can be no doubt that, aside from what Paul absorbed of Greek culture through his daily life, he sought and found those schools and teachers who introduced him to the depths of Greek spiritual striving.

Yet, in the midst of this wealth of Hellenistic life, the world of the Old Testament must have become increasingly important and ultimately dominant in the life of the young Paul. The scriptures of the Old Covenant, from the Books of Moses to those of the Prophets, were known to him initially in the Greek version. At that time, not only the original Hebrew texts but also the Greek translations were considered by diaspora Jewry to be inspired. It was said that seventy renowned scribes proceeded to translate the Holy Scriptures; the astonishing result was that all of them arrived independently at the identical wording. For this reason the Greek text was known as the *Septuagint,* the Seventy.

The fact of his father's membership of the order of the Pharisees does however suggest that, from early on, Paul was instructed in the Hebrew language and in the use of the sacred original text of the Old Testament. Behind the bright, thought-transparent words that had brought the Holy Scriptures so close to non-Jewish contemporary philosophy and morals, there echoed for Paul the darkly solemn, primordial sound. It must have been as if only here did he learn to know the complete inner truth and earnestness of the Old Testament, in which the stern will of Yahweh pulsed. So, from the Greek wording adapted to the world, he found his way to the original Hebrew sound of the voice of God. This experience inevitably produced a direction of striving for his innermost being, and the profound earnestness of it induced him to search ever more deeply in the soul discipline of the Pharisees.

While belonging to the order of Pharisees, Paul's father probably was not numbered among the innermost circle. Originally, the Order had upheld the sternest monastic and ascetic observance. Through radical segregation from all worldly things, particularly all pagan elements, a path of strict ascetic and meditative exercises was followed by those who decided to accept the Order's discipline. The Pharisees were intended to be the crack troops among those preparing for the coming of the Messiah and the Last Judgment. When, in the centuries after Alexander the Great, Hellenistic Judaism arose full of zeal for missionary activity, the Order of the Pharisees ceased to be exclusively concerned with strict segregation from the world. The Order assumed the work of extending the Jewish influence, as a means of preparing humankind for the approaching Messianic event. Around a narrow core which maintained stern discipline, the Order probably instituted a larger circle of lay-members with relaxed rules, not unlike the lay Tertiaries of the medieval orders of monks. Just as the parents of the boy Jesus in Nazareth were lay-members of the Order of Essenes, so Paul's father may have been one of the lay-members of the Order of Pharisees.

While becoming familiar with the sacred Hebrew word of the Bible, Paul must have penetrated into the innermost aims of Pharisaism. Here, too, the stern impact of the biblical Yahweh presented itself behind the semblance that had been allowed to arise under Hellenistic influence. Paul accepted radically all that prepared him for membership of the inner circle. And if there had never existed a genuine Pharisee in the original, founding sense, *he* would be that man. The eschatological Messianic concept, taught esoterically, took hold of him: the Messiah will come as the cosmic judge, at whose appearance the world passes away.

It had always been the father's idea to send his son to the

noble school of the Old Covenant in Jerusalem once Paul had reached the required age. Now, in Paul himself too, an inner urge had awoken that guided him from Tarsus to Jerusalem.

With this new resolve, the young Paul had already undergone a 'conversion.' The same term, applied so inappropriately to what he was to experience near Damascus, was a true description for this inner revolution and focus, to be carried out so thoroughly that it involved a complete departure from the 'world.'

4. From Jerusalem to Damascus

Arriving in Jerusalem from the colourful and bustling metropolis of Tarsus, the young Paul must have felt as if he had been transported from a world of seductive appearances into one of profound realities, since, despite changes in Hellene times, the temple area of Jerusalem still retained much of its age-old character. Given his precocious and deeply serious nature, Paul only now really became himself.

Two types of schooling awaited him here at the spiritual centre of the Old World. To start with, the emphasis was naturally on theological instruction from the most distinguished teachers among the scribes. Moving on from the academic classes, when admission into the higher degrees of Pharisaic monastic life came under consideration, the focus was increasingly on spiritual exercises intended to transform the deeper soul forces and, above all, the will. The theological element of the scribes' erudition, namely, the study of the Torah, was based on those Old Testament books that look back into history beyond Moses and Abraham to the beginnings of creation when the Elohim fashioned the Earth aeon. Similar to an initiation, the spiritual path of the Order was linked to the prophetic element, hence also to the Old Testament prophets who directed their gaze into the Messianic future. Just as the prophets had become heralds of future events through a higher form of perception and hearing, so, too, the neophyte was to achieve the stage of having visions and hearing directly the word of the deity. Ardent conviction that the Messiah would eventually, or even imminently, come, motivated the soul to diligent practice, driving it towards an awakening of higher perception. Undisturbed by the decadence that was beginning to affect the Order, all true Pharisees aspired to encounter the One in the spirit realm who was on his way to meet humankind.

Paul's period of learning and teaching in Jerusalem must have lasted for many years, perhaps more than a decade. Yet it is possible that it did not pass entirely without interruptions; if Paul entered the esteemed school of the scribes at the age of fifteen, as was frequently the practice, it is quite feasible that at frequent intervals in his training he may have returned to Tarsus.

When he arrived in Jerusalem, some of his first teachers may well have been the very same scholars who, only a few years earlier, were so astonished at the wisdom of a twelve-year-old Nazarene boy, during the Easter festival in the Temple. With his exceptional gifts and eager progress in learning, the youth from Tarsus met with their approval, though his sombre earnestness may have appeared uncanny on occasion, to at least one of his teachers. Paul, who here in Jerusalem was known by his Hebrew name, Saul (Shaul), had among his later teachers one called Gamaliel. He was the grandson of the renowned Rabbi Hillel, greatly revered for his patient kindness and wisdom. Many of the sentiments felt for his grandfather were transferred to Gamaliel, who had a striking similarity of character. Although Gamaliel was still one of the younger rabbis, the strength of his fatherly love transformed discord into peace and offered consolation for the suffering. Far from being zealous or fanatical, he advocated understanding and justice towards all. Thus, we see him intercede in the Sanhedrin for the apostles Peter and John, about to be condemned without a hearing.

It is not impossible that, reacting against Gamaliel's nature, his pupil developed a disposition towards zealous impatience. Since, in any case, something in Saul urged him beyond the theological preliminaries to the actual mysteries of the Order to which he had dedicated himself, the unshaken calm and wisdom of his teacher was almost bound to present him with a difficult and puzzling question.

The tempestuous impatience of Paul's nature confronted the fundamental limitation of the Pharisees' beliefs. To hold the view that the coming of the Messiah was imminent and that his appearance heralded the end of the Earth aeon, hence the Day of Judgment — for, 'he who beholds God must die!' — operated in the soul like an incessant fear. The 'fear of God,' elicited by thoughts of the stern Yahweh deity, could only intensify as 'Messianic terror' in anticipation of the one who was preparing to be the cosmic judge of sinful humanity. Was there still time to go on with life as usual, if the hour was already approaching when the merciless judgment of human souls would take place?

In the face of Gamaliel's patient benevolence, Paul had to ask himself: Doesn't one who has been initiated into the innermost secrets of the Order know what is about to happen? How can he speak of God's fatherly love, expressed through his very nature and occasionally in words, when, in fact, we face God's discipline and have to prepare ourselves for His wrath? Perhaps, on occasion, the pupil braved his teacher to ask why he drew the curtain of love over the terrifying mystery of wrath.*

How could the tension-filled Messianic eschatology (the teaching of the last things), the equation of the Messiah's arrival with the Last Judgment, actually come about? It resulted of necessity from the special form of visionary perception which was striven for and practised in the esoteric circle of the Order of Pharisees. From the outset, an extreme element was inherent in this soul discipline. With violent jolts, so to speak, the soul was torn out of the relationship with the body; and like from the string of the overstrained bow, the arrow shot off from space and time into infinity. The curtain opened prophetically on the most distant future. Due to a basic soul attitude determined by their impatient intellect, a utopian disposition infused the eschatological vision striven for by the Pharisees. Then, woven as if out of blinding lightning flashes, the figure of the Messiah appeared; the time between the present and the earth's end contracted into a single moment as if in an overwhelming shock of terror. All future epochs telescoped into one. There is no more evolution, for time is no more. Through the divine lightning flash of the Messiah's arrival, the great cosmic selection takes place. That phase of the Earth aeon, which is moving forward to the next cosmic cycle, takes with it those human beings who pass the test of the Last Judgment. The damned are swept along by that fragment of the earth that plummets in the cosmic conflagration like a cinder into the abyss.

* Franz Werfel's drama *Paulus unter den Juden* [Paul among the Jews] seems to touch on the true facts where it probes into the issues which came between Gamaliel and Paul.

The character of this world picture, which dramatically leaps over time and space, can be illustrated by the manner in which the devout of the Old Testament formed a concept of God himself. Properly speaking, the monotheistic concept is not contradicted by a world view which, beyond mineral, plant, animal and man, assumes a hierarchy rising from angels and archangels all the way to Cherubim and Seraphim. All realms of existence, the earthly and the super-earthly, can serve the *one* God as limbs and organs of his corporeality. An attitude, on the other hand, which, driven by the impatience of intellectual thought, hastens directly towards the ultimate and highest aspect; which, instead of contemplating the wealth of phenomena, immediately takes hold of the all-encompassing idea of oneness, is not at ease with any mention of the hierarchies. It wishes to know nothing of a 'divine world'; it aims only for God. Thus, although there are passages in the Old Testament that mention angels and Cherubim, one can sense on the whole a concern that the concept of the *one* God might thereby be impaired. This aversion to the hierarchies extends all the way into intellectual Protestantism — despite the fact that the New Testament speaks of them on every page. Just as an abstractly conceived monotheism effaces the realms of the angels, the eschatological vision of the Messiah causes everything lying in between in time to vanish into nothing. We are dealing here with a fundamental short-circuit that has deeply affected Christian concepts of the world.

One cannot deny a certain greatness inherent in the Pharisaic vision of Christ (the Greek 'Christ' corresponds to the Hebrew word, 'Messiah'). The Christ-being was pictured in world-shattering loftiness. The path subsequently chosen by Christ himself was quite outside their field of vision, namely, to relinquish divine greatness and assume the plain and humble form of the sinful human being, so that a seed of transformation and salvation could be sown, not only for humanity but for the earth itself, until the old aeon would pass into a new one. The terms, the 'Coming One,' *ho erchomenos,* and the 'coming aeon,' *ho aiōn erchomenos,* are intimately related, but only through a profound short-circuit in conceptualization could both be identified as one. Through the *coming* of Christ the foundation was laid for the future possibility of the *coming* of the 'new Earth' at the end of the Earth aeon.

By virtue of his soul constitution, Paul was predestined to experience the eschatological vision of the future. Since the Messianic idea already gripped him so totally when he came from Tarsus to Jerusalem, it probably required only a few steps on the path of Pharisaic training to lead him to the threshold where the lightning of the Messianic event could reveal itself to him.

A vigorous commitment to the future enshrined this prophetic vision in Paul. He was born prematurely, ahead of his time. Where, in the First Letter to the Corinthians, he calls himself 'one untimely born,' (1Cor.15:8) he first of all expresses a general sense of being deeply out of tune with the time of his incarnation. But he also indicates quite concretely that his mother gave birth to him prematurely at only seven months.

Such a shortened embryonic period has much stronger soul-spirit effects than mere physical and biological observations can recognize. The human being that is preparing to incarnate comes from the worlds in which the future is safeguarded until it can become the earthly present. Just as the archaeological strata under our feet preserve the successive layers of the past, so the gradational realms of the hierarchies above our heads bear the future which will descend to the earth stage by stage. During the embryonic period, the human being draws ever closer to the present from spheres of the future. If the mother carries the child to full term, it has arrived truly and fully in the present when it is born. If the child enters the world prematurely, it will have to struggle all its life to balance a discrepancy which can sometimes be felt only slightly, at others, however, quite noticeably. It will not be easy for such a person to dwell in a well-adjusted, healthy manner in his earthly body and to stand with both feet in the present. He will all too easily be inclined to hover somewhat above himself and reality. On the other hand, he will have a sensitivity to the future, towards matters for which the time has not yet arrived. He lives ahead of his time without always being able to give himself a full account of it. If he is prematurely born in the physical sense, then, in regard to the development of earthly conditions also, he has been born too soon; he is a premature birth in regard to humanity.

This applies to Paul in an archetypal way. Providence placed him in time in such a way that he followed the laws of a future age of humankind, at the same time preparing the way for them. To begin with, however, the futuristic bias of his character fitted him to enter more intensely and unreservedly than anyone before him into the eschatological convictions and visions of Pharisaism.

It is quite probable that Paul was not spared the temptations resulting from the Pharisaic view of the future. Would he not have seen other attitudes as lukewarm and indecisive, including those of other religious groups filled with the Messianic expectation? Conceptual impatience drove him to fanaticism. The more he encountered the 'quiet ones in the land' with their Essene humility, the more passionately he displayed Pharisaic haughtiness. Fascinated by the almost logical course of his own experience and behaviour, he could not help but consider all the others inconsistent, particularly those who also set their hope on the Messiah, and he turned against them with an increasingly self-consuming rage.

Theologians have puzzled a great deal over the word, *ektrōma*, which has been translated as 'untimely birth.' Many proceeded from the assumption that this word frequently means, 'miscarriage'; consequently, they have tried to figure out what Paul referred to when he applied this term to himself. It was Rudolf Steiner who pointed out the fact that, even in the physical sense, Paul's birth was premature. The following passage from one of Rudolf Steiner's lectures speaks of this. Earlier, mention has been made of how Paul was guided by the wisdom and grace of destiny to the Damascus experience:

> Paul was an initiate in wisdom but not a clairvoyant. He did, however, possess a prerequisite for becoming clairvoyant in an abnormal manner, and he himself mentions this. He refers to it as 'grace,' bestowed upon him from above; he tells us that he was born prematurely — usually translated 'untimely born.' He was not carried to full term in the maternal womb, but descended from the spiritual to the physical world before being wholly immersed in all

> the elements of earthly existence; that is, he came into the world before the moment when ordinarily the unconscious ties which bind men to the spiritual powers are broken. The vision on the road to Damascus was made possible for one whose spiritual eyes had been opened through the agency of an untimely birth.
>
> Having had his spiritual vision bestowed upon him as a consequence of his premature birth, he now gazed into the earth's aura and there beheld the Christ. Therefore the span of time during which this Christ had walked the earth must have already lapsed. Here was proof that it was Christ who had died on the Cross ...[14]

Even if Paul, after the age of twenty-eight, was not constantly in Jerusalem but spent periods of time in Tarsus or perhaps elsewhere on instructions of his Order, he surely followed events in Judea with close attention. The stir surrounding the appearance of John the Baptist would therefore not have escaped his notice, and the anxious question must have posed itself whether those who had allowed themselves to be baptized by John would rise to some kind of coherent action? In the end, the gruesome demands of Herodias terminated the Baptist's earthly life. Saul may well have looked upon the activities of John's disciples after the death of their master with bitter disappointment, if not with contempt, particularly those who now gathered around Jesus of Nazareth. What a pitiful glimmer had the blazing flame of the Messianic proclamation, kindled by John, now become! Where now was the soul-stirring majesty which had called upon the approaching judgment of the world? And this Jesus! How could serious disciples of the Baptist see in him a continuation, let alone a climactic fulfilment, of John's message! *There* had been a roaring storm; *here,* at most, blew a gentle breeze. *There* had stood a superhuman form; *here,* the man was so human, quiet and unassuming.

In the circle of the disciples who followed Jesus there was one who believed that here the Messiah *had* come. But this one simply did not understand why the fire that would destroy the yoke of Roman rule did not blaze forth out of Jesus. Thus, he, Judas, was consumed with impatience, waiting for the moment when

Jesus would finally assert his world-dominating sovereignty. Paul, who observed everything from a distance, was also driven by impatience and intense expectation. The possibility, however, that the Christ could have already appeared in Jesus did not enter his mind; he entertained too elevated a notion of the Christ whom the world awaited. Jesus disappointed him because he suppressed the stirring message of John instead of expanding it. And worse, there came the dark hour of Golgotha in which the Galilean died an ignominious, detestable death on the cross. Without resistance, he allowed everything to happen to him; not to mention the fact that at the very least his imminent death should have induced him to cast some word of awakening like a flaming torch into humankind.

It is really not possible to imagine that Paul remained untouched by the events of Holy Week. Though he was not yet an executive member of the Sanhedrin, in the way he was later on during the proceedings against Stephen, he may well have been present as an observer when Jesus stood before Caiaphas. Peter, who watched from the courtyard, retreated in the face of the incomprehensible riddle inherent in those events. Saul may have battled with himself so as not to give open vent to his passionate contempt.

Indeed, this zealous Pharisee could have told himself: 'Nothing more can be expected from this direction; I must seek elsewhere for companions in the actions that I owe to deluded humanity.' But on a deeper level, a mysterious attraction was exerting itself which drew him again and again towards the adherents of Jesus. And this very attraction, which ran counter to his conscious mind, turned into hate which became increasingly violent.

This became especially the case when confused Easter reports reached Saul from the bereft circle of Jesus' disciples, and when it became clear that some in this group were more than ever convinced that the Messiah had in fact appeared in Jesus. Saul did not pass over the foolish delusion of a small, insignificant circle that had no idea of the magic greatness and power of the Messiah to engage with this new reality. What he knew of this 'insignificant group' evoked ever greater outrage in him. For newcomers now joined this circle who had not previously belonged, having sympathized at most from a distance. Perhaps there is some truth in the frequently voiced tradition that some of these newcomers to the developing Christian community were fellow pupils of Saul's on the spiritual path. Time and again, Barnabas and Stephen have been mentioned in this connection. In any case, it must have been extremely upsetting and irritating for Saul that one of the most illustrious members of the Pharisees, Nicodemus, more and more clearly took the side of the Nazarene.

All of Saul's sympathies were with those who considered the growing severance of Jesus' supporters from the Jewish community a disgrace and danger for Judaism, and therefore proceeded with all possible means against them. He surely also believed that their movement represented not only a gross simplification of the true elevated Messianic concept, but was also a dangerous distraction from the necessarily tense period of Messianic expectation.

Then came the decisive day. In the High Priest's palace on Mount Zion, Stephen, recently appointed as one of the seven deacons in the circle of the Christians, was brought before the Sanhedrin accused of blasphemy. He stood in the very place where Jesus had faced the same charges and endured the questions of Caiaphas. Filled with the Spirit, Stephen illuminated the path of God's will through the history of the Old Testament, leading to the life, death and resurrection of the Christ in Jesus of Nazareth. And it was not only in Stephen's words that something higher and spiritual was present, but in his whole being. His countenance became luminous so that even his accusers and judges believed they beheld before their eyes an angel incarnate. The feeling that the ground was reeling under their feet, however, caused them to succumb to an ecstasy of hate. Stephen was condemned and then led out of the nearby Gate of the Essenes — all this taking place in the vicinity of the Cenacle, where Jesus had washed the feet of the disciples and had given them bread and wine; where the Apostles had experienced the Resurrected One in their midst for forty days as well as the fire of Pentecost. Outside the walls of the city, Stephen was stoned to death.

At this point in Acts, Saul is mentioned for the first time. Outwardly, he was merely playing a minor part in the scene involving Stephen. Inwardly, however, he was more passionately concerned than most about the issues. The word, *syneudokōn,* found here in the biblical text, has been quite inadequately understood and translated to mean merely that Saul 'took delight' in Stephen's death.* It really indicates that he was caught up by the ecstatic, visionary experience which overcame them all at the sight of Stephen illuminated. For what else could be re-kindled in the young Pharisee's soul — and perhaps now more blindingly bright than ever before — but the great Messianic vision of the Day of Judgment? The acute paradox that had long and deeply agitated Saul now reached its climax, namely, that any contact with Jesus' environment, which attracted him so magically and through which his tragic error could have been refuted, only intensified his hatred and fanaticism.

Saul now placed himself at the head of the inquisition about to be pitted against the nascent Christian community. By obtaining written authorization, he had himself installed as the leading judge against those who were so scandalously forsaking the faith of their fathers at a time when every effort should have been made to prepare for the fulfilment of the Messianic prophecy.

Saul moved through the land like a scourge of divine wrath, an instrument of the approaching Day of Judgment. But when his passion for God reached its boiling point, the sphere that he believed he was serving intervened. At the noon hour, as he was travelling from the blinding, hot desert into the greenness of the oasis surrounding Damascus, he was granted a vision that thoroughly overthrew his compulsions and left all his existing perceptions healed, rectified and extended. Stilling the unrest of his soul, the one whom Saul had despised because of his humble being and shameful death on the Cross appeared before him in sunlike glory and greatness. Saul had believed that his own concept of the Christ was loftier than that of the circle who revered Christ in the unassuming human being, Jesus. Now he was forced to realize that what he had taken for greatness was a

* The German text of Acts 8:1 has the sense of: 'But Saul took delight *(Wohlgefallen)* in his death.' The Revised Standard Version has: 'And Saul was consenting to his death.' The author's interpretation makes it clear that neither the German nor the English conveys the full sense of the Greek. (Translator).

product of his own fear and impatience, and that true greatness was concealed in what he had looked down upon.

His misguided fanaticism was now refuted. And yet Saul did not have to feel contradicted and undone. His focus had not been directed to the wrong object; his ardent longing and service had always been intended for Christ, for the Messiah. But his vision had been wrong. Having arrived at visionary insight along the path of his training, the strength of this very vision had made him blind. A glaring light had dazzled him. Too much discord and, on that account, finally also hateful arrogance had infused the visionary experience which had guided him so far. Now Saul felt a new peace and harmony healing his soul and his vision, streaming from the one whom he was encountering, despite the fact that he believed himself to be crushed by the encounter.

How was the image which Saul had up to now held in his mind altered?

A person who looks quietly into the future reckons with *developments.* Regardless of whether it is arrived at by thinking or through visionary prescience, he beholds stages ahead which must be gone through until, finally, a goal can be reached. A seed must take time to germinate, to sprout and, at last, come to fruition. If impatience interferes in the pictures that man forms of the future, the necessary intervals between stages are all too easily eliminated; finally, even the time between the present and the final goal is obscured. Present and future collide with each other; in all his imperfection, man finds himself placed directly before the goal and the demands for perfection contained in it. Now fear can really grip him. If inward weakness and anxiety have already been the root of impatience, its fruit only makes them worse.

In the eschatological vision which the order of the Pharisees cultivated and which Saul had so passionately made into his guideline, time — which makes possible all developments and stages — was eliminated. In the Pharisees' view, three fundamental experiences of humanity's Messianic evolution were telescoped into one: the first Christ event which begins with the human incarnation and culminates in the drama of death and Resurrection; the second Christ event, which, in the biblical scriptures, is designated as the Coming of the Son of Man on the clouds of heaven; finally, the transition of the Earth aeon into the new planetary condition, which John's Apocalypse terms the 'new Earth and the new Heaven.' Along with the third event, time and space lose the validity they possess during the Earth aeon. The first two events, on the other hand, definitely still presuppose the existence of the world of time and space; after all, the first event occurs on the level of earthly incarnation. Because of the merging of these fundamental events that are actually separated by time and space, the Messiah was pictured in such a manner that through his coming space and time were done away with.

Correctly understood, each fundamental experience plants the seed for the next, and, in the revealing light of Damascus, Paul's eschatological vision was filled with understanding. The effect of the first Christ event is that the Resurrected One is united with the spiritual component of earth existence. Although eluding the sense perception of the human being, the actual developments really begin only now. The etheric world which is connected to the earth is increasingly permeated by the essential effects of the Easter event. At the same time, through intensification of the inner force rendered possible by Christ, human beings must grow beyond mere sense perception until they are able to encounter the Christ in the etheric realm. This is when the Second Coming begins which takes its course in the supersensory sphere and extends over long periods of time. The part of humanity that links itself with the Christ can truly become Man and, at the end of the Earth aeon, move into the new aeon. The other part sinks away into the subhuman level and joins the lunar, hardened formation which the earth eliminates from itself as it turns into a sun. Therefore, it is indeed the Christ through whom humanity and worlds are separated; in so far as this is true, he is the cosmic judge. But God's great patience grants humankind the favour of time. The image of the field can therefore take the place of the vision of terror — the field on which the seed of Christ grows and bears fruit if the human being cultivates it properly.

The fundamental error of the Pharisees, which could be called a spiritual optical illusion, continued its effects far into Christian history despite the correction at Damascus. From the earliest times after the first Christ event, there were Christian circles for whom the two subsequent fundamental events merged into one. Here too, the cause was always a form of impatience, with accompanying fanaticism and intolerance. Such eschatological circles feverishly pictured the Second Coming as if the Christ descending 'on the clouds of heaven' would preside over the Day of Judgment. This Christian version of the Pharisaic vision became almost a permanent view, not only of certain sects, but of the Church itself. The great paintings by Signorelli, Michelangelo and Rubens which depict the Last Judgment, for example the classic depiction on the altar wall of the Sistine Chapel, witness to this eschatological conception. And the part which the pictorial conception of the Day of Judgment plays in the exercises of the Jesuit order established by Ignatius of Loyola can seem like the restoration of Pharisaic secrets on a Christian basis. A correct understanding of Paul makes it clear that the benevolence and patience of God has inserted a period of grace and evolution between the second and third fundamental events, which Paul's original viewpoint had merged into one.

Because of the Damascus experience, Paul found the way from Christ to Jesus. What he had so fanatically rejected was now revealed as true, namely, that the Messiah could appear as a humble human being who did not even distinguish himself from other men through his office and rank and finally suffered such an ignominious death as that of a criminal. The light-form that appeared to Paul at Damascus bore the stamp of the man, Jesus, who had served the Christ for three years as a sheath, because the spiritual 'body,' the etheric form in which Christ now revealed himself, was the etheric body of the man, Jesus, the substance of which had been transubstantiated through the victory of the spirit. In essence, the content of the Gospels, the life of Christ on earth, now became clear to Paul.

Thereby, a full view of the future opened up as well, with a gradual understanding of its grace-filled processes of growth. An insight arose which could loosen like nothing else the spell of fear and terror in which Paul found himself through his religious fervour. The Messiah came not as the cosmic judge, but as the Redeemer, the Saviour; indeed, he had already come. While the past stage of human evolution had been to endure the progressive Fall, its future stage would be the soil on which the seed of redemption blossomed. The redemption that occurred through Christ would henceforth be the theme of inner world history.

'Time' is nothing formal; it is humankind's grace-filled gift of reprieve preceding the ultimate decisions. The merciless spell of the Old Testament's concept of God and — in its extreme — of the Pharisees' idea of the Messiah had come about because, in it, the continuous fear of the eschatological short circuit was effective and time was not really taken into account.

Just as Paul — in retrospect — understood the human being, Jesus, he comprehended the mystery of human incarnation as such. This was not limited, after all, to the unique historical fact of Christ's incarnation in the man, Jesus; it is a principle that continues to work on into the future. As yet, is man not still in the process of becoming man? Did the progressive tragedy of the Fall not begin by man losing the perfection of paradisal creation bestowed on him: God's image in the human form? Did the Messiah not become man, in order that man could become *Man,* meaning that he could recover the lost true humanity made in God's image? As Paul began to comprehend the human being, Jesus, it dawned on him for the first time what man is. He discovered the secret of the 'Son of Man.' 'Becoming truly man' is the meaning of all future development. And the path to it was opened through the redeeming power of the first coming of Christ. By entering into humanity himself, Christ planted in man the potential to recover his true human image. It was not only in a quite general way that Damascus permitted Paul to look anew into past and future. One may say that he did so, too, as the first participant in the second cosmic event.

The first Christ event was achieved. It had included the grace-filled encounters granted to those who were united with him until Ascension and Pentecost, and took place entirely on the plane of physical existence. Now the Resurrected One continued to be present but in a sphere where, initially, human consciousness could not follow him, having become blind to the spirit. When would the prediction of the 'two men in white robes' be fulfilled, who said to the disciples on the mountain of the Ascension: 'This Jesus ... will come in the same way as you saw him go into heaven' (Acts 1:11)? The time will come when, through inner strengthening, human beings will expand their perception and consciousness. Then the world of the etheric will open to them, and there they will behold the light-form of Christ. In the fifteenth chapter of the First Letter to the Corinthians, Paul himself listed his Damascus encounter among the sequence of Easter phenomena. In reality, however, it was something new. In advance of normal human development, Paul, the premature first-born of future humankind, was 'seeing Christ in the etheric realm.' Paul was privileged to experience ahead of time what would start to become possible for humanity in general only two thousand years later. Thus he was the early herald of the second Christ event which, in our time, is now due to take hold of and fill the whole consciousness of man.

The hour of Damascus liberated Paul from the sombre spell of the Old Covenant and brought him into the light-filled kingdom of the New Covenant.

5. Paul and Moses

Christian theology has nearly always viewed the Damascus event as a complete break in the development of Paul's life. In reality, while we are dealing in one sense with a break, on another level we find a hidden continuity. Although they appeared in radical contradiction of what followed, earlier events had been an essential preparation for Damascus. Despite the erroneous and, to make it worse, fanatically held conceptions that went with it, Paul's fervent expectation of the Messiah, his longing for the Christ, had powerfully affected his soul. Only a thin wall in the end separated him from the one for whom in his own manner he had striven so zealously. Not evil but error, intensified by a blinding visionary light, had created this partition. Then the scales fell from his eyes. The approaching grace encountered in Paul a deeply concealed process of maturation originating from an ancient destiny. Thus it came about that Paul brought a quintessential element of the cultural past into his now totally changed life. One of the leading individualities of his day, a focal point in that culture, was recast in the light and fire of the Christ-being.

After the lightning of Damascus had struck him, Paul was a different person to the very last fibre of his being. But in reality, his innermost being, having been buried, was only now freed and awakened.

Through his strict observance of the Pharisaic rule he had penetrated to the point where the supersensory world begins to stand before the soul in images. Yet, at the same time, the approach to the threshold signifies entry into trial. Fear and terror grip the soul, the more so as the intellectual contents predominate in consciousness. Only if the soul is able to let go of consciousness without sinking into faintness, and then penetrate through the imaginative picture experience and hear inspirationally the spiritual word, only then is it also strong enough to cross the guarded threshold and make itself at home in the spirit realm. The path on which Paul had been directed led only as far as the threshold.

Thus, those images accompanying the initial awakening of a higher perceptual capability assumed visionary character, that is, filled with terror at proximity to the threshold. In this way they remained suspended, as it were, between the world of the senses and the world of the spirit. This encouraged the misinterpretation that these initial images would eventually be fulfilled in physical, perceptual form. Hence, in particular, the terrifying vision of the Last Judgment, with Christ appearing as the cosmic judge. The very thought that the Messiah would descend upon humankind in this way was bound to infuse fear into longing for those who waited. A world view characterized by fear of the threshold, as in the Pharisaic-Jewish view, has to be dualistic in the extreme: God and man, heaven and earth are completely incommensurable and incompatible. How can the living light of God impinge upon the darkness of earthly man, how can the power of His spirit meet the perishable earth-substance without the earth splitting asunder and burning up?

Before the gates of Damascus, Paul was delivered from the terrifying Messianic paradox. From beyond the threshold, a benevolent, helping power approached him, releasing his essential being from terror of the divine and awakening in him the force that he himself would later on call 'faith.' Through this power, the dividing barrier between this world and the beyond disappeared; he was allowed to take the first step across the threshold. This occurred as he was led forward from the element of vision, which he only knew as visionary lightning, into that of inner hearing.

The accounts that we have of what took place in that noon hour before the gates of Damascus remain incomprehensible and even contradictory unless we cease to imagine in physical-sensory terms what were supersensory events and experiences. Neither the overwhelmingly powerful light, 'brighter than the sun' (Acts 26:13), which shone round Paul, nor the voice that spoke to him, could be perceived by earthly senses. If, in the account given by Acts, mention had been made of a clearly outlined form risen from out of the light, we would still have to transpose this light-image completely into the inner sphere in order to comprehend it; and we would have to 'de-word' the words in which the voice announced itself and allow them to sound forth anew inwardly in order to do them justice. Still, the biblical report does not speak of a figure. The vision towards which Paul had earlier found his way and experienced not as tranquillity but as overwhelming brightness, now blossomed forth: the golden glory of the spiritual sun proclaimed itself behind the external sunlight. Now hearing was added to vision; the inspirative penetrated the imaginative. The experience became concrete and gave him certainty of comprehension. Paul found the field of supersensory experience suited to his nature. Not in the picture, but in the word did Paul inwardly feel at home.*

Paul *heard* the light. Notwithstanding all the power of that voice, it was still an inner hearing when he felt himself called by his name twice and when the question broke in upon him which compelled him to become conscious of the essential motives of his persecuting zeal: 'Saul, Saul, why do you persecute me?' It was a dawning of awareness in which, simultaneously, the voice of his own conscience sounded. In his own inner being, a voice arose which yet only belonged to him. A higher one peremptorily proclaimed himself to Paul. His whole being trembled with the anxious question of who this higher one was: 'Who are you, Lord?' (Acts 9:4f) The intensity and sincerity of the question unlocked the answer which now came forth as hearing became seeing. A figure and a countenance could now be perceived. The divine light-force of the Christ-being appeared in a form that bore human traits. Paul beheld the countenance of the Messiah whom he believed he was serving and realized that this countenance was indeed marked by the consummated human incarnation in the man, Jesus of Nazareth.

Only now did a mature and complete vision begin to unfold within Paul. The brightness of the Pharisaic vision, which had

* In his lecture cycle, *The Gospel of Luke,*[15] in reference to the words, 'self-seer' and 'servants of the word' in Luke's prologue, Rudolf Steiner makes a significant distinction between two types of searcher for the spirit in the early Christian period. There were those who, in developing their soul forces, passed through the normal sequence of steps in supersensory experience: through Imagination (picture), Inspiration (word) and Intuition (being.) Then there were others who were predisposed first to develop the capacity of inspired cognition in a state lacking any pictorial quality, and who only subsequently perceived images. Paul is undoubtedly representative of the second type.

filled the soul with so much terror and restlessness, was superseded and healed. It was as if the sun had risen to quieten the lightning flashes of a nocturnal thunderstorm. Nonetheless, a profound shock in Paul's soul came with this mighty easing and relaxing of tension. What an appalling error he had succumbed to! What evil he had perpetrated under its fanatical duress! The insight gained as a consequence of the true vision struck him so powerfully that his eyes were blinded.

Then it became clear that he of whom Paul had been so deeply afraid was living benevolence and love itself. The experience of feeling himself touched and permeated, of surrendering himself in faith to the One whose will is nothing but help and redemption, allowed Paul to sense a way out of the helplessness of the moment; and this escape would be the beginning of many paths — leading him towards his world-wide mission. The hate-filled passion of persecution would be transformed into the untiring work of apostolic activity.

Even the element of intuition, in which the listening vision and the visionary hearing culminated, made itself known in spiritual words, in accord with Paul's nature which above all was inclined to inspiration. Yet it was seeds of will, slowly dawning vistas of activity, that arose in Paul. His human will was henceforth tied to and received into the will of Christ itself, receiving guidance from above. This became clear when Paul, though blind outwardly but inwardly fully awake and able to perceive, encountered less conspicuous people who had attained to the indwelling of the Resurrected One in their souls. The seer, Ananias, engaged in the ministry among the Christians of Damascus, having been able spiritually to observe and accompany the destiny of the erstwhile persecutor without having been physically present, now became Christ's instrument in Paul. Three days later, Ananias performed the laying on of hands which, even then, was the confirming expression of baptism by the Spirit. And the resolution into which Paul's crisis was thus guided, at the same time lifted the spell of blindness which had covered his physical eyes.

The account of the Damascus event in Acts 9 (subsequently also in chapters 22 and 26), largely takes the form of a normal conversation such as takes place between two people in the flesh. If we fail to penetrate through this style of representation to the supersensory event, we face the danger of being trapped at a trivialized level, of by-passing the grandeur of the supersensory reality. If this happens, we cannot come to grips with the contradiction posed by Paul himself, where he characterizes the whole event exclusively as an *inner* process (Gal.1:15f).*

It is only by searching for the supersensory realities behind the words in Acts employing outward-earthly, pictorial analogies, that we can resolve the contradictions in regard to the experience of Paul's companions in the event of Damascus. At one point it is said that although the men who were with him heard the voice, they saw no one (9:7). Another place in Acts has Paul saying: 'Now those who were with me saw the light but did not hear the voice of the one who was speaking to me' (22:9). These two passages lead one to conclude that the impact of what Paul experienced also touched the souls of his companions, so that reflections of the light-phenomenon as well as the sound element reached them. The possibility is ruled out, however, that they could distinguish a figure in the light and the speech of a concrete being in the sound. They perhaps believed they were perceiving physical lightning and thunder, just as it says in the Gospel of John (12:29) when a spiritual revelation of words resounded: 'The crowd standing by heard it and said that it had thundered.' In the descriptions of Acts, the reason why a light experience is mentioned in one instance and, in another, an experience of sound, may relate to the fact that depending on their basic soul configuration the participants were either more aware of the lightning or the thunder.

Paul's experience has inspired many creative attempts at retelling or dramatic representation. Frequently, novels and dramas on the subject have suggested valuable nuances which have escaped merely theological consideration. Describing the human events that followed directly after the Damascus hour, Martin

* RSV main text has 'But when he who had set me apart before I was born ... was pleased to reveal his Son *to* me ...' However a note gives: Greek *in*.

Beheim-Schwarzbach's laudable and unpretentious booklet on Paul has the following:

> The startled companions rushed to his side to lift him up. He hung limply in their arms, listening to something within ... He was blind, and they directed him to Damascus ...
>
> As a blind man, helplessly led by the hands, the representative of the High Council arrived in Damascus. His companions knew not what to do ... They had come as officials and hangmen. Saul, however, no longer seemed to have any of this in mind. He did not eat or drink, yet appeared not to be concerned about his eyesight. He was caught up in intense musing. Then people took him to the house of a man by the name of Justus and tried to care for him. Apathetically, he allowed everything to be done to him. This lasted for three days.
>
> Then there came a man who called himself Ananias and asked to speak to Saul of Tarsus ... Saul had been expecting him. The voice had not been deceptive. He had had no doubt. A hundred senses now seemed to open to him which formerly he had not known. And now his physical eyes, too, became clear again. He looked around; he saw Ananias standing in front of him — the first brother of his new life. Ananias admitted that he had been afraid to come to him, but Saul reassured him. For many hours, Saul and Ananias spoke with each other.
>
> Ananias had to instruct him in all the details of his faith in Jesus ... Yet, strangely enough, Saul hardly had to learn anything. It seemed to him as if he had known this all along ...[16]

At Damascus, the step that Paul was permitted to take across the threshold between this world and the world beyond was at the same time the decisive step within; he moved towards the centre of his being and destiny. This came about because he encountered that entity which is the central point of everything, not only of space and time but of each individual human being. It was not a being outside his own self that was revealed to Paul. To his great astonishment, he recognized his own higher self, yet at the same time the higher self of all humankind. Not *a* man but *the* man, not any 'I' but *the* 'I' revealed itself to him. An organ had opened up in Paul that could perceive the spirit-sun of the Christ because they were essentially akin. Just as the eye of the body has been, in Goethe's words, 'fashioned through the light for the light,' and can only perceive the light because it is itself of a solar nature, so a hidden relationship exists between seeing the Christ and his indwelling in the individual. The 'Christ in him' opened Paul's eyes to the vision of Christ. It is for this reason that Paul characterized the Damascus event as a process of the inner soul: 'When it pleased God to reveal his Son *in* me.' (Gal. 1:15*B*) It is no coincidence that this phrasing occurs in the same letter where we find the classic statement: 'Not I but Christ in me.' (Gal. 2:20*B*)* Earlier, Paul had asserted: Not I but the Christ (the Messiah); man is nothing, God is everything. Now he added two significant words: 'not I, but the Christ *in me.'* The lower, earthly human nature was not set aside, but the path became free for the affirmation and growth of the higher true self in man. Formerly, Paul measured the human being by the outwardly established law. He pictured the Messiah as the judge who approaches from outside and judges according to the outer law. Now he began to fathom the *inner reality*. Christ does not judge according to the Law of Moses. He is himself the inner reality that can be heard in the centre of being in each man. The human incarnation of Christ laid the foundation and planted the seed for the freedom and sovereignty of the human being and thereby, generally, for man to become truly Man. Through the Damascus light Paul was not *taught* better in the sense that he now acquired different, more fitting contents for his conceptual life. A new *how* of conceiving and thinking came alive in him. Paulinism was not a new system of doctrines, but a new principle of the spiritual life.

Paul felt, and again and again expressed it in a radical manner, that through the light of Damascus he had found the path *from Moses to Christ*. If we take this not merely as a general truth which, as such, goes without saying, but as the appearance of a

* RSV: 'It is no longer I who live, but Christ who lives in me.'

completely new principle of thinking and life, then a surprising light falls on Paul's life immediately after the Damascus event.

If we take only the account in Acts, the impression could arise that Paul *immediately* made contact with the original Apostles. However, in the Letter to the Galatians, Paul emphasises that he did not go first of all from Damascus to Peter and the other Apostles, who represented the centre of the nascent Christian congregations in Jerusalem. He took this step only after three years. Of the interim period, he merely says that he travelled to Arabia. (Gal.1:16-18)

No clear ideas have been arrived at concerning Paul's sojourn in Arabia, though that would be of fundamental importance. Even theologians with a greater sense of empathy have remained quite vague here. Adolf Deissmann says:

> It is not certain whether he was already involved there in missionary activity; it is as unlikely that he conceived of the system of Paulinism there as it is likely that he had the desire for a period of quiet contemplation.[17]

In the same Letter to the Galatians, Paul answers the seemingly open question concerning the significance that Arabia had for him during the three years of seclusion. In the fourth chapter, 'Arabia' is mentioned once more, as the region of Mount Sinai.* There, long ago, Moses had received the Law out of thunder and lightning and had brought it forth. The inner confrontation with the Mosaic Law had to be the foremost task for Paul to fulfil after the lightning and thunder of Damascus. Do we not feel a sense of world history when we picture how, for his time of inner contemplation, Paul journeyed from Damascus to where Moses had once accepted the Sinai revelation for humankind? Instead of taking counsel with Peter and the other Apostles, at the very outset Paul deliberated with the genius of Moses himself. What was born on Mount Sinai reached its culmination at Damascus, for, as the new Moses, Paul's task was

* In my book, *Moses*, it was explained in detail that the biblical Sinai cannot be identified with the primeval rock massif on the so-called Sinai peninsula. The biblical Sinai, outwardly much more insignificant but still active in half-volcanic processes during Moses' time, is an elevation in 'Arabia Petrea,' the rocky Arabia directly south of Palestine in the neighbourhood of the biblical locality, Kadesh.

to replace the Law of Moses with the law of Christ, the law of freedom.

We can consider the Letter to the Galatians as Paul's account of the Moses journey which he undertook in those three years. He was addressing a congregation which wanted to transfer the Mosaic Law, which, after all, had been set aside by Christ, into Christian life. Therefore, through his description of the Damascus event as well as through the statement, 'Christ in us,' he gave testimony to the fact that he had found the way from the outer to the inner authority of the Law. Now, however, citing the holy scriptures of the Old Covenant, he could represent the Mosaic Law as an instrument that was to serve for a time but not forever. Here we must quote in full Paul's summing up of his position:

> Tell me, you who desire to remain under the duress of the Law, do you not hear what the Law itself says?
>
> For it is written that Abraham had two sons, one by the maid-servant, one by a free woman. The son of the maid-servant was born according to the flesh; the son of the free woman through the power of the Word of the Spirit.
>
> This is a significant allegory. In pictures, the twofold covenant with God, the two testaments, stand before us. The first covenant with God is the one from Mount Sinai. It leads to loss of freedom. This is Hagar. Now, in Arabian, Hagar means Mount Sinai. This corresponds in meaning to the temporal Jerusalem, for it is in slavery with all its children. But the new Jerusalem is the free one. She is the mother of all of us ... You, dear brothers, like Isaac, are children born of the Word of the Spirit. But as at that time he who was born according to the flesh persecuted him who was born according to the Spirit, so it is now.
>
> But what does the scripture say?
>
> Cast out the maid-servant and her son; for the son of the maid-servant shall not inherit together with the son of the free woman. So, brethren, we are not children of the maid-servant but of the free woman! (Gal.4:21-31*B*)

Until now, theology has seen nothing more in this passage of the Letter to the Galatians than an example of allegorical interpretation of biblical scripture — considered today to be playfully trivial — extended into Christian life. Yet, even on this basis, it shows that Paul demands the 'expulsion of the Law,' just as Abraham once expelled the 'Egyptian maid,' Hagar, along with their son, Ishmael, following a divine command. A profoundly wise insight into the meaning and course of Old Testament history is concealed behind the apparent allegorizing by Paul.

When the time should be fulfilled, the hereditary line and folk development proceeding from Abraham, the arch-patriarch, was intended to offer the human sheath in which the Christ-being could incarnate. Abraham's oldest son, Ishmael, to whom Hagar gave birth, was not suited, however, to continue this line. Together with his mother he was excluded from the developing folk relationship. From him descended the Arabian tribes. The Israelite line found its continuation in Isaac, the son of Abraham and Sarah, who was born when his parents were already of advanced age. Given the natural conditions of the time, his birth had to be viewed as a miracle, an event brought about by the Spirit. Although the actual element of heredity was not eliminated, it was reduced to a minimum. The Ishmael stream distinguished itself from the Israelite line of Isaac and Jacob by a more rapid development of the abstract intellect, while retaining a wilful, untamed character.

What had to be eliminated from the stream of heredity because it would have interfered with its regular development had to be reabsorbed into the nation's history as a stimulus to the development of consciousness once the Israelites were strong and confident enough to receive it. This took place through Moses in the form of the revelation on Sinai. When Moses had to flee from Egypt, he went to 'Arabia.' There, in Kadesh, in the Horeb-Sinai region, he became the disciple of the most important Ishmaelite teaching and mystery centre of that period. Jethro, the initiated leader of the sanctuary, helped to make Moses into the great creator of the thinking force springing from the forehead of man, turning Moses into the liberator and leader not only of the Israelites, but of all humankind. When, later on, Moses guided his people out of Egypt, the achievement of the forty-year sojourn in the wilderness consisted in his leading the whole tribe into the school in which he himself had been Jethro's disciple. As a pupil of the Sinai mysteries, he became the inaugurator of the sacred Law of Yahweh. In the far-off future, humanity would awake to the freedom of the ego-endowed human being through a spirit-permeated thinking. The path to this goal had to lead through the Law, which did draw man deeply into intellectual consciousness, yet made him unfree by subjecting him to an external authority in regard to his moral and social life.[18]

Among the insights that Paul brought back from his period of contemplation in Sinai, he saw through the foreign origin of the Mosaic Law. More than an interesting allegory was intended when he indicated the linguistic relationship of the name, Hagar, with the term, 'Mount Sinai.' The revelation on Sinai was an Arabism within Israel's spiritual history. It did not even originate from the spiritual sources from which the Old Covenant as such had emerged. In a certain sense it was indeed a distortion of the original. Even one who wanted to lead the Israelite-Jewish development back to its very own sources so as to purify it, would have had to repeat Hagar's expulsion by expelling the Law of Sinai. At Damascus, it became clear that the Law received by the son of the maid-servant and his sons, had served its time. The sun of freedom had risen above the horizon and would tear apart the bonds of serfdom. The 'inner authority' replaced the Law with its instructions and commands.[19]

The period in Arabia by no means caused Paul to view his task only in complete contrast to that of Moses. Rather, it enabled him to forge an immediate inner connection to it, so that he could consider his future activity as continuing the work of Moses on a higher level.

To look back into the age of Moses meant to become submerged in an early stage of the Old Testament development long before this had assumed its most extreme form, turning away from nature. At that time, the radical *contrast between paganism and Judaism* which emerged and intensified especially in the age of the great prophets, did not yet exist. The age of Moses represented a kind of middle-point between the patriarchs and the prophets. The folk coming into being around the patriarchs, Abraham, Isaac and Jacob still retained their sacred high places, groves and wells.[20] The people did not yet distinguish themselves so sharply from the surrounding pagan tribes, who worshipped the spiritual beings in the kingdoms of nature.* As the ferment of something pertaining to the future, however, the Israelite-Jewish stream had to develop in such a way that it turned away increasingly from the spirituality of nature, in order more and more exclusively to cultivate a religious life based only on the human-moral element. All intrusions of outer nature were distilled out of the religious consciousness; in this way, Judaism — though relatively small in numbers — emerged in the end as qualitatively different from the rest of humanity.

When Moses led the Israelites out of Egypt, this signified an important step on this path. Indeed, Egyptian life represented *the* religion founded on the cosmic, magical primal powers. The ensuing 'wilderness' was a fitting arena for the *inner* exodus from Egypt that had to follow; in other words, for the people to receive instruction intended to move the focus of religious life from outside to the inside. In the school of the Sinai wilderness, Moses gave the Law to the people. It was to direct all the soul's power of attention from the cosmic natural element to the human moral one. This turning away from the kingdoms of nature in favour of an initially abstract inwardness could be understood as an incarnation process which was finally to ground souls on a mineral earth foundation. The stone tablets of the Law were an allegorical expression of this.

For the completion of this mission by Moses, there was still need for a specific nature-spirituality, but one that, disregarding organic, living elements, belonged exclusively to the mineral earth element. In the Sinai region, the earth had not yet hardened totally to cold, rigid mineral. It still boiled and steamed with the forces of fire smouldering in its ground. The whole area through which the Israelite journey took place still possessed a solfatara-like, half volcanic character. Not that molten lava still broke

* The word 'heathen' originally designated those who prayed 'on the heath,' that is, outside in nature to their gods. The Latin *paganus* has the same origin.

through the earth's surface, but there were still many places where, because of its volcanic atmosphere, vapours could arise which, during the daytime, appeared like a pillar of smoke, and at night glowed like fire.

From the midst of these telluric phenomena, now long extinct but at that time vibrant and active, the spirit voice had already spoken to Moses when he first fled from Egypt and arrived in the realm of the Midianite mysteries. To this period belongs the secret of the 'burning bush.' Yet, this landscape, this earth, was also the natural surroundings of all that Moses and his people experienced during the forty years of the desert journey. Like a divining rod, the incense rising from the Ark of the Covenant led the people through the main areas of these telluric activities. The centre of all this was the sacred mountain with its double-summit, Sinai and Horeb, surrounded by tempests of steam and fire issuing as if from an oracular mouth. Here, Moses heard the highest and fullest message of the voice which had once addressed him out of the burning bush. Thus, the Law came into being in the Arabian land of the Midianites. Guided by the new Law, the people finally discarded even the links with nature which Moses himself had still retained, and now developed towards a moral-religious outlook that was radically withdrawn from nature, indeed, opposed to it.

With intense Pharisaic fervour, Paul had participated in this inner orientation of Judaism, leading to a gradual diminution of all affinity with nature. Then came the hour of Damascus, unprecedented in its nature, for up to this time the curtain had not torn apart for him as, divorced from the world, he had descended into his inner being in deepest contemplation. Now the cosmic environment of earthly nature was not only part of the stage of the event, it helped to bring it about. Just like Moses' experience before the burning bush, Paul's Damascus experience also possessed an important connection with nature. The light of the Resurrected One did not merely shine inwardly; it emerged from the etheric environment. During their journey across the barren Syrian plateau, Paul and his companions had been exposed to the piercing, burning rays of the noontide sun. Now they reached the green living belt which encircled the city spread out in the valley, and made it into a heavenly oasis. They were embraced by the mystery of shade, in which the merciless external aspect of light is removed and the inner essence of light, the spiritual component of the sun's effect, is exposed. Where the cruelly consuming light of the physical sun was subdued; where the lifeless desert gave way to a garden of living things, there it was that all at once the spirit sun's light shone forth overwhelmingly for Paul and his companions. Just as Moses out of the fire of Sinai, so now Paul heard the word of his calling out of a light that had moved into nature's etheric sphere.* Here was refuted not only the eschatology of the Messiah as Final Judge, but also the fundamental thesis of post-Mosaic Judaism that nature no longer revealed divinity and that, therefore, all pagan elements were impure and evil. An epoch was announced in which everything would be made new and in which both paganism and Judaism could find a synthesis on a higher level. Paul who, like no other, had trodden the anti-nature path of Judaism, knew from the hour of Damascus that he was now called upon to be the Apostle of nations. He would be carrying the Christ message to the non-Jewish, pagan nations of the world; he would proclaim to them that not only the hopes and prophecies of the Jews but also those of the heathens were being fulfilled.

During Paul's three years of reflection in Arabia, he also learned to penetrate the Sinaitic mystery. Not that any traces of the former telluric activity were still evident. On the spot where, a few centuries earlier, the divinity had spoken to Moses out of thunder and lightning, fire and smoke, Elijah experienced that God was no longer to be found in earth-nature, but only in the quiet inner voice. Paul, on the other hand, comprehended how Moses in his time could still receive the revelation of God, before humankind's ancient clairvoyance had finally faded from the

* In reference to this, see Rudolf Steiner, 'Spiritual Bells of Easter II': 'Through the Christ event the material fire (of Sinai) was spiritualized ... It was seen again when the eyes of Saul, illumined by clairvoyance on the road to Damascus, beheld and recognized in the radiance of heavenly fire the One who had fulfilled the Mystery of Golgotha ... Matter and Spirit are related in the evolution of worlds as the miraculous, material fire of the thorn-bush and of Sinai is related to the glory of the *fire from the clouds* that shone before Saul who had now become Paul.'[21]

domain of geological forces. At that time, had Christ not approached close to the terrestrial sphere on his path towards human incarnation? Was it not he who, through the power of Yahweh, had revealed himself to Moses and the children of Israel? Later, in the Letters to the Corinthians, Paul put into words what the now dead nature of Sinai had told him. The miracle of the Rock, which had accompanied the sons of Israel throughout their wandering through the wasteland, was the Christ! (1Cor.10:4) Though Moses had participated actively in the effects of the Sinai miracle, he could not comprehend their Messianic secret; thus, at the 'well of doubt and trial' (Massa-Meriba), he had confronted the prediction of his tragic destiny, namely, that he himself would die without having set foot in the Promised Land.[22] Looking back, Paul recognized what Moses had been unable to grasp.

On the hard rock-summit of the 'Place of the Skull,' the path of the Christ himself passed through the vanishing point of humanity's religious experience of nature. The reason why Paul could encounter him subsequently in the ether-weaving of nature at Damascus was that Christ's path rejoined a superhuman cosmic element after his passage through death. Quietly, the garden of a new earth germinated in the dead mineral. In the etheric realm appeared the first traces of the spiritual sun that seeks to unite with earth existence. Just as the environment of Sinai represented the sphere which Christ passed through prior to his becoming man, so that of Damascus indicated the sphere in which the Resurrected One sought his further path.

At Damascus, Paul ceased to be a Jew concerned with the denial of nature and separation from it. Later on, when he went his way as a world traveller and Apostle of the nations, a significant nuance of his relationship with nature emerged even more clearly. This was noted by Adolf Deissmann who almost alone among Protestant theologians, was endowed with true insight into the Anatolian world and climate of early Christianity, specifically the journeys by Paul. In his book on Paul, published in 1911, he added a map from which it can be seen that the world of Paul coincides with the habitat of the olive tree. No real motivation is expressed in the text for the inclusion of this map, for although

Deissmann sensed the significance of his discovery, he was unable to express it conceptually. It is in fact most instructive how the paths of Paul's journeys remain always in those areas where the olive tree grows — something that certainly could not have been the conscious intention of the Apostle. There are no olive trees in Egypt, and it is known that Paul did not travel there, although Alexandria was one of the most important cultural centres of those days. On the other hand, the fact that Spain belongs in the olive tree zone throws a certain light on the early Christian tradition that Paul is reputed to have made an apostolic journey to Spain during his period in Rome as a prisoner.[23]

In his lecture cycle, *Christ and the Spiritual World,* Rudolf Steiner spoke in some detail on the subject of 'Paul and the olive tree.' We can thus decipher the geographical connections between the various pre-Christian spiritual streams and the coincidence of Paul's travels with the habitat of the olive tree. Chronology, astrology, meteorology and geology successively characterize the ancient Persian, Egypto-Chaldean, Graeco-Roman and Old Testament spirituality. The olive tree, by virtue of its gnarled root system and trunk, its foliage and oil-bearing fruit, appears like an allegory of nature for the transition from geology to Christology; thus, the transition from the Old to the New Testament.

An illuminating symmetry of correspondences now results between the different landscapes of the activities of both Moses and Paul. Sinai shows us the last condition of earth substance prior to the final hardening into rock. By comparison, the olive tree represents those processes on earth which lead the dead element out of itself back into the living one. This is not meant to indicate those etheric processes received rhythmically by our earth from the cosmos, only those that originate through a natural etherization and spiritualization of the earthly element. In forming the oil, the olive tree takes from the earth those forces which can be etherized. The volatile oils which spread the aroma of blossoms across the meadows as they evaporate, do not originate from the earthly realm but from the celestial spaces. On the other hand, what the olive tree gathers in its fruits is not oil from above but oil from below. It is the oil of the earth; in it, the inanimate earth substance becomes etherized.

This is indeed the mysterious element that impresses the traveller from the north so much when he encounters olive groves for the first time in Italy or Greece. The grey, gnarled and crooked, often hollow trunks of the trees, appear like withered and fantastically formed rock-like continuations of the ground. One cannot really imagine that any sap still rises through this wood. Likewise, the narrow, silvery leaves that feel hard and almost a little glassy to the touch, remaining throughout the years on the tree without changing, truly reflect the element 'earth.' Everything in the tree seems akin to mineral and rock. No fresh, sap-filled element is contained there. The olive tree gives us the appearance of being a hoary old man. Yet, through an olive grove, around the wrinkled shapes of the trunks and through the silvery-green foliage, a light-ether magic weaves and is wafted like the veil of a mysteriously emerging sphere of life. Afterwards, the ripe olives are proof of the reality of the life forces that remained concealed. Etherized earth element is lavished upon us in the pure olive oil.

It is surely no coincidence that the landscape of Golgotha was determined so abundantly and strongly by the olive tree and its secret. On the summit of the Mount of Olives, as he took his leave of them, Christ gave his disciples apocalyptic instructions for the future like a last testament. At the foot of the Mount of Olives, between the olive trees of Gethsemane (the very name means 'Oil Garden'), Christ struggled with death, inwardly abandoned by his followers. Again, on the summit of the Mount of Olives, the Apostles beheld the Resurrected One at the end of the forty days as he united with the whole earth sphere. Is not the breath of Resurrection, henceforth pervading the whole earth creation, symbolized in the natural life of the olive tree? Etherization of what is dead, spiritualization of earth substance — in all instances as a spiritual process, this signifies the path of the Resurrected One wherever human beings prepare for him a place in their hearts. The wisdom of Providence directed matters in such a way that the torch of this spiritual process was first carried through those regions of the earth where the processes of nature corresponded prophetically. This is the secret correspondence between the world of Paul's journeys and the world of the olive tree.

The desert wandering of Moses and the apostolic journeys of Paul stand over against each other in a world-historical correspondence. Moses' activity *still* had a natural foundation in the smoke and fire of the Sinai territory. Paul's mission *once again* had a natural basis in the quiet light of the world of the olive tree. Unlike Judaism, Christianity does not stand in such an extreme contrast to paganism. Rather, the triad — paganism, Judaism and Christendom — outlines the mighty course of evolution. The heathen nature religions were oriented towards the starry cosmos of sun, moon and earth. The history of the Old Covenant had the purpose of disengaging the human being from nature and of referring him to his inner being. Through the Resurrection of Christ, nature, meaning the whole earth, has also been included again in a completely new way in the process of redemption and the sphere of religious life. In Paul, the new step incarnated, as it were: coming from the most extreme Judaism, he turned into the Apostle for paganism. He bore the new cosmic message to those human beings who still remained within the subsiding forces of the ancient cosmic experience of divinity.

Although much is only fully comprehensible in the context of the lectures, some of the explanations by Rudolf Steiner concerning Paul and the olive tree shall be quoted here:

> And now the geology characteristic of the Jewish people was to be permeated by the spiritual being whom we ... have studied as having a particular activity in relation to the earth. Geology was to be Christened. The spirit of the earth was to be experienced in a new way by men ... But this was possible only if there came a power which could free the spirit of the earth from the earth forces. This was accomplished when the earth's aura was permeated by the power of Christ and consequently a change came over the earth itself. The Christ entered into the forces which the Yahweh deity had released and gave them a different character.

Steiner goes on to discuss the laurel dedicated to Apollo, which receives its shape from 'meteorology,' the nature element of Graeco-Roman life. He then continues:

Another plant is much more closely bound up with the earth; it is, so to speak, the expression of geological relationships. If one really feels how the oil penetrates the olive tree, so that in one's own soul the elemental forces are stirred by the way in which the olive tree allows a new sprout to be grafted on to it and to flourish best there, — then one feels how intimately the olive tree is permeated with the oil of the earth. One can feel the earthly element pulsing through the oil. And now recall ... [mention had been made of this in an earlier lecture] that Paul was destined to build the bridge between Hebrew antiquity and Christianity, between geology and Christology. As we said, Paul's activity extends through the sphere of the olive tree ... We can feel the elemental forces that stream through the olive tree into the environment, and these are forces familiar to the soul of Paul. We ... feel them in his words. He immerses himself, as it were, in geology in order to experience the elemental forces in the aura of the olive tree and to let its aura inspire him in that geographical realm where his work lies.

Nowadays, people read these things ... much too abstractly ... They do not reflect how not only intellect and reason, but all the forces of the soul can be connected in a primal earthly sense with all that lends a certain region its particular character. It was the olive tree that gave its stamp to the Pauline region. And when Paul sought to raise Jewish geology up to himself, then he expressed the most important things — inspired by the olive tree — concerning the relationships of the Christ-filled human beings to those who are distant from Christ. Let us hear the strange words Paul uses when he wishes to bring the Gentile Christians into relation with the Jews. They are not to be taken abstractly, but as words that rise new-minted from the elemental depths of his soul ...

In the following words from his letter to the Romans, Paul speaks to the pagans as the Apostle of the pagans. But he makes it known how it is his heart's desire to win as many as possible of those related to him by ties of blood, people of the Old Covenant. These are like an olive tree of which many branches have been broken off, meaning, that many do not penetrate to the fulfilment of the prophecy given to them. In place of the broken-off branches, branches are taken from a wild olive tree and grafted onto the old, cultivated tree. They are those who, from among the pagan nations, find their way to the Messianic fulfilment:

> But if some of the branches were broken off, and you, a wild olive shoot, were grafted in their place to share the richness of the olive tree, do not boast over the branches. If you do boast, remember it is not you that support the root, but the root that supports you. You will say, 'Branches were broken off so that I might be grafted in.' That is true. They were broken off because of their unbelief, but you stand fast only through faith. So do not become proud, but stand in awe. For if God did not spare the natural branches, neither will he spare you. Note then the kindness and the severity of God: severity toward those who have fallen, but God's kindness to you, provided you continue in his kindness; otherwise you too will be cut off. And even the others, if they do not persist in their unbelief, will be grafted in, for God has the power to graft them in again. For if you have been cut from what is by nature a wild olive tree, and grafted, contrary to nature, into a cultivated olive tree, how much more will these natural branches be grafted back into their own olive tree. (Rom.11:17-24)

Quoting this passage, Rudolf Steiner continues:

> Thus he spoke ... showing how he took what he had to say from the geology characterised by Judaism, drawing a superb picture of the elemental forces which rise up from the earth and hold sway in the olive tree.[24]

6. Law and Conscience

As a Pharisee, Paul had pictured the Messiah in the Mosaic tradition, as the cosmic judge who descends into the world in order to judge humanity according to the Law. Through the Damascus light, Paul now recognized the inwardly appearing Messiah who bestows on humanity and the world a new direction. But Christ does not resemble a flash of lightning that breaks in on the world from outside; rather he resembles a sun-seed which, germinating, fills the world with light; a leaven which, from within, renews what has died into the risen bread of life.

After this turning point, Paul was forced to look back on the pre-Christian spiritual development in a completely different manner. The cultural stream of the Old Covenant had prepared humankind in a special way for the Christ through 'the Law and the prophets.' Above all, it had done so through the fire of longing which the prophets had enkindled with their Messianic prophecy. The Law, too, in its time, had played its instructive part. Yet its effect had now become ambiguous, indeed, unbalanced. Paul had personally experienced how, through the Law, a wall of rigidity had come about which caused the human being to have no sight for the true sphere of the Christ.

At the same time, as if he were suddenly discovering all this afresh, Paul could not help but gain a positive understanding of certain fruits of Greek spiritual life with which he had become acquainted so vividly during his youth in Tarsus. He had to recognize that a significant form of preparation and education, orientated towards the Christ and equalling that of Mosaic, prophetic Judaism, existed in the European traditions within non-Jewish, pagan cultures. In particular the ethical wisdom derived from classical Greek philosophy, holding sway in the circles of the Stoa, also pointed in the direction of Christ. First and foremost, the stream of the Old Testament had had the mission of helping to bring about the earthly incarnation of the Messiah. Could the Greek cultural stream perhaps offer a way towards *understanding* the Christ, now that he had arrived? Did the Mosaic Law not almost stand in the way of a proper perception of the Christ? And had an insight not emerged from what the Greek and Roman philosophers were able to state about 'conscience' as the inner authority of the striving human being, an insight which could be further developed towards a comprehension of the Christ? How did 'Law' and 'conscience' relate to each other?

Of the two mighty evolutionary streams — one of which produced the culture of the Law, and the other which gave rise to the impulse of conscience — the first goes back to the most ancient periods of earth development. The second stream, younger and more orientated towards the future, emerges only later, not long before the turning point of time.

The stream of the Law accompanies the whole path of humanity which we term 'history' but which is basically nothing else but the expulsion from paradise that passes through many stages, the progressive Fall.

We could call the original state of this development *'the Law of the deity itself.'* More intimately than the babe at its mother's breast, the human being was embedded and integrated into the world of his divine origin. As yet, he had no individual existence. God's essence supported and flowed through the essence of man. Just as the water droplet and the wave in the ocean follow the laws and movements of the greater whole, so the human being lived and weaved in God. No other body of law existed which man could have obeyed other than the law of the deity itself.

Then came the moment when the tragic primordial event occurred through which man began to fall away and separate from the original paradisal union. This event *had* to happen, for otherwise man would never have awakened from the sleep and dreams of his childhood, nor would he have outgrown his infancy. But the profound tragedy was inherent in the *manner* in which it happened. Beings who, in preceding aeons, had already forfeited their accord with the highest divine will, brought impatience and precipitancy into the evolutionary process. What should have been an organic growing and maturing process turned into one of falling and descent. The soul-spiritual human being plunged more deeply into physical matter, and the realm of earth itself condensed more quickly and became hard, stony ground.

For a long time, however, a benevolent echo of the paradisal law of God accompanied humanity's earthly path. Though the human being had fallen away from its immersion in the cosmos of the divine hierarchies, it still remained for ages in the bosom of the maternal earth-nature. Thus, the Greeks' mythical consciousness of history looked back into the primal age of nearness to the gods in which the *Law of Demeter* prevailed. Mother Earth followed her own law in the wondrous, heavenly rhythms of her life of nature, and the law she bestowed upon men consisted in allowing them to participate in her life. In a dreamy, natural manner, human beings followed after her. The law of the mother was their law, too. They did not have to become aware of it in order to obey it. The law of nature was identical with the moral law. Thus humanity remained close to heaven, though already moved from the blessed heights of heaven into dark depths of earth. Men did not lose their innocence; the pulse beat of pure nature passed through them as though through the many members of one body. Though the child no longer lay at the breast of its mother, it now learned to tread its earthly path holding its mother's hand. In his poem, *Das Eleusische Fest* (The Eleusinian Festival), Schiller nostalgically looked back to the times when Demeter-Ceres gave her laws to human existence, thus banishing the dangers of savagery.

In the course of history, however, it was inevitable that the faculty for freedom and choice developed in the human soul, while at the same time recollection of the divine diminished. Due to the densifying and hardening bodily sheath, the human being was increasingly cut off from the primeval relationship with nature. Man now confronted nature as a stranger. A schism tore his world in two.

Placed in a position of having to rely upon himself, would man now find his way according to the divine will? Would he strive for the good and do it, or would he descend to evil? This concern brought about the appearance of the great lawgivers, from Hammurabi to Solon. The greatest was Moses. The *Mosaic Law* replaced the Law of Demeter.

With this, an important but considerably one-sided factor entered the history of human morality. Earlier, 'morality' had also existed but it was childlike and innocent. It required no directions or laws, for, originating from paradise, it was simply present still in the feelings and instincts. The moral law established by Moses and the other lawgivers did not proceed from the paradisal origin of man but from his Fall. It no longer reckoned with his innocence but with man's sinfulness and alienation from God. Thus sin becomes an earthly fact which is held up to consciousness. The German language offers an especially spatial description of the concept of 'sin' in the words *Sünde/Sonderung* from which we get the English 'sunder' meaning 'to separate.' The Law, in the form of revealed commands by God, speaks across the deep abyss to the human being who, bridgeless and separated, confronts the deity. 'From outside,' the stern, judgmental voice addresses man and tells him what is good and what must be avoided in order for him not to fall into the abyss in which there blazes the annihilating fire of divine wrath. Ever since the stern word of the Law resounded, the dualism of existence has prevailed: in the world beyond, the pure and holy deity is enthroned; here below, man, full of fear, a member of a fallen, unholy secular world, lifts up his glance to God.

This tragic bias in the Law of Moses is also demonstrated in the following. The age of Demeter drew to a close because the human being outgrew his beautiful childlike immaturity. But now the maturity slowly developing in him was not allowed any room to grow. The stern deity of the Old Covenant could have no confidence in man that he would find the right directions. Thus, immaturity was replaced by a basic dependence on the part of the maturing human being.

Something else is connected with this. Out of the act of establishing the Law, far more extensive consequences resulted for the *consciousness* of man than for his moral life. After all, the mission of Moses consisted, first and foremost, in bringing about a new consciousness; thus, the Law, transmitted through him to the people, had to serve this goal.

The Law permeated the lives of those for whom it had binding power with an unheard-of degree of awareness. This had already been brought about through the basic Ten Commandments, but also through the all-encompassing catalogue of rules and directions for all areas of social and personal life, including matters of hygiene. No room was left for any instinctive discovering and doing of good, nor for any impulse arising creatively out of the soul's inner being. Compliance with the Law was not possible without thoughtful attentiveness throughout life to the commandments applicable to every situation. Thus, the Mosaic Law was not only the ruler of the moral life, but above all prompted the awakening of the conscious mind.

A new interplay between being and consciousness commenced. The Law was given from outside; its commands could be learned. Thus, it became the moral primer with the aid of which human beings, not only a handful of leaders but the whole nation, trained their thinking and memory. Now the Law also contained a great number of God-given, sacred aims for human will and actions. Nobody could escape the feeling that a chasm remained between his being and what he thus received into his consciousness. The fear of God's anger and punishment, which could be unleashed through each non-compliance or — worse — transgression of the Law, was the main impulse for striving after the good. The Law established what was good and what was bad. The light of awareness had been enkindled in the human being, but at the same time the seed of a discrepancy between being and consciousness was implanted in his nature. The rift which separated God and the world, hence also God and man, now also passed through the human being itself.

We must clearly envisage the nature of the thought-imbued consciousness that was now aroused. It was distinctly a 'thinking-about-something,' namely, a thinking about a content already given authoritatively. Greek mythology pictured this rational brain-bound thinking in the figure of Epimetheus. In the figure of Prometheus, it is contrasted with creative thinking in which will is also at work, hence, a thinking capable of bringing the fire of the gods' thinking from heaven down to earth. Fundamentally, the mode of thinking initiated by Moses is not of Promethean nature.

From it arose the capability of abstraction and finally modern intellectualism. It emerged as the Epimethean head intellect, which then brought with it the tragic rift between being and consciousness which is such an acute problem in modern life.

The consciousness produced by the Law of Moses involved a sudden acceleration if not a violent jolt in the gradual breakdown of man's ancient union with nature. It was not without reason that the rocky desert became the stage where the people of the Old Covenant entered the training ground of the Law. On the other hand, the exodus from Egypt which ushered in the desert journey was a necessity. An ancient cosmic magic was retained in Egypt which, as such, could never have allowed the birth of an ego in the human being and which would never have opened the path into freedom.

Later on, the Law of Moses, which was still valid for all twelve tribes of the Israelite nation, was superseded by a second Law which applied only to the small Jewish remnant of the whole nation — the *Law of Ezra.* This was established during the exodus from Babylon where the people had lived in exile, just as the Law of Moses had been given during the exodus from Egypt. The extension of the Law instituted by Ezra was the stern rule of the Order of Pharisees.[25] We have mentioned how, in Pharisaic esotericism, intellectual consciousness accompanying the discipline of the Law was intensified to a visionary level, and that Paul had matured in that school until the light of Damascus surrounded him.

Ultimately, the stream of the Law extends into our own civilization, where it not only flows into the endless forms of political legislation, but where it has very nearly produced a culture of *natural law.* Instead of standing before the deity, the human being stands before godless nature. In it, he seeks for laws. The natural law, in a sense the most extreme dilution of what was once 'the Law of the deity,' dominates all modern, intellectual thinking. It is the last stage in the history of consciousness which, brought about by the stream of the Law, ran in a direction parallel with it. Having created the concept of the natural scientific world based on natural law, the human being who was once so intimately linked to nature finds himself at last completely cut off from it. To situate his own being in this world conception in his thoughts is possible for him only to the degree that stone, plant and animal are part of him. The specifically human element, above all the world of morality, has no place in this world view.

In traditional Christianity, people hold fast to the Old Testament's basic thesis of the unbridgeable chasm between God and man. In the meantime, modern scientific thinking, the most advanced offspring of Mosaic legalistic thinking, draws the final conclusions leading towards self-exclusion of the human being. The expulsion from paradise culminates in the intellectual Fall. The consequence of man having fallen consists in the fact that today he is in danger of being eliminated from the world view that he himself has thought out. Law leads to the ultimate culmination of 'sin' in the sense of man's ultimate separation from the divine world-configuration.

In its various forms during the course of evolution, law was an important means of educating humankind towards egohood. It is, however, inherent in its nature that it accompanied and finally even promoted the ego development more in its negative aspects, in particular, the separation and isolation of the individual from the original universal unity. The Law could not really be effective in strengthening and encouraging man's innermost being, for it made use of the fear of punishment and hope for reward. It educated the human being who was evolving towards ego consciousness but did not direct him beyond his inner dependence. In other words, on the path of the Law and the state of mind produced by it, the human being was moulded so as to acquire an ego form. The question remained open as to whether and how the form would be able to fill its being with the true ego content. The moulding of self was not possible without a progressive hardening of the earthly sheaths. Only a body that had become completely physical, particularly in the human head and brain, offered a suitable mirror for developing sensory and intellectual consciousness. Hence the Old Testament folk stream as custodian of Yahweh's Law had the task of silencing the ancient visionary organs and faculties by contracting man's supersensory being — in particular the etheric body — to coincide with the physical.

Even the great prophets had to place their proclamation into this service. Hence, Isaiah was given the task: 'Go and harden the hearts of the people.' It was not on account of the wickedness of men, but the intention of the Yahweh deity itself that, finally, even the hearts of men became hardened and stonelike, as if in accommodation and subjugation to the mineralized brain. The stream of the Law followed so closely the hardening consequences of the progressive Fall that the question of how the rigid ego form could possibly be capable of receiving as its content the true ego, the spiritual entelechy hovering above the human being, led to anxiety, and was indeed humankind's cry of distress. And this alarming question is not outdated even now; on the contrary, it has become an acute omnipresent danger.

The solution to this question and salvation from the anguish related to it, has come into the world through the incarnation, death and Resurrection of Christ. To experience and to recognize this was the grace bestowed on Paul through the light at Damascus. He then became the Apostle of the heathen, bearing his message of Christ first and foremost to the non-Jewish nations, especially those in Europe, through the fact that, aside from the stream of the Law, another, younger stream existed. It had the purpose of preparing for the Christ impulse the more western branches of humanity living in a Europe only recently awakened from sleep. We can call this stream the *stream of conscience.* Where the Law trained human beings, the ego form came about; where conscience awakened and gave direction to life, humankind prepared for the reception of a higher ego-content.

It is perhaps one of the most revealing observations which can be made in philology that the term 'conscience' only emerged in literature at a late period which can be precisely designated. What Rudolf Steiner pointed out, later research has since confirmed.[26]

The word 'conscience' does not occur at all in the Old Testament. For that matter, it does not exist in the Hebrew and Aramaic languages. This, of course, does not imply that in the books of the Old Covenant there is no evidence of profound soul conflicts dealing with moral issues. But this is not 'conscience'; it is the voice of the Law indicating to the human being his imperfections and rebellions against God. In the spiritual life of Greece, we witness the birth of the concept of conscience. Here, too, the word does not seem to have existed in earlier times. Even Plato's writings are not familiar with it. We look for it in vain in Aeschylus and Sophocles. Then it suddenly surfaces in Euripides, the youngest among the three great tragic dramatists, in his dramas, *Medea* and *Orestes*. From that moment on, the word 'conscience' becomes one of the most illuminating concepts of Greek philosophy; finally, in the writings on ethics by the Stoics — now no longer in the Greek language but in Latin — it appears in the foreground. Given its absence from the Old Testament, its mention in the New Testament is filled with significance. It is Paul especially who vitally incorporated this word into Christian vocabulary.

Rudolf Steiner calls attention to the fact that, with the appearance of the concept of conscience, the underlying transformation of consciousness can be discerned in the development of Greek tragedy from Aeschylus and Sophocles to Euripides. In his dramas, Aeschylus introduces aspects of clairvoyance, the ancient property of humankind, wherever man becomes conscious of guilt. As if witnessing an outer soul world, the guilt-laden person perceives entities who pursue him in order to mete out punishment and revenge.

> The soul becomes clairvoyant ... in order to perceive what it has wrought in the physical world through its misdeed ... The misdeed produces quite definite processes in the spiritual world ...[27]

Thus the Furies appear to the guilty one in a terrifying and recriminatory manner and rob him of his peace.

By the age of Aeschylus, ancient clairvoyance had already become extinguished in Greece. But in poetry, its contents still lived on for a while as a memory. Then, however, it became possible to take the experience of guilt, which had moved completely into the inner life of the human soul, and express it in a new form which was fruitful for dramatic poetry.

> When the ancient clairvoyance began to disappear ... the human being ... perceived ... the effects brought about by the cosmic spirit only in a reflection within his inner being. This reflection of the rectifying cosmic spirit,

which stands guard by the side of the ego, appeared to the human being as the conscience watching over him.[28]

The experience of a divine voice speaking within man's being did not originate at the same time that the term, 'conscience,' made its appearance in literature. Long since, in the 'sentient sphere of the naive folk,'[28] it had taken the place of the revengeful spirit forms of ancient vision. Through the moral bearing which proceeded from it, it had already made a major contribution to the reorientation of Attic-Greek life. Although Socrates and his great disciple, Plato, did not yet employ the word 'conscience' — Socrates spoke rather of the *daimonion* who whispered words to him at important moments — he did die a martyr's death as the very representative of the urging of conscience.

In the Greek language, the word for 'conscience' first appeared in a provisional form as *synesis;* but soon, beginning with Democritus and Demosthenes, it is found in its complete form: *syneidēsis.* The corresponding Latin is: *conscientia.* Today, it is not possible readily to experience the original, richly image-saturated value of these words. For, in the course of time, an additional meaning developed which the same word can imply. The German language is one of the very few which, for the second, younger concept, formed a word of its own, namely, *Bewußtsein* (consciousness). In particular the Latin *conscientia,* and the modern words derived from it in French *(la conscience)* and English (conscience) signify both awareness and the sense of right and wrong. The original meaning of conscience is almost overshadowed and devalued by the newly added meaning. We have spoken of the fact that it was particularly the stream of the Law which established 'consciousness.' It made the human being conscious in a quite specific way. But the light which thus filled the human being with wakefulness did not spring from a creative source within himself. It resulted as a side effect and consequence of a discipline and culture shaping man from outside. It is therefore characteristic that the stream of the Law, including the language of the Old Testament, did not produce a word for 'consciousness' itself. For that to happen, it would have been necessary for the human spirit to rise to a creative 'consciousness of consciousness.' While consciousness did come into being, it was not the kind that could have carried out the act of becoming conscious of and giving a name to itself. It had to wait until the other fundamental spiritual stream had progressed to the creation of the word 'conscience' in order to adopt this word, which thus faced the danger of paling in meaning.

The word, *syneidēsis* (conscience), designates the awakening of a quite specific consciousness. It is not 'consciousness in and for itself,' but a 'becoming conscious of self' on the part of the human being. Yet it is by no means simply what we denote as 'self-awareness.' Man becomes conscious of himself in a higher light, through the assistance, as it were, and cooperation of an invisible higher being. He is not alone when the conscience speaks, although it raises its voice within his own inner being. The Greek prefix *syn* means 'together with' (Latin, *con-).* Thus, the activity of conscience flows out of the cooperation of the human being with another mysterious entity who dwells within him. This is why conscience can relentlessly pronounce guilty the person in whom it is aroused. And this inner authority not only expresses itself completely independently of any externally established law, it avails itself of an incontestability and absoluteness which a law can never have.

Concerning the origin of the 'stream of conscience,' surprising insight can be attained through the perspectives which Rudolf Steiner has opened up. He describes how, after passing through the ancient Indian and Persian stages, and having evolved the human 'sentient soul' in the third great cultural epoch which had as its scene Egypt, Babylon and Chaldea, the regular development of culture and consciousness led to the blossoming of the 'rational and mind soul' in the fourth, the Graeco-Roman culture which began approximately with the founding of Rome and lasted until the fifteenth Christian century. In the fourth cultural epoch, the 'central epoch,' in the middle of which fell the Christ event, the nature of man was so far imbued with culture and structure, particularly by means of developing the capability of thought, that it could receive into itself the ego impulse. From the east, the stream of the Law stood at the back of humanity's ego birth. In Israelite-Jewish history, it had assumed its most extreme form.

Through completely distilling all ancient cosmic relationships out of human nature and through a special refinement of the brain-bound intellectual consciousness, it contributed the most to the fact that the ego impulse, the principle of the ego form that is enclosed within itself, took hold of the human being.

Aside from mainstream cultural development, however, away from regions which were the focal points of history, different evolutionary processes ran their course. Thus, at the time of the Egypto-Babylonian civilization, northern and western Europe were by no means an area of cultural stagnation. Of course, nothing existed there that was comparable to the high culture of the magic temples and pyramids by the Nile and between the Euphrates and Tigris rivers. Inwardly, on the other hand, enveloped in a still dreamlike mythical life of seership and bards, an important process was taking place. There, the ego awakened in the sentient soul which was still completely opened up to the cosmos.

> The lofty culture of ancient Chaldea and Egypt was poured into a sentient soul as yet unconscious of its ego. Here in the North, no such lofty culture was implanted into the soul. The soul, therefore, remained more or less uncultivated; but in this very lack ... it developed an ego consciousness ... Among the peoples of Egypt and Chaldea, ego consciousness was late in coming ... In Europe, however, the ego did not delay but developed immediately in the sentient soul. On the other hand, it waited until the later soul principles had developed before absorbing certain qualities pertaining to the treasures of civilization.

The development of conscience was prepared by:

> the mutual inter-permeation of the sentient soul by the ego feeling. In them [the northern Europeans], the ego feeling, which lifts men up from the lowest to the highest, already spoke in the sentient soul like a voice from God. Before this, nothing spoke in them but instincts, desires and passions, but now, like a voice from God, they were urged to do right so that they might rise to the higher ego.[29]

In the people of ancient northern and western Europe, the birth of the ego impulse in a soul still completely united with the cosmos and borne by the gods led by no means to a human self-consciousness resembling that of today. What now took on life as a spiritual element in the soul's foundations was experienced as a divine-hierarchical being indwelling the soul. Human beings felt themselves to be direct descendants of the gods. Only this makes it comprehensible that as late as the age of the great Germanic migrations, important branches of these folk groups designated themselves as Goths, meaning 'gods,' and that others who, together with the Saxon tribes, later inhabited the British Isles, called themselves Angles, meaning, 'angels.'

The early ego birth in the still dreaming ancient Europe is the origin of the stream of conscience. The fundamental feeling of life determined through divine indwelling, the intuitive knowledge of the divine voice in the human soul, flowed also during the third cultural epoch into eastern and south-eastern regions of Europe. In the south and the east, enveloped in mythical dreams, the Graeco-Roman world still awaited its hour. Particularly in Greece, perhaps beginning with the period of Homer — a few centuries after Moses — an encounter may have taken place between the waves borne from the east by the stream of the Law, and in the west by the stream of conscience. When the ego impulse then awakened as well during the fourth cultural epoch within the mainstream of culture, the Greek world was already protected against the merely formal character which, for example, had been assumed by this impulse in the Israelite-Jewish development. The original European stream, which was ensouled by the higher ego content, added its effects; thus, the ego impulse could come alive as the impulse of conscience among the Greeks and, later, the Romans. Where this occurred, the young 'I' had a divine support against the danger of sinking down into the mere egoistic ego. The day came when, through the lips of the poet, the wondrous word, *synesis, syneidēsis,* could be uttered for the first time, thus to become incorporated into the vocabulary of all peoples.

It is possible to say that the word 'conscience' unfolded its fullest sound and brightest light-force when Paul uttered it. He who had passed through the sternest school of the Law became the greatest herald of conscience.

In his case, the word, *syneidēsis,* joined the sequence of words, heavy with meaning, which he coined creatively out of his closeness to Christ. They all begin with the prefix, *syn-: syn-pathein, syn-stauromenai* — 'to suffer with Christ,' 'to be crucified with Christ,' 'to die with Christ,' 'to arise with Christ.' Interpreted literally, the term, *syneidēsis* (conscience) designates a sacred, mysterious accessory to knowledge. A knowledge is referred to here which is not merely human. The human being is allowed to 'know together with' a higher being. The Pauline words normally appear with the phrase, 'with Christ,' but *syneidēsis* was used by Paul without this addition; but here was it someone else's knowledge that Paul felt privileged to share?

Several times in his letters, Paul calls on his conscience as a witness: 'I am speaking the truth in Christ, I am not lying; my conscience, which is guided by the Holy Spirit, is my witness.' (Rom.9:1*B*) 'We are allowed to boast, for the testimony of our conscience speaks for us' (2Cor.1:12*B*). How can a human being call upon his conscience to be a witness for his own statements unless he distinguishes it from himself? The human being speaks, but there is another who adds his say. Indeed, only because the other one says the same thing, can man dare to speak up. Since the hour of Damascus, Paul could claim to be speaking no longer merely out of his own self, but out of that higher knowledge. His conscience was for him the organ for Christ. And yet it was not a matter of a stranger adding his say from outside. As Paul spoke, Christ spoke through and with him; and just because of this, it was Paul himself who spoke in the fullest sense of the word.

Properly understood, Paul's Damascus experience stands in the centre of human history as *the classic experience of conscience.* Here are revealed in a grand, archetypal way, both the negative note of the voice of conscience which brings error and guilt to man's awareness, and its positive authority which permits the light of truth, of right and of divine aims to shine out that much more powerfully against the dark background. On Golgotha, the greatest wrong of all time had occurred. Because humanity had not recognized him, it had nailed the Lord of its own redemption on the Cross. At Damascus, in Paul, humanity became aware of this greatest of all injustices. The veil of the tragic error was torn apart. But the matter did not rest as emotional shock at becoming aware of humankind's abysmal guilt; the truth was revealed which had not yet been recognized. The light-being, against whom the spears of darkness had been directed, appeared in its totality, namely as the sun and central point of the world, to the sight of that human being who, at this moment, was the conscience of humankind. Truth itself came in person, in pure magnitude of grace without a reproachful, judgmental attitude; with this, the profound error was refuted, humanity's wrong was forgiven.

Paul himself characterized what he had experienced at Damascus as a revelation of conscience, by describing it as an inner process of becoming aware, not as an encounter with a spirit form approaching him from outside, as it were: 'When it pleased God to reveal his son *in* me ...' Paul had entered more and more exclusively into the school of the intensified Law of Moses, the educational result of which produced the enclosed, contoured ego form of the human being. But secretly, a higher ego-content had matured in Paul — perhaps its slumbering seed had germinated in his early youth in Tarsus by means of the fact that the bright spirit of the Greek language as well as awareness of the word, 'conscience,' had fallen on it like a warming ray from the circles around Athenodorus.

In his lectures dealing with conscience, Rudolf Steiner has also spoken of the 'further development of conscience.' He says that within Christian life the role of conscience, which preceded Christianity as an important cultural preparation, does not cease but only now actually finds its fulfilment. The power of conscience was originally like a bud which could bloom only when the rays of the Christ-sun fell on it. What kind of flower was it which then unfolded out of this bud?

Conscience came into being when the ancient clairvoyance, which still beheld the avenging Furies, finally became extinguished in humanity. One day in the future — and this future begins now in our twentieth century — a new clairvoyant vision would awaken in the human being under the rays of the Christ-sun. As with Paul before Damascus, the eyes of our inner being will open to the light of the Christ-being, and the whole sphere of morality and the guidance of destiny will be illuminated. This will be the blossoming of the bud which formed once when the old clairvoyance centred itself in the force of conscience. Thus, the Damascus experience of Paul is at the same time the anticipated unfolding and further development of conscience that will be available one day to all human beings. A direct Christ experience, not dependent on any external tradition, is available to those in whom conscience blossoms forth into an organ of vision:

> Human beings ... must learn to recognize that it is possible to know Christ as the historical Jesus even without historical documents for the reason that the Damascus event can be renewed for any person through training or, in the near future, for the whole of humankind.

This significant 'new faculty' can awaken in the human being, 'because the soul has stood for a while under the light of conscience.'[30]

During his three years of isolation and contemplation in Arabia, in that region where Moses was active and received the Law, Paul acquired full surety over the step from the Law to conscience, from the outer to the inner authority, which the grace of destiny had allowed him to make. There is a profound inner reason why, later on, in the same Letter to the Galatians in which he described overcoming the Arabism of the Law in terms of the new expulsion of Hagar, he expressed the key to his Christened insight resulting from the Damascus event with the words: 'Not I, but Christ in me.' At the beginning of this letter, testifying to the Damascus event, he described it as an event of the inner soul: 'When it pleased God to reveal His son *in me.*' The Pauline formulation of 'Christ in us' was designated as replacing the Mosaic principle of the Law: 'For I through the Law died to the Law, that I might live to God. I have been crucified with Christ; it is no longer I who live, but Christ who lives in me' (Gal.2:19f).

The 'Christ in me' is the form which conscience now assumed. The European-Greek experience of conscience was the Messianic prophecy of western, pagan humanity. The Pauline 'Christ in me' was the first fulfilment of this prophecy prior to the time when the bud will fully open up to the vision of Christ.

The 'Christ in me' is the key for everything that Paul was able to teach and to proclaim. When the day comes that this can be recognized and utilized concretely, only then will Paul actually be discovered and comprehended. In the letter to the Galatians, the Pauline phrase occurs once more, as the expression of concern and struggle for human souls: 'My little children, with whom I am again in travail until Christ be formed *in you* ...' (Gal.4:19)

Paul finally went so far as to designate the 'Christ in us' as the new cosmic principle:

> The mystery hidden for ages to the generations of men has now been made manifest to those who sanctify themselves to it. To them God chose to make known the riches of the glory which this mystery is to unfold among the peoples of the world: It is the *Christ in you,* the seed of hope of all new revelation. (Col.1:26f*B*)

These words make it evident at the same time how clearly Paul discerned his mission within the various streams of humanity. Not among the people belonging to the stream of the Law, hence also not among the chosen people of the Old Covenant, was the revealing light of 'Christ in us' to arise, but in the 'peoples of the world,' in the pagan stream of the West to whom had been given the impulse of conscience as first instalment of what was promised for the future.

One of the most sublime utterances by Paul concerning conscience demonstrates with what absolute mastery he surveyed the two main streams of humanity:

> When the nations of the world who have not the Law do by nature what the Law requires, then those who have no external law bear a law of their own in their hearts. They show that what the Law requires is written in their hearts: the *conscience* that speaks in them, expresses the same thing ... (Rom.2:14f*B*)

It is clear that Paul is not referring to the secondary, exclusively negative expressions of conscience, which emerge as 'guilty conscience' after one has transgressed the Law. Since the traditional Christianity of the Churches has retained the Old

Testament mood of the Law despite Paul, most of what appears to this day as an activity of the conscience in the Christian sphere of life belongs as a 'guilty conscience' more to the direction of the Law. Conscience as the pure inner authority however is not only an accusing voice recalling the past, but it points to positive ideals and goals of the future.

One can say that through the Damascus event Paul became a *European* in the spiritual sense due to the fact that this occurrence separated him from the stream of the Law and fitted him into that branch of humanity which had developed the idea of conscience. With innermost necessity, his apostolic path was to lead him finally westward into the European countries, because it had been through a providential meeting of East and West that his eyes had been opened. The East not only would develop the ego-form through the Law, but also would offer up the bodily sheath as the earth-form in which the Christ could incarnate. Along with the impulse of conscience, the West had to prepare the higher ego-content and with it the organ for inner comprehension and ultimately the beholding of Christ.

> Through the Christ impulse, humanity at last was given the possibility to understand that the God who is the creator of all things ... and of the outer sheaths of the human being, can be comprehended and conceived in our inner being. Only by grasping the truth of Christ Jesus' divine humanness could humankind become capable of understanding that God can be something that can speak to us in our own inner nature. In order that man could find within his inner nature the nature of God, it was necessary for Christ to enter the evolution of mankind in an external historical event ... Thus, we see how the *external* comprehension for the idea of the divinity of Christ Jesus is born in the East, — but how what the human consciousness develops as the conscience approaches this from the West ... Thus East and West co-operate with each other. We see how the sun of the Christ nature dawns in the East; and we see how the Christ-eye in the human conscience is prepared in the West in order to understand the Christ. This is why we see the

victorious march of Christendom developing, not towards the East but westward ... Christianity takes hold of the western world because it was in the West that Christendom had to fashion its organ in the first place. There we see Christendom linked to what has become the most profound factor of culture for the West: the concept of conscience, tied to Christianity.[31]

7. Paul and the other Apostles

Within a short time, news of the sudden change which had occurred at Damascus in the life of the Pharisee, Saul, must have reached the circle of those gathered around the Apostles in Jerusalem. With his departure for Damascus, the hate-filled raging of the persecutor had moved towards a frightening culmination; everyone awaited the first reports with trembling hearts. But what were the bewildering new questions that arose along with the sense of relief now that the danger was averted? Something incalculably mysterious must have taken place. Would the change in Saul's soul be genuine and enduring? And what attitude should they adopt if the news, brought by messengers, turned out to be true: that he who had been filled with hatred had turned into a confessor of the faith, that the persecutor had become a proclaimer? Did that sombre, fanatical man actually cease to be sinister now, or did he not appear even more enigmatic? Shock, mistrust and fear mingled with feelings of relief and did not really allow joy to arise.

From what the congregation at Jerusalem learned, it became clear that Saul had by no means simply turned into one of those who, like the other newcomers, joined their ranks. A radical difference, the breath of something new, made itself felt, something that would eventually confront the Apostles with hitherto unknown questions. Was the recently established, quietly growing realm to be subjected already to the tempests of a revolution? The most diverse opinions were expressed, and in a way that revealed once again the differences present even among the leading individuals in Jerusalem. Peter may initially have been enthusiastic, but then he began to have doubts. Others who were less Galilean, more Jewish and rooted in the thinking of the Law, raised darkly pessimistic points. John may silently have looked into the future which stood dramatically enough before his inner eye. On occasion, he may well have admonished everybody to be open-minded and patient.

To begin with, the Apostles in Jerusalem were spared the anxious encounter which they had anticipated. Paul vanished from sight. From day to day, people tensely expected his arrival. Finally, however, when three years had gone by since anybody had heard of him, messengers from Damascus came who reported that he had returned, and that he was calmer, more assured and determined than could ever have been imagined. Yet, what he now proclaimed as a result of his long inner self-communion revived the old questions and concerns to an intensified degree. Paul announced that the age of the Law instituted by Moses had come to an end; that he who stood above the Law had appeared. It was not long before it became known that Paul was being attacked and threatened in Damascus in the most vehement manner. The deadly persecution, whose leader and instigator he had been, now turned against him. Those whom he had ceased to persecute did not know whether they should take his side wholeheartedly. The brethren of the congregation in Damascus believed that they could no longer protect him. They helped him escape by lowering him at night in a basket down the outside of the city wall.

Paul now took the step which the congregation in Jerusalem, in suspense, had long awaited. He set out to make contact with the first Apostles and to come to terms with them concerning his mission in relation to theirs. One day it was reported that he was in Jerusalem. It is understandable that a natural, joyful and frank meeting could not come about immediately. The leading men of the original congregation probably would have avoided Paul even longer if there had not been one individual who was anxious to build a bridge of understanding and reconciliation, namely, Barnabas, who had looked forward to Paul's coming with enthusiastic expectation.

Upon Paul's return from Arabia, following his three-year silence, everything that happened in Damascus and Jerusalem must be considered against the background of a fearful uproar throughout Jewry. Caligula, the mad Caesar, had arrived at the point where he identified the nocturnal spectres that were plaguing him with Judaism. Thus, he staged the most cruel persecutions of Jews everywhere. It could be that Paul's arrival in

Jerusalem coincided with dreadful reports of the first great Jewish massacre of recent history which had claimed many thousands of lives in Alexandria. Subsequently, Caligula ordered the deathblow against the central sanctuary of the Jews in the Temple of Jerusalem. Petronius, the Roman governor of Syria, was ordered to march with his legions to Jerusalem and erect a larger than life-size statue of Caesar in the inner sanctum for the purpose of seizing the Temple. Again and again, Petronius, in league with others of insight, delayed execution of the order. They recoiled from the immeasurable bloodshed which a worldwide revolt of the Jews would entail. Everywhere, the most terrible fear gripped the Jews, including those living in Jerusalem. Then, with the assassination of Caligula, the danger was averted. Claudius, the next Caesar, renewed the protective rights granted to the Jews. The congregation around the Apostles in Jerusalem certainly shared in the fear aroused during Caligula's lifetime, for they were seen as nothing more than a Jewish sect. It was far from the minds of the Apostles, too, to view themselves as detached from the religion of their fathers. In the prevailing circumstances, not only the actual representatives of the Jewish religion but also many of the first congregation in Jerusalem were now particularly sensitive to any criticism and attack against the Law entrusted to their forefathers. Although it goes without saying that nothing connected Paul with the Caesarian persecution of Jews, he was, nevertheless, now seen as an opponent of the Law of Moses.

When Paul arrived in Jerusalem, the life of the first congregation was directed by two men. One was Peter, whom the Lord himself had entrusted with the leadership of the future community. At his side stood James, the stepbrother of Jesus.* Dedicated to the strict asceticism and prayer discipline of the Nazirites, which bordered on fanaticism, James, prior to the event of Golgotha, had been incapable of tolerance and understanding for Jesus and the circle

* He is always designated as 'the brother of the Lord.' In my book, *Kindheit und Jugend Jesu*, it was pointed out that he was the brother of the Solomon Jesus youth who died young. Later, when through the marriage of the widowed Luke-Joseph with the likewise widowed Matthew-Mary, both families had become one, James became the stepbrother of the Jesus whose birth is narrated in the Gospel of Luke.

linked to him. Only subsequently, as visions overcame his soul shortly before the festival of Pentecost, had he begun to recognize what had occurred.[32]

During the first weeks after the mysteries in the spring of the year 33, Peter, who rose only gradually and with uncertain soul to the task imposed on him, had had the disciple whom Jesus loved at his side like a helping genius. The precious sequence of scenes in which Peter and John work together continues for quite a while from the Gospels into Acts. In the passages where Acts refers to the first encounters between Paul and the other Apostles, John has already disappeared from the scene. Perhaps he was no longer in Jerusalem at that time; in any case, he was absent from the city at that moment. Now Peter relied on James who possessed a nature and orientation, however, quite different from John's. Since the resurrection drama of Bethany, the eagle of the Lazarus-John genius had soared to heights encompassing all humanity. By contrast, hardly anybody had linked himself more deeply and solidly with the spiritual mission of Judaism than had the Nazirite James. Probably it was he who had come closest to the fervour of the Pharisee Saul *prior* to the Damascus transformation. Thus, when Paul now arrived in Jerusalem as a fundamentally changed person, he not only encountered in the leading Apostles the new light of the sun which had arisen at Easter and Pentecost; he also met up with the ancient Saturnian, sombre world of the Law.

The difficulties dividing the leaders of the first congregation from Paul did not really stem from their being angry with Paul for his former opposition and persecution. Had Peter not denied the Lord three times, and did James not have to reproach himself for having misjudged and rejected as a visionary the one who had been his brother? Rather, it was the far-reaching differences of consciousness that made mutual understanding so difficult.

Peter and the other Apostles proceeded from the human figure of Jesus. Their destiny had brought that about. This is even true of the 'brother of the Lord,' James, although in his case it was a subsequent contact. The extent to which they rose from there to recognition and acknowledgment of Christ himself remained an open question and differed with each person. Paul, on the other hand, could only proceed from his experience of the Christ-being; he could only discover the earthly, historical facts of the life of Jesus in the higher light revealed to him. He did not depend on the reports of others. The light of Damascus placed him in a position resembling that of the evangelists who, without having to rely on external traditions, deciphered the content of the 'three years' from the book of spiritual retrospection and subsequently interpreted it in human words. The empirical path of the other Apostles was confronted in Paul's case by the path of transformation and illumination of consciousness, something that certainly also included a supersensible viewpoint. Paul acknowledged the significance of the simple, existential relationship which the other Apostles had to the Christ events. Without reservation he gave precedence to the special destiny of those who had been true witnesses of the incarnation of Christ. But this could not mean that he also subjugated himself to them in questions of consciousness. In regard to this he was so advanced in comparison — with the exception of John — that he was capable of surveying the special feature of the Christ relationship of each Apostle as well as the one-sided elements and limitations inherent in it.

In the books of numerous theological scholars of early Christianity, mention is made repeatedly of the Jesus cult of the first congregation. This expression is, of course, largely the result of the fact that an exact differentiation between Jesus and Christ is impossible within a world conception which rejects all supersensory phenomena. On the other hand, the designation, 'Jesus cult,' is actually quite appropriate for the community-building principle predominantly effective in the circle of the first Apostles. As in Peter's case at the moment of his spontaneous confession of Christ in Caesarea Philippi, the other disciples, too, must repeatedly have experienced flashes of pregnant insight or felt in moments of quiet contemplation that the Christ, the Messiah, had become man in Jesus. But who, actually, was the Messiah? And how were they supposed to picture him? If he was God, how could he assume human form without the world thereby coming to an end? The thoughts which formerly had induced Paul resolutely to deny the Messiahship of Jesus may have passed as questions through the souls of even those disciples who 'believed' in Jesus.

As such, the lofty Easter experiences of the forty days did not lead beyond the Jesus-faith to the final Christ-certainty. The miracle of the Resurrection, which made itself known to them by extending even to physical sense perception, referred particularly to the man, Jesus, who had moved among the disciples in living flesh and blood. The great chasm of consciousness between Paul and the others would perhaps have become evident most clearly if the question had been raised as to how the coming of the Messiah, anticipated with longing by humanity, related to what Jesus himself had designated as the 'Second Coming,' the coming of the Son of Man 'on the clouds of heaven.' Not all the disciples would have replied: The Messiah has already come and the Second Coming will be his new revelation when, one day, humanity will be mature enough for it. A few, in particular the brother of the Lord, James, believed that the actual event was yet to occur; the Second Coming, which they pictured to be imminent, would signify the true and real coming of the Messiah. As a Pharisee, Paul had never been able to picture the Messianic event other than in the form of a Second Coming entailing the ultimate end of the world and the creation of a new one; yet at Damascus he had received the insight that the Messiah had in fact already appeared in humble human form and, through death and resurrection, was inseparably united with humanity and the earth. In addition, he was aware now that a new Christ revelation in the etheric realm was going to be bestowed on humanity in the future; that on him, Paul, as humanity's untimely birth, an early ray of this future sun had already fallen so that he could become the one to prepare its arrival.

Owing to their numerous uncertainties and unexpressed differences of opinion, the Apostles in Jerusalem reacted with reserve to the radicalism which could be observed in Paul. No real contact would therefore have been established without the intervention of Barnabas.

Barnabas was a Levite from Cyprus. His original name was Joseph. He must have occupied a special place in the congregation in Jerusalem. It was the Apostles who had given him the Hebrew name, Barnabas, in Greek, *huios paraklēseōs,* or 'Son of Spirit-Consolation,' in recognition of his standing in the Christian community. The word *paraklesis* contained in the name, points to the 'Paraclete,' the Holy Spirit. Thus, the choice of this name may have referred to an important service which Barnabas had been able to render to the Apostles in connection with the event of Pentecost. As in the case of Joseph of Arimathea, Simon of Cyrene and Nicodemus, it is probably not amiss if we place this 'Joseph of Cyprus' in the same category as those individuals who, as representatives of related spiritual streams, possessed a certain inner rank and, as helpers and friends, were more loosely connected with the congregation. The assumption arises that Barnabas came from the social circles of the Essene Order.

To a much greater extent than has hitherto been realized, Essenism formed the basis for the first Christian congregations both in regard to its members as well as its institutions and social forms. Whether it was members of the Order itself or individuals and families active in Essene settlements and colonies, the great majority, particularly the most spiritually advanced, soon realized after the events of the year 33 that the prophecies they held sacred had found fulfilment, and that Essene life would henceforth continue in the Christian congregations.

The house where the first congregation of Jerusalem customarily gathered illustrates most clearly this joining of Essene life with that of Christianity. It had been the house of the Order of the Essenes, erected at the holy site above the original location of the Ark of the Covenant and the grave of David. At the same time, it had served travelling members of the Order as one of the many hospices situated in towns around the Mediterranean. In this house on Mount Zion, friendly Essenes had made the Cenacle, the room of their daily sacred meal, available to Jesus and his disciples for the celebration of the Last Supper. Here, on Maundy Thursday, the Washing of the Feet and the sacred ceremony of bread and wine had taken place. That same night, the disciples fled from the Garden of Gethsemane back to this house, where they could seek the right of asylum in the sanctuary in order to escape the clutches of the officials. There they remained during the following weeks. During the forty days of the Easter encounters, the Cenacle now became their true temple until, on the morn of the fiftieth day, the flames and rush of the Spirit came over them.[33]

In the period that followed, the house of the Cenacle became the home of the Apostles and the developing congregation. There exists no example more unequivocal than this of notable sections of Essenism making way for Christian life. Mary, the sister of Barnabas, was already installed there as housekeeper. Her young son, John Mark, later became the Mark evangelist. We must therefore imagine Barnabas as having close links with the house of the Cenacle.

The Messianic conceptions and expectations of Essenism were widely different from those of the Pharisees; yet they contained a certainty equally great. The lightning of eschatological terror did not flash through them; neither were they obscured by the distractions of earthly political aspirations. The Essenes counted on the long-term patience of God in humanity's history. Therefore, they pictured the longed-for Messiah more as a healer than an avenger and judge. In many countries, the Essenes called themselves 'Therapeutae,' and many of their representatives, travelling in pairs throughout the countryside, worked as folk doctors always ready to render medical care. When the Messiah came, he would bring down from heaven by word and deed the cosmic remedy for an ailing creation which would otherwise fall hopelessly under the spell of death.

They were not opponents of the Mosaic Law, but they adhered to a version from which the acute, axiomatic lack of confidence in man was expunged. They were related more to Naziritism, also inaugurated by Moses; thus their rule, consisting of directions for the ascetic and meditative life, represented a kind of intermediate level between the Nazirite vows and the Mosaic Law.

The fact must not be overlooked, however, that a one-sidedness and weakness was inherent in Essenism as a matter of principle. The Essenes strove for a 'pure' life *away* from the world and material concerns, even where involvement with the world could not be completely avoided. Weapons and money were strictly prohibited; anyone who came into contact with them was contaminated. All food and drink which drew the soul-spiritual part of man more deeply into the body was avoided; this, naturally, included any partaking of meat and wine. As for the grape, even the unfermented juice was shunned, because this imbued man with egotistic qualities. Everything was dominated by a tendency toward isolation by bringing about special conditions for the conduct of life. In the midst of the ocean of impurity, an island exempt from original sin and evil was to be established. The fact that, thereby, the remainder of humanity only fell all the more under the tragic, compulsory grip of matter and, in addition, had to contend with the demons banished and held off by the Essenes, brought about the Luciferic and socially self-centred one-sidedness of these circles. It is the same element which later on clung to Christian monkhood and monastic institutions, and which, incidentally, was a direct continuation of Essene establishments within Christianity.

In any case, if we picture Barnabas as having stood in some way in an intimate relationship with Essenism, it becomes comprehensible that he was open to Paul's transformation and present convictions. Like him, he could clearly acknowledge that Christ, the world-healer, had become man in Jesus. He could also understand what Paul meant when he declared that the age of the Mosaic Law had come to an end. And had Paul not been living for three long years in the desert as an ascetic and hermit, just like those who belonged to the innermost circle of the Essene Order? Barnabas cleared the way for Paul in Jerusalem. He brought about detailed conversations between Paul and Peter and, subsequently, James. It is probably due to the efforts of Barnabas that a certain understanding was achieved, at least to the extent that Peter and James no longer wished to impede the missionary activity of Paul.

Surely, it was not only now that Paul and Barnabas became acquainted. Perhaps the frequently expressed conjectures are correct that Stephen, Barnabas and Paul had once been fellow students — possibly during the time when Paul was among the pupils of Gamaliel. In any case, their ways parted during Stephen's martyrdom. Paul thereby became a fanatical opponent; Barnabas may have been most profoundly confirmed in his leanings towards the Christian circle.

Though it may appear like a break in the narrative, certain aspects shall be pointed out here that make clear the union between Essene institutions and impulses and the life of the first Christian community. The installation of seven deacons — Stephen was one of them — belongs here, something which the circle of the Twelve decided on soon after the initial events. The Acts of the Apostles indicates as a reason for this installation certain complaints raised by the Greek members against the Hebrew faction of the congregation concerning the 'daily *diaconia.'* As no comprehension existed, particularly in Protestant theology, for the early ritual life of the community, the expression *diaconia* was misunderstood. It was translated as 'daily assistance' [or 'help']. The deacons, who were installed for the purpose of accommodating those complaints, were taken to be subordinate parish helpers or almoners of sorts. At this point in the New Testament, however, the term, *'diaconia'* decidedly refers to 'divine service.' Literally, it simply means 'service,' and, for the sake of comparison, we need only consider the meaning inherent even today in the simple English word 'service,' which is unequivocally understood to mean ritual ceremony and worship, to realize that here in the Acts of the Apostles reference is being made to a lack of and — for the purpose of remedy — the creation of an institution in the ritual life of the congregations.

The stern Judaism of the Law had carried out a mighty concentration of worship whereby only one temple existed, the Temple in Jerusalem. In addition, there was only one important ritual ceremony — the one at Yom Kippur, the autumnal Day of Atonement. Basically, there was only one priest — the high priest of any given period who, once a year, on the occasion of the single service, entered the Holy of Holies behind the curtain. The Old Testament mood deriving from this attitude has continued into the present in the tendency in the extreme forms of Protestantism to celebrate Holy Communion just once a year.

A diametrically opposed attitude had developed among the Essenes. There, adorned in festive garments, people gathered together daily for the 'sacred meal' in the Cenacle of the monastery or the home of the Order. The daily meal together, the breaking of the 'daily bread,' was the 'daily *diaconia*' — the sacred ceremony carried out every day.

In the inception of the first congregation which took place in Jerusalem, the polarity between the ritually impoverished Hebrew-Jewish faction and the Hellenistic side orientated towards a stronger life of ritual became apparent. Particularly from the time that James, together with Peter, had assumed the leadership, the Apostles tended more towards the Hebrew point of view and conceived their task above all to be the proclamation of the word. But in so far as they followed the urging of those Hellenistic members of Essene leanings and installed Stephen and the other deacons, they made room for the ritual-priestly element against their own fundamental attitude. Thus, the daily celebration of breaking bread, the 'daily *diaconia,*' ceased to be in danger of becoming neglected. The sacred substance of both the evening of Maundy Thursday and the forty days of the Easter encounters, which indeed had always entered into the communal sitting at table, received its own channel, pulsing like blood in the artery through Christian history as the most significant stream. Destiny brought it about that the 'daily *diaconia*' had as its location the same Cenacle at the holy site on Mount Zion in which the disciples had been privileged to experience the mysteries of the sacred meal with Christ himself before Good Friday as well as after Easter morning. In close proximity to the Cenacle, in front of the Gate of the Essenes, at the nearest city gate next to the palace of the high priest, Stephen had been stoned, and Paul had supported those who had thrown the stones.

Stephen, the exponent of the newly-developing priestly element, had become the first martyr. Barnabas, whom we can assume dwelt with his sister in the Cenacle, may have considered himself the representative and perpetuator of the impulse which had been embodied in Stephen. In any case, it was due to him that the actually divergent opinions of the original community remained in balance with one another. Although belonging to the Greek faction himself, he had understanding and reverence for the Apostles and enjoyed their greatest confidence. Because of his special position within the congregation, he could then also build the bridge between Paul and the other Apostles, for Paul had himself switched sides, as it were, from the Hebrew to the Greek element as a result of his experience.

Significantly, it was not the event of Pentecost but only the death of Stephen that gave the signal for apostolic expansion. The Apostles themselves, however, were not the first to go out as missionaries but those who belonged to the Hellenistic, diaconal faction of the community. They were close to Stephen and now may have felt sent forth and accompanied by his genius. Thus we see another of the seven deacons, Philip, travelling at once through the region of Samaria as a bearer of the missionary proclamation of the word.* Above all, a group of 'men from Cyprus and Cyrene' set out on the task of spreading the gospel in an astoundingly new and daring manner, so that only a short while later a new centre of Christian life came into being in the world capital of Antioch. Henceforth, the focal points of the Jewish Christian and pagan Christian wings confronted each other in Jerusalem and Antioch.

The Acts emphatically characterizes this turning point in the development:

> Now those who were scattered because of the persecution that arose over Stephen travelled as far as Phoenicia and Cyprus and Antioch, speaking the word to none except Jews. But there were some of them, men of Cyprus and Cyrene, who on coming to Antioch spoke to the (non-Jewish) Greeks also, preaching the Lord Jesus (Acts 11:19f).

The men who are mentioned here, who were travelling out into the world on a missionary endeavour, were predominantly those who, coming from Essene or related groups, had found a connection to the Christian community. Their decision to depart may have been determined by two reasons. The hatred of the Jews which had led to Stephen's death had not only been incited because he had confessed his faith in Christ. If this had been the

* Acts 8:5ff. Here, it becomes clearly evident that the deacons were by no means limited to offering assistance in nursing care, and did not leave the proclaiming of the Gospel only to the Apostles.

only reason, their hatred would have been directed just as much against Peter or James. What angered his opponents most was that Stephen, by confessing his adherence to Christ, had intensified his Essenism to the point of an open and consistent break with the Mosaic Law. When the more general persecutions were unleashed in which the Pharisee Saul played such a fanatical, instigating role, they were directed especially against the Hellenistic section of the congregation which, along with its adherence to Christ, combined a clear break with the Law of the Old Testament. It is very likely that this also brought about the danger of dissension and alienation within the congregation. Those members of the Hebrew faction who were less exposed to persecution may frequently have been upset about their Hellenistic brothers who, in their estimation, were too radical. They may have been relieved when the latter departed from Jerusalem.

On the other hand, it could not really have been the intention of the friends of Essenism who had come from all the countries around the Mediterranean to remain permanently settled in Jerusalem. Quite apart from all the dangers, they felt drawn to their homelands or to the people among whom they had earlier been active as travelling messengers of the Essenes or Therapeutae. Hence, a number of fateful conditions encouraged the expansion which finally led to the establishment of the centre in Antioch.

When we are told that those who travelled northward initially addressed themselves only to Jews, this indicates the obvious possibility that the Essenes who had become Christians could hope to find understanding in other countries among those people who dwelt in the surroundings of the Essene Order. Therefore, the *coenacula,* the rooms of the sacred meal in the Essene homes, may frequently have been the locations where the proclamation of the word occurred. This very fact is clearly discernible in the descriptions of Acts. In a number of passages mention is made of an 'upper room.' The Latin Bible always refers here to a *coenaculum.* It corresponded to the Essenes' fundamental attitude of retreat from all material things that in their cloisters and hospices the room that was to serve as a sanctuary was never located on ground level. It was always an upper room, for they believed that in this way they could protect it from the direct emanations of the earth. Even the Cenacle in Jerusalem, which to this day exists in the Gothic form bestowed on it by the Crusaders, lies one level above the ground floor. In early days the healing and resurrection of Tabitha by Peter took place in Joppa (Jaffa) in a cenacle built as an 'upper room' (Acts 9). It was in a cenacle that Peter experienced the vision which beckoned him to go to the house of the Roman centurion, Cornelius. The narration begins with the words, 'Peter went up on the housetop' (Acts 10:9). The scenes referring to 'upper rooms' extend even to the description of Paul's journeys. Thus, a cenacle was the location of the long midnight sermon at Troas during which young Eutychus was overcome by sleep and fell out of the window. 'There were many lights in the upper chamber where we were gathered' (Acts 20:8).

The radical new step which that special group of missionaries, the men from Cyprus and Cyrene, dared to take in Antioch, consisted in the fact that they carried the message of Christ to pagan Greeks, to people who had no connection whatsoever with Judaism and the Law of Moses. To those who proved to be open to their proclamation, acknowledgment and adherence to the Old Testament Law was not made a condition for acceptance into the circle of people confessing themselves to Christ. This was the first actual elimination of the Law.

It may well have been the impulse for missionary promulgation of the Christian Gospel that brought Paul and Barnabas enthusiastically together. After all, Barnabas was wholeheartedly on the side of the 'men from Cyprus and Cyrene,' to whom he doubtless belonged as one of their leaders, and as whose representative and contact he had remained in Jerusalem. What Barnabas could tell Paul of his friends who, following Stephen's death, had journeyed forth into the world, did perhaps give rise in Paul to images of his coming travels as the Apostle of the nations. He had always felt drawn beyond the realm of the Law. How would he succeed in breaking through the confines of the Old Testament, bringing the message of Christ to the non-Jewish nations who, in their religious culture, had undergone such a completely different, more inward preparation for Christ?

After the first communication which had opened up positive

avenues with the other Apostles despite many weighty problems, Paul did not remain long in Jerusalem. Because of Caligula's hatred of the Jews and the reports of the horrible bloodbath in Alexandria, everything was in too much of a state of feverish excitement. Even the Jewish members of the first congregation, gathered around James and Peter, felt themselves more Jewish now that such terrible dangers threatened Jewry. They were therefore particularly sensitive to any criticism of the Law. There were tensions and heated discussions until Paul realized, amid the urging of the others, that it would fare better for all of them if he were to depart from Jerusalem. Adjustment to community interests was a natural dictate for Paul. When similar difficulties and tensions became evident in Caesarea, the harbour town on the Mediterranean, Paul came to a far-reaching decision. Just as he had withdrawn after the Damascus event into the Arabian desert for three years, so he now went back home to Tarsus in order to immerse himself in renewed reflection. In Arabia he had held discourse with Moses and the genius of Judaism. In Tarsus, not now in the seclusion of the desert but in the midst of city life, pursuing the paternal trade of carpet-knotting and tent-making in patient self-effacement, Paul held discourse with the genius of Greece, from its mystery-origins all the way to the philosophy of the Stoics. Now, in connection with what he had already absorbed during his youth, Paul caught up on integrating European spiritual life into his own being.

This went on for a long time, hardly shorter than the seclusion in Arabia, until suddenly, one day, Barnabas, who had not rested until he had found Paul in the bustle of the city, stood in his workshop.

What brought Barnabas to Tarsus? Problems and concerns similar to those caused by Paul had arisen after all for the leaders of the first congregation through the activity of those 'men from Cyprus and Cyrene' who had finally brought it about that the centre of a pagan Christian community, no longer connected with the Old Testament, was established in Antioch. Constant reports arrived in Jerusalem, where the congregation was not growing larger but instead had finally shrunk down to a small group, that an ever growing number of people from heathen backgrounds were flocking to the congregation in Antioch. Events now swept across the sternly held convictions of those who, like James, viewed the Law of the Old Covenant as the indispensable precondition for the new faith. The Apostles sought for a way to remain in constant and close connection with the developments occurring in Antioch. To this end, they sent Barnabas. He accepted joyfully — after all, he was going to see for himself the successful activity of those who had been his close friends. When Barnabas arrived in Antioch, he was initially delighted — the seed of the new faith was growing in rich abundance — but finally even he could not quite ignore the worries which posed such difficulties to the friends in Jerusalem. For him, a radical break with the religion of the fathers was less urgent, since he had always lived within a religious structure that eliminated much of the oppressive weight of the Law's yoke.

Then, suddenly, Barnabas realized — like a revelation — that what he knew to be Paul's fully conscious conviction was being put into action here in Antioch. Much more so than himself, Paul was the man for the developments under way here. Thus he proceeded to Tarsus to look up Paul in his seclusion and win him for the great mission in Antioch.

For Paul, Barnabas obviously came just at the right moment. Sufficient time had been devoted to renewed reflection. Since Barnabas came to him as the delegate of the leaders in Jerusalem, he could comply with this summons without having to fear a revival of the earlier differences.

Thus, Paul arrived in Antioch. This was an even larger world capital than Tarsus. The power-hungry Seleucid Diadochi, to whom the Syrian-Phoenician part of Alexander's kingdom had fallen, had established this city in a majestic location in the corner between the western coast of Syria running from north to south and the southern coast of Asia Minor running from east to west. Here, the northern spurs of the Lebanon and the Anti-Lebanon sink down and turn into the extensive plain by the Mediterranean, guiding the Orontes river to the ocean. In the age of the Apostles, the city was a world in itself. A spiritual life like the one nurtured in the great schools of Tarsus was not to be found here. The harbour by the sea was also too far removed for the throng of commerce to have filled the city with the din of activity. It was a city of military garrisons and luxury which had grown to immense proportions. Comprised of several lanes, wide, sumptuous avenues with pillars ran for several kilometres towards the slope of the mountains. Where they ended, a gigantic marble statue of Jupiter rose high into the sky. The city walls were decorated with between three and four hundred towers up to twenty-five metres high. Life there was unrestrained and modern in the sense that all cultic and moral deviations of the decadent Orient met here. But side by side with much addiction, there was just as much ardent longing. Thus, the word of the Christian Apostles found many open ears and hearts.

There followed a year of fruitful cooperation between Barnabas and Paul. Though Paul still imposed some restraint on himself since he acknowledged Barnabas' main responsibility, the enkindling fire of his spirit made itself clearly perceptible.

Here, something really new came into being. Nothing can bring this to expression more distinctly than the name which arose in Antioch for those who confessed themselves to Christ. Here, for the first time, they were called 'Christians' *(Christianoi).* The name, 'Nazarenes,' by which they had been denoted in Jerusalem and elsewhere, made it clear that the human figure of Jesus of Nazareth still occupied the central position as the subject of devout worship. The designation arising in Antioch replaced the mere connection to Jesus with the fuller connection to the Christ-being who had entered into incarnation in the man, Jesus. It was frequently thought that the name had been put forth by non-Christians who, to begin with, had employed it in a derogatory, sarcastic sense. But it is more likely to assume that it was an expression coined directly by Paul, for in it resounds the fundamental Pauline principle of the experience of indwelling; a Christian is one who can say: Christ in me.

In those days, a bitter time of deprivation came over the congregation in Jerusalem which, as far as external assets were concerned, had become most unassuming and poverty-stricken, but yet was always acknowledged and experienced as the sacred centre. Since Claudius had replaced Caligula on the throne of the

Caesars, the spectre of the great persecutions of Jews had been put to rest. But now, just as in the days of the birth of Jesus and the time of the baptism in the Jordan, there existed another Herod — King Herod Agrippa. Since he sensed that a special mystery of soul and spirit was involved here, he became possessed with mad envy and hatred against the congregation. A severe famine caused people everywhere to be seized by panic-stricken fear. The group that was gathered around the Apostles remained steadfast like a rock in a gale. This was when Herod struck. Just as Herod Antipas had once ordered the beheading of John the Baptist, Agrippa had the older James beheaded, the only one among the Apostles to have travelled further into the world, westward as far as Spain. Now one of the Twelve had become a martyr. There are many indications to support the likelihood that James was killed on a Good Friday. Eleven years had gone by since the Good Friday on Golgotha and now, to the profoundly sad memories, a heart-rending sorrow was added. But this was not all — Herod Agrippa even ordered Peter, the head of the congregation, to be arrested and thrown into prison. Everybody feared and trembled for his life.

News of the first congregation's distress had prompted a plan of special brotherly aid in the already large community in Antioch. Generous donations were collected which were to be presented solemnly in Jerusalem as a gift expressing community spirit. In Acts, this gift is designated by the same term as is the 'daily service,' namely as *diaconia.* Just as the gifts were handed out by human beings at the sacred table and yet came from God, so it was meant to be with this gift of fellowship. Barnabas and Paul were dispatched to hand it over. The festival of Easter may have been scheduled as the date for the presentation.

During the night preceding the morning of Easter, the congregation was gathered in the Cenacle in the 'house of Mary, the mother of John Mark,' the sister of Barnabas (Acts 12:12), not only to await the rising of the Easter sun, but primarily to pray for Peter. There was a knock at the gate. The friends were frightened, believing it might be the officials come to claim new victims. Finally, when the maidservant went to the door, she heard Peter's voice. Her joy was so great that instead of opening the gate, she ran back to the others to bring them the tidings. They did not believe her and said that it could not be Peter; perhaps it was his angel (Acts 12:15). But then, when the door was finally opened, Peter stood in their midst and gave testimony of how he had been led miraculously, in an enraptured state of consciousness, by an angel out of the prison, and how, in front of the house of the Cenacle, he regained his senses. In the souls of all those gathered here, the remembrance of the joy of Easter morn joined with the present jubilation at this experience of the helping guidance of the spirit. The brotherly gift from Antioch, presented by Barnabas and Paul, became an outer form for the experience of God's help. The attacking demons were repulsed by invisible hands. Just like Herod who had ordered the infanticide at Bethlehem, so Herod Agrippa was now seized by a horrible disease and succumbed to it.

The fact that Peter and Paul met again under such circumstances doubtless removed many emotional barriers between them and gave rise to spontaneous affection.

Primarily, however, the bond of activity between Paul and Barnabas was strengthened. When they returned to Antioch they took along as a helper John Mark, the nephew of Barnabas. Upon arrival, they soon embarked on an apostolic journey together, accompanied by John Mark. This journey is referred to, not with full justification, as the first of Paul's missionary travels. Even now, Paul did not feel that his very own hour had come. This was a journey by Barnabas accompanied by Paul and John Mark. This is seen clearly in the fact that their journey led initially to the isle of Cyprus, the home of Barnabas. Like his friends, the men from Cyprus and Cyrene, Barnabas could finally proclaim the Gospel of Christ in the world from which he came. And he was grateful to his destiny that no less a person than Paul had been placed by his side in this endeavour. When they journeyed on from Cyprus into the interior of Asia Minor, the alien inhabitants of these regions, on one occasion, became aware in their own way of the balance of responsibility between Barnabas and Paul. Through the wondrous spiritual activity of the two men, they were transported into ecstasy. Believing that the gods themselves had appeared among them in human form, they wanted to worship and offer up gifts of sacrifice to Barnabas as Jupiter, and to Paul, as the spokesman, the messenger of the gods, Hermes.

On this journey Paul may well have become occasionally impatient to the point where the restraint which he had imposed upon himself out of consideration for the gentler, conciliatory attitude of Barnabas was hard on him. The radical insights to which he had penetrated in his inner struggles drove his fiery temperament forward. Filled with admiration and reverence for Paul, Barnabas sought to keep in step with him. Once, however, the discrepancy which existed latently between them emerged in an indirect manner. When Paul energetically moved forward into regions where, for Barnabas, his earlier connections no longer existed, Barnabas himself was able to give in for his friend's sake. John Mark, on the other hand, must have considered his uncle's yielding to Paul a weakness; out of inner opposition, he went home by himself.

Later on, when Paul and Barnabas, having returned to Antioch, were considering a new apostolic venture, matters finally reached the stage where their activities separated; in particular over the question whether they ought to take John Mark along again as a companion. Paul decided to take the initiative himself. Instead of going with Barnabas who did not wish to part from his nephew, Paul began the new journey with Silas. Now he was able to follow his own radically different insights and inner directions. Thus, henceforth, the following characteristic developments of the Christian impulse confronted each other: on the one side, led by the Lord's brother, James, there was the Jewish Christian group which adhered to the Mosaic Law; on the other side was the pagan Christian wing which linked up with the innermost fruits of the European development of the ego.

The people surrounding Barnabas represented an advanced Christianized form of Essenism that moved beyond the egotistical, Luciferic one-sidedness of the earlier Essene life owing to the apostolic impulse of expansion, thereby forming a middle ground. Peter finally became their apostolic representative when Barnabas' friends, who early on had established a congregation in Rome, asked him to go there. In Rome, John Mark, too, became Peter's pupil and in the end matured into the evangelist to whom we owe the second Gospel. As the third city, Rome was added to Jerusalem and Antioch and, when these two cities later declined in importance, remained the most important historically.

After the return from their joint travels, Barnabas and Paul constantly had to defend themselves against the sharp criticism and vehement attacks of those holding to the Jewish Christian standpoint. Finally they ventured to Jerusalem in order to arrive at agreements with the other Apostles which safeguarded the interests of the general community, but which were also intended to give the individual Apostle freedom for his manner of activity. This meeting has been called the 'Apostles' Council.'

Paul now had a well-founded right to demand freedom for his work amongst the non-Jewish peoples. Not only had he accomplished great things, he had also demonstrated his willingness to subordinate himself and join with the general community and those responsible for its leadership. On the other hand, he could point out that in important instances Peter himself had disregarded the stern world of the Law — for example, when he baptized the members of the house of the Roman captain, Cornelius, all of them non-Jews. It is true that Peter had been induced to ignore the Law by powerful spiritual experiences, and the Holy Spirit, becoming manifest in a pentecostal way in the circle around Cornelius, justified his actions. As he candidly related later in the Letter to the Galatians, Paul probably also brought up the fact that Peter did not behave consistently in regard to the rules which a Jew had to observe in his relations with non-Jews, for example, in the case of joint meals. He reproachfully hinted that Peter allowed himself greater freedom in the absence of witnesses than if he knew he was being observed by any of the Law's advocates. Paul well knew how to demonstrate the impossible attitude of those wishing to include the Law of Moses in Christianity. True and consistent observance of the Law, which was what the Lord's brother James intended to carry through, could only lead in the end to the total isolation of a small Jewish sect. Paul, on the other hand, had already offered proof that actual observance of the freedom brought by Christ opened the way to the whole of humankind.

Following Paul's own account of this Apostles' council in Galatians (Gal.2), we can assume that John was also back in Jerusalem by then. Thus it was that Peter, John and James together had to come to a decision concerning Paul's demand. Perhaps it was partially due to John's presence that Paul received the freedom he had requested for his apostolic work. In any case, the Nazirite James also displayed magnanimity and judgment when, on his part, he opened the way for Paul's free activity beyond the Law. To prevent any relapse into the decadent magic of pagan cults, only a few, essential parts of the Old Testament Law were acknowledged by all as binding rules even for the pagan Christian congregations.

From this time forward, several forms of Christian life developed by mutual agreement. More than could become apparent in the conditions existing at that time, it could hardly be seen that the Pauline form was the preparation of epochs yet to come. Together with the form represented by James, the Petrine character was to dominate Christian history for the present.

8. The Journeys: The Step towards Europe

In comparing himself with the other Apostles, Paul once uttered proud words that seem almost arrogant at first glance, 'I worked harder than any of them' (1Cor.15:10). Indeed, he immediately adds that it was not really his own ego but a higher power, dwelling within him in grace, that worked through him. He stands amazed before the unheard-of number of achievements which could be attained through him. Thus, he writes to the Romans:

> For I will not venture to speak of anything except what Christ has wrought through me ... by word and deed ... so that from Jerusalem and as far round as Illyricum I have fully preached the gospel of Christ (15:18f).

Apart from the elder James, who travelled as far west as Spain, Paul was the first to heed the impulse of the Resurrected One and follow the apostolic way. We should remember that the way in which the first two Gospels express the evangelical task of the Resurrected One at the culmination of the Easter events was not in outwardly uttered words. After his Resurrection, the Christ spoke to his disciples with his whole being. His being was the word with which he made himself known to them. And his being was in the process of world-wide expansion. The Ascension experience of the disciples was but an imaginative reflection of this. The Christ-being pouring itself into the whole of humanity, his union with the earth for the purpose of being ever present in a dimension transcending space, this in reality was the apostolic impulse that swept along the disciples.

Decades before this mystery of Easter and Pentecost occurred, a great restlessness of soul had already awakened in humanity. Whether expressed in the wanderings of brothers from the Orders of the Essenes or Therapeutae, in the Stoic and Cynic travelling preachers, in the proselytizing of Pharisaic Judaism or in the oriental cultural stream flowing into Europe — everywhere a premonition was felt which aroused among the separated nations a sense of universal humanity and common purpose. Through

Easter and Pentecost, the event was fulfilled of which all these conscious or unconscious Messianic stirrings were merely a prophecy. Paul was at the focal point of this fulfilment. Although he had not been present at the disciples' experience of Pentecost, nor at their Easter encounters, since Damascus the apostolic impulse had gripped him most directly: 'For necessity is laid upon me. Woe to me if I do not preach the gospel' (1Cor.9:16). But to obey this necessity was for him the greatest freedom and noblest grace. For a whole lifetime he wandered the world, travelling greater distances than all the others. Seemingly insignificant and persisting in his humble trade, he nevertheless took his mission into the great centres of civilization of that period.

> By means of the travels undertaken by Paul, lines are drawn from the most important cities of eastern culture to the most significant western centres of traffic. When perusing a map of the *Imperium Romanum,* a person who no more than hears the names of the stopping-places in Paul's journeys will have to admire the worldwide scope of his field of action. Tarsus, Jerusalem, Damascus, Antioch, Cyprus, Iconium, Galatia, Phrygia, Ephesus, Troas, Philippi, Thessalonica, Athens, Corinth, Illyricum, Rome, perhaps even Crete and Spain — the sower who furrows and scatters the seeds in these regions deserves to have the Master's words applied to him: 'The field is the world' (Matt.13:38). The world capitals in particular were his sphere of activity. Paul, the man from a big city, spread the gospel in the big city ... Almost without exception, the sites of Paul's work are those that are marked even on the smallest maps ... It is only another expression for the same observation that since the modernization of Mediterranean traffic, we can reach almost all of Paul's important locations by steamer, by train or by both means of transport. The routes taken by steamships as well as trains follow the basically unchanged geographic necessities for traffic to which the routes and streets of antiquity had adjusted on land and at sea.

Thus writes Deissmann, and he adds that the inhabitants of Lystra were not completely in error when they saw in Paul the winged messenger of the gods, Mercury.[34]

If we also reflect that Paul nearly always travelled the land routes on foot — the New Testament describes him as only once riding a horse when, as a prisoner, he was brought from Jerusalem to Caesarea — and that on occasion he even preferred travelling on foot to the sea route (Acts 20:13), a rare physical accomplishment is added to those of soul and spirit in the picture we have of him. If we imagine how Paul addressed the people in the synagogues as well as the marketplaces of the big cities, we certainly must not forget that in order to reach these locations perhaps the steepest mountains had to be scaled.

> Customarily, one only considers the points where they [the Apostles] were active, not the endless and much more wearisome intervals in between. The reports are silent concerning these; no fame is linked to the countless hours on the road through dust and desert, crossing over bare boulders in the heat of the sun where a sip of water or a few figs are a delectable rarity, or to the hard resting places at night out of doors, where chilling coldness closes in. These intervals by means of which the goals were so dearly attained are no less worthy of fame than the goals themselves.[35]

The fact that Christianity also spread to the nations of humanity on the physical plane and could begin to turn into a world movement is above all attributable to Paul's untiring and enthusiastic achievement. Only because of the wide-ranging impulse of his apostleship, were Peter and the other disciples finally drawn out of their narrow confines into the activity of spreading the Gospel. Thus, the paradox came about that those men, who on the physical plane had been privileged for three sacred years to witness the incarnation and earthly sojourn of Christ, would perhaps have been unable by themselves to turn Christianity into a factor to be reckoned with by all humankind. On the other hand, he who had turned into an Apostle purely because of spiritual, supersensory experiences, possessed the strength of initiative to translate what had taken place for the redemption of the earth into the existing conditions of humanity.

Since it is always simply presumed that Luke's Acts of the Apostles is meant in today's sense as a biographical account of Paul's life and activity, it has become customary to speak of the 'four journeys by Paul.' But it is not difficult to recognize that there can be no question of even an approximate completeness of description. Not only is no mention made of the last part of Paul's life and his death; it also becomes unquestionably clear from the Apostle's letters, for example, that the so-called third journey, somewhere within the last stay in Ephesus, includes many journeys of which Acts says nothing. The sum total of routes and work loads that Paul coped with is very much greater than can be inferred from Luke's description alone.

Luke does not direct his gaze only upon the external course of events. He is concerned about certain inner converging points and transitions of development. The standpoint of objective reporting is foreign to him. We follow the inner intention of the description if we pay heed to the configurations of destiny and providence that are woven into the tapestry of Paul's activity.

It would be quite misleading if, among the so-called 'four journeys,' one were simply to consider the first and the fourth as comparable with the two journeys in the middle. At the beginning and at the end, Acts describes journeys that destiny imposes from outside, so to speak. As we have seen, the first is not actually a journey by Paul but by Barnabas. Paul goes along as Barnabas' companion, largely conforming to the latter's plans. He purposely holds back as far as his own apostolic intention is concerned. Paul embarks on the final journey not out of a free decision of his own but as a prisoner. Yet now, although outwardly unfree, in reality he is inwardly freer than ever. He is master over what is happening. Therefore, those whose task it is to guard and escort him have to take him to Rome where he wishes and has to go.

The non-stop activity of travelling which lies in between these two journeys conditioned by fate, is in fact one great totality. Just because, at one point, there is a brief stay in Jerusalem, two journeys, the second and the third, were made of it. Here, Paul's own apostolic will unfolds, motivated by the inner impulse of the Spirit and the Resurrected One.

The journey of Barnabas occurs in close connection with the destinies of birth and homeland. It may have been a sacrifice for Barnabas that following Stephen's death and in consideration of the special tasks which had arisen for him in Jerusalem, he had not been able to depart with the other 'men from Cyprus and Cyrene.' Only now, it had proved to be spiritually right and necessary for him to begin an apostolic mission as had the others. Perhaps he even sensed that ultimately it was not so much his destiny as his companion's, whose all-embracing mission for humanity was now to be prepared. To begin with, however, following the transformation which occurred in him on his joining the circle of the Apostles, Barnabas willingly obeyed the need to travel to his home country and to relate his present spiritual endeavour to that of his youth.

Miracles of the spirit accompanied his and Paul's route through Cyprus, the island of Venus and copper. But more so than Barnabas, Paul here came into his own. As in reflected images, important stations of his own development appeared to Paul's soul. When the magician, Elymas, who opposed the apostolic mission, was defeated by the higher power in Paul's speech and became blind, was Paul not reminded of his own experience in that hour when the lightning of Damascus struck him? In this instance, the one blinded did not receive sight through the same flash of lightning. Instead, the eyes of another were opened, those of Sergius Paulus, the highest-ranking Roman official on Cyprus, so that he perceived who had sent Barnabas and Paul. The fact that this convert was also named 'Paul' caused Paul to feel confirmed in his own development. Henceforth, he dropped his Jewish name Shaul or Saul once and for all, a name shared in common with the first king of Israel who, like him, was from the tribe of Benjamin. Now only his Hellenistic name, Paul, 'the little one,' was to be valid, thus acknowledging the importance of the higher being dwelling within him.

After they had travelled through Cyprus, Barnabas' home island, it became necessary to move on. The obvious thing to do would have been to turn directly towards Paul's home territory of Cilicia. It was probably Paul himself, however, who gave the impetus to turn from the most direct route. After crossing over to the mainland of Asia Minor, they proceeded on a path describing a vast curve to the north and east that would in the end lead to Cilicia but first rose to the mountain summits and the extensive highland. Barnabas was able to make Paul's tempestuous will his own. Yet he surely had to overcome feelings similar to those that caused his nephew John Mark to become reluctant and finally depart for home, shortly after arriving on the mainland.

It has to be borne in mind that although people in those days could not yet avail themselves of maps on which the specific political borders of countries were outlined, human beings were instead equipped with an elementary instinct for the etheric and astral qualities and characteristics of landscapes and countries. From the eastern Mediterranean region with its special soul configuration, towards the east and northeast into the primal dimensions of Asia, as well as westward and towards the northwest into the lands of Europe, a threshold had to be crossed, filling the soul with anxiety and fear, and requiring inner fortitude and courage. It was as if one departed the known world in order to venture into a mysterious and impenetrable void; thus it was that people experienced the various regions of the earth as characteristically different. In Palestine, one already took such a step when crossing the Jordan. In the land east of the Jordan, a traveller entered a different dimension on reaching the Moabite mountains or Arabia's highland — one could sense this even until recently — an experience that not only transformed one's breathing but, indeed, one's whole being. One had arrived in Asia, in the realm of humanity's ancient mother. A similar experience could be undergone ascending from the sea on the southern coast of Asia Minor, proceeding from Tarsus across the Cilician passes into the interior highlands. In a special sense this passage signified a threshold between Europe and Asia or, in the reverse direction, from Asia to Europe. Two mighty entities of fundamentally different soul physiognomy confronted each other here.

Since the two men did not select the short route across the sea or along the coastal area leading from the homeland of Barnabas into that of Paul, a vague yearning for distant places may still have held sway in Paul. It was not actually the highland-interior of Asia Minor that attracted him. The call he obeyed came from further away and was even of a polarically different nature. This could only become clear however, when, later on, he chose his routes on his own apostolic responsibility under the guidance of the Spirit.

The world of 'little Asia' reacted with ancient ecstatic soul faculties to the proclamation of the Gospel, as well as to the healing deeds that emanated from both Apostles. Nearly everywhere, they were greeted with a large crowd; but then, incited by Jewish circles, the people's mood switched to the other extreme, and hostilities and persecutions set in. Here was a world in which the seed of a personal faculty of judgment had not yet been sown in souls. Nevertheless, what Barnabas and Paul now entrusted to this ground as sowers was not in vain. Along with the uplifting religious experiences arising from the Apostles' activity, the seed of the ego-like power of conviction also grew.

In Lystra, it was particularly the healing of a man who had never walked that evoked ecstatic jubilation and the gathering of a great crowd. People paid homage to the Apostles as if they were gods who had descended from Olympus and assumed human form, and the priests prepared a great sacrificial feast. When, however, the Apostles rejected and dampened this intoxication with all the emphasis at their disposal, the mood of the crowd soon changed to rage under the influence of the Jewish persecutors and Paul suffered his first severe martyrdom. He was stoned, his tormentors convinced that it was his corpse which they were dragging out of the city to throw outside the walls. Only a small group of the faithful were witnesses of how Paul rose and returned to life as if nothing had happened to him.

We should conclude wrongly from the events in Lystra that Paul travelled through these lands not merely as an apostle but also as a miracle worker. In those days, Apollonius of Tyana, the acclaimed miracle worker, was also on his travels. We have already mentioned that he was an approximate contemporary of Paul's, from a town located almost the same distance north of the mighty Taurus pass, the Cilician Gates, as Tarsus was south of them. As a last great initiate of the pre-Christian mysteries that were superseded by the Mystery of Golgotha, Apollonius unhesitatingly made use of the suggestive, magical means of ancient times. Paul was not the same kind of miracle worker, just as the so-called 'miracles of Jesus' certainly must not be placed in the same category as the deeds of Apollonius.[36] Because of his links to Essene Therapeutism, Barnabas may more easily have been capable of exercising psychic healing. He was credited with a major share in the healing of the cripple in Lystra, a fact that becomes clear in the crowd viewing him as the father of the gods, Jupiter-Zeus, whereas in Paul they saw only Mercury-Hermes, the messenger of the gods. This healing can be compared with that of the man who had been lame from birth, which occurred soon after the great Pentecostal festival when Peter and John were approaching 'the Beautiful Gate' of the Temple in Jerusalem (Acts 3). Just as had happened then, the sustaining power of two Apostles' interaction had such an effect that only the kindling spark of a word, uttered in this case by Paul, needed to be spoken for the ego of the stricken person to take hold inwardly of the paralysed limbs and move them.

In the life of Jesus, in the activity of the first Apostles, and now, finally, in Paul, the so-called 'miracles' are found at the outset. The power of a new beginning, a *status nascendi,* was felt. As this process continued, it operated more deeply and became ever more inconspicuous. Still, this does not mean that the miracles ceased or became less numerous. They only moved more to the inner realm. The real miracle of Lystra consisted in the fact that for the first time, in a powerfully physical manner, Paul was privileged to experience what he later called 'dying with Christ,' and 're-arising with Christ.' The human power to go through a dying process into new life was infinitely elevated and blessed through the power of the 'Christ in him.'

In the events of Lystra, the reflections of destiny, interwoven with the experiences of this first journey, continued. In outward happenings, the deeper insights of Paul's progressive self-discovery became objectified. On Cyprus, the memory of his own blindness at Damascus was reflected in another person turning blind. In Lystra, his stoning echoed the earlier stoning of

Stephen carried out with his cooperation outside the city walls of Jerusalem.

Barnabas' journey became Paul's significant destiny. In Lystra and Derbe, the great northern sweep of their route had already come quite close to Paul's homeland, to Cilicia and Tarsus. Through the miracle of Lystra, however, the actual inner goal was attained. The journey did not continue to Tarsus. Taking the same route on which they had come, Barnabas and Paul returned to the seacoast. On the way, they took pains to encourage and to organize in practical ways the groups that had formed through their activity. Then, without stopping again at Cyprus, they chose the direct sea-route for the return to Antioch.

The agreements of the so-called 'Council of the Apostles' that were confirmed in a solemn document and made public in Antioch by special messengers, paved the way for Paul's own apostolic impulse. He had demonstrated that for the sake of unity he was willing to undergo any necessary restraint. Now his genius could move its wings freely in pursuing the aims revealed by the voice of spiritual guidance.

Paul pressed for a new departure. He was ready to continue their joint travels and activities. Barnabas, however, felt too constrained and therefore could not fall in with the idea that through Paul's leadership a fresh direction was to emerge. What he envisioned was basically a repetition of the same journey he had already undertaken with Paul. Therefore, he wanted John Mark to be their travelling companion once again. Paul could not agree to this. He knew only too well that now it was a matter of being free to venture towards completely new shores. Thus he chose as his companion Silas, one of the delegates who had carried the document formulated in Jerusalem to Antioch. Thrilled by the prospects that opened up here, Silas had not returned to Jerusalem. He had been active in the first congregation in Jerusalem as a teacher but also as the bearer of a specifically prophetic gift. He was eager to exercise these special spiritual gifts, wherever possible, in cooperation with Paul. Together with John Mark, Barnabas departed on a journey of his own and went again to Cyprus, his homeland.

Paul did not travel according to a preconceived set plan. He was confident that at the proper time he would be shown the right path. He felt as if he were following in the footsteps of a mightier sower who — although invisible to earthly senses — had set out on *his* path through humanity.

Paul started out hesitantly and expectantly. It seems natural that initially he felt drawn towards his homeland. Yet he was not in a hurry. This is evident in the fact that he did not travel by ship, preferring instead to journey on foot. This required more time and physical hardship but it allowed him to divine within himself the spiritually suitable paths.

Thus, the two companions prepared to take the overland route on their journey to Cilicia. Surely one of their stopping places was Tarsus, though Acts does not mention it. Then, crossing over the high passes through the Taurus, they arrived at Derbe and Lystra in Lycaonia where, during the journey with Barnabas, the deification drama had been followed by that of the stoning. Here and in the towns located still further in the interior of Asia Minor which had been visited earlier, the abandoned threads of activity were taken up again. Everywhere Paul and Silas made known the decisions reached in Jerusalem by the first Apostles. For those who had found their way from non-Jewish backgrounds to the newly established communities — and doubtless this was true of most of them — this signified the sounds of a fanfare of freedom. The constraint of the Law dwindled away. The fact that strict limitations had been drawn at certain points in regard to the pagan rituals of magic caused no dampening of this sense of relief. It must have been a heart-warming sign for Paul that in Lystra of all places — in a sense as the fruit of the destiny undergone there — a Greek youth, Timothy, entered his discipleship. Henceforth, Timothy accompanied Paul on his journeys; he was his first associate who, although having a Jewish mother, had grown up completely outside the school of the Law, purely in the light of Greek spiritual life. Yet, so that he could be active also among those who came from the sphere of the Law, Paul nevertheless freely let him accept the Law of Moses, including circumcision, as a principle of schooling.

Something strange and puzzling resulted when Paul and his companions continued on their way across Asia Minor beyond the region of the previously visited congregations. Following their inner directions they travelled through Galatia, Phrygia and Mysia. But in none of their stopping places were they able to appear before the people to proclaim the Gospel. They received clear signs that it was not their task here and now to undertake any apostolic activity. Future events, not yet clearly discernible, seemed to await them and call them on.

When they finally had arrived in the northwestern corner of the peninsula of Asia Minor, the event occurred. If they had followed their own ideas, they would now have turned northeast into the regions that extend along the south of the Black Sea. Now, however, an invisible guidance not only forbade them to preach but to proceed further. They were not to turn but to continue in the straight direction which they had followed up to now in crossing Asia Minor. Thus, not far from the Dardanelles where Asia is separated from Europe only by a narrow channel, they arrived in Troas on the coast of the Aegean Sea, where from dark, dreaming Asia, one looks across to bright, awake Europe.

The 'prophetic sense,' the charisma of Silas, had doubtless played a part in the spiritual guidance of the route that they had taken. Since Damascus, Paul had been gifted with the faculty of supersensory perception. He was not dependent on those charismatic talents, vestiges of former spiritual capacities that were cultivated in the congregations and placed at the service of Christian soul life. If things had gone according to his inclination, some of these faculties, such as the speaking in tongues, would no longer have been practised at all. We shall have to speak of this later. Most likely, he expected something from a further cultivation of the prophetic sense, something that he recommended for this reason to the congregations (for example, 1Cor.14:39). In the Old Testament development, this mental aptitude had moved increasingly from the domain of sleep into the waking state. Previously there had been the 'seers,' foremost among them Samuel. They possessed the gift of discerning in sleep the answer to questions that were posed to them, and proclaiming it when they awakened the following morning. Then came the time of the prophets who even in the waking state could receive the answer of the spiritual world in order, then, to express it in human words. A variation of this gift, weaker on the one hand and yet further developed on the other, played a part in the life of the Christian congregations. Silas was one of its representatives. It must have been a matter of a special interposition into the conceptual life of the will which, properly speaking, was asleep and therefore open to the spirit. Thereby, inner certainty arose concerning the will of higher, leading powers, even concerning the intentions of God himself. The reason that Paul consented to this prophetic gift and, in Silas, made one of its bearers his closest associate, was based on the fact that through the transformation of his own soul faculties at Damascus he beheld a future stage of the human capacity of thinking. Through overcoming the mere head element and through the cooperation of heart and will, this faculty of thought will itself assume prophetic, apocalyptic character.[37]

In Troas, a window to the west of humanity opened for Paul. He had arrived at a decisive turning point of his life and work. Now he recognized that the guidelines of his life had all along been quietly leading to this moment.

During the night, Paul had a dream that was more than a mere dream; it was a true spiritual encounter. The figure of a man with the countenance and attire of a Macedonian stood before him and called him across the sea into his country. In this figure, Europe itself beseeched Paul for help. Now the actual goal of this journey became clear. The step across to Europe had to be taken. Only there could the word and power of the Resurrected One enter creatively into the progressive evolution of humanity.

Even the location where Paul received Europe's summons expressed the importance of the step now to be taken. Close by lay the last ruins of Troy where, long ago, the Greek nation, the first-born of a new humanity, had struggled free of Asia's magic spell and tutelage so as to come of age. Then, after almost a thousand years of the development of Greek culture, the young Macedonian king, Alexander, had landed with his ships at the same site in the golden armour of Achilles in order to bring to Mother Asia the fruits of the free daughter, Europe. From here,

Alexander's expeditions, which sprang much more from spiritual than political aims, proceeded deep into the interior of Asia. Were the journeys that Paul now prepared to embark upon not Alexander's expeditions, only in the opposite direction? And were they not the hidden and humble journeys of a craftsman rather than a royal advance of a splendid army? Now a craftsman went his way — not from West to East, but from East to West, from Asia to Europe. In the East, humanity had received the most sublime gift of heaven. They were able to comprehend it with full consciousness only by means of those soul faculties attained in the West's vigorously advancing life. The West had come as far as it could by means of merely human forces. Now it required the higher impulse of divine help capable of breaking the terrestrial spell, the seed of which had already been implanted on eastern soil. As the herald and bearer of the force needed by Europe, Paul now prepared to take the decisive step.

Now, a new wind filled the sails. This becomes evident even in the style of Acts. Suddenly Luke becomes involved in so lively a manner that he abruptly lapses into the we-style, which henceforth he makes use of again and again:

> And when Paul had seen the vision, immediately we sought to sail on into Macedonia. We were filled with the certainty that it was the divine world itself which had called us to preach the gospel there (Acts 16:10*B*).

For theologians preoccupied with questions of literary authenticity in the scriptures, the 'we-passages' in Acts have a special interest. In them they see the trace of a source-text which, in all probability, went back to Luke himself, whereas the other parts of the scripture remain questionable to them. Or they draw the conclusion from the suddenly appearing 'we-style' of the Troas scene that Luke was present as Paul's companion only from this point onward, and that none of the preceding events in his book had as yet the value of an eyewitness report. Luke was a Greek. The change that occurred in Troas concerned him personally. Europe itself now speaks through him in the 'we-style.' It may be that Luke only became Paul's disciple and companion during the crossing from Asia to Europe. In that case, this event is a confirmation of the new elemental impulse. Nothing is thereby imputed against those parts of Acts that are not composed in the 'we-style.' The fact that Luke was able to write his Gospel and the Acts of the Apostles is not due to his having been an eye-witness at some of these events. It is due to his having matured in his discipleship with Paul to a higher consciousness that permitted him to draw from real Imagination and Inspiration and thereby read from a more sublime chronicle than merely his personal memory.

9. The Journeys: Paul, the European

A fetter was shaken off, a spell was lifted. It was the spell of his own origin and legacy. Since his youth, Paul had inwardly yearned for distant expanses, for lands where the light-filled Greek language had originally been spoken.

The ship carrying Paul and his companions sailed under a brisk wind in a northwesterly direction. Its first port of call was an island which rose solemnly from the sea like the mighty crown of a king. Greek temples of glittering white marble shone in the sunlight not far from where the ship had dropped anchor. This was Samothrace, the island of the mysteries of the Cabeiri. Here, where Europe had awakened from deep sleep in ancient times, Paul first set foot on European soil. All during the voyage, the Thracian coast, the European continent, had shimmered in azure hues in the distance. The ship landed at the adjoining coast of Macedonia and the group soon arrived in Philippi, the former capital of the country. From here the father of Alexander the Great, the Macedonian king Philip, from whom the town had received its name, had brought to an end Greece's independence. At the same time, he had laid the foundation for the possibility that, through his son, in the form of Hellenism, the Greek spirit could conquer and penetrate the whole world. In a certain sense, Philippi, the starting point for Alexander the Great's world empire, also became later on the starting point for the Caesarian empire of the Romans. Here, in the year 42 BC, Octavian, later to become Caesar Augustus, defeated once and for all the resistance of Brutus and Cassius, the last champions of democratic Rome.

Philippi had long since sunk to the rank of a provincial town. It was situated where the broad fertile coastal strip is bounded by the baseline of the mountains. A part of the town crept up the slopes of the castle-topped mountain which looked out far across the sea. Yet how different it was compared with the southern coast of Asia Minor, also running from east to west, where the Taurus mountains rise from the plain where Tarsus was situated! Here mountains, plain and sea possess nothing of the East's majestic divine proportions. Rather, a glow of loveliness is poured out over nature. Everything is more human. Here even the sun that casts its golden rays over the waves of the sea speaks more the language of beauty than of majesty. Paul and his companions may have felt as if a friendly landscape received them here. The people, too, met them in a friendly manner. Divine and human elements appeared in balance.

How could it be that this pleasant and harmonious world called for help in the dream-figure of the 'man from Macedonia'? For these people, too, the future must have been harbouring in its womb some tragic threat and danger. It was an equilibrium bestowed by nature that illumined these men's faces with a quiet pride of freedom. What would it be like however, if the tempests and labour pains of ego-birth were to commence? If the benevolent spirits were to let go of the human beings whom they had so far guided, they would be spared neither the experience of disharmony nor that of the abyss. Therefore, at the proper time, European humanity in particular needed the higher ego-content which it was unable to bring forth on its own. The humanness that gave such a friendly, harmonious impression was nothing but a presentiment and deeply unconscious longing. As yet, the archetypes were close. Paul knew that he was the herald of the power by means of which human beings, traversing any chaos and void, can draw near again to their archetype, beyond the abyss.

Lydia, a seller of purple garments, who had come to Philippi from Thyatira in Asia Minor, was a representative of that human nature which grows into Christian experience in a straightforward, organic manner. The divine substance finds an open chalice held up to it. The power of the Christ becomes the fulfilment of the true being of man. Lydia and her circle not only offered a hospitable home to Paul and his companions but also to the one whom they proclaimed. A congregation was formed which we know received the most human of Paul's letters that have come down to us, a letter filled with undiminished affirmation: 'Rejoice in the Lord always; again I will say, Rejoice!' (Phil.4:4).

However, the days in Philippi did not come to an end in serene harmony. It is most instructive to note that Paul inspired dissent and brutal animosity simply because he inaugurated harmony in the world of Philippi which did not as yet possess it. A woman, who had Sibylline-Pythian faculties, belonged to the circle that was open to the Christian message. She entered with facility into abnormal states in which her own ego consciousness receded, and as a result certain spiritual beings could speak through her in an oracular manner. Her master made a business of her mediumistic gift, demanding payment from those who sought out the maidservant's gifts of divination. Now it so happened that when the woman lapsed into these abnormal mental states, she broke out again and again in hymns of praise over Paul and his companions and the significance of their mission. In response, Paul addressed her in such a manner that he healed her. He strengthened her ego to such an extent that the interruptions of her ego-consciousness ceased. These were, on the one hand, vestiges of once generally prevailing psychic faculties, yet they were pathological phenomena as well. The essentially healthy element of the Christian principle, which terminates any sort of mediumship, asserted itself, for the Christ's indwelling signifies the true ego's fulfilment.

The healing that was effected on the maidservant was, however, against the business interests of those who had profited from her trance conditions. The individuals who were aggrieved managed to enkindle such a wave of obsessive hatred that Paul and his people were severely mistreated and finally thrown into prison.

This quick reversal of the prevailing mood of friendliness demonstrated that the harmony with which people in Philippi were gifted was not yet self-acquired but bestowed by nature, hence a last paradisal reflection. The Sibylline capacities of the maidservant, too, were echoes of ancient soul capacities. As paradoxical as it may sound, a new force had to enter the human being that would strengthen and heal the soul within its ego centre, even where the soul did not yet appear to be weak and ailing at all. The ancient openness to the spirit was going to be lost one way or another and would, as it diminished, allow all manner of demons to gain entry. Blessed were those in whom the evening twilight could change into the dawn of a new day without inner disturbances.

Among the Europeans who were illumined by archetypal openness to the spirit, the male figure of the jailer joined the female figure of Lydia. During the night after the imprisonment of the 'troublemakers,' an earthquake forced open the locked gates of the prison. When the jailer, who was already in despair over the prisoners' presumed escape, discovered them still in their cell, the joyous shock opened his inner eye and he recognized the truth of their proclamation. In his house as well as in that of Lydia, a germinal beginning came about for the miracle of the community of Christ.

In Thessalonica, Paul for the first time entered a city in Europe which, although not as large as Tarsus, nevertheless had something of the character of a metropolis with its throng of ships in the harbour and people in the bustling city. It spread along the extensive beach of a huge circular bay. The houses rose from the blue expanse of the sea, ascending the slopes of the mountains, reaching the highest point inland towards the north, where even today castle ramparts crown the rim of the summit as they did long ago. Looking southwards from the beach as well as from the mountain top, one sees the majestic and awe-inspiring sight of Olympus, the summit of the gods. Despite the warm Mediterranean sun, the broad triangle of the mountain's silhouette reaches up to the region of eternal snow. Even from Philippi, the white summit of Mount Olympus could be seen in the distance. In Thessalonica, the mountain is so tangibly close one cannot avoid sensing the nearness of the deities whose throne it is.

Throughout history this place was a crossroads for humanity. Like arteries, ancient roads that later turned into army roads between Rome and Byzantium allowed the life of nations to intermingle. Here commerce is dominated to this day by a special colourfulness of costumes and languages. It is not as if the cosmopolitan exchange that took place here was ever of quantitative significance; but as if symbolizing destiny, an archetypal pattern always arose for the striving, future-orientated life of humanity. Olympus does not really proclaim gods who belong to the past; it seems to stand as a guardian and herald for distant future goals. At the same time, it appears like a symbol of the patience of gods who reckon with eternities.

In Thessalonica, nothing could be sensed of the harmonious paradisal legacy of Philippi. Here a man was placed into conflicting forces in which he had to prove his worth and develop his character. Here angels and demons fought for him, and man, involved in the struggle himself, had to choose on which side he wished to be. Future apocalyptic conflicts between Christ and Antichrist made themselves felt germinally. It is no coincidence that Paul would later on be writing letters to the congregation about to be established here. These letters would stand in close proximity to John's Apocalypse, because they speak of the mysteries of the Antichrist but also of the grace of a new coming of Christ.

Paul followed the principle that he maintained everywhere. He first carried his message to the synagogue in order, with the divining rod of the word, to pick out those individuals within Judaism who were open to the being of Christ. He must have known that here more than elsewhere he challenged the forces of opposition. A persecution of Christians, allegedly carried out in the name of the Roman Caesar, broke over the circle of the faithful ones. Paul and his companions were taken away from the focal point of danger by a special group of people and led to Beroea, a quiet town situated about a day's journey away. It must have been a circle of 'quiet ones in the land' who, in the manner of the Essenes and in connection with their holy scriptures, cultivated an esoteric spiritual life and therefore understood immediately what Paul and his friends were proclaiming. Confidently, Paul could entrust to them his concern for the development of the congregational life in Thessalonica.

This circle helped in Paul's activities. When Beroea became dangerous as well, they accompanied Paul to Athens while allowing the co-workers of the Apostle to remain behind among them.

Suddenly, Paul was transported to the spiritual fountainhead and centre of Greek life. Like Jerusalem, Athens was an ancient city, but a younger and completely different one. Enveloped in the warm, golden brilliance of beauty, how infinitely more sunlike was the temple of Athena on the Acropolis, in comparison with the stern Yahweh temple on the rock plateau of Moriah! Surely Paul arrived with high expectations at the place where, once, Socrates had been the teacher of Plato, the mentor of Aristotle who, in turn, was the tutor of Alexander the Great. But how profoundly disappointed and ultimately angered Paul must have been by what he actually encountered here!

Politically Athens had long since forfeited its freedom and lost its proud glamour and wealth. It also no longer possessed the earnestness and reverence with which, long ago, it looked up to the higher worlds. The temples no longer revealed truth. Mockery of their gods by the people or empty iconolatry alone remained.

We should not assume that Paul's indignation was directed against the spiritual realities that were originally experienced by the Greeks, worshipped in the temples and given expression in the sculptures of Greek art. Since the scales had fallen from his eyes outside the gates of Damascus, Paul had beheld and known the entities who are creators, protectors and guides of the kingdoms of nature and human existence. He now stood as a genuine Greek among those who were Greek from birth. The divine image of Athena, sculpted by the masterly art of Phidias, still stood in the temple above. Born from the forehead of Zeus, she was the embodiment of living divine thinking. Who among those living still felt a sacred obligation to cultivate and develop that thinking entrusted to human beings by the gods? Who but Athena moving from the realm of the gods into the being and destiny of humanity!

In the days during which Paul traversed the Greek city in all directions, the pictureless curtain of Judaism may have torn open more than once for him, so that in the mirror of Greek imagery he recognized once again this or that insight or task which he bore within his soul. On the Acropolis in the Erechtheion, the ancient sanctuary of the city, he perhaps also stood before the sacred olive tree of which it was said that Pallas Athena had once made it grow forth from the bare rock. Was the character of that world in which he was supposed to work not expressed with elementary force in the olive tree's growth, the sacred tree of Athena? And if his activity was to bear the proper fruits was it not to lead in the future to the redemption through Christ of that once divine power of thought, which had subsequently fallen and died in man? The Athenians had become unfaithful to the goddess after whom they were named. Without realizing it, they had trodden her under foot. Humanity would continue to desecrate and slay Athena on its future paths. In Paul, on the other hand, a view had opened towards a progressive resurrection of Athena through the Christ who had moved into the souls of men.

Here as well, Paul braced himself to speak up. As always he did so first in the synagogue but then later in the open market-place. Soon there occurred something that he was prepared for: members of various schools of philosophy began to debate with him. Naturally, they had no intention of having a serious discussion with him. Full of disdain and mockery, they who were so proud of their cleverness made fun of him. What could a travelling tradesman know of philosophy! 'What would this babbler say?' some of them asked.*

Others who had begun to take some notice arranged that on the Areopagus Paul was given the opportunity to speak to the leading figures of the schools as well as of the city government. The Areopagus, the 'Hill of Ares,' was always a quiet but distinguished spot in the townscape of Athens. It was part of the gentlest of the three city hills, the Philopappos, which is situated closest to the sea. In ancient times, it housed the spiritual fountainhead of the city's life, the mystery school. Today, the aromatic black-

* Acts 17:18. The Greek word, *spermologos*, commonly translated as 'babbler,' actually means, 'kernel picker.' (See Deissmann: *Paulus*, 2nd edition, p. 173, footnote).

green forest of short coniferous trees, covering the wavy slopes of the hillside, still retains something of the mood of mysterious silence. From the proudly enthroned Acropolis, the eye travels across the shining sea towards the islands of Aegina and Salamis, and landward to the mountain slopes covered by the spruce forests of the Hymettos. From the mystery hill and the Areopagus, one looks up to the ochre-yellow, shining temples on the Acropolis.

The Areopagus, a rock held up by the landscape like a sacrificial gift, was the site where the decisions that had been reached in the secluded council, formerly in the circle of the 'seven sages of Athens,' were proclaimed. This was also the reason why it was the place where legal judgments were made, a task reserved for the leaders of the city. Adjacent to the Areopagus, the slightly higher and more open rock plateau of the Pnyx is where Pericles spoke to the people.

In Paul's age, the 'School of Athens,' the council of the wise men, still existed; but it was no longer a matter of course for genuine initiation-wisdom to determine their judgments. After all, four and a half centuries before Paul, Socrates had had to defend himself on the Areopagus, and the 'Council of Sages' had not heard through him the voice of an awakening humanity's conscience; instead, it had forced him to drink the cup of hemlock. Nevertheless, it would be wrong to think that in Paul's days no possibility survived in the School of Athens for a continuing flow of a still living mystery knowledge.

The mystery centre belonging to Athens was that of Eleusis down at the shore across from the island of Salamis. There, though only like a last, weak rivulet, the genuine stream of Dionysian initiation still existed which knew the secrets of death and resurrection even as late as the days of Julian the Apostate in the fourth Christian century. And this raises the question: was there not perhaps one among those who listened to the words of Paul on the Areopagus who, by grace of genuine experience of the Dionysian mysteries, was open to the message of the One who had passed through death and Resurrection for all humanity?

With practised skill, Paul appeared before the teachers and

leaders of the Greek people. No master of rhetoric, an art in which antiquity felt such pride, could have surpassed Paul in his Areopagus address. He told his amazed listeners: You yourselves have already erected altars to the god whom I proclaim! The gathering realized that a man was speaking here who had acquainted himself not only outwardly with the temples and rituals of Athenian life. He spoke as one familiar with intimate secrets. He said to them: I have seen in your city the altar in which are inscribed the words, 'To the Unknown God.'* Therefore, you bear within your hearts the expectation and hope of a divine being that is yet to come. I proclaim to you: he whom you await has already come. He has become man and has placed the mystery of death and resurrection openly before the world, accessible to all human beings. In seclusion, you have cultivated this mystery in your temples. Gradually it is becoming extinct there; nor does it matter, for it was nothing but the continuous prophecy of the One who was to come; this prophecy has already been replaced by its fulfilment.

Paul, however, proved to be not only knowledgeable in Greek religious life; he was also familiar with the writings of Greek philosophers and poets. He said: Haven't some of your poets said, 'We are indeed his offspring?'† This does not only refer to the fact that humanity descends from the gods. It means: he whom you are awaiting, who has already come, is the actual human god. The true being of man, only a reflection of which dwells within us, is fully present in him, and thus he, the Resurrected One, 'is not far from each one of us.' 'In him we live and move and have our being.'

As yet, Paul did not proclaim the 'Christ in us' to the Greeks on the Areopagus; rather, he revealed to them the other secret: 'We in Christ.' One statement does not contradict the other. For he of whom Paul can say, 'Not I, but the Christ in me,' is the greater, the all-encompassing one. We are enveloped in the one

* Altar stones with this inscription have been found more than once. Reproductions of them are contained in Deissmann's book on Paul.

† These words are found, for example, in a hymn by Cleanthes (about 300 BC).

who dwells within us. He is the whole man of whom we can only be a part.*

The *elite* of Greek culture, gathered on the Areopagus, did not have an ear for what Paul proclaimed. Their own religious conceptions no longer contained any life; they had become formal and schematic. Thus, these people were unable to recognize that this message was indeed the fulfilment of Greek prophecies and longings.

The Acts reports that only a very small number of people were able to recognize the truth in Paul's words. Evidently no congregation came into being at that time in Athens. Was it here of all places at the centre of European thinking that Paul was destined to fail? If anywhere at all, it was in this place that the spell of denominational, narrow thinking had to be broken — a thinking that allowed itself to be impressed again and again by quantitative viewpoints, ignoring esoteric realities.

In actual fact, Paul's Areopagus speech caused the noblest mystery wisdom in Europe to join the stream of Christian thinking. Instead of the establishment of a congregation, it led to the creation of a school which for many centuries cultivated a significant stream of esoteric Christianity.

Among the very few whom Paul won over on the Areopagus was one who can almost be designated as the embodiment of esoteric, spiritual Europe. This cannot be deduced from the text of the Bible, which only says: 'Among them was Dionysius, one

* Goethe's *Proömion* contains a paraphrase of just this section of the address on the Areopagus. Neither Paul's words nor Goethe's verse should be understood in a pantheistic sense. Without even so much as hinting at the name, Christ, the poetic utterance leads from 'Christ in us' to 'we in Christ.'

Was wär ein Gott, der nur von außen stieße,
Im Kreis das All am Finger laufen ließe!
Ihm ziemt's, die Welt im Innern zu bewegen,
Natur in Sich, Sich in Natur zu hegen,
So daß, was in Ihm lebt und webt und ist,
Nie Seine Kraft, nie Seinen Geist vermißt.
[What kind of God would only push from outside,
and let the cosmos run around his finger!
To move the world within befits him,
to nurture nature in himself, himself in nature,
so that what in him lives and weaves and is
will never lack his power nor his spirit.]

from the council.' In the Greek, this Dionysius is called 'the Areopagite.' He not only had a leading position in the 'Council of the Sages,' which proclaimed its decisions on the Areopagus, but had been initiated into the Eleusinian mysteries. He was familiar with the secret of death and resurrection in the symbol of the grain of seed from the ear of corn — which Demeter holds in her hands — not only in the manner in which it was taught, but above all in the way it was practised by the mystics. It may well be that the name Dionysius was not the personal name of the great Areopagite but one that had been acquired through initiation into the mysteries of Dionysius.

Thus, in Athens, a man whom the world already recognized and revered as a great teacher became the disciple of Paul. In the Damascus light, which opened up to him through the words of the Apostle, the mysteries of expectation blossomed into the mysteries of fulfilment. He discovered the one whom he had still sought on the sun to be present here on earth.

Dionysius the Areopagite has exercised an important influence on the development of Christianity, not only in early Christian times but far into the late Middle Ages. In that respect he surpassed most of the twelve Apostles. In paintings and sculptures depicting the death of Mary which existed in large numbers in medieval times, we almost always find the figure of Dionysius the Areopagite next to the Apostles who have hastened from all over the world to the deathbed of the holy mother.

Dionysius was directly involved in the history of Christian thinking. From the sixth century onwards, a number of texts appeared that were written in Greek and were reputed to have been written by him. The most important were *Concerning the Celestial Hierarchies* and *Concerning the Divine Names*. The great theological thinkers of the Middle Ages like Albertus Magnus and Thomas Aquinas acquired more training and knowledge from these Dionysian writings than from any other book apart from the Bible. And as long as theology was fructified from this wellspring, it still wore the cloak of divine wisdom and was permeated by substance as if it were the blood of Christ. After all, it signified much more than merely an intellectual knowledge to be familiar with the nine angelic hierarchies and their differing tasks in the cosmos and humanity. It bestowed clarity and certainty on the heart's meeting with the individual entities of a higher world.

It is understandable that doubts concerning the authenticity of the Dionysian texts should surface in recent times. Numerous details make it clear that the texts could not have been written in their present form during the first century of our Christian era. Here, however, we are dealing with a classic example of the fact that the standards of normal literary criticism fail in regard to writings that originate from esoteric sources. As is true of almost all esoteric literary treasures, the teachings by Dionysius the Areopagite were initially handed down for centuries by word of mouth; Rudolf Steiner has pointed this out in detail. They did not originate in the period when they were finally written, expressed in the conceptual forms of that particular age. On the contrary, people wrote them down so as to prevent them from becoming lost when the ancient memory faculties of the heart were replaced by intellectual forms of consciousness.

Since the days of Paul and his great Athenian disciple, there has always existed a school of teaching directed in the spirit of Dionysius in which, at any given time, the leading instructor was known as Dionysius the Areopagite. It is also noteworthy that this cultivation of the Pauline spirit was located farther west than Athens. St Denis is as close to Paris as Eleusis is to Athens. The townscape of Paris is closely linked with that of Athens by means of secrets of history and destiny that in part are revealed and in part concealed in the images of legend. They relate that Dionysius the Areopagite is supposed to have come to Paris where, in the end, he died a martyr's death. As befell Paul in Rome, he is reputed to have been beheaded on the top of the hill of Montmartre. The original name of it was *Mons Martis,* mountain of Mars. This, however, is the exact Latin translation of the Greek *Areopagos.* Hence, there also existed an Areopagus in Paris, and according to legend it was upon this hill that the judgment was pronounced and carried out on Dionysius the Areopagite. Only later on was 'Mount of Mars' changed into 'Mount of Martyrs' or *Mons Martyrum* — Montmartre.

Legend relates the following, miraculous course of events: Dionysius still retained the strength to take his severed head and mount a horse. Then he rode northward and, at the spot which he was able to reach before he died, a place of worship was erected in his honour: St Dionysius which became St Denis. Today, from Montmartre at the northern edge of the ancient city centre of Paris, one sees below a wide, straight avenue leading northward to St Denis, where the cathedral is a major national sanctuary, comparable to Westminster Abbey in London. Apart from the cathedral with its external historical significance — and of equal importance for humanity's spiritual history — there existed in St Denis the relocated 'School of Athens,' as it were. In it, allied and united, Greek and Christian mystery-wisdom was cultivated throughout many centuries. While the legend was later transferred to a younger Dionysius the better to master the riddles it poses, it is a striking, pictorial expression of an influence lasting throughout a whole era. It points to the inspiring effect after death exerted by the genius who had been shown the way to Christ by Paul's address on the Areopagus.

Frequently and with great emphasis, Rudolf Steiner has pointed out the significance of Dionysius the Areopagite, as the following two passages from his lectures shows:

> ... The newest path available for ascending to wisdom is the Rosicrucian path. This path does not direct the human being into the past but into the future ... Here, by means of certain methods, man is taught to develop on his own the wisdom inherently within him ...
>
> In part, this path was already prepared long before Christianity. It assumed a special form through that great initiate who, as Dionysius the Areopagite, established a discipline in the esoteric school of Paul in Athens from which originated all later esoteric wisdom and schooling.[38]

> A genuine occultist ... knows that esoteric Christian schools of initiation have existed and that the profound meaning of the Christian scriptures was taught in them ... If we are to consider one school which, in this regard, appeared the most on the surface of external history, it is the great esoteric Christian school that the Apostle Paul himself inaugurated in Athens, the school of Dionysius

> the Areopagite ... What the disciples of such a school had to acquire was direction, a certain mood and attitude in regard to the highest truths ...
>
> This was true, also, of that school of Paul's, which revealed the highest truths only after intimate preparation. While Paul preached Christianity to all the world, his pupils in Athens experienced the esoteric side. And as the spirit of this school continued for long periods of time, the representative of the esoteric truth was always called by the same name. The School of Athens continued on for centuries, and he who was its leading teacher, actually the most profoundly initiated one of the school, always bore the name Dionysius. This is the reason why the individual who recorded these matters in the sixth century — when writing had become more customary — was also called by that name.[39]

In Corinth, Europe once again presented a completely new appearance. This was a large and modern metropolis. The two oriental sister cities, Tarsus and Antioch, were left far behind. The size of the plain that was covered by the city seemed infinite. Two centuries earlier the Romans had razed the city to the ground. Now, a wall, thirteen miles long, surrounded the metropolis which was so large that it took an hour to walk from the city centre to the outskirts. The city on the isthmus, surrounded by mountains, extended from one sea to the other and was a bustling port. Corinth had five marketplaces, five large arcades, five thermal springs, and a number of theatres. One of the amphitheatres had 22000 seats. The huge town was nestled in wheat fields, olive groves and vineyards along the shores. Like a paternal guardian, the town's mountain, the round rocky knoll of Acrocorinth, rose above it.

The colourful life of the cosmopolitan population was not conducive to philosophical contemplation and tranquillity. People abandoned themselves here to the intoxicating beauty of nature. Here it was not Athena, the princess of thought, who ruled but Venus-Aphrodite, the goddess of celestial and earthly love. When from the temple of Athena on the Acropolis in Athens, one sees the round elevation of Acrocorinth in the distance across land and sea, shining in the golden light of the evening sun, one absorbs something of the diversity possessed by Greek life even in Paul's age. For on the summit of Acrocorinth stood the temple of Aphrodite which put such a special stamp on the city. It was almost a Babylonian-Oriental enclave on European soil. Nearly a thousand neophytes served the goddess Aphrodite in a fervour of sexual ecstasy. This metropolis on the isthmus was the location for the culmination of a decadent paganism.

It is significant that here Paul changed the style of his activity. For the first time since his joint efforts with Barnabas in Antioch, he paused on his journey and remained for a year and a half in the same place. The fact that he decided shortly after his arrival to stay longer than planned becomes evident when Silas and Timothy, who had remained behind in Macedonia, now joined up with him again. A well planned joint effort was indicated. Corinth, like no other city, posed such great challenges when it came to developing a congregation.

The people who gathered together here in a Christian community understandably brought with them many attitudes and habits of their former pagan religious life-styles. Paul and his companions faced tasks here fundamentally different from those occasions when it had been a matter primarily of dealing with the Jewish Christians. Where the Law continued its domination over the congregation, much rigidity had to be loosened, fear had to be illuminated by joyful confidence. In Corinth, the opposite was required. Here quiet earnestness had to take the place of unrestrained agitation, firm steadfastness and formative energy had to structure the ecstatic chaos.

In Corinth too, Paul was engaged in proclaiming the Gospel. However, here the ritual element took precedence over teaching. The Christian ritual, the Christian sacramental life, had to become effective in the midst of Luciferically inspired pagan forms of worship. It must have been in Corinth above all, where work was done on the actual structuring of the Christian sacrament. As the enlightened inaugurator, Paul contributed more in this area than theology has realized up to now. Large portions of the letters to the Corinthians in particular were placed at the service of this special mission. When Paul quoted Christ's words at the Last Supper (1Cor.11), he considered it important to point out that he was not dependent on eyewitness accounts but that he could experience and receive the words in a direct way from the Lord himself. In this context also belongs 'The Great Hymn to Love' (1Cor.13), the very essence of all the words of Paul that we know. It is no coincidence that it is a component part of the letters addressed to the Corinthians. What is here called 'love' transforms, orders, sanctifies and redeems the element which, proceeding from the rites of the goddess of love, turned the city into the maze of love. The Greek term for the love which was blossoming in the sphere of Christ, *agapē,* was initially synonymous with the Christian sacrament of bread and wine.

At Corinth, Paul's thoughts began to turn even more vividly towards the west, to Rome, the political centre of Europe. Shortly after his arrival he was hospitably received into the home of Aquila and Priscilla, who, being carpet weavers, practised the same trade as himself. They had only recently come to Corinth from Rome, having been forced to leave during a general expulsion of Jews under Caesar Claudius. Aquila as a Jew and Priscilla as a member of a noble Roman family had found their way into the Christian community which already existed in Rome. It can be assumed that both had played an active and leading role in this circle. Now they stood by Paul's side, not only as his hosts but as his first co-workers in the metropolis of Corinth. Through them Paul heard much about the beginnings of the Roman congregation. The breath of future destinies touched him in a personal as well as a general sense. Often he may have felt as if he were already among the brothers and sisters in Rome, perceiving through their souls the pulse beat of the great world-historical event as well as the tension directly present there between the sphere of Christ and that of Caesar.

On a second occasion the thought of Rome confronted Paul like a calling. Gallio, Seneca's brother, came to Corinth as the new Roman proconsul.* He was also a famous teacher of Stoic

* From inscriptions on fragments of marble plates found in Delphi, it becomes clear that Gallio assumed office in Corinth in the summer of the year AD 51 (see Deissmann: *Paulus).*

philosophy, and commanded the greatest respect and veneration everywhere in the world. Seneca himself viewed Gallio as the greater before whom he bowed in awe. Later on, both brothers were forced to end their lives on Nero's orders.

In Corinth, as he had always done, Paul turned initially to the Jewish circles. The latter, however, finding themselves naturally in an extreme state of tension with the pagan life of Greece, reacted on the whole with fanatical rejection. When Paul's activity now extended to ever wider circles among the non-Jewish people, it finally led to a vehement outbreak of hatred and Paul was dragged before the Roman proconsul under serious accusations. Yet before Paul could even take the floor in his own defence, Gallio refused to pronounce judgment in matters of faith. There can hardly be any doubt that Gallio was well aware of who Paul was and in his own way sympathized with Paul's doings. When the Jews refused to be turned away, he did not prevent the Greeks who were present from driving Sosthenes, the leader of the accusers, out of the tribunal by beating him. Later on, Sosthenes became a Christian and associate of Paul's; thus, at the beginning of his letters to the Corinthians, Paul listed him as one who also sent greetings. So it was his persecutors who thus brought about an important encounter for Paul with one of his greatest Roman contemporaries.

The hour had not yet come to continue the apostolic journeys further to the west, perhaps even to Rome. A pause ensued. Paul felt called upon to briefly return home on a pilgrimage to the Temple in the Holy City. The fact that it would be possible to visit once again those congregations which had come into being in Asia Minor may also have decided Paul to turn eastward. Aquila and Priscilla went with him.

The journey to Jerusalem did not really take place primarily to carry out the apostolic mission. Paul therefore deviated from his custom of wandering on foot and chose the quickest way. Soon, the ship carried him and his companions to the coast of Asia Minor. He arrived at Ephesus; the third great city after Jerusalem and Athens. Here, at the site of ancient, sacred mysteries, Mother

Asia herself had helped her daughter, Europa, to take her first groping steps.

It must have been decisive for Paul to come here. He wanted to go to Jerusalem once more to find a new beginning; and he discovered Ephesus. It was not as if he were taking a backward step from Europe to Asia. He retained the principle and the impulses of his European destiny, never again to lose them. But along with the feeling for Europe's inner fruits, he discovered the East in a new manner in Ephesus. Previously, Europe had had to descend from its dream-enveloped prenatal existence to proceed on its earthly paths. And indeed, this had taken place in Ephesus and its sister cities along the Ionian coast in the ages preceding Homer as well as in Homeric times. Thus, in Ephesus, echoes of an ancient age turned simultaneously into pictures and forebodings of the future.

The congregation that already existed in Ephesus pleaded with Paul to remain. However, he could not comply immediately with this wish. Faithful to his pledge, he first had to continue with his journey to Jerusalem. Yet having arrived there, he did not stay long. When the festival was over to which he had come as a pilgrim, he soon departed. Now Ephesus was his goal. Since he had selected the land route this time, he was able to visit on the way the congregations in which he had earlier been active, both in Antioch as well as in a number of other cities of Asia Minor. Ephesus now remained his post for three years. As he had done in Corinth, he dedicated himself to the cultivating and developing of the congregation. Yet the situation was a different one here. It permitted him to move constantly about within a large area towards the East as well as the West.

It is usual to refer to the work which Paul carried out after his brief stay in Jerusalem as his third journey. In reality, his work culminated here in a completely new form of activity. After all, it is quite evident that from this point onward Acts no longer lists all the stopping-places of his travels and work. Many of the destinations that are mentioned in the Letters but are not reported in Acts belong to the three Ephesian years. A number of journeys on land as well as on sea took place. There is, for instance, the one where Paul penetrated westward past Corinth as far as Illyria.

There is also a quiet sojourn of longer duration in Corinth; finally, a number of instances of severe martyrdom, shipwrecks, tortures, imprisonments, and so on (2Cor.11:23-33).

In Ephesus, Paul found access to deeper levels of history and therefore turned increasingly into the Apostle of Europe, the new world. He fared like a person who, having taken a firm grip on his present destiny, is also able to transform consciously what slumbered as fruits of former earth incarnations in the depths of his being.

In the millennium that had passed since the days of Homer, important phases of human development had been located within the neighbourhood of the temple of Ephesus, until the night when Alexander the Great was born and Herostratus' torch-brand had caused the temple to be consumed by flames. Had Pythagoras not taught here before the Asian conquerors surrounded the peaceful temple with a large and noisy city? When the quiet of the mystery site had been protected only with difficulty against the encroachments of the profane world, was it not here that Heraclitus had taught and written down his thoughts? Were these not the thoughts of the fire from which all existence has emerged, the element of the creative Logos, the Universal Word; thoughts of the inescapable, progressive, ever-changing stream of evolution? Something of the future breath of freedom touched Paul here from ages of the distant past.

The activity of the Apostle now had two focal points: Corinth and Ephesus. To begin with it might seem that Asia, where the spiritual call towards Europe had resounded, was once more taken into account and that a balance and equality had thus been established between East and West. In reality, however, Asia now saw Paul as the herald of the European genius who was connected with Christ. Asia's value was reflected, as it were, out of the past into the future. The ancient spirituality signalled the new one; the heights which it is humanity's task to scale in the future became visible in images.

During his moves back and forth between Corinth and Ephesus, a figure stood by the side of Paul who, because he belonged more to the ancient spirituality, brought Paul's proclamation even more clearly into focus — the Alexandrian, Apollos. He began his enthusiastic activity in Ephesus, believing he was working in the service of Christ. He did not encounter Paul during the latter's first brief stay there. Some joint work did originate, however, between him and Aquila and Priscilla, who had accompanied Paul from Corinth to Ephesus and then stayed on without him. In their exchanges, Apollos soon became aware that he was still lacking the final certainty concerning his comprehension and proclamation of Christ. Willingly he accepted what his two friends could relate to him. Nevertheless, full satisfaction still eluded him. Therefore he made the decision to go and work in Corinth in the hope of penetrating more deeply into the Gospel of Christ. This was why Paul did not encounter Apollos upon his return to Ephesus. It was not long, though, before Paul came across traces of Apollos' activity there, especially when he met up with twelve of his disciples. Later on, when he again left Ephesus to go to Corinth, Paul did work with Apollos but not without an essential difference in their spiritual orientation becoming clearly evident.

Having come from Jewish schools of learning, Apollos was a scholarly and eloquent philosopher. In his thinking, he was quite close to Philo of Alexandria, the great contemporary of the Apostles. Perhaps he had been Philo's student or, more likely, his schoolmate. As his writings, *Of the Contemplative Life* and *Every Virtuous One is Free*[40] demonstrate, Philo had a strong sympathy with Essenism and Therapeutism, in which his allegorical interpretation of the books of the Old Testament received an occult nuance and emphasis. More than Philo, Apollos seems to have become involved in the meditative element of initiation that streamed through the Essene Order. Because of this, as happened to so many other Essenes, it appears that he found access to the Christian conviction. He now took his spiritualized, allegorical interpretation of the scriptures and joined it with the insight that Jesus of Nazareth was the Christ; that the longings and prophecies of the Old Testament had thus been fulfilled. He had great successes with his lectures, particularly in Jewish circles.

Only too frequently Paul has been compared to Philo, especially by Protestant theologians. The manner of thinking in his letters was characterized as Alexandrian allegorizing, though this was not limited to the Old Testament but extended to the contents of the New Testament as well. This conception of Paul as a Jewish theologian who advanced himself further by acceptance of new teachings confuses Paul with Apollos. It would be correct in regard to Apollos; Paul could not be more misunderstood. It is therefore important to focus clearly on the fundamental difference between the outlook of Paul and that of Apollos.

In Acts, we learn of Apollos as well as his twelve disciples that their share in the Christian mysteries only extended as far as the 'baptism by John' (18:25; 19:3). What is meant by this?

The baptism by John signifies the level to which humanity had been able to aspire before the coming of Christ. The Christ idea was a profoundly familiar one to John. In his presentiments, he too could recognize the secret of the human incarnation of Christ in the one whom he had baptized. Yet the power and the ever-present being of Christ could only be experienced after the events of Good Friday and Easter. Thereby, a new principle of spiritual experience entered humanity. John the Baptist himself had indicated this prophetically, inasmuch as he had contrasted the baptism with water carried out by him, to 'the baptism with the Holy Spirit,' which in the future would proceed from the Christ-being. The report that Acts gives of Paul's encounter in Ephesus with the twelve disciples of Apollos is one of the passages from which we can derive a concrete picture of how, even at that time, the 'baptism with the Holy Spirit' was an important ingredient of the original Christian congregational practices. Paul asked the twelve men whether they had received the baptism with the Spirit. It was evident from their answer that the mystery of the Holy Spirit was still unknown to them and that the source of their participation in the Christian life was purely and solely the baptism of John which they had received. The manner in which Paul subsequently spoke to them of Christ brought about the beginning of a decisive transformation in their minds. They longed for full incorporation into the Christian life. The baptism of John was now not considered sufficient for joining the congregation. A twofold rite of baptism was carried out. First they received the baptism by water, then, however, Paul added the so-called baptism by fire and performed on them the laying on of hands. The inner transformation in the twelve men continued; their soul was enkindled, their spirit enlightened.

Such insight into the early handling of the sacrament poses a number of questions. They begin to be resolved, however, if one considers that the dual rite of baptism carried out on adults in the early ages of Christianity contained the seed for the sacraments of baptism and confirmation. The two were moved to an earlier age of life only later — baptism to the beginning of childhood and confirmation to the onset of youth.

All pre-Christian initiation was based on the principle of ecstasy. The extreme and complete form consisted in the neophyte being placed into the deathlike temple sleep, the 'mystical death,' after undergoing the preparatory instructions and soul trials. The ecstasy lifted the fallen being of man to the divine heights from where, transformed and gifted with higher knowledge, it returned after three days into the bodily sheaths. In the late ages of antiquity when the ancient spiritual vision in humanity had virtually shrunk to intellectual thought, only a certain aspect of the ancient initiation remained in some places, for instance among the Nazirites and Essenes. After long, ascetic preparation by means of certain baptismal rites with water, the souls were loosened from their bondage to the body so that a certain revival of the ancient clairvoyance occurred. Thus, in this manner, as a last shadow of the supersensory world, a half imaginative, allegorical picture element became mixed in with the now abstract thinking. With the baptism carried out by long submersion in the waters of the Jordan, John the Baptist still brought it about that the souls experienced a death-like liberation from the body, even if only for a short time. As a result of their entering the higher worlds, they then brought back an awareness of their own mental darkness and of the approach of a divine light into everyday life. Apollos and his disciples who laid claim to the baptism of John had doubtless encountered only quite diminished versions of this. Thereby, they had attained to a slightly enlightened thinking that also enabled them to find theological, doctrinal access to the fact of Christ's human incarnation.

The transformation that was now brought about in the spiritual life of humanity through the Christ event consisted in the principle of ecstasy being replaced by that of incorporation. The Pauline principle of 'Christ in us' became operative. The principle of ecstasy was at an end; that of incorporation, a new beginning. The difference between the two makes clear the distinction between Apollos and Paul.

With this new beginning, the seed existed for a form of consciousness that does not arrive at its insights outwardly, but comes to them from within. The intellectual, brain-bound thinking, which was still to have a dramatically rich history reaching from the Neoplatonic and Alexandrian philosophy all the way to the mode of thinking of modern natural science, was and is a cognition leading from without to within. Today it is an appendage to sense perception directed solely to the external world. It came into being as the shrunken product of ancient, half-clairvoyant perception. The principle of incorporation viewed in the Pauline sense, must give birth one day to a new, creative thinking that will grasp the world from out of the core of the human being and, because of this, will also penetrate through the outer surface of things into their inner spiritual essence. In the baptism by the Spirit or by fire, early Christendom had a means to the awakening of man's supra-personal centre of being. It was not an outward warmth, not an external fire, with which this baptism was carried out. Indeed, it was not something that one person carried out actively, while another allowed it passively to happen. It was the loving, blessing help that could be offered by the congregation to the one who seemingly received something, but actually did it himself. The fire of the Spirit already had to be burning in the inner warmth of soul, then the laying on of hands could sanctify the flame by aiding it in attaining peace and harmony, turning it into a source of light, into a spiritual organ of perception. When the fountainhead of the 'Holy Spirit' sprang forth, the fiery tongues of Pentecost morning did not simply descend on the Apostles from outside or above. The flames were enkindled within; then, a higher spiritual element could come to meet the indwelling spiritual essence and be recognized by it. The more clearly the secret of incorporation is understood, the more all misunderstandings vanish which would view as ecstatic conditions the Pentecostal experience of the Apostles or what occurred in souls during the act of the baptism with the Spirit. The secret of these experiences consists in the exact opposite of ecstasy and rapture.

The twelve men in Ephesus took the step from the world of Apollos to that of Paul when they found their way from John's baptism to the Christian baptism. With it, the fulcrum of their spiritual life was moved from the head to the heart. Theology changed into religion. Not that they now changed from 'knowledge to faith,' from an experience in thinking to one of feeling. From intellectual head-thinking, they penetrated to an intensified thinking elevated and illumined by soul warmth and spiritual light, which corresponded to the spiritual element indwelling them creatively in the core of their being. What thinking can develop into in the future when it becomes Christian and is produced by the true Christ-permeated ego of man, was prophetically evident in the perception of those who were baptized 'with fire and the Holy Spirit' in the first days of Christendom. Though he had not been present on Whitsun morn, Paul was the actual guardian and cultivator of the baptism of the Spirit. Since Damascus, he was able to cognize exactly the portent of the future. He saw in this baptism the seed of an initiation into which Christian humanity would have to grow, particularly in those ages when the Damascus mystery will become an event for all humanity. Then Christendom will one day be able to enter into its 'era of the Holy Spirit.'

A 'confirmation' in the exact sense, an acknowledgment and strengthening of man's innermost being, took place through the baptism by fire and the Spirit. The first part of the dual rite of baptism, carried out predominantly with water, had relinquished the magical initiation character of John's baptism. It represented the symbolic conclusion and sealing of the catharsis, the purification by which the one who wished to fit into the community of Christ had prepared himself. By means of this baptism, the vessel was made ready and worthy of receiving something. The baptism with the Holy Spirit brought to life the higher content in the vessel. As in the course of time the first part turned into the baptism carried out on the child, and the second into the confirmation of the young person, the archetypal relationship becomes even more evident. Through birth, the human spirit and soul have begun to dwell in an earthly sheath; baptism sanctifies this vessel. After two times seven years, the inner man is born in the maturing earth man; he attains to his own soul that is gradually maturing into a sense of self. Confirmation is the blessing and sanctification of what henceforth lives in the earthly dwelling as celestial content. Confirmation is therefore the sacrament of the Holy Spirit. Yet within a properly comprehended Christian sacramentalism, baptism and confirmation are not only to be connected to those moments in life when they are outwardly performed. They signify processes of development and goals of human striving which continue to develop further throughout life. Expressed in Pauline terminology, they are the mysteries of both the child of God and divine sonship which, proceeding from the archetypes of baptism and confirmation, or from baptism by water and fire, are to penetrate the whole of life.

10. The Journeys: Trial and Martyrdom

At the end of the three Ephesian years, Paul's life moves into a completely new phase and assumes a different style.

In his younger years, Paul had believed that the direction of his life arose out of his own convictions. Before the gates of Damascus, however, he discovered that his life became true only through what happened *to him.* On this new basis and in unison with his overpowering destiny, he once again discovered an activity that flowed out of his own will. This was made possible because, within his own 'I,' he could simultaneously feel a higher 'I' and allow it to work with him. Now everything would change again. He felt something approaching that would happen *to him.* He knew that his own mission would be fulfilled in the very act of placing himself totally in the service of destiny, yet without it dampening the fire of his own inner activity.

Perhaps it gave him strength to occasionally recall in all humility that the turning point being ushered in resembled that moment in the life of Jesus when, after entering Jerusalem, the stations of the Passion began, beyond which, however, the greatest deed, the final sacrifice and revelation, was still concealed.

In the Gospels, the description of the events that took place in the days of Holy Week occupies as much if not more space than the rest of Jesus' life. Thus, we also note in Acts how after having represented the dramatic period of the apostolic journeys in a few, scanty sketches — quite incomplete for the taste of the traditional historian — the style changes into a broadly flowing, detailed description at the point where the story of the passion in Paul's life begins.

The change was heralded one day when the populace in Ephesus erupted in fury and feverish ecstasy. The uproar, directed against Paul, placed him in the greatest danger. Until then, the attacks and persecutions which Paul had endured had mainly proceeded from the Jewish side. Paul himself had anticipated the dangers connected with this, for he never deviated from the rule that his sense of deep fateful obligation had imposed on him: to take the message that he had to proclaim and bring it initially to those who lived with the scriptures of the Old Covenant. Disappointed and persecuted by the Jews, he had turned towards the world of Greek paganism where he had always met with understanding, but it now revolted against him for the first time.

Rebuilt in pompous proportions after having been burned down by Herostratus, the temple of Artemis, once the quiet maternal source of the holiest mysteries, was still one of the most important centres of Greek spiritual life. There the air still harboured a faint echo of the feelings formerly evoked in human souls by the devout worship of the virginal mother, Artemis-Diana, who bestowed life and wisdom in abundance. Particularly in May, the month of Artemis, the ceremonies of this pre-Christian Mariolatry reached a culmination; the large number of priestesses who served in the temple appeared in impressive processions before all the world.

Now however, through the growing spiritual tension between the fibre of Christian life and the gradually dying ancient life of the gods, the discrepancy which had arisen between the sacred past and the decadent present of Ephesus suddenly became evident. The goldsmith, Demetrius, in whose workshop small silver replicas of the Artemis temple and probably also reproductions of the famous statue of the many-breasted goddess were produced, blamed the decline of his business on the successful Christian competition instead of on the diminution of the ancient spirituality. He knew how to unleash furious agitation among the people against Paul. It culminated in a tremendous scene in the amphitheatre. Obeying the entreaties of his friends, Paul remained completely in the background. The whole affair came to nothing when the people regained their senses and realized that in fact no reasonable charges could be brought against Paul. Paul however, could not help but sense a sign and signal in this event. What he had divined for some time now became quite obvious to him: something was calling him and he had to obey.

Two kinds of feelings and thoughts determined the plans which he now made. One was that he had to go to Jerusalem although he knew that a grievous destiny awaited him there. Had not Jesus of Nazareth also been impelled to take the decisive step from Galilee to Judea? In Paul's companions, feelings may have surfaced similar to those of the Apostles when Jesus revealed to them the impending path of suffering and sacrifice: 'Behold, we are going up to Jerusalem.' The other was that Paul sensed that he would also be going to Rome (Acts 19:21). This conviction was so firm that alongside the sombre prospect of Jerusalem, a bright image arose of the continuing possibilities of destiny and work.

He departed from Ephesus but did not choose the direct route to Jerusalem. First, he visited the congregations in Macedonia and Greece; then he even spent several months in Corinth, continuing with the special care that he had always lavished on this congregation. Then he planned to continue travelling to Palestine on the most direct route. The threat of Jewish plots against him, however, made him embark for his return journey by the same route as had led him from Ephesus. He realized that now it was a matter of bidding farewell to the congregations in which he had been active until then, particularly those in Asia Minor. This became the underlying tone for everything he now undertook in his apostolic activity.

Among the particular effects of his nature which, apart from his teachings, were evoked through the premonition of destiny emanating from his words, the events in Troas stand out symbolically. Troas was the place where the call to Europe had reached him; now, where there had once been a beginning, there came a moment of culmination. In the cenacle, located in an upper room, Paul celebrated the sacred meal, then gave out instructions which turned into farewell addresses of a truly testamentary character and kept the friends together until midnight. Eutychus, a youth who sat in a window of the crowded room, was so moved by Paul's words that he succumbed to a deathlike condition (similar to the one which the neophytes had to undergo during initiation in the ancient mystery centres) and fell from a height of three floors. Paul attended to him with all his devotional power. Having calmed his terrified audience, he continued with his instructions until daybreak when Eutychus returned to full life and consciousness. It was not coincidental that this particular stage in Paul's journeys was accompanied by a living sign of death and resurrection.

To take leave of his congregation in Ephesus was a poignant moment for Paul, as all the congregations of Asia Minor were gathered there as their spiritual centre. Yet Paul could not return to Ephesus again, feeling impelled to go to Jerusalem. The Pentecostal festival was imminent in which the ancient sacred celebration, offering the first fruits of the year, was now combined with the new celebration of the baptism with the Holy Spirit. On the occasion of this festival, Paul planned to make a sacrifice in the Temple in which he would place the inner harvest of his work at the disposal of the spiritual worlds as a gift of first fruits. As he had done before with Barnabas from Antioch, he would bring a donation to the original Christian congregation from the communities where he had been active. In this way a parallel offering would be expressed on the human level, reflecting the divine offering made in the promised Temple-sacrifice.

Therefore, Paul hit upon the expedient of asking the presbyters from the congregation of Ephesus and the communities all around to come to Miletus. They were dismayed when he announced his imminent farewell, adding that he would see them no more in this life. The thought of death darkened their souls like thunder clouds.

Paul, however, did not wish to sadden the friends gathered around him. He counted on their strength and courage. Just as Jesus once took his leave from his most intimate disciples during Holy Week on the Mount of Olives by allowing them to see into the apocalyptic drama of humanity's future, so also did Paul before the Ephesian congregation that was so close to his heart. There would be no time of peace for the development of the young congregations. Paul had to speak to the shepherds about the wolves who would attack and maul the flock. He also had to speak to them of the distortions and reversals that the Christ mystery, which is at the same time the mystery of true humanness, would suffer in their own ranks. Counter images would be brought to bear against the archetypes as if they were truth. Yet such apocalyptic tensions would only witness to the vital progress occurring on a spiritual level. Devoted and unselfish pastoral service would triumph over all dangers and would bring the followers safely through, for any help needed would flow from the higher spheres of true evolution.

The closer Paul approached to Jerusalem, the more numerous and insistent became the warning voices of those who tried to induce him not to go there now. In particular some beseeched him who, owing to special prophetic faculties, beheld the ominous clouds gathering over his fate. Paul himself, however, had long seen clearly the darkness awaiting him in the Holy City. He was aware that he was intent on a path of sacrifice. But he also knew that he *had* to take this path and could not avoid the threatening evil. He wore the armour of courage and determination; he knew he would be able to draw the sword of the spirit.

In Jerusalem, leadership lay in the hands of James, the brother of the Lord. Despite the important centres which Christian life had established elsewhere through his efforts, it was natural for Paul to acknowledge the original congregation in Jerusalem as the authoritative centre. He thus appeared before the circle of presbyters gathered around James in order to present the collected gifts and to report on his work in the wider world.

For the first time, the two men confronted each other without any of the other Apostles being present. Neither Peter nor John knew how to ease the tension between these two who, as representatives of the sternly Jewish Christian element and the pagan Christian stream, stood at different poles. James and his followers could not help but receive Paul's report with admiration, joy and gratitude. Yet their own closeness to the Law of the Old Testament brought about reserve and concern. To their sombre earnestness, the freedom and clarity of the Pauline spirit appeared completely foreign.

James posed questions that seemed to border on reproach and accusation. He adhered to the dispensation from the Mosaic Law in regard to all those from non-Jewish, pagan circles who were becoming Christian, something which had previously been decided upon unanimously in the group of participating Apostles. No Greek or Roman would be brought under the yoke of the Law as a precondition for becoming a Christian; he had to agree only to a few rules that represented a dividing line against the most extreme pagan ritual magic. But how had Paul dealt with those who had come from Judaism to the Christian faith and life? It was the unalterable opinion of James that, for any Jew, turning Christian could in no way signify abrogation or easing of the obligation to the Law. Now was it true, as the rumours coming from all sides would have it, that even in regard to the Jews Paul had lessened the importance of the Law or even declared it to be invalid?

Paul was in a position of having to justify himself. Thus, his renewed encounter with the original congregation turned into the first act in the drama of the trial against him. The ancient world placed the new one in the dock.

Yet he did not wish to justify himself in the place where he now stood. Naturally, all his teaching led to the insight that the Law of Moses had only a preparatory mission. 'The Law was our teacher until Christ' (Gal.3:24*B*). But he had never invited or even encouraged anybody approaching him from the background of Judaism to break the Law. In his heart, he was still close to the people from whom he had come and to the special mission that Providence had bestowed on the Jews. His most ardent wish was that those who had grown up in the world of the Law would find the way that he had discovered, so that the light could break the spell of darkness.

James demanded that Paul demonstrate before all the world that in regard to his own person he still acknowledged and followed the demands of the Law. Paul ignored the insulting aspect of this unreasonable expectation. After all, aware of the change that was becoming evident in his destiny, he had come to Jerusalem intending to seal through an outer act of sacrifice the offering taking place in his inner being. He could do that without difficulty in the form suggested by James. More consciously than ever, he could now offer up the sacrifice in the form of an intercessory prayer for the fate of the nation that was at the point of forfeiting its rank of the chosen.

The very prayers and sacrifices that Paul now offered up in the Temple brought into motion the wheel of misfortune. But had it not been the same at the beginning of the mighty Passion drama during Holy Week? It was after entering Jerusalem, when Jesus went into the Temple in order to observe the offering of the holy festival, that the floodgates of hatred and persecution opened. Jesus' entrance into the precincts of the Temple subsequently proved to be a crushing judgment against the dying past. With Paul, too, the new element entered the sanctuary of a dying world. And although he now wished to do nothing but pay a tribute of respect and faithfulness to the Temple and spirit of the past, the ancient world hissed and roared under this touch of the new. The Jews could no longer acknowledge the apostate as one of their own. They viewed it as a desecration of the Temple if he entered it or prayed there. They did not wish for a fresh shoot to grow from the dying tree trunk.

His furious opponents expelled Paul by force from the Temple and locked its gates. They whipped him — had not men even scourged one who was more than a human being? — and attempted to kill him. Only the intercession of the Roman Temple guard who took him under protective custody saved his life.

In Caiaphas, Pilate and Herod, before whom Jesus had to defend himself during Holy Week, three basic streams of humanity came together in order to slay the one who had come to bring new life. The Ahrimanically dark and cold element took the stage in Caiaphas and the Jewish Sanhedrin. The Luciferically flickering element, the impure fire of egotism, stood at its side in Herod and Herodias. Between the two extremes, the merely human element without backbone assumed the figure of Pilate. And when Jesus was led all round, men could assume that they were weighing him on all their scales of justice.

Paul's trial also passed through a number of acts; he, too, was sent from pillar to post. On three occasions, the world of Caiaphas first confronted him. In a certain sense even the scene that actually was only a prologue of the case against Paul belongs here: Paul before James and the presbyters of the first congregation. In the second and third acts, the world of Pilate played an assisting role: in the presence of the Roman captain, Claudius Lysias, and his cohorts, Paul had to defend himself to the Jewish people and the Sanhedrin. Up to this point, Jerusalem was the stage of the drama.

Subsequently, in Caesarea, where a gigantic monument of Caesar Augustus looked out over the Mediterranean, four acts followed in which the world of Pilate and Herod appeared. Two Roman procurators, Felix and Festus, assumed the place of Pilate. Three members of the family of Herod joined in as a sensation-seeking audience: Drusilla who, along with Felix, posed questions to Paul; King Agrippa II and his sister Berenice who, as the guests of Festus, listened to Paul. They were the three children of King Herod Agrippa I who, at Easter time in the year 44, when Paul and Barnabas brought the gifts of the Antiochenes to Jerusalem, had the elder James beheaded and caused Peter to be imprisoned. After these seven stages of the trial, Paul was brought before the ruler of the Imperium Romanum.

The Roman centurion, Lysias, allowed Paul to address the people from the stairs of the Temple. The multitude seethed with fury and only became silent when Paul began speaking in the Hebrew tongue. The people were permitted to hear how the lightning strike of Damascus had shown him the very real fulfilment of all Messianic prophecies and hopes. They were also told that when Paul subsequently came back for the first time to Jerusalem, he was privileged to hear the word of Christ in the Temple from which he had just now been dragged out. It prophesied to him that, tragically, it would not be the people of the Old Covenant but the pagan nations that would be open to his message. Thus retrospectively, we also learn something concerning which Acts had remained silent — that Paul had received a concrete direction from Christ for his apostolic journeys when the first Apostles, whose directions and help he had sought, failed him.

After Paul had addressed the people, the Roman captain knew even less than before about whether Paul was being justly or unjustly accused and persecuted in such fanatical manner. Through interrogation and, if necessary, through torture, he wanted to find out what he was dealing with here. Yet Paul now posed a new puzzle to him by invoking the rights that he possessed as a Roman citizen. The centurion had no choice but to make sure that the prisoner received a fair trial by the Jewish Sanhedrin. Proudly, Paul stepped before this council in which the high priests, representatives of the party of the Sadducees, had to pronounce judgment, together with the Pharisees and scribes attached to them. Paul himself had once been the product of one of these two major factions. The Pharisaic eschatology that spoke of the resurrection of the dead at the coming of the Messiah had filled and guided him until the hour of Damascus. From his youth, he was only too well aware of the unbridgeable chasm that separated the Pharisees and their highly strung spiritual life from the materialistic and political thinking of the Sadducees, even in regard to the Messiah.[41] How could they pronounce judgment over him, given that they were divided among themselves on such crucial questions? Paul took command of the situation by raising in the debate the question of the resurrection of the dead. Although he knew since Damascus how wrong the Pharisees were in their conception of this mystery, he could still declare his faith in the resurrection. What he had anticipated came about: the various factions gathered in the Sanhedrin began fighting furiously among themselves when the catchword sounded. The centurion helped Paul escape from the general fracas. During the following night, as a spiritual response to the chaos of men, Paul heard the ordering word of God's will. Christ himself was comfortingly close to him, allowing him to become aware of the certainty that he would now take the historic step from Jerusalem to Rome which, in his thoughts and spiritual experiences, he had already foreseen so clearly (Acts 23:11).

Because of their hateful designs, the Jews brought it about that Paul was removed from their influence in Jerusalem and taken a first decisive step closer to Rome, the goal of his destiny. A group of zealots, binding themselves with sacred oaths and pledges of fasting, conspired to kill Paul. They would ask Lysias to bring him once again before the Sanhedrin; on the way there, the ambush was to be carried out. Like Barnabas, Paul had a sister who lived in Jerusalem and by chance the young son of this sister happened to overhear something of the conspirators' deliberations. He found a way to reach Paul and communicated what he had heard. Paul sent him to Lysias who immediately gave the order that the prisoner be brought under heavy guard to Caesarea to the Roman procurator. At this point of the drama, in place of the successors of Caiaphas came those of Pilate and Herod.

When the Jewish accusers arrived, governor Felix staged a court assembly. The high priest had gone to the trouble of bringing along an advocate, the Roman orator, Tertullus, who was to sway the representative of Caesar to pronounce against Paul. As one who familiarized himself thoroughly with local events, Felix was not completely ignorant of the questions being dealt with here, and the points brought forward by Paul in his justification were not new to him. Felix, however, lacked depth; he did not possess the courage to pronounce a judgment in favour of the accused. He dragged out the trial under the pretence that the centurion Lysias would first have to be interrogated as a witness.

Just as Herod Antipas had once demanded out of curiosity to hear the words of John the Baptist, so Felix wished to listen to Paul. Together with Drusilla, a member of Herod's family, he made Paul present to him the substance of his message and teaching, but time and again they were frightened off by the moral earnestness pervading Paul's words. Secretly, Felix hoped for a bribe after the excitement of the trial had subsided. He calculated that Paul must have acquired a great number of friends who would be ready to purchase his freedom with money.

Paul remained in the prisons of Caesarea for two years. Surely he did not remain inactive during that time. Through many letters — the letters of Paul in the New Testament are doubtless only a small selection from the original number — he continued with his leadership and care of the congregations. Perhaps, as was the case later on in Rome too, he was to some extent free to continue quietly spreading the Gospel outside the prisons.

After the two-year tenure of his office had run its course, Felix was replaced by the new governor, Festus. Just as Paul had confronted Felix on two different occasions, once in the presence of the Jews, once when Drusilla was present, so also he would face Festus twice.

The Jews urged Festus to pursue the trial against Paul in Jerusalem, planning to carry out the assassination, plotted long ago, on the way. But Festus remained firm and proceeded with the case in Caesarea. After listening to the accusations and to Paul's replies however, he realized that it would be impossible for him to come to a decision. He asked Paul whether he would agree to a continuation of the proceedings in Jerusalem. At this moment, Paul did the only thing that could bring him closer to his destiny, for the sake of which he had patiently endured all his suffering so far. He appealed against the way the trial was being conducted and called on the highest authority, Caesar in Rome. The governor then decided to have him brought to Rome. Once again, having tried with Satanic motives to bring Paul to Jerusalem, the Jews in effect brought it about that Paul's way led all the more inexorably towards Rome.

At this point, the house of Herod now joined the successor of Pilate. King Herod Agrippa II and Berenice, brother and sister of Drusilla, came to visit the Roman governor. When they heard of Paul, they too asked to hear him, and so Festus made it appear that he wished to consult Herod Agrippa who was considered knowledgeable in Jewish teachings. In a solemn gathering, Paul was presented to the royal guests and, for the sake of justifying himself, was invited to freely proclaim his message to humanity.

As he had done in his Hebraic address to the people on the terraced, outdoor staircase of the Temple in Jerusalem, here again Paul described the light-drama of Damascus. The fire of the spirit blazed in his words. The secret of Christ's Resurrection and the resurrection of man's being which it made possible, shone forth from him. Festus was filled with fear by the power that issued from Paul's words and wanted to subdue, as he termed it, the madness of the Apostle. Inclining towards the ecstatic element, the Herodian brother and sister had to admit that it would not have taken much more to convince them. What was missing however, was the true depth of earnestness in their souls, the only means with which to apprehend and understand the truth of Christ.

They were thus of one mind that they could have freed Paul had he not appealed to Caesar. Now the step to Rome had to be taken. The seven steps of preparation led to the court of the highest power then existing on earth.

The journey that brought the Apostle to Rome is normally referred to as Paul's fourth journey. Within the outline presented by Acts, this designation is accurate. Yet, how completely different everything was now! Although this journey had the same destination that he would have hastened towards if he had been freed, it was one Paul had to endure, not something he carried out. It was a prison transport accompanied by a military force. And yet the prisoner in question was the freest of men. While he had been effective before by means of his word, he had now completely matured to the point of being effective above all by means of his being. His fate was ever more clearly sealed with the destiny of Christ. Through the mystery of suffering-with-Christ and dying-with-Christ, he attained a Christ-permeated nobility. What was being done to him and the manner in which he fulfilled his destiny from within both proclaimed simultaneously the apostolic mission that he carried through the world. This is why Acts describes the dramatic sequence of the ocean voyage in such detail, although in a direct sense it did not serve the promulgation of Christ's Gospel.

In the way that Paul's trial ends in a stormy, danger-filled voyage, his whole apostolic life becomes recognizable as a Christian Odyssey. The 'adventures' of this Odysseus are the external expressions for stages of inner transformation and permeation by Christ.

It was late in the year when the centurion Julius of the Augustinian cohort set out with his soldiers, who were returning to Italy, and the prisoner placed under his charge. The autumnal storms were in evidence and made it necessary to steer a course close to the mainland. Even here too, many alterations of course were necessary; thus, the voyage proceeded only slowly. Paul was allowed to move about freely; a few of his friends, among them Luke, had been permitted to accompany him. At the southwestern corner of Asia Minor, they had to transfer to another vessel; it was a grain-ship from Egypt on its way to Italy that had been driven off course by the winds. Even as it sailed on, the vessel had to bow to the increasingly vehement force of the elements and initially had to steer a southward course, then veer along the southern coast of Crete. There, a lengthy stop was required. Finally, when the weather was more favourable for sailing, all seagoing traffic on the Mediterranean had ceased for the winter. Paul, much experienced in sea voyages, advised anchoring the ship for the duration of the winter at this very spot, even though he felt urgently impelled to move on toward his goal. While the sailors realized that they would not be able to reach Italy before the onset of winter, they did want to continue the voyage to a more favourable harbour. Even the centurion and his soldiers disregarded Paul's warning. The ship departed in good weather, but hardly had it reached the high seas when it was overtaken by a tremendous storm. There could be no more thought of steering a predetermined course. All efforts were devoted to preventing the vessel breaking up or capsizing by girding up the ship's hull, reefing the sails, throwing the ballast overboard and eventually dumping even the cargo of grain into the sea. Yet the wild tempest continued and tossed the ship around like a toy. For many days pitch darkness continued and the sun and the stars no longer seemed to exist.

There was no prospect of being saved and, faced with almost certain death, the three hundred or so people aboard the ship were going mad with despair. Paul alone, the prisoner, stood out like a rock of calm and confidence in the midst of the storm. His words had a quietening power, as if a higher being were speaking through him, one who could also command the waves of the storm. Paul made it clear that the confidence he was trying to show did not emanate from his own resources. He allowed the terrified people to share in his spiritual experience. In the midst of the storm's din, the voice of the one by whom Paul felt sent out had once again spoken of his destined goal; no power in the world would be allowed to obstruct the path leading to it. The people aboard the ship were told that Paul's certainty of reaching Rome alive included the possibility of deliverance for them all.

After thirteen days and nights of the raging storm, the proximity of land was ascertained through soundings. Anchors were laid out astern so that the ship would not be thrown against rocks. However, now there was a chance of deliverance, the sailors attempted to abandon ship and save their own skins by means of the ship's boat. They did not reckon with Paul who, though imprisoned, was the real captain and leader. Paul warned the soldiers who immediately cut loose the boat, thus thwarting the contemptible intention of the sailors.

At daybreak, Paul called together all those aboard ship and invited them to partake of some nourishment after the long enforced fast. A simple but solemn meal took place. Paul stood in the middle and broke bread as was customary in the Christian congregations during the sacred meal. Following him, all present ate of the bread. None could be unaffected by the wonderfully succouring and healing power that was shared through the bread. What Paul was doing was like the administering of communion.

Meanwhile, it had become daylight. The anchor ropes were cast off and the sails set so that the wind could drive the ship towards the now visible land. When the vessel hit a sandbank, the bow ran aground and the hull split asunder. The ship had to be abandoned but all the passengers reached land safely. Previously, when Paul had taken the first step towards Europe, following the call of the Spirit, it was on the mystery-island of Samothrace that he set foot on land. Now, amid dramatic dangers and trials, he came once more to Europe, and again set foot upon an island that had harboured ancient mysteries — Malta.

The winter storm at sea had lasted thirteen days and thirteen nights. A surprising light is thus shed on this voyage. For the mysterious time between the old and the new year, from Christmas Eve to the feast of the Epiphany, also lasts for thirteen days and nights. From the dark womb of midwinter, in the quiet glimmer of the Christmas light, the new year is born.

It is not impossible that it was over the Christmas period when Paul's ship withstood the storm. Yet even if the storm occurred somewhat earlier and perhaps fell during Advent, something of their secret nevertheless becomes evident because of the suggestion of Christmas standing over them like a star. From these thirteen days and nights, too, a new year was born; a new age for humanity had dawned in which the light of peace shines through the darkness of raging storms.

Let us take the two books by Luke contained in the New Testament, the Gospel of Luke and the Acts of the Apostles, and consider them as a whole. We are led from a lyric, intimate Christmas night to the finale of apocalyptic Christmas drama; from the Christmas peace of Bethlehem to the Christmas storm on the wildly tossing waves of the sea. By means of this we are led to discover the developing Christmas mystery. The light of the first Christ events was fittingly embedded in the intimacy of Bethlehem. In our age, this element moves increasingly further away from us due to the progressing destinies of humanity. Yet it is not only the loss that we should bemoan. A new Christ event is approaching which will take us not into peace but into strife; not into tranquillity but into the storm. Its light is like the lightning flashes in a thunderstorm. Where apocalyptic courage dwells it can inaugurate peace on a completely new level. At the same time, human beings who believe they stand increasingly firm on earth are in reality on the verge of losing the solid ground under their feet. Without being clearly aware of it themselves, they have had to sail forth on the sea of stormy destinies. It is questionable whether there are always people on board the ship who, like Paul, can bring forth the calming power of inner assurance.

Having escaped the storm, the voyagers awaited the spring on land. Again, they experienced the radiant healing force in Paul. The inhabitants of Malta shared in these blessings and expressed their gratitude by heartfelt hospitality which they extended to all the shipwrecked people until the winter drew to an end.

With the beginning of spring, their voyage continued on a vessel which, like the one wrecked by the storm, had come from Egypt and had spent the winter on the coast of the island. It bore the sign of Gemini on its crest. The journey proceeded northward. Stops of longer duration in Syracuse on the east coast of Sicily and in Puteoli, the harbour of Naples, made it possible for Paul, who enjoyed considerable liberty, to visit existing Christian congregations and live with them for several days. Having its origins in the foundation of Greek life which once blossomed there, Syracuse was one of the great metropoles of that period. In size, Naples was still a young city but the Caesars' preference for it had furnished it with much luxury and with the ambition likewise to become a metropolis. Above all, the landscape spoke to Paul through a mighty cosmic sign: the great volcanos sent their columns of fire and smoke up to heaven. In Sicily, it was the majestically outspread, paternally olympic Etna. In Puteoli, one beheld the more dramatic, temperamentally changeable Vesuvius. Here the region all around still emitted smoke in many places through half volcanic processes of fire and sulphur. In Puteoli, people to this day relate the story that when Paul was on his way to Rome he preached in the impressive circus that resembled an amphitheatre and which was situated on the slope above the harbour. In its immediate vicinity steamed the gigantic crater field of the solfatara. Once before Paul had come face to face with an earth not yet completely cooled but steaming in fiery manner. This was during the three years following the Damascus event when he withdrew into the Arabian desert of Sinai and became acquainted with the cosmic foundation of the Mosaic revelation. Now the volcanic element attracted the Caesars, who for that reason located their residences and summer villas around Naples. Their striving for superhuman power was mirrored in the unpredictable nature of the fire and smoke.

Proceeding from Naples, the party continued the journey on foot over the land route. When they were about halfway to Rome, Paul was already being welcomed by brethren of the Roman congregation. They came to meet him in order to turn his entrance into Rome on the Via Appia into a solemn event of joy despite the chain of imprisonment which he wore. For a long time, warm, intimate relations had linked Paul with the congregation in Rome, and not just because of his friendship with Aquila and his wife, Priscilla. The men of Cyprus and Cyrene had founded the congregation. Thus, it had become the centre of the Barnabas stream which represented a bridge between the Jewish Christianity of James and Paul's pagan Christendom. The congregation in Rome had invited Peter to work in their midst. They probably had no inkling as yet that because of this the centre of the whole Christian community would very soon be transferred to Rome, following the extinction of the first congregation in the destruction of Jerusalem and the death of James. During those years, Peter must have stayed in Rome much of the time. Although Acts and Paul's letters are silent concerning this, no doubt a self-evident understanding must have existed between the two great Apostles, Peter and Paul. The circle of helpers who stood by Peter's side also came to the aid of Paul who lived and was active in quite different fields. John Mark, for example, the nephew of Barnabas and later the evangelist, was among Peter's closest disciples and assistants in Rome. But Paul too, who had once sent him away and even separated from Barnabas on his account, experienced his obligingness and named him in letters written to other congregations (2Tim.4:11; Col.4:10; Philem.24).

Peter's environment, which was identical with the life of the congregation, differed from the Roman surroundings of Paul. The numerically insignificant Christian community was not completely unknown in Rome. There were whispers abroad about it. But the congregation did not care to be in the public eye. It pursued its inner path quietly, and serious seekers found their way to it. There were good reasons for seeking a certain invisibility. Among the Romans who had become Christians there were many who as friends of pre-Caesarian Rome and clinging steadfastly to the ancient Roman civic virtues, were repelled by the Caesarian decadence. Inwardly they had always refused to give approval to the worship of Caesar. Therefore, not just as Christians but even as Romans, they were considered suspect and were disliked by the state.

This is how it came about that Peter along with the congregation was more or less submerged in the city's immeasurable throng of people. Tradition relates that he lived in the house of a senator, Pudens, who was probably a true Old Roman. There the congregation is said to have gathered to celebrate its services. The house was located on the descending, broad southern side of the Esquilin and Viminal, thickly populated by middle class families in the principal ancient street of this part of town, which to this day is called Via Urbana. The church, Santa Pudentiana, stands there as a quiet monument of the martyrdom that the Roman congregation had endured. It is said that in the days when the Christians were blamed for the great fire in Rome, one night the officials of Caesar came here and forcefully dragged away the devoutly gathered congregation. In the pleasure gardens of Nero situated not very far away — at the site where later the Colosseum was built — the Christians were then said to have been burned as living torches to illuminate the orgies raging there. The daughters of Pudens, Pudentia and Praxedis, are said to have escaped imprisonment by chance; in the early dawn, they carried the charred corpses of their friends to their father's house and entombed them in the cistern.

Unlike Peter and the congregation, Paul could not remain in quiet seclusion in Rome. This resulted from the manner in which he had arrived there: as Caesar's prisoner upon trial. Though he was generously granted a certain freedom of movement and even the possibility of working, he was never completely without a guard and remained confined to a restricted area. And this happened to be the direct environment of soldiers and officials of the royal court, the official centre of the Roman world empire. When at the conclusion of the Letter to the Philippians that was written in Rome, Paul conveyed greetings from the friends around him, and among them especially named those belonging to 'Caesar's household,' the milieu in which he lived and worked becomes visible for a moment.

A local tradition exists in Rome concerning the place where Paul is supposed to have lived during the first two years there: 'And he lived there two whole years in his own rented dwelling' (Acts 28:30*B*). This tradition has remained as good as unnoticed. It does, however, contain an extraordinary inner evidence, and even in the event that it should eventually prove to be historically inaccurate, it is exceedingly instructive in illustrating Paul's Roman environment.

In ancient Rome, the government quarter was situated on the Via Lata, the 'broad avenue,' which at the Capitol and the Forum Romanum continued as the Via Flaminia, the famous trunk road to the north. Today, the Via Lata is the Corso, the proud old main street where Goethe watched the famous Roman carnival pass by. It leads towards the great white marble monument of King Victor Emmanuel I, which is built on the slope of the Capitol, concealing the view of the old Forum Romanum towards the inner city. In front of the monument, the Corso ends in the Piazza Venezia, where, in its palaces, the most important offices of administration were located even in Mussolini's days. Shortly before the point where the Corso comes to an end, next to the Palazzo Doria, the baroque church Santa Maria in Via Lata is squeezed into the closely compressed buildings. And under this church, in the silt-filled lower basement dripping with water, old foundations can be seen, remnants of the building in which Paul is supposed to have lived.

It is quite plausible to locate this point in the official centre of ancient Rome. In those days, the area was less built up. Where the church stands, Diocletian's triumphal arch was erected around the year 300, and was only torn down towards the end of the fifteenth century. It was to mark the border between the life of the city and the realm of the ruler. In Augustus' time the plan had been to decorate the Via Lata from here with a long arcade all the way to the Milvian bridge, hence almost through the whole city. The plan remained unexecuted, but it corresponded to the sentiments which Romans always entertained in regard to this street and its ending in the seat of power.

Julius Caesar had constructed a great hall, the Diribitorium, which initially served as the gathering and voting place for the centurions, the army and the arms-bearing citizens, where Diocletian's arch and Santa Maria in Via Lata later stood. The vote-tablets were delivered and counted there during popular elections. In Nero's time, the original purpose of the hall had already receded into the background. In Caesarian rule, voting was no longer given so much importance. It was then that the Diribitorium served a more popular purpose: free grain was distributed there to the populace, whereby the Caesars sought to maintain the favour of the multitude that called for *panem et circenses* (bread and circuses!).

Tradition relates that in the days when Paul came to Rome, the office of distributing grain was in the hands of a Roman official by the name of Martianus who was leaning towards the Christian faith. Following his own wish, Paul is said to have been assigned to him as a helper. And there he could also dwell together with Luke.* In the course of time, Paul began to address the people who gathered here in great numbers, among them several who in some sense belonged to the household of Nero's court. The fact that this local tradition has never been taken seriously but was dismissed long ago as legendary by the Church may be connected with the uncertainty that almost always dominated Petrine Rome in regard to the figure of Paul. Perhaps the polaric juxtaposition of the milieux around Santa Pudentiana and Santa Maria in Via Lata will eventually be acknowledged as illuminating for Rome's history in the apostolic era. Regardless of whether Paul, the prisoner, actually did or did not distribute grain for bread to Rome's populace, his word and being were nevertheless a sustenance for the people gathering round him, just as it had been on the ship that night when, on the black, stormy sea, he had stood in the midst of his terrified companions.†

The years remaining to Paul after the dramatic storm-filled voyage that had brought him to Rome pose many riddles to historians. Luke, who faithfully stayed with Paul during the journey of imprisonment and also never moved from his side in Rome, drops the thread of narration in his description of the Acts of the Apostles at the moment when the goal, Rome, had been

* The words, *en idiō misthōmati,* 'in his own hired dwelling,' are in most cases understood to mean that Paul was able to stay in his own rented house for those two years. But it is not impossible that this indicates the kind of professional activity for which Paul had allowed himself to be 'hired.'

There exists still another local tradition that speaks of a Pauline domicile. It is even mentioned by the apocryphal text, *Passio Petri et Pauli.* According to it, Paul is supposed to have had his last lodging on the left bank of the Tiber in the eleventh region *ad Arenulam* (*arenula,* washed ashore Tiber-sand) — the Diribitorium was situated in the first region — close by the island in the Tiber. He is supposed to have preached in an empty granary near the Porta Ostiensis. There, it is said that soldiers were also among his listeners. At this site stands an ancient little church, San Paolo alla Regola. Since Paul in all probability stayed in Rome much longer than two years or returned there again and again, the various traditions are not mutually exclusive. Still, it is probably not a coincidence that both traditions mention a hall where corn is distributed, and an audience composed of the circles of soldiers and courtiers.

reached. He does speak of the two years after Paul's arrival in Rome. But we are no longer informed of what took place in these two years, nor are we told how much time elapsed between the end of these two years and Paul's martyrdom. All traditions are in agreement on the point that as his most intimate disciple and most faithful servant Luke remained with Paul and was present at his execution. Why does he fall silent so soon? The kind of biblical exegesis, pursued above all by Protestant theology, which could only comprehend Acts in the light of present-day reporting and biographies, tried to assume that Luke's second book was written during Paul's lifetime, and for that reason did not describe the last period of the Apostle's life and his death. Nothing is said, however, about the content of the two years that are mentioned so briefly. The only possible conclusion is that with their arrival in Rome a certain development had come to an end for Luke and something new was beginning, which was no longer part of his task as an evangelist. Once this is clearly recognized, we may begin to consider tentative ideas concerning this considerable span of time. Actually, it was only the opinion that where nothing is reported nothing actually happened which led to the assumption that, after the two years had gone by, Paul was executed. Catholic theology, which did not allow itself to be deterred quite so much by principles of biblical criticism, often adduces a further three years of life that remained to Paul after the two years mentioned at the end of Acts.

In Rome, Paul had to be prepared from one day to the next to be called before Nero for interrogation, since he had himself appealed to Caesar in the trial against him. It does appear that the prosecution of Paul's case was prolonged for two years, during which it is inconceivable that Paul's presence did not come to the attention of Nero and his entourage. In the first place, the appeal proceedings for which the accused had been brought to Rome from a distant part of the world, sparing no expense, not only had to be reported but had to be taken in hand in some form. Secondly, Paul's activity occurred so near the central places of government, and so frequently were persons who belonged to Caesar's court drawn into the circles that listened to the Apostle, that to remain hidden or forgotten was out of the question. The apocryphal traditions, in fact, abound in stories that suggest contacts or even encounters between Paul and Nero. It is said for example of Patroclus, the cup-bearer and beloved of Caesar, that he belonged to the followers of Paul. One day, seated high above on a window-ledge because of the great throng, he fell like young Eutychus in Troas and was thought to be dead. When Nero heard about it, he was filled not only with sorrow over the youth's death but with wrath against Paul. Called back to life by Paul however, Patroclus then returned to Nero. Completely confusing emotions now arose in Nero, causing him to summon Paul to appear before him. It is also reported that Acte, a female slave from Asia Minor who was the mistress and first wife of Nero, having been rejected in the end by him, became an eager pupil of Paul's.

In those days, one man lived in Nero's entourage as his former teacher and present advisor who, surrounded by the hell of Caesarian madness, attempted to remain a guardian of reason and humanitarianism. He was the Stoic philosopher, Seneca. Perhaps his brother Gallio, before whose tribunal the Jews of Corinth had dragged Paul a decade earlier, was even then in Rome and able to stand behind his brother who revered him as the ideal of a Stoic sage. It is quite possible that Paul came in touch with Seneca. Gallio, who doubtless remembered Paul, could have played a part in bringing about such an encounter. Thanks to the two brothers' familiarity with the idea of conscience as a divine principle in humanity, the thought of late antiquity attained in them its closest approximation to the ideas of Pauline Christianity. Beyond that, their rapidly approaching future created a link between the two brothers and Paul. Gallio and Seneca only appeared to share in Caesar's power. They must have been aware that because of Nero's growing hate against all reason and genuine philosophical striving, a Damoclean sword hung over their heads, just as it did over the prisoner Paul. We may assume that Paul even survived the two brothers by one or two years, for during the chaotic conditions unleashed by the great fire in Rome Nero forced Seneca and Gallio to commit suicide.

In all probability, Paul was declared a free man when the trial was finally continued and the decisive proceedings took place.

Perhaps those who assumed that Seneca might have had a hand in it were not so much in error. After all, the accusations arose from the basis of the Jewish faith. Harsh persecutions of Jews had occurred in Rome, long before the Christian convictions were clearly seen as being opposed to the Roman principle. Nero, too, was at that time still open to reason to some extent.

If events took this course, it may well be that it was just the impression made by Paul on Nero that contributed to the last, wildest outburst of Caesarian madness. The apocryphal Acts of the Apostles reports that Paul warned Nero of the approaching world conflagration (Acts of Paul IV): 'Allow yourself to be saved from the fire that is breaking in upon the whole earth. We are not fighting for an earthly king, as you may believe, but for a celestial one ...' The image of an impending world conflagration that would pass sentence on him may have affected Nero, who considered himself to be the ruler of the world's destiny, in such a way as to produce the mad idea that it would be better to cause the conflagration himself rather than fall victim to the Last Judgment. This is how it may have come to pass that in the year 64 Nero staged the burning of Rome, and subsequently used this as a motive for the cruel persecution of the Christians and philosophers. Apocalyptic apparitions made their ghostly appearance in world history.

If it is true that Paul was given back his long denied freedom, what did he then undertake? How did he make use of the reprieve that destiny granted him after he was already done with life? The silence surrounding the remainder of Paul's life is no coincidence; it is a falling silent in the face of a mystery. A completely different and higher element must have pervaded any course of action that was still possible to him. Perhaps it was Paul himself who spread the veil of secrecy over his further travels and activities, beginning with that hour just prior to the burning of Rome. There are scholars of the opinion that Paul made long journeys for two or three more years, making use of the unexpected opportunity to revisit the congregations in Greece and Asia Minor that he had previously established. To assume such an unswerving continuation of his activity would be to misunderstand the mystery in which the remainder of Paul's life culminated. Such a path would belie Paul's own certainty concerning his fate, which had prompted him to bid farewell forever in Miletus to the delegates of the congregation in Ephesus.

One aspect of this final period emerges in faint contours, concerning which the New Testament is silent. It actually appears that Paul spent part of the period of grace bestowed upon him in Spain. The early Christian voices that have come down to us speak of this as of something generally known, although they are silent concerning any details. One most important testimony is the Letter to the Corinthians by Clemens Romanus, one of the first bishops in the Roman congregation following Peter. Written approximately three decades later, it says there:

> A herald he was in the East and the West ...
> He reached the outermost border of the West
> (Clem.1:5).

Regarding the arguments that have been raised to support the idea of a journey by Paul to Spain, one fact should be referred to again which is not conclusive but which prompts speculation. Adolf Deissmann published his Pauline map in order to demonstrate that in all instances Paul's journeys followed the habitat of the olive tree. On the one hand, he points out that Paul never went to Egypt where olive trees do not grow, something that is not a matter of course considering Egypt's cultural importance in those days. On the other hand, Deissmann shows that one country — Spain — lies within the zone of the olive tree; going only by the Acts of the Apostles, however, we must assume that Paul did not travel there, but nonetheless it seems to belong within the range of Paul's journeys.

It follows the consistency of Paul's apostolic activity that he penetrated further west beyond Rome. The first step that he had to take consciously following the behest of the Spirit led to Europe, as far as Greece and Illyricum. The next step was to Rome, not only into the centre of Europe but also into the midst of a newly fashioned world. The next step would have had to lead to the extreme west of Europe, hence indicating that the western world was intended as the stage of humanity's future, just as the Orient had been the stage of the civilizations of the past.

Like the apostolic journey two decades earlier that had led the elder James, who became the patron saint of seafaring people and world travellers, to Spain, so Paul's journey to Spain also ended in something like a mystery. We know nothing regarding the activities of James or Paul while in Spain. It is most unlikely that Paul was active there in the same way depicted in Acts. Yet he may well have sown the seed of Christ's Gospel into the ground of secret mystery sites, which were dedicated to the task of preparing for the future when the ancient principle, *ex oriente lux,* would have to be replaced by the new one, *ex occidente lux.* The light of the Spirit that rays forth from West to East was the goal of striving in later centuries for the circles around the Holy Grail. Perhaps it was motives similar to those that induced Titurel, according to legendary tradition, to erect the Grail castle in Spain, which made Paul journey there at a time when he should have been dead, yet mercifully was spared.

It must have been approximately two years after Nero's burning of Rome in the year 66 or 67 — an equal length of time had passed since the thirty-three years of the life of Christ — that with the increasing persecutions of Christians Paul was imprisoned again. This time, things proceeded quickly. His insistence on his rights as a Roman citizen could now influence only the manner of his execution. He was granted the privilege of being beheaded by the sword rather than being hanged, crucified or burned to death. Of his faithful companions, Luke and Titus were present when, far from the gates of the city toward the south in Trefontane, the Apostle died the martyr's death.

It is said that three fountains, to which the name *Trefontane* refers, sprang forth from the spots where the blood of Paul spurted on the ground. The truth contained in this may be that from this moment, a higher soul and life element streamed in the three springs which, earlier, had indicated a quiet, etheric centre at the edge of the Campagna landscape. Until our time — only now is the relentless advance of technology and modern development bringing an end to the miracle — a sacred cosmic element could be sensed under the eucalyptus trees by the springs of Trefontane; any sensitive person was awe-struck before them and felt transported to the most holy places of Palestine. Not only in an outer sense did one find oneself in an oasis, for the monks of that monastery have created a fertile realm from the marshy terrain by planting tall eucalyptus trees. Here more than anywhere else, one could sense the miracle of transformation, the radiance of a quiet golden glory within earth. Trefontane was and still is the most important of the three Roman sites of the martyrs around which something of the atmosphere of the apostolic age continues to linger. Sceptical historians have spared no effort to discredit these locations and to declare them not to be genuine. Yet they were and still are tranquil points of light within the turbulent life of the big city and its surroundings.

The location where Peter is reputed to have been crucified head downwards — most probably one or two years before Paul's execution, but on the same day at the height of summer — is situated outside the region of the seven hills on the Janiculo, high above the whole city spreading out below. A round little temple constructed by Bramante, San Pietro in Montorio, situated today in the narrow courtyard of large baroque buildings, marks the site.

In the south at the Porta Latina, today just within but formerly outside the city wall, another little round temple, also built by Bramante, indicates the spot where the ancient presbyter, John from Ephesus, is supposed to have suffered his Roman martyrdom, San Giovanni in Oleo. There, legend relates, he was tortured by being submerged in boiling oil. Since he remained steadfast, he was returned to Asia Minor and banished as a prisoner to the island of Patmos.

Thus we see Peter, Paul and John reach out to Rome with their destinies. Peter, allowing himself to be guided more instinctively by fate, had left the world of the East behind where the new Christian life was connected with the Asian maternal womb as if by an umbilical cord. Through this action, Peter had made a confession in favour of the West and sealed it with the martyr's death on the cross.

Paul had consciously taken the step to Europe and had thereby cut the umbilical cord. He came to Rome in outward lack of freedom but not against his free will. Thus he implanted into the Occident the potential for developing a future not only out of technological, soulless thinking, but Christian, inspired knowledge.

John came to the West only as a prisoner and tortured being. Through this it became evident that the still distant future of the Holy Spirit, which he prepared and conserved through his activity, would one day benefit the Occident.

The Apocryphal Letters between Paul and Seneca

The traditions which, since ancient times, have spoken of a friendship and spiritual exchange between Paul and Seneca, are supported in concrete form by fourteen short letters (eight letters from Seneca to Paul, six by Paul to Seneca) that have come down to us with a preface by St Jerome (*c.*340–420).[42] Understandably, many objections, probably justified, have been raised against the authenticity of these letters. Nevertheless, since it places a historically possible relationship vividly before us, this tradition puts an interesting emphasis on the last chapter of Paul's destiny. Therefore this apocryphal exchange of letters is inserted here in translation from the Latin, without any further detailed interpretation.

1. Seneca to Paul:
I assume that you, Paul, have already heard that yesterday, together with my friend Lucilius, I had a conversation concerning the 'hidden things' (*de apocrifis*) and other matters. Some of your pupils were present. We had withdrawn to the gardens of Sallust. There, it came to pass that we were seen by the above-mentioned pupils who then joined us, although they actually wished to go elsewhere. You must believe that we would have liked to have had you present. Therefore, I want to tell you that we felt wonderfully refreshed after we had read one of your texts, namely, one of the many letters with the splendid exhortation that you had sent to some town or the centre of a province in order to stimulate the moral life.

I believe it was not you that expressed these thoughts; they were spoken through you, although in some passages one could also say they were spoken by you as well as through you. They are so lofty and of such noble clarity that I believe many generations of men will not suffice to comprehend them completely.

I wish you health, my brother.

2. Paul to Seneca:
With great joy, I received your letter yesterday and I would have liked to answer it immediately, if a suitable messenger had been at hand. As you know, it is not a matter of indifference when and through whom, at what hour and to whom something is entrusted. Therefore, please do not consider yourself treated in a slighting manner because I place such value on the suitability of the messenger. You do write that my letter found favour with you and I consider myself fortunate to have the recognition of such a distinguished man. You, being a critical and philosophical spirit, the teacher of such a powerful ruler, would not say something like this if you did not also mean it.

I wish you lasting well-being.

3. Seneca to Paul:
I have laid out a few volumes of my works which I have arranged according to their contents. I would also like to read them to Caesar. If only destiny is favourable and I bring him to the point of showing interest once again, perhaps you can be present. If not, then I would like to indicate a day to you when we can go through these matters together. I do not want to come out with these writings until I have discussed them with you first. We must only be intent on an auspicious opportunity in this regard so that we do not encounter trouble. You should know that I have not forgotten you.

I wish you good health, my brother.

4. Paul to Seneca:
Each time I hear letters from you read to me, I sense your presence and can have no other feeling save that I perceive you in our midst. Therefore, come as soon as you can so that we can see each other face to face. May all be well with you.

5. Seneca to Paul:
We are greatly distressed over your long silence. What has happened? What is the reason for your long absence? If it is the displeasure of our mistress about the fact that you have turned away from your old ritual and faith, then you can tell her that you have had to follow your insight and did not act thoughtlessly. Farewell.

6. Paul to Seneca and Lucilius:
Concerning what you have written to me, it is not possible to speak by means of quill and ink. The quill holds it firm and outlines it, the ink makes it only too visible. This is true, above all, ever since I know that among you, within your circle and surroundings, there are those who think my thoughts. We must have respect for everyone, and this is all the more the case because we also deal with those who could take offence. If we have patience with them, we shall in some way and in regard to something manage with them. This is assuming that they are people who are able to admit to faults. Farewell.

7. Seneca to Paul and Theophilus:
It has been rewarding for me to read your letters to the Galatians, the Corinthians and those in Achaia. May our exchange become imbued with something of the mood of God's nearness with which you ensoul these letters. For the Holy Spirit that is in you and is exalted over everything expresses with pure lips an abundance of awe-inspiring thoughts. Therefore, it is my wish that you will never lack the proper words for these majestic thoughts since you have to present such grand things.

Since I cannot conceal anything from you and thus might burden my conscience, I also want to tell you that the emperor was moved by your thoughts. When the treatise concerning virtue containing your thoughts was read to him, he said he was surprised that somebody who had not undergone the customary course of learning could present such ideas. I answered him that the gods always speak through the mouths of the simple, not through the mouths of those who forever mix their own erudition into everything. And when I made this clear to him by the example of Vatienus, the farmer, before whom two men appeared in the field of Reate, who were afterwards recognized as Castor and Pollux, the Caesar seemed convinced. Farewell.

8. Paul to Seneca:
I know very well that when he is in this frame of mind, our Caesar can be open to miracles; still, he does not wish to be taken by surprise but wants to be convinced. Therefore, I believe that you have made a mistake when you directed his attention to something that is in contradiction to his customs and views. Since he is devoted to the pagan gods, I do not understand what you had in mind when you afforded him a glimpse into my thoughts, unless you did it only out of love for me. I implore you not to do that in the future. You must avoid doing something out of love for me that could offend the mistress. Her antipathy cannot hurt us if it remains as such, but it cannot help us either if it ceases. As queen she does not wish to be insulted, as a woman she will be angered in any case. Farewell.

9. Seneca to Paul:
I know that you were not concerned for yourself when you became upset because I wrote you that I had read your letters to Caesar. You had objective reasons, because he estranges people inwardly from all arts and moral customs. I am no longer surprised about this, for I have realized it myself in the light of numerous examples. Therefore, let us make a new start and if I took matters too lightly in the past, you will forgive me. I have sent you a book concerning 'the use of the word.'

Farewell, beloved Paul.

10. Paul to Seneca:
Every time I write to you and sign my name, I do something of grave significance which is actually not in accord with my religious conviction. For, as I have often pointed out, I am obliged to be everything to everybody. Therefore, in regard to you, I should have to be aware of the honour that the Senate has awarded to you; I should put my name only at the very end of the letter, for otherwise I run counter to proper custom and place my own will too much in the foreground. Farewell, most honoured teacher.

Written on June 27, during the third consulate of Nero and Messalla.

11. Seneca to Paul:
I send you greetings, dearest Paul. Believe me that I was deeply saddened and troubled about the fact that despite your innocence, all of you are being punished so severely. It also saddens me that the whole population considers you people to be so hard-headed and criminal and is blaming you for all injustice that occurs in the city. Let us bear it with a calm state of mind and let us utilize any favourable possibility that destiny still allots to us, until, finally, the unvanquishable happiness puts an end to the evil. Thus did earlier times bear up under the Macedonian, the son of Philip, a Cyrus, a Darius and Dionysius, and our age under a Gaius Caesar — all men who simply did anything that they wanted to do. It is clear how the fires came about under which Rome has to suffer again and again. If, in our dark age, without being punished immediately, the people were allowed freely to talk about who bears the guilt, soon they would all know everything. The Christians and the Jews are put down as those responsible for the fires; it has always been like this. The rapacious spirit, whoever he may be, whose desire is murdering and whose mask is the lie, will be called to account in his own good time. Just as a good man sacrifices his life for many, he above all must be thrown into the fire for all. One hundred and thirty-two large houses and four thousand small ones burned for six days. Only

the seventh day brought a reprieve. I hope, dear brother, that you are well.

Written on March 28, during the consulate of Frugi and Bassus [AD 64].

12. Seneca to Paul:

I greet you, dearly beloved Paul. If one who is as important and beloved by God as you are is not only linked with my name and myself, but is most closely united with me in all things, then this affords your Seneca the greatest satisfaction. Since you are the summit of all mountains, does it not fill you with joy that I am so close to you and would like to be your *alter ego?* Therefore, do not consider yourself unworthy of placing your name right away at the beginning of your letters; do not believe that you have to praise me considering the fact that you are a Roman citizen. As far as I am concerned, you have the same rank that I have, and I the same as you. Farewell, beloved Paul.

Written on March 23, during the consulate of Apronianus and Capito.

13. Seneca to Paul:

Much in your writings is allegorical and puzzling, and therefore, with the power and creative genius available to you, you must be concerned not so much with decorative words but with thorough inner form. You must not be afraid, as I have probably often told you already, that you thereby ruin the meaning of the words and weaken the force that is supposed to be expressed. You will certainly want to follow me and be intent on the pure Latin style so that the concepts that you utilize acquire a noble sound. In that, you make use of your great gifts in a worthy manner. Farewell.

Written on July 6, during the consulate of Lurco and Sabinus.

14. Paul to Seneca:
Things have been revealed to you in your train of thought as are granted to few men by the deity. I am also certain that I sow abundant seed on fertile ground, namely nothing that is subject to mortality, but the lasting word of God that comes from him who increases and remains in eternity. The judgment at which you arrive owing to your clever mind cannot go wrong, and therefore you will not allow yourself to be led astray by either the pagan or the Israelite forms. You will become a new citizen of Jesus Christ and with a herald's words proclaim the pure wisdom to which you have penetrated. You will transmit it to the earthly king and his house and friends, whom you will convince only with difficulty or not at all, for most of them will turn a deaf ear to you. Once, the word of God enkindled the spark of life in them; now, however, it wishes to create the New Man, free of distortions, gifted with an eternal soul, striving forward on the path to God. Farewell Seneca, you who are so dear to me.

Written on August 1, during the consulate of Lurco and Sabinus.

The Epistles

11. The Letters

We do not have any kind of outward portrait from the apostolic age, not even a suggestion of a description that could give us an idea of the countenance and figure of Paul.* Instead, we possess an exceedingly lively soul-portrait of him in his letters. Apart from their lofty Gospel message, they are also revealing personal documents. In their words, the pulse beat of Paul, his personal feelings and will, his human temperament, can be directly experienced.

In his lecture series, *The Bhagavad Gita and the Epistles of Paul,* Rudolf Steiner pointed emphatically to the personal note that sounds everywhere throughout the Pauline letters. After having described how the *Bhagavad Gita* soars aloft beyond the level of mundane human experiences to a sphere of detachment, composure and absence of passion, he says:

> With the Pauline Epistles all this is different. The ... dispassionateness of the *Gita* is lacking ... We feel over and over again that what Paul says comes from a person

* Only because people do not take the visionary and imaginative character of the Gnostic and apocryphal scriptures into account, a passage from the *Documents of Paul and Thekla* is frequently interpreted as containing a description of how Paul looked. It is said: 'He [Onesiphorus] saw Paul coming, a man slight of stature with a bald head and bent legs; with noble bearing, eyebrows grown together, a slightly protruding nose, filled with friendliness, he appeared at times like a man, then at times he had the form of an angel.' From these words, we can ascertain with certainty merely that when Paul spoke and acted under the inspiration of the Spirit, he rose beyond the merely human level to a complete change in appearance. The transformation that he then underwent must have been the more impressive just because he was of unassuming physical appearance. The details in the description in regard to his physical looks should not be taken literally but imaginatively. More than many of the other Gnostic apocrypha, the pictorial style of the *Documents of Paul and Thekla* extends to the visionary, fantastic element.

> who is passionately indignant at what has happened. Sometimes the tone is harsh and scolding ... even ... condemning ... in every sentence one hears a Pauline note. Every sentence reminds us that a man is speaking who ... is either ... expressing justified anger over this or that which others have done ... or who speaks in such a way about the highest concepts of Christianity that we feel he is personally involved ... How personal all this is! A breath of the personal surely runs through these Epistles.[43]

For a long time, the rigidly dogmatic concept of inspiration with which the scriptures of the New Testament were approached brought it about that the personal note in Paul's letters was not heard. And if notice was taken of it, people concluded that it was out of the question that these texts could have flowed from divine inspiration.

It can only signify a gain however, and free the way for a new Christian conception appropriate to the recent development of consciousness, to see the human element contributing its part in the New Testament scriptures. Only on this basis do we properly learn to appreciate the marvellous intensifying of the word of the Spirit; for example, when something like anger, uttered for a particular reason, then blossoms into a hymn of humanity like the 'Great Hymn to Love' (1Cor.13:1-13). The fire that blazed in Paul when he was the zealot campaigning against the young Christian congregations was not extinguished, but redeemed and transformed. If previously it had been sinister and mean, now it burned as generously and brightly as the growing flame of Pentecost.

For Adolf Deissmann's studies of the New Testament, it was an important starting point to view the Pauline letters from within the general *history of letter writing*. He was aware of the role that letters, intended as a literary not as a personal communication, played in late antiquity: the epistle, the doctrinal letter, the message. But it was against his instincts to place Paul's letters in this category. For him, it was a relief to be able to prove that particularly around that time the personal writing of letters, the mutual exchange of greetings and communications, became widely fashionable in the Mediterranean region. He surveyed innumerable fragments of letters written on scraps of papyrus or shards of clay. In his book, *Licht vom Osten,* he published a selection of these and eagerly proposed the idea that the Pauline letters were not to be counted among the epistles of literature but as non-literary, *genuine letters.* He speaks of the 'misunderstanding, fraught with consequences, whereby something living was up-rooted and placed into an herbarium.'

> Together with their author ... the letters by Paul share the fate of having frequently been judged in the wrong way ... People have misunderstood their intimate character, their soul. They were considered as essays, as pamphlets in letter-form, in any case as literary accomplishments, as the theological works of the first Christian dogmatist ...
>
> [It is] evident that these texts were born of a specific, unrepeatable situation, and, intended only for this single situation, are not products of literary art but of real life ..., documents of primal apostolic ministry from man to man ... the missionary work of the Apostle, the leadership of his congregations ... Paul wrote these letters or ... dictated them to the pen of a companion in the storm and stress of his wanderer's life, rich in deeply stirring experiences. Then, in the form of a single copy, he had them carried to the place of their destination by trustworthy messengers, across sea and land, from Ephesus to Corinth, from Corinth to Rome and to Ephesus, without the world at large or even the whole of Christendom immediately knowing anything of the existence of these pages. Paul neither intended nor imagined that a part of these intimate epistles would still exist centuries later.[44]

Deissmann did not find many attentive ears for his efforts to bring into view the human character of the Apostle in his letters so as to free them from theological and dogmatic stereotyping. In the final analysis, the reason probably is that making them more natural and humanizing them is only the first step. After all, those of Paul's letters that have come down to us were accepted into the spiritually exact composition of the New Testament canon by people of great insight, and acknowledged as texts from super-human sources. Certainly, Paul was no theologian in the sense of a traditional, dogmatic or intellectual theology. He was a human being who, out of the very foundation of his being, had received again in one decisive moment the ingenuousness that had been his only as a child. But in the hour of Damascus that had once more turned him into a child, he simultaneously became one of the greatest initiates of humanity. Therefore, the word that he spoke or wrote was both completely human and yet God-given.

Once the spell of a dogmatic conception of divine inspiration has been broken, and leaving aside for the moment the divine content of the scriptures, it is fascinating to decipher the history of the spirit and human consciousness from the composition of the Old as well as the New Testament canon. In the Old as well as the New Testament, the biblical scriptures are placed together in three groups that follow each other in the trinity of image, word and being. This is because they respectively originate out of Imaginative (seeing), Inspirative (spiritual hearing) and Intuitive (touching in being) spiritual perception.* In the Old Testament, the level of images is filled with the 'historical books'; in the New Testament, with the Gospels and Acts. The poetic scriptures in the Old and the letters in the New Testament represent the 'inspiration of the word.' The intuitive element characterizes the prophetic books of the Old Covenant. In the New Testament, only the Apocalypse of John corresponds to them. The first and the third groups — imaginative review of the past, intuitive preview of future events — hold sway completely in the supra-personal sphere. In the middle-group, however, which permits the ever-living present to have its say between past and future, pulses the personal element that strives towards its own self and beyond itself to the spirit. Here turning points in the history of consciousness stand out.

In the so-called 'poetic books' of the Old Testament, the Psalms of David, for example, represent a classic stage in the development of the liturgical and poetic word emerging from the other-worldly temple darkness of the magic ritual acts, as the sound of personal inner struggle pervades it for the first time.

* See the author's studies, *Das Evangelium*. In the chapter, 'Inspiration,' a description is given of the new paths which Rudolf Steiner indicated for a comprehension of the inspirational origin of the Bible.

This is at the same point in time when, in the dawn of Greek spiritual life, Homer, the visionary bard singing of the gods, allows the supra-personal myth to stream into poetic verse.

Apart from the Psalms by David, there resounds the Song of Songs by Solomon. It represents the birth of song in humanity. Nevertheless, like the psalms, it was reserved for the liturgical sphere for a long time yet — the individual, devotional use of religious texts became possible in mankind only with the Middle Ages. Yet in the Song of Songs, as in a prophecy enveloped in beauty, the myth was sketched of what would one day take place in the individual person between soul and spirit and would lead to the birth of the 'I.' In the folk songs of all nations, which flowed for three millennia from the wellspring of Solomon, longing, presentiment and the gradual fulfilment of the God-loving and spirit-loving birth of the ego became woven together.

In the middle group of the New Testament scriptures, we observe a similar new beginning. In the letters of Paul and the other Apostles, we see the personal 'letter,' as we understand it, struggling to be born. It is the freely uttered word that allows the other to be free; it is the word of one personality to another or to a group of persons. (Initially there had been the authoritative decree of the ruler — a tendency that has continued into our own times in the encyclicals of the Pope.) The documents on which Deissmann's differentiation between epistle and letter is based demonstrate how, around this time, something began to change within humanity in regard to written communications. Through the expansion of the Roman Empire communications had developed to the point where a form of private exchange of letters became possible. In addition, a new impulse can be noted during that time in the history of the epistle, the literary doctrinal letter. Since the age of Socrates, particularly within Stoicism, there had existed a teaching which abandoned the authoritative principle and addressed the free insight of the one seeking for knowledge. The 'diatribe' was a special form of the didactic letter developed by Stoicism and employed by the Stoic travelling speakers. Paul also made use of this form. For his letters are at the same time epistles and rightfully have been used since the early days of Christianity as texts for the ritual reading in the congregations.

Now into this form as well, there poured the rich, warm blood-stream of personal experience and insight. At the dawn of a new age, what appeared sporadically and hesitantly in the world at large found its concentrated form, filled with creative promise for the future, in Paul's letters.

Not all the letters written by Paul have come down to us. Those included in the New Testament canon are certainly but a small part of the whole. Paul had to share abundantly what had been given to him; without doubt, he was untiring in sending out letters. It follows from the two preserved letters to the Corinthians, for instance, that the congregation at Corinth had received additional letters from him. Nevertheless, we can be certain of possessing in those that have come down to us a quintessence, in itself complete, of the letters actually written by Paul.

When, around the middle of the second century, the canon of the New Testament was selected and composed from the wealth of apocryphal Gospels, Apocalypses, Letters and Apostles' Acts, this effort was similarly permeated by the wisdom and insight that was present in the origin of the writings thus pronounced to be the Holy Scriptures.* At that time a larger number of Paul's letters might still have been included in the canon. It was not the case that all the texts which were of genuine apostolic origin were chosen. A selective principle was employed but one which did not rely on intellectual analysis and dogmatic methods of censure. The spiritual inspiration, perceived as a real being in the individual writings and also in the arrangement and inclusion of groups of texts, served as the criteria for inclusion in the canon. After all, such texts were not read silently, in thought; they were loudly intoned and heard. Thus together, the letters of Paul known to us

* Only later did dogmatic tendencies in the Church lead to the impoverishment of the Holy Scripture and its related texts. Along with the Gnostic literature, countless apocryphal texts, earlier considered as belonging in the environment of the New Testament, were eradicated, because too much concerning the supersensory world had come to expression in them. For the same reason, the scriptures that were included in the canon were in many instances amended in conformity with Church dictates. The Latin version of the Gospel of Matthew, originally written in Hebrew, is the prime example of this.

form a unity. They are also an organism, like the four Gospels, although in a different, quieter manner.

The variety, the wealth of outer and inner possibilities of formulation becomes evident at first glance. Already the polarity between *letter* and *epistle* is classically represented. The letter addressed to Philemon is not only the shortest but also the most 'letter-like letter by Paul' (Deissmann). It is the type of letter written on a certain occasion, for a concrete reason, and expressing a personal, benevolent intention. Philemon, one of the leading men in the congregation at Colossae, had a slave by the name of Onesimus. He searched for him, for the slave had run away from him without paying the ransom. Now fate brought it about that Onesimus came to Paul and became his faithful pupil and assistant. This was far away from Colossae, perhaps even in Rome where Paul, himself Nero's prisoner, showed special concern for the man who had fled from bondage. It is also possible that it was in Ephesus that Onesimus, as a result of his master's search, was put in prison and there encountered Paul as a prisoner. Paul, however, did not wish to keep Onesimus by his side. He sent him to Philemon with a short letter asking his master to acknowledge the unfaithful slave as his brother in the Lord, and to grant him his freedom. And from then on, Onesimus belonged to the close circle of assistants through whom Paul guided his congregations.

This short letter, which concludes the letters of Paul in the New Testament, stands in direct contrast to the Letter to the Romans which opens the sequence. Romans is the only letter that Paul wrote to a congregation as yet unknown to him. There was no immediate, personal reason for it, and therefore out of all of Paul's letters, it could most easily be designated as an epistle. Yet it is not a letter of teaching to the extent that Protestant theology since Luther's days has repeatedly claimed. Some of those who laid claim to this letter for their own theological opinions, did not even notice how they only picked out certain passages from it, thus doing injustice to the spirit of the whole. Much less were they aware of how they narrowed down and impoverished Paulinism through their prejudiced interpretation of a few verses, overlooking the tremendously varied abundance of Christian knowledge that speaks from the remaining letters of Paul. The epistle to the Romans is nevertheless a genuine letter, written freely and confidently to an unknown group of people without a dialectical introduction or systematic catechizing. This genuine letter to the Romans more radically than all the other letters expresses the new element of Christ's love as contrasted with the world of the Old Testament Law.

The canonical letters of Paul are grouped according to the recipients. They are addressed to seven congregations and three individuals.

By their very volume, the letters to the congregations appear to have the main emphasis. It would be wrong, however, to consider the texts addressed to Timothy, Titus and Philemon as less important, or mere appendages. From the earliest times they have been known as 'pastoral letters.' While people also made use of this term in Protestantism, they could no longer connect a special meaning to the designation in a framework in which the priestly cult had been abandoned; where the ritual life as well as the office of the ministry had been placed in the hands of laymen. On the other hand, from its apostolic beginning, the nature of early Christianity was certainly determined by the supra-personal element that flows through liturgy and priesthood. Therefore, the pastoral letters occupy an important place within the canon as priestly texts, as words spoken strictly from priest to priest. They represent a transition from the second to the third group, from the Letters to the Apocalypse. The Apocalypse was the esoteric book of the priests. As a vestibule to this temple, the small group of priestly letters emerged. What is meant here becomes quite clear only when we consider the Letter to the Hebrews apart from the Pauline pastoral letters. Hebrews is not a letter by Paul as has been frequently assumed. It arose from the same source from which, through John, the Fourth Gospel and Revelation have originated. It is an instruction for those who were involved in the transition from the ministry of the Old Testament to the Christian ministry. (The name 'Hebrew' does not denote the blood-related folk relationship but a spiritual rank attained within the life of the nation.) In the most specific sense, this 'Johannine pastoral letter' is a prelude to and preliminary schooling for the Revelation of

John.* Notwithstanding the fact that they differ in tone and content, the Pauline pastoral letters similarly draw near to the sphere of revelation.

The seven communities to which Paul's nine congregational letters are addressed remind us of the seven archetypal communities to which the seven letters of the Apocalypse are directed. As closely united circles of human beings, the congregations of Ephesus, Smyrna, Pergamum, Thyatira, Sardis, Philadelphia and Laodicea existed in an earthly sense in the aged John's sphere of activity. In Revelation, on the other hand, these communities become transparent and appear as a scale of evolutionary stages that must be undergone by the spiritual vanguard of humanity. There the inner curve leads first of all from the after-effects of the ancient spirituality, still close to heaven, to the descent and impoverishment of earth, then up again to a gradual attainment of a new spirituality related to human freedom. Just as the seven physical locations, where the seven Johannine communities had originated, form a line resembling a half-circle from the Ionian coast up to the highlands of Asia Minor, so, too, the spiritual archetypes that become visible in them express a path of stages to be undergone by humanity.

Does a sign also appear out of the seven Pauline congregations indicating, beyond the tangible earthly facts of early Christian life, a spiritual order contained within them? If so, it is by no means as evident as in the letters of the Apocalypse. It is also not readily expressed in the canonical sequence.

Of the seven Pauline congregations, three belong to Asia, four to Europe. The European ones are Rome, Corinth, Philippi and Thessalonica; those of Asia Minor are Ephesus, Galatia and Colossae. Consequently, by far the larger part of Paul's surviving words is addressed to Europe. The Letter to the Romans and the Letters to the Corinthians considerably surpass in size the remaining Pauline letters.

* It was Rudolf Steiner who, in a conversation, first pointed out the Johannine character of the Letter to the Hebrews. The more attention is paid to the intimate relationship of the Letter to the Hebrews and Revelation, the more plausible is this initially surprising indication.

The three letters to congregations in Asia Minor, to the Ephesians, the Colossians and the Galatians, represent a smaller volume than those directed to Europe. Yet if surveyed together, they present an exceedingly important triangle. Their geographical boundaries touch most closely the curve of the seven apocalyptic communities, which without exception are located 'in Asia.' Both Paul and John wrote letters to the Ephesian congregation. The atmosphere of Ephesus was still imbued with something of the ancient spirituality, of divine presence, and was for this reason the first among the Johannine congregations. The three Asian letters by Paul also touch the end of the apocalyptic sequence of seven. While we do not possess a letter by Paul addressed specifically to the Laodiceans, as Colossae was in the vicinity of Laodicea it was Paul's wish that his letter directed to Colossae should also be intended for the neighbouring community: 'And when this letter has been read among you, have it read also in the church of the Laodiceans; and see that you read also the letter from Laodicea' (Col.4:16).

Geographically speaking, with the letter to the Galatians Paul reached far beyond the realm of the seven Johannine letters, the curve of which closes its circle in the west of Asia Minor. The province of Galatia was located far inland in the primitive highlands. Today, the capital of Turkey, Ankara, at the centre of this mountainous country, has long since attracted modern civilization. While the region between Ephesus and Colossae was still imbued with the breath of Ionic-Greek life, orientated towards Europe and illuminated by Homer, Galatia was surrounded by the more elemental atmosphere of Asia. Just as Paul's letter to the Romans goes furthest westward so the letter to the Galatians goes furthest east. Here the polarity between the European and the Asian appears most clearly.

The predominance of European letters over Asian reflects the historically significant step towards Europe which Paul had to carry out in his apostolic destiny. Still, it was Paul who encompassed both East and West. He could readily be a champion and admirer of progress for the future and the new world, for the very reason that at the same time he was also an exponent and a bearer of the 'ancient wisdom,' the divine values of the past.

Destiny had willed it that Paul, a scholar and adherent of the Old Testament *par excellence,* turned into the Apostle of the Gentile nations, advocating the free sovereignty of Christian faith over Mosaic Law. He was opposed in this by the Jewish Christian factions in the congregations. They held that those who turned Christian should still continue to obey the Old Testament obligations to the Law. In addition to James, the strictest representative and leader of this direction, some of the original Apostles, in particular Peter, inclined to adhere to some aspects of the Law.

The canon of the New Testament makes room for both sides. However, the abundance of words from the Gentile faction, represented by the wealth of the Pauline letters, is opposed only by the Letter of James as an expressly Jewish Christian text.

A shadow of this fundamental polarity belonging to the early Christian period also influences Paul's letters and characteristically determines their whole form. Whereas Paul generally operated freely within a broad impartiality towards all people, in two of his letters — a European and an Asian one — he had to expound on Jewish Christian tendencies, noticeable in the congregations in question, which he could only consider as a relapse into bondage under the Law. This is what distinguishes the Letter to the Romans and the Letter to the Galatians from the rest of Paul's letters.

For very different and yet related reasons, parts of the Christian congregations in Rome and Galatia tended toward the Jewish Christian position. Rome's essential contribution to the civilized world was its juridical element: the *corpus juris,* a collection of the laws valid for civil life. Here, the Jewish and the Roman cultures touched most closely. People who came from Judaism could view Roman jurisprudence as a more modern, cosmopolitan form of the Mosaic Law, inasmuch as the latter contained directions for all imaginable details of life. Thus, the Roman milieu encouraged an intensification of the restrictions of the Law among recently converted Jewish Christians. In addition, under the Caesars, a fever nurtured by Oriental ecstasy and magic had penetrated Roman life, which more than ever induced all earnest people to revert to ancient, genuine Romanism with its civic virtues, morality and sense of justice. In the midst of moral chaos, the confluence of the Jewish and Roman elements allowed a kind of bastion of pious adherence to the Law to arise that extended even to the initial establishment of a Christian community.

The population of the province of Galatia in the mountainous country of Asia Minor, where Paul had been active during his first journeys and had established congregations, were predominantly of Celtic origin, as shown by the name 'Galatian.' A few centuries earlier, a movement prompted by the feeling of an impending cosmic twilight had entered among western European Celts that brought about easterly migrations as far as the region of the Caucasus (Georgia). This is the reason for a widespread Celtic settlement in the interior of Asia Minor.

It is not hard to understand why, particularly in this region, Paul had readily found open ears and hearts. Here he had in fact encountered 'Europe' before the call of the Spirit had caused him to take the step from Asia to Europe. A European openness and receptivity of spirit responded to the spiritual substance of his proclamation. Through their contact with the Christ impulse, the Celtic Galatians strongly sensed the inner contrast in which they lived, surrounded as they were by the orgiastic, ecstatic character of Asia Minor. By becoming Christians, they simultaneously became Celts again in a stricter sense.

The genius of the Celtic culture, which was already drawing to a close, was expressed in the way human social life was organized. For the Celts, the social structure combined an aristocratic principle of leadership with egalitarianism of the religious order or lodge. King Arthur and his Round Table of twelve knights was the mythical archetype for the social life the Celts envisioned. In it was contained the readiness for common battle in favour of the good and noble against all that was unorganized and base. It is therefore understandable that among the Galatians the tendency towards stern morality reacted again and again against the Oriental environment. This must have been even more the case when Christian congregations formed. An alliance between the Celtic striving for morality and the Mosaic Law was clear and easy. And Paul had to tell them in no uncertain terms that they should have more faith and patience until a completely new morality, but now one free of any law, would result from the cradle of Christian experience. He appealed to the essentially European level within them when he called out to them, 'You are destined to freedom!'

It is tragic that the letters to the Romans and Galatians, which were written to repulse Jewish Christian tendencies and reversion to the Old Testament, have frequently been misinterpreted in the history of Christendom — above all since Luther — in the sense of a more modern form of Judaic Christianity. In particular the Letter to the Romans, which represents the most clear-cut abandonment of the Law of the Old Testament, is comprehended by means of concepts belonging to Old Testament Law and Roman jurisprudence even by modern Protestant theology. The dialectical conception concerning Paul often seems to drag Paul back to the pettifogging rabbinical element, the spell of which he had broken once and for all.

Over against the two letters concerned with the problems of the Jewish Christian stream, stands the whole variety of the remaining letters by Paul in which pagan Christian life and thinking unfolds in a free way. Paul was serious about the fact that not only the Jewish Old Testament but also Greek mythology and philosophy had been a preparatory school for Christianity. Among the European letters, those addressed to the Corinthians hold the balance against the letter to the Romans. Among the Asian ones, those written to the Ephesians and the Colossians balance out the Letter to the Galatians. Whereas in the letters to the Romans and Galatians Paul dealt mainly with 'faith' and Christ's effects on the human personality due to the problematic issues surrounding 'law and freedom,' in the expressly 'pagan Christian' letters, the dimension of Christ's love was revealed to the growing congregation. Therefore, the letters to the Corinthians mention above all the mysteries of the sacrament and the forming of the congregation. Inasmuch as he was the author of both letters to the Corinthians and the one to the Romans, Paul combined in himself polar opposites which, in the development of ecclesiastical Christendom, divided into the contrast of Catholicism and Protestantism. From the totality of Paul's letters, the Christianity of the future can and must find the way to a new synthesis of these contrasting values.

Wishing to survey the Pauline letters in the sequence of their origin, hence to view them chronologically within Paul's biography, theology hit on the idea of distinguishing between the early ones, written during his activity while free, and the so-called 'letters of the imprisonment.' Originally, this was only to make a distinction between the period before and after the trial in Rome as a prisoner of Caesar. Accordingly, the 'letters of imprisonment' would be those that Paul sent off to the congregations during the last, most mature part of his life, particularly those from Rome.

Perhaps scholars strayed from the main drift of Paul's destiny when the question was raised whether this or that 'letter of imprisonment' could possibly have been written during an earlier period of prosecution or imprisonment. Deissmann, for example, along with many other theologians, put forward the hypothesis that all 'letters of imprisonment,' or at least a number of them, could be attributed to a lengthy time of imprisonment suffered by Paul during his sojourn in Ephesus. Accordingly, the Letter to Philemon, for example, would not presuppose that the slave, Onesimus, who had escaped in Colossae, encountered Paul no earlier than in Rome; he could well have chanced upon him already in the prison of Ephesus.

Yet the difference between Paul's letters written in freedom and those written during imprisonment should not be over-estimated. Paul felt free regardless of whether he was a prisoner or not. He felt and described himself as a *doulos Christou,* a 'slave of Christ,' whether he dwelt in freedom or in imprisonment.

The biographical sequence of the Pauline letters is not clearly evident everywhere. In this regard, it may be possible to adhere by and large to the ancient traditions. According to these, Paul emerged as the proclaimer of the written word only after having taken the step from Asia to Europe. In Athens, the first great European centre on which he set foot, he wrote to the Thessalonians, one of his first European congregations. Among the scriptures of the New Testament, it may therefore be likely that the First Letter to the Thessalonians is the first text to be written down. Paul wrote the letter when Timothy, whom he had sent to Thessalonica, had returned with good tidings. To the joy of the moment was joined the enthusiastic vitality and courage of the future vision of Europe as the soil of a new life.

The great European letters, addressed to the Romans and to the Corinthians, also breathe the new impulse which entered Paul's activity through the nocturnal vision of Troas. When he dared to write to Rome from Corinth, where the Roman congregation, still unknown to him, was represented in Aquila and Priscilla, this makes clear how he felt at home and justified to work in Europe. Nero was not the only one who was in control of Europe and thus of the whole world. Paul appeared on the stage as the herald of a higher Lord.

Among the letters of imprisonment — most likely, they were dispatched from Rome — belong, above all, those to the Asian congregations in Ephesus and Colossae, perhaps even the Letter to the Galatians. To think of the congregations in Asia and to write to them from Europe, from Rome itself, became possible through an awareness that encompassed East and West, the Old and the New world. And seen from the centre of Europe, the breath of ancient wisdom which characterized the milieu in Ephesus and Colossae and which was now becoming receptive to the new wisdom made accessible through Christ, appeared more than ever in its elevated greatness.

In Ephesus and Rome, Paul's sphere of activity encountered and influenced those of John and Peter. As if to emphasize this even more, two important letters by Paul were directed to congregations where the two great Apostles also worked: to Ephesus where John was influential as well; and to Rome where Peter was also active. It has always been puzzling that Paul in these letters did not refer even in passing to the other Apostles. Certainly the Pauline letters, which on the one hand were the first personal documents as such, possessed above all a supra-personal character. They were words of proclamation and direction to the congregation and were meant to be read as ritual texts. Yet this does not completely solve the riddle. It is more easily solvable when we imagine that Paul was able to cultivate a relationship and an exchange of insight in an inward way with Peter and John that amounted to more than any outward correspondence.

Thus there arises before us a configuration of apostolic life that was drawn by a mighty destiny: James, the 'brother of the Lord,' remains in Jerusalem and dies there as well: he maintains the link of the new with the old. Peter is guided westward to Rome by his destiny, though more on account of deeper forces of will than of conscious thought, and lends strength there to what is coming into being. John goes eastward and unfolds his activity of blessing and love from Ephesus: he transforms the ancient wisdom into the new knowledge of the heart, which he prepares and preserves for a future epoch of Christianity. Paul transcends all opposites: he combines East and West and paves the way for a conscious Christianity.

12. The Language of the Letters

Two elements that seem to be far apart flow together in the language and vocabulary of the letters by Paul. On the one hand, a human being speaks completely from his heart and personal temperament without any concern for literary style. On the other hand, here is one who knows more and has deeper insight than others into the world-configurations of spirit, soul and body; but again, he speaks in accordance with his human temperament. Totally unconcerned, he speaks on the basis of his knowledge and vision as if he, the initiate, were addressing not the common folk but his equals.

As we have seen, Deissmann gave emphasis to the first characteristic, for it was his overall concern to prove the popular and original character of the New Testament scriptures as opposed to Attic-Greek prose composition. At the beginning of our century, philologists — a particular example is Reitzenstein — investigated the second area. People began to notice that the vocabulary of the Greek New Testament, especially the Pauline letters, was to a surprising degree interspersed with typical expressions from pre-Christian mystery religions. Here we touch upon one of the main reasons why for many centuries and at least since Luther, theology misinterpreted or could only inadequately understand essential points in Paul's texts.

It goes without saying that Paul would not have had to enter the Greek mystery schools in order to become acquainted with the specific technical terms that he subsequently used in the language of his letters. Through his early inner training and initiation which had blossomed in a completely new fashion after Damascus, he had drawn close to the realities of supersensory existence in the cosmos and in the human being. Not only the book of the sense world lay open before his eyes; the 'world behind the curtain' also lay open before him, clearly decipherable. He was no longer dependent on abstract philosophical and theological concepts in regard to spiritual matters. Concreteness pervaded his thought and speech when it concerned the world of the spirit, a concreteness equal to if not greater than that of the realm of sense perception. In his own right, he was fluent in the mystery language in which the descendants of the Greek mystery schools spoke of the spheres of the spirit, although more now out of a sense of tradition than out of direct experience.

To be concerned about keeping secret the knowledge of initiation as had been customary in the earlier mystery centres, speaking in one language to those who knew and in another to the 'common people,' was now quite impossible for Paul. It contradicted the very essence of his nature, his temperament and even the living aims of his activity. He was eagerly rushing forward to meet the future, a world transformed right to its foundations. In him pulsed a will and a genius belonging not to his age but to a future one. This brought about in him the radical urge to make public what he knew. Had Christ not died and been resurrected for *all* humanity? The ancient principle of secrecy preserved a distinction between a small, privileged group and 'mere laymen.' In Greece, the whole wealth of the age of Pericles, the dramatic art of a man like Aeschylus, the sculptures of Phidias, the philosophy of a Plato had emerged owing to an irresistible urge to make the mysteries public.[45] What had been exclusively taught and practised in a restricted circle as secret knowledge was now recast in a generally communicable artistic and philosophical form. For Paul, the law of antiquity was long since untimely. What did it matter if much of what he said and wrote was not fully comprehensible to one or other of his contemporaries! In the circle where he was active, Paul relied on the gently growing light which, through the baptism of the Spirit and the indwelling of Christ, illumined hearts and made them an organ of comprehension. In full awareness, Paul wrote his letters as 'humanity's untimely birth,' as the precursor of future ages. From this emanated the unconcern with which he employed his spiritually concrete vocabulary irradiated by the light of Damascus.

It is clear that the more the ancient, still half-visionary relationship to the world of the spirit dimmed, the more texts such as the letters of Paul would become misunderstood and incomprehensible. The special radiance within illumined hearts which still existed in the early Christian centuries, was all too quickly drawn into the mighty twilight of the gods that followed in humanity's history of consciousness. Paul had indeed raised his voice as a forerunner and spokesman for a future era. Yet initially, a future dawned — and it extends even into our time — in which the human mind grew increasingly distant from the light-filled, spiritual concreteness of the Pauline language. It is only in passing through the 'dark age' of mere intellectual reasoning that the future is arising, the language of which Paul uttered ahead of time.

A passage in one of the letters by Peter shows us that even in Paul's lifetime, indeed within the circle of the first Apostles, understanding the language of the Pauline letters was considered to be difficult:

> So also our beloved brother Paul wrote to you according to the wisdom given him, speaking of this as he does in all his letters. There are some things in them hard to understand, so that they can be twisted by the ignorant and unstable ones ... (2Pet.3:15f*B*).

Much of the theological literature concerning Paul would not exist, or at least would have been written quite differently, given an awareness that the spiritual realities, in the sight of which Paul spoke and wrote, have vanished from modern humanity's field of vision. Unfortunately, such insight has hardly existed; instead, in almost all instances and with dogmatic self-assurance, theologians equated the Pauline principles with the intellectually abstract concepts of our age. It is not hard to realize, for example, how differently the word 'God' sounds and is heard depending upon whether the one speaking or listening feels himself confronting merely a world of sense perception or a substantial supersensory world with its own abundant configuration.

To the honest person of today, the Apocalypse of John must seem the strangest text in the New Testament. At best, he can interpret in an allegorical manner the celestial content that emerges there in pictorial form. Thus, devoid of spiritual substance, he can add these contents to the abstractions which alone are accessible to his thinking. Luther frankly admitted that 'his spirit could not adapt to this book.' And he added to this that he did not like to imagine Jesus and the Apostles as people who had had 'visions.' Luther should have admitted to the same difficulty regarding the letters of Paul. For in numerous passages they reach directly into the dimension of the Apocalypse. During Paul's lifetime, John's revelations as yet did not exist in book form. But even then they could be read in the spiritual realm, for the realities existed of which his revelations spoke in images. And Paul belonged to those who were familiar with them.

When Paul speaks of the sounding of the 'last trumpet' (1Cor. 15:52), this is no vague expression of emotion and fear. From among the seven levels of the apocalyptic cycles of time, he sees precisely before him, as if looking at a cosmic clock, the particular one whose hourly chimes are the resounding of the seven trumpets. When the seventh trumpet resounds, then the last hour of this cosmic aeon has begun.

When Paul brings out the contrast between the Old and the New Covenant in the dual image of the 'temporal' Jerusalem and the Jerusalem 'above' (Gal.4:25f), he moves his glance in the same spiritual direction as does the writer of the Apocalypse, whose descriptions culminate in the vision of the celestial Jerusalem.

The more we are again in a position to form ideas of a real supersensory world, the more we must marvel at the sovereign way in which Paul, in the style of his letters, simply took for granted a familiarity with the signs and structures of this higher world. Even his reference to the hierarchies belongs here. Without wanting to admit to it, Protestant theology, having joined ranks with materialistically orientated natural science, and not having retained a traditional knowledge of the hierarchies, unlike Catholic dogmatism, easily falters where Paul speaks of the hierarchical beings beginning with angels and going all the way to the Seraphim. Modern theology cannot understand that Paul bases what he says on a hierarchical world-conception as if such a view were a matter of course. Many theologians are inclined to believe that in this regard Paul laboured under ancient superstitions. One or the other has even attempted to read into such passages of Paul a negation of the hierarchical beings (particularly in Rom.8:38f).

At no point is the impoverishment of spirit — suffered since early Christian times on the part of human thinking which is so proud of its 'progress' — more evident than where we deal with the extension of the kingdoms of creation: stone, plant, animal, the human being, and beyond. In the age of the Apostles, the names of the three times three hierarchical levels of being were not even among the special words and names known only in the closed circle of the mysteries. Everywhere among the common people there existed living experiences of these spheres of existence, hence also the possibility of a linguistic expression for them. The new and unknown subject matter that until then had been taught exclusively in esoteric schools and that Paul brought out openly in his letters, dealt mainly with the Christ-being's position within the hierarchies, or in other words the change which had occurred in this relationship through Christ's human incarnation, death and Resurrection.

A passage from the Letter to the Colossians can serve as an example:

> For in him the whole fullness of deity dwells bodily; and through him you too are filled with him, who is the head of the primal powers and the spirits of earth's creation (Elohim) (Col.2:9f*B*).

The word, *pleroma* — fullness — is one of the fundamental concepts belonging to the late Greek mysteries and continues even into Gnostic texts, although it gradually fell into disuse as a widely employed technical term. It is more than an emotive concept meant to express the infinite majesty and greatness of the deity. It is an exact expression for the structured variety of hierarchical beings, who represent a unity inasmuch as they are organs and members of a superordinate divine being. Through Christ's incarnation as man, the relationship of all the hierarchies to humanity has become a fundamentally different one. In Christ, they are all participants in the incarnation, the beginning of a new spiritual permeation of the human being, impoverished because of its alienation from God.*

* The word, *plērōma*, also occurs with the same meaning in the prologue of the Gospel of St John (1:16): 'And from his fullness have we all received, grace upon grace.'

Lacking the faculties for sensing the mystery-character of the Pauline language, theological research on Paul arrived at the most egregious misinterpretations where Paul speaks in a first-person style about the awakening of supersensory perception in the human being. In the twelfth chapter of the Second Letter to the Corinthians, Paul has reason to refer to himself. He states that he has at his disposal the possibility of imaginative and intuitive spiritual perception and cognition (visions and apocalyptic revelations). But he scorns to boast of this as if it was the result of personal merit. As far as his own human condition is concerned, it places difficulties in the way of his cognitive intercourse with the spiritual worlds. The description he gives is as follows:

> I know a man, borne by the power of Christ — it is now fourteen years ago — who was caught up to the third heaven — whether in the body or out of the body I do not know, God knows. And I know, too, that this man was caught up into paradise — whether in the body or out of the body I do not know, God knows — and there he heard unspoken words which no human mouth can utter ... But to keep me from being proud and arrogant over the abundance of these revelations, a thorn was placed in my physical body, a Satanic angel tortures me. Three times I besought the Lord that this torture should leave me, but he said to me, 'Keep to the grace that I grant you. This power can only become effective on the basis of the greatest weakness of the human being.' So I would rather boast of the weakness and illness of my nature, for it is due to them that the power of Christ can work in me (2Cor.12:2-9*B*).

It was on the basis of this passage that an age which no longer had at its disposal any imaginative, inspirative and intuitive perception, gave rise to the idea that Paul was an epileptic. It was thought that the attacks which overcame Paul did place him in ecstatic conditions, but that they were basically of an unhealthy, pathological nature. Thus even Franz Werfel placed Paul on the stage in epileptic contortions in his otherwise brilliant drama, *Paul among the Jews,* thereby demeaning him to a repulsive caricature.

What does Paul try to say in these almost legendary words? Does he only wish to report on one unique experience of transcendence which had overcome him a long time ago despite a puzzling weakness that adheres to the nature of his soul and body? One can actually think this way only if one is unable to conceive of any form of supersensory experiences and insights other than in connection with the pathological states observed in people even today. Such a view disregards the fundamental transformation that occurred in Paul through the Damascus experience.

Even though he exemplifies it through his own experience, Paul wished to speak of an inner conformity to moral laws that are of general validity. Logically speaking, he needed to only present the fact, not the form, of *his* supersensory experiences; but he spoke from the heart and gave of himself. Thus we are privileged to see into the intimate nature of his inner path and development.

The uniqueness of what Paul had experienced two-times-seven years ago, of which he could now speak, consisted in the fact that in all quietness a fruit of the Damascus experience now ripened in his soul — a breakthrough occurred. It was not as if he had brought this about by means of his human faculties. Because the inner prerequisites were now fulfilled, a higher power came to meet him and allowed his soul to grow beyond itself. It was not an ecstasy and translation as in the spiritual experiences of the past where the soul departed the body and unfolded spiritual vision in the place of a day-dreaming consciousness. The miracle that took place was that the soul remained awake *in* the body — and yet did not find itself in exactly the same relationship to its body as before. It was greater than the body, therefore it was *also* but not *only* outside the body. The principle of translation was replaced by that of indwelling. The higher power that came to meet Paul and allowed his soul to grow beyond itself, now indwelt him. And because it was mightier than his soul, it permitted his soul to partake of its own greatness, thus allowing an experience of ascent and intensification. In a classic example, Paul expressed this transition which had significance for all humanity: that henceforth the higher world wishes to reveal itself to the *waking* human being. This is reflected in the two related questions that he raised during his description: 'Was he in the body? Was he outside the body? I do not know, God knows.' The miracle lay in the fact that both states, which until then had been mutually exclusive, now occurred simultaneously: the soul was in the body and yet outside it.

Following this, Paul employed words which are enigmatic for an age that lives with the Copernican world conception; they were, however, basic elements of the cosmic spiritual experience of ancient humanity as well as of the ancient wisdom still cultivated then in the mysteries. In regard to the sojourn of the soul outside the body in sleep, in death, and also in the translation during initiation, the world view was valid — and is still valid today — which holds that the earth is surrounded and enveloped by the seven planetary spheres, the seven heavens. Paul felt himself lifted up to the third of these spiritual spheres during his breakthrough. Subsequently, the inner, mercifully bestowed possibility was intensified, and paradise, the fourth, the central heaven, the spiritual sun-sphere, received Paul.

What is it that Paul wanted to indicate when he placed a dark shadow by the side of his experience, even including it as one of the prerequisites and foundations of the light? Luther's interpretation of the 'thorn in the flesh' almost suggests a moral peculiarity that Paul could not deal with. The Greek text speaks of a thorn that indwells the physical body. What is meant here is an incitement (Latin: *stimulus),* from the physical nature, by means of which the body tries to become the driving force in place of the spirit.* On the one hand, Paul was touching upon a tragedy common to all humanity; on the other, he made clear a heavy burden that he alone had to bear.

The fact that Paul was not a man of his times but 'one born prematurely,' the precursor of a future epoch and consciousness, opened for him possibilities of grace but also a particularly painful tragedy. In the time between then and now, humanity has recorded many external advances; inwardly, however, men went the way of an ever increasing impoverishment. The progressive

* Note by translator: The German text says *Anstachelung* here, literally, 'being prodded with a thorn.' *Stachel* is 'thorn' in German.

Fall of humankind brought it about that the last vestiges of the paradisal legacy were finally used up. Since the beginning of the so-called modern age, man has attained to high degrees of alertness but he has paid a great price for his wakeful state. His soul and spirit were ever more chained to the earthly body and thus drawn into the processes of decline and death holding sway there. Humanity is passing through a decisive point where either death will at last prevail over the soul, or the spirit will tear the human being away from the gravity of death and guide it toward a new ascent. During this crisis, people will not readily know what 'spirit' signifies, and will mistakenly understand it to refer to the brain-bound intellect. But it is just this intellect that would precipitate the soul's dying, finally making the victory of matter complete.

Ahead of his time, Paul was already a man of the consciousness soul. This means that even then, he experienced the impoverishment and emptiness of soul which, one day, would have to be undergone by all human beings as a necessary transitional stage. Today the cultural advance of humanity bears within it the 'thorn of the physical nature.' As yet, the danger to the human condition, arising from the increasing preponderance of matter over spirit, the outer over the inner, has not been clearly recognized. The isolation of man from God and from the spiritual sphere will finally become evident in increasing phenomena of illness and debility, not immediately definable medically. Paul was clearly aware of the precarious condition which he had to bear owing to his special form of incarnation. In his physical body, he sensed the angel of death, the Ahrimanic power, who, at the point of nothingness and transition, wishes to hand over dominion to dead matter. Often Paul reached the limits of his strength and beseeched the deity to free him from this trial. But he was given the answer that it was just this condition of emptiness, lying between debility and illness — the Greek word, *astheneia,* signifies this — which, if rightly experienced, would make him receptive to the most abundant spiritual endowments. Was not the great light of Damascus the beginning of those gifts which he could enjoy as a first-born ahead of time, as an early bearer of the consciousness soul that passes through the vanishing point? This is really what Paul wanted to convey to the Corinthians when he revealed to them the law of his own spiritual experience: in order to find the spirit the human being cannot do or contribute anything except to be conscious of his emptiness and inadequacy. Then he can experience the grace of Christ's indwelling; as the true, higher 'I,' Christ will then work out of and through him.

In a lecture dealing with the subject, 'Where do I find the Christ?' Rudolf Steiner discussed this issue in the following terms. He said that in the seventh century, around AD 666, a sudden disturbance occurred in the evolution of human consciousness, as the 'intellectual Fall' advanced:

> At that time ... humanity ... suffered an internal injury extending all the way to the corporeality ... This disease was inoculated into mankind and when it comes fully to expression it leads to the denial of the Father God ...
>
> In so far as human beings are part of civilized humanity, they bear a thorn in their body today ... Paul refers a lot to this thorn; he speaks prophetically, for, being an especially advanced person, he already possessed it in his age. Others only received it in the seventh century. But this thorn will become increasingly prevalent and will be more and more significant. When you encounter a person today who surrenders completely to this thorn, to this illness — for this is a thorn in the physical body, it is a real disease — then this person is an atheist ..., one who denies God. Actually, anybody who is a member of modern civilization has the predisposition to such atheism ... In a manner of speaking, our nature was mineralized somewhat at that time, retarded in its development, so that all of us bear within us the illness of atheism ...
>
> This disease of denying God brings about any number of effects in the human being ... In a sense, the soul is chained more closely to the body ... Death, which is destined only for the body, would ... also have become the soul's fate. This has been counteracted by the Mystery of Golgotha ... Whereas, on the one side, a certain stream

> in world evolution brought about a stronger kinship of the soul to the human body than was destined for man; in order to keep the balance, Christ has bound the soul more strongly to the spirit than was predestined ... Just as our body has within it a force leading to illness which tends towards the denial of God, so, when we have the Christ-force within us ... we have a health-bestowing, healing force within us. In the truest sense of the word, Christ is for us the healing Saviour ['Heiland' in German], the physician for the disease that can turn the human being into one who denies God.[46]

It would require a discussion of the whole totality of Paul's letters in order to cite all the pertinent examples of how the Apostle's language, notwithstanding its personal character, is interspersed with mystery terminology. The more clearly this is recognized, the more clearly the style and language of the letters also proclaim the mighty course of evolution. Through Christ's incarnation, death and Resurrection, the mysteries have moved out of the darkness of secrets into the open arena of human existence; no curtain hinders our access any longer to the universal secrets.

Teaching

13. The Old and the New Adam

Through the light of Damascus, Paul discovered *the archetypal man.* Formerly, he had known only God and despised the human being. As a mere man, he now experienced Christ in his own inner nature; the bridge was suddenly thrown across the terrible abyss between God and man. At the same time he became aware of the secret he had so fanatically denied: that in the man, Jesus, the Christ had truly become man and had linked his destiny in a unique and intimate way with humanity.

Now a source of light had entered man's inner being; a bright radiance illumined the soul and spirit so that they became clearly visible and could be deciphered. Paul was thus the first initiated scholar and herald of a *Christian anthropology.* And this anthropology was able to describe exactly the change in structure that occurred in the human being through the relationship to Christ. As with other Pauline terms, the concepts that Paul employed when referring to the human being have traditionally been interpreted until now in a religious, edifying sense, as *soul*-concepts. They were misunderstood as pictorial paraphrases, whereas, in reality, they were *exact spiritual* concepts, fundamental terms of a solid framework of insight. The misconception was encouraged — something we have already discussed but have to emphasize once again here — because Paul rejected any systematic, catechismal instruction and, as if addressing members of the mystery schools, simply presumed that all the terms were familiar.

We begin to fathom the wondrous order of spiritual perception — in the higher sense also a 'system' — that Paul enjoyed and from which he could draw freely, if we gather together the many passages in which the word, *anthrōpos* (man), occurs in the letters that have come down to us. Solemnly pronounced pairs of concepts, triads or individually coined phrases stand out:

ho palaios anthrōpos, the old man
ho kainos anthrōpos, the new man
(Rom.6:6; Eph.2:15; 4:22-24; Col.3:9)

ho exō anthrōpos, the outer man
ho esō anthrōpos, the inner man
(Rom.7:22; 2 Cor.4:16; Eph.3:16)

ho prōtos anthrōpos, the first man
ho deuteros anthrōpos, the second man
ho eschatos anthrōpos, the last man
(1Cor.15:45f)

(ho anthrōpos sōmatikos, the physical man)
ho anthrōpos psychikos, the soul man
ho anthrōpos pneumatikos, the spiritual man
(1Cor.2:14f; in this passage, the first member of the triad is not mentioned but presupposed)

ho anthrōpos choïkos, the earthly man, formed from earth substance
ho anthrōpos epouranios, the celestial man, fashioned after the spheres of heaven
(1Cor.15:47f)

Examples of classically coined, individual phrases are:

ho phthartos anthrōpos, the temporal man (Rom.1:23)
ho talaipōros anthrōpos, the man standing under a tragic curse (Rom.7:24)
ho hairetikos anthrōpos, the erring man (Tit.3:10)
ho anthrōpos tēs anomias, the man of chaos (2Thess.2:3)
ho anthrōpos teleios and *ho anēr teleios,* the consecrated man (Col.1:18; Eph.4:13).

The anthropology of the Pauline letters is a dynamic one. It does not waste time enumerating the various members of which the human being consists. This was taken for granted by Paul. It becomes clear in passing that he by no means acknowledged merely the physical as the sheath of incarnation for the human being and the other terrestrial kingdoms of creation. He was familiar with supersensory sheaths as well, known to modern anthroposophy as the life or etheric body, and the soul or astral body. Therefore, in order to indicate that the mystery of resurrection does not take place in man's earthly, physical body, he said: 'There are terrestrial bodies and there are spheric, celestial bodies' (1Cor.15:40*B*).

Paul principally viewed the human being as involved in a mighty evolution. His attention therefore was directed above all on how man's structure would be fundamentally altered through connecting with the event of Christ. This is the reason why most of the pairs of concepts referring to the human being are of antithetic character. The fundamental example is, 'the old man and the new man,' according to whether the human being is perceived prior to the coming of Christ or turned towards Christ.

For example, if we approach Paul's letters with the question whether the human being consists of body, soul and spirit, or whether he consists of body and soul as laid down by the church dogma of the year 869 AD, we discover no direct, systematic answer. It is unmistakable however, that Paul viewed man as a trichotomy, not a duality. The point is that his pressing interest only begins where the effects of Christ bring proper order into this trichotomy. The natural human being has his sheath-nature, the physical and the soul sheath. His true 'I,' the spiritual part of his nature that is to dwell in the sheaths, merely hovers over him. The tragic hardened state of the sheaths brings it about that man remains fragmented; his spiritual part does not find its way into the earthly man. It is only through the work of Christ that the human being begins to become a complete being, for through the freeing of the soul which occurs as a result of the indwelling of Christ, the true self, the spiritual part of man, draws into the sheaths and can become effective within them. It can therefore easily remain an abstract and not fully accurate statement to say that man consists of body, soul and spirit. The man of body and soul has his spiritual element, yet without Christ he does not have it. Only the Christ is the whole, complete man.

The essential core of Paulinism relates equally to man and Christ. It is the basic key to Christian anthropology as well as to spiritual Christology, for it is the teaching of the 'old and the new Adam.' At the same time, it is here that we confront the prime example of how Paul crystallizes and concentrates whole worlds into the words and formulations he coins. Here a merely intellectual and logical comprehension is totally insufficient. In his lectures, *From Jesus to Christ,* in connection with the formulations, 'first and second Adam,' Rudolf Steiner emphatically pointed out how 'Paul utilized the whole evolution of humanity for the concept and idea of Christ.' And he adds:

> If we let the Pauline epistles work upon us, we have finally something which, through its extraordinary simplicity and through the deep penetrating quality of the words and sentences, makes a most significant impression. But this is so only because Paul, through his own initiation, had worked his way up to that simplicity which is not the starting-point of what is true, but the consequence of the goal. If we wish to penetrate into what Paul was able finally to express in wonderful, monumental, simple words concerning the Christ-Being, we must come nearer to an understanding of human nature, for whose further development on earth the Christ-Impulse came.[47]

'Adam' means 'the man.' To that extent, to speak of the first and second Adam would signify that a new creation of man has taken place in and through Christ. Yet this would be much too general and unclear a statement. More exactly, 'Adam' means 'the man who is incarnated in an earthly physical body,' for the Hebrew term 'Adamah' means 'earth substance.' Hence, where the story of creation speaks of the creation of Adam in the first book of the Bible, it does not refer to a creation out of nothing, a very first appearance of existence. As a supersensory being, man was present already. In Adam he entered a new condition:

he became an *earth being*. Henceforth, there existed a reciprocal effect between his soul and spiritual being and the physical earthly sheath with which the Elohim adorned him.

Subsequently, when mention is made of the new Adam, this includes a transformation and renewal that takes place within the physical body of man, hence in the realm of earth substance. This implies that through this transformation the human being is newly created even in his physical body; that he receives a new body that is developing within the material sphere in which he incarnates. From the first Adam all the way to Christ, the evolution of the earthly human body, hence that of earthly substance in general, was a descending one. Through the Fall, death drew into the earthly body. A constant increase of the power which death exercises over the human body and which it tries to expand over the whole human being, extends throughout the cosmic and historical epochs of humanity's history on earth. This forms the sombre background, in front of which man's inner development, consisting of a progressive process of awakening, takes place.

The new development, inaugurated through the life of Christ in the middle of time and in a place far from the world's mainstream, was not limited to the inner realm of man's soul. A power began to be effective that would break the spell of death under which the earthly nature of man suffers. Through this power, the process of degeneration and death, increasing in the course of time, is complemented by a process directed towards growth and regeneration; and where this power truly can take hold, the process of decline is finally arrested. The cosmic significance of Christ's Resurrection consists in the effect that it is constantly increasing in strength. The new Adam is Christ from whom, henceforth, human beings are descended in regard to the renewed body, just as all natural human beings are descendants of the first Adam.

Paul acquired the certainty with which he was able to utter the mystery of the 'old and the new Adam' from his Damascus experience. The entity who had revealed himself so overwhelmingly to Paul in that hour had been more than a human being. And yet, to the very core of his own humanness, Paul realized that he was dealing here with something involving *the human being*. A new seed of divinity had been implanted into man, liberating human nature from its traditional distance from God; redeeming it from the loss of the condition in which it had been an image of God. The entity who revealed himself to Paul was no physical human figure; it was flaming spirit. And yet, at this moment, even within his own earthly body, Paul experienced the mystery of the triumphant sovereignty of spirit over matter, of life over death; the sovereign entity revealing itself to him was the one who had become man, the Resurrected One. Illuminating future redemption, a sun of transformation had risen over the human being and earthly substance.

The Pharisaic schooling of the Old Testament had taught Paul to look down on and despise the human being and the world of earthly nature. It was of benefit to him that during his youthful development he had also been in contact with the European spirit of Greece and its mystery practice where the human being was held in such high esteem that even the gods were depicted in human form; in which people were so fond of the body that the world of those who had departed the body was experienced as the sombre world of the shades. This now helped Paul escape the influence of the Old Testament.

In Rudolf Steiner's lectures, *From Jesus to Christ,* we read of the close connection between Paul's view of the 'old and the new Adam' and his proclamation of Christ's Resurrection:

> Paul then affirms that through Christian evolution men are gradually made ready to put on the second Adam in place of the first Adam; the incorruptible body of the second Adam, Christ, in place of the corruptible body of the first Adam ... As the first corruptible body is descended from Adam, so must the incorruptible body originate from the second Adam, from Christ ... For Paul, this view shines out directly from the experience of Damascus ... If man, as regards his corruptible body, is descended from the first Adam, then, by receiving the Being of Christ into his own being, he has the possibility of having a second ancestor. This ancestor, however, is He who, on the third day after His body had been laid in the earth, rose out of the grave ...

> I would like to add the remark here that an assertion such as this, made by Paul after he had reached the summit of his initiation through the event of Damascus — the assertion concerning the second Adam and His rising from the grave — could be made only by someone whose whole mode of thought and outlook had been derived from Greek thought; whose roots were in Greece, even if he were also a Hebrew; by one who in a certain respect had brought all his Hebraism as an offering to the Greek mind ... That which the Greeks valued most highly (the human body) was given back to them with (the thought of) the Resurrection by Paul the Jew, who had been steeped in Greek culture.[48]

> In a certain sense Paul was an initiate *before* the Event of Damascus. His initiation had combined the ancient Hebrew principle and the Greek principle. He knew that an initiate became, in his etheric body, independent of the physical body, and could appear in the purest form of his etheric body to those who were capable of seeing it. If, prior to Damascus, Paul had had the vision of a pure etheric body, independent of a physical body, he would have spoken differently. He would have said that he had seen someone who had been initiated and would be living on further in the course of earth-evolution, independently of the physical body. He would not have found this particularly surprising. What Paul experienced on the road to Damascus could not have been that. He had experienced something which he knew could be experienced only when 'the Scriptures were fulfilled'; when a perfect human Phantom, a human body risen from the grave in a supersensible form, would appear in the spiritual atmosphere of the earth ... That is what appeared to him on the road to Damascus and convinced him.[49]

In two places, the key concept of the old and new Adam emerges in Paul's letters as if from a quiet mystery background: in the fifth chapter of the Letter to the Romans (12-19) and in the fifteenth chapter of the First Letter to the Corinthians (21-49).

We would misunderstand in principle everything being said there, were we to interpret it as meaning that Adam, the progenitor of all men and at the same time the instigator of their Fall, were to be placed over against Christ, a divine saviour and redeemer working from outside. For then it would merely be a symbolic gesture to call Christ the second Adam. Every emphasis is placed on the fact that *man* stands at the earth's beginning as well as at the new beginning made possible by Christ. Quite unmistakably, this is expressed at the beginning of the passage in the First Letter to the Corinthians. 'For as by man came death, by man the resurrection of the dead has come into the world' (1Cor.15:21*B*). This has hardly ever been noted seriously, because there is a similarly sounding passage — but on close inspection significantly different — in the beginning of the Letter to the Romans:

> Therefore as sin came into the world through *one* man and death through sin ... how much greater is the grace of God, which, through the *one* man, Jesus Christ, has been bestowed on the many (Rom.5:12-15*B*).

It is possible to translate the beginning of the passage in Corinthians also in this way: 'For as by one man ... ' But since the numerical term, 'one,' is missing in the Greek text, the word 'man' has to bear the full emphasis. Therefore, whether we say, 'as by man came death' or 'as by one man came death,' in either case, *man* is specifically placed at the initial as well as at the new beginning, except that at the beginning of earthly humanity's destinies stands the incomplete man, whereas the new beginning has been brought about by him whom we may term the complete man. The first, descending evolution was brought about and continued through man, for each human being bore within him the fragmentary and flawed nature of Adam. Likewise, the ascending development, the increasing sovereignty of life over death, is not simply placed among humanity as a unique miracle in the Resurrection of Christ. Every individual human being turns into the subject and bearer of this development inasmuch as he receives Christ into his being and thereby becomes man in the true and complete sense. Through man, the world is led into death in so far as the human being has to admit: Not I but Adam in me! In like manner, the world can be guided to life again through man, when, with inner justification, human beings say: Not I but Christ in me!

One of the passages in which the anthropological aspect of the mighty transition in evolution brought about by the new Adam becomes clear, as if in passing, is the following sentence: 'The first man, Adam, became a life-bearing soul, the last Adam became a life-engendering spirit' (1Cor.15:45*B*). Here we confront a fulcrum. The Pauline wording itself obliges us to advance from the blurred, merely emotional content to clear, spiritual principles that are part of a higher form of anthropology. Rudolf Steiner has called the modern spiritual science inaugurated by him, 'anthroposophy,' for in it the 'wisdom of man,' an anthropology of a higher kind that includes the supersensory, is the foundation and essence of an encompassing cognition and world view. In reading the Pauline texts, the basic principles worked out by anthroposophy can help us become aware of the complete view — knowledge of which was always taken for granted by Paul — and, in comprehending it, to take it into account. Those who are labouring for a new understanding of the Bible will encounter many a surprise concerning how closely Paulinism and anthroposophy are related to each other in this regard, frequently even coinciding in the wording.

We have mentioned already that we cannot be content with the simple formulation that man consists of body, soul and spirit. The interaction of body and soul becomes comprehensible only when a more complete view is acquired of those members of man's being which possess the nature of sheaths. In progressing from the soul to the spirit, from the sheaths to the actual core and essence, our understanding must become dynamic and include the drama of the Fall and Redemption.

The sheath-nature of man is already a threefold one. Here, instead of speaking merely of body and soul, we must speak of body, life and soul. Anthroposophy calls the three sheaths:

physical body
etheric body, life-body, formative forces body
astral body, soul-body

In germinal form, man received these three members of his being during the three aeons which preceded the specific Earth-aeon ('Saturn,' 'Sun,' 'Moon').[50] (Note that the spiritual human entity was present prior to its sheaths! Inasmuch as these were prepared for it through the creative activity of higher beings, who guided evolution from one aeon to the next — slowly and in increasing measure, the presentiment of individual life and self-existence drew into the human being.) At the beginning, borne and sheltered by the angelic kingdoms, the actual being of man, which is of spiritual nature, hovered above the nascent sheath-nature. Distantly, as if dreaming, it became aware of itself when it began to be reflected in a corporeality of its own.

The purport of the specific Earth-aeon was the incorporation of the spiritual core, the 'I,' into the threefold sheath-nature. With that, the fourth member, the ego, would relate to the three as the content to the vessel. Only now in a real sense could man himself become the subject of inner and outer activities. And the ego's activity would now have effect, not only on the world around it but also on its own human nature. This would imply that the transforming influence of the imprint of the spiritual 'I' would be conveyed to the three sheaths.

This organic evolution experienced a profound interruption in a primordial period of the Earth-aeon, described by biblical mythology in the image of the Fall. The Luciferic power implanted in man a premature ego-impulse. The true spiritual 'I,' whose time had not yet come, remained in its condition of hovering above. What was added was a lower self-will of the soul, a false 'I,' which became active in the soul-body. This awakening and desiring, illusory 'I' turned towards the earthly sense world and bound itself ever more strongly to its own physical body, which, after all, is an essential part and organ of the terrestrial sense world. The human being exchanged its childlike, dreaming existence in the spheres of the heavenly hierarchies, the world of God, with the perceiving and grasping urges of the earthly realm. Thereby, it not only separated itself from God but even from its own true self which still remained in the spiritual dimension and hovered above the earthly sphere. 'Sin' in the sense of separation came into the world. The German language makes this clear in the words 'Sünde' or 'sin' and 'Sonderung,' 'separation.' Separation became the condition of humanity. Death, too, entered earth existence. Between the soul-body behaving as if it were an 'I,' and the physical body, man's life-body was caught up in a tragic state of strangulation. Increasingly, it was drawn more deeply into the lifeless mineral substance of the hardening physical body and became spellbound there, so that in the course of humanity's earthly evolution the degenerative processes finally outweighed the constant regeneration provided through the life forces. The deficit of life, the tyranny of death, became ever greater. The life-body could no longer keep the physical body alive and let it slip to the ground as a corpse. Finally, even the soul participated in the body's fate of death. Like a 'second death,' the soul's death was added to that of the body.

This is the tragedy of the first Adam: he is a 'life-bearing soul being'; he possesses life and soul; but the life is tragically consumed and at last the soul begins to die along with the body.

How could a corrective measure be taken? A change could occur if, despite the stranglehold in which the threefold sheath-nature had become entangled, the true self, the spiritual part of man, could gain entry and become effective. The spirit would be capable of tearing the soul away from the spell of bodily imprisonment. Facing the spiritual world rather than merely the sense realm, the soul would become the first member of man's constitution to be permeated and transformed by the spirit. Through this the life-forces, too, would be liberated. The etheric body of man would once more be able to flow and be nourished by the true 'waters of life.' Instead of being delivered up only to the powers of death, the life-body and physical body would be opened up also to the transforming effect of the spirit. This is what is meant when Paul called the new Adam a 'life-engendering spirit form':

> The first man, Adam, has turned into a being possessing (self-consuming) life and soul,
> the last Adam will be an (inexhaustibly) life-engendering spirit form.

The change is effected by Christ. Into the fragmentary human world, cut off from its own true being, he bears the undefiled, whole image of man. Christ opens the way for man's spirit, his true self, to enter into the sheath-nature which has fallen into the clutches of death. As the human being begins truly to consist of body, soul and spirit, an ascending world of life replaces the descending one under the tyranny of death. With his own resources, man cannot overcome the tragic separation. Yet he can accomplish this if he allows the death-vanquishing power of the new Adam to enter him and to work alongside his being.

What matters is to discern ever more clearly in Paul's writings the signs of an objective language of cognition. Only then will it become possible to recognize how radically Paul departed from the sentient element of the Old Testament. Martin Luther's translation of the Bible places Paul back into the sentiment of the Old Testament by not comprehending him spiritually but through moral, self-absorbed soul concepts. When Paul speaks, it is certainly true that a genuine, stern morality is present, but in an objective, supra-personal sense. The cosmic aspects which Luther, like almost all of Protestant theology, did not want to recognize in the books of the New Testament, actually play the dominant role; personal morality is embedded in a higher, morally viewed cosmos.

This can be exemplified in a sentence from the passage in Romans concerning the old and the new Adam: 'For as by one man's 'disobedience' many were made sinners, so by one man's 'obedience' many will be placed into the state of true being' (Rom.5:19*B*).

The words *parakoē* and *hypakoē*, 'disobedience' and 'obedience,' can only be comprehended in a human and moralistic sense through an unconscious assumption that the human being in the earlier periods of our planet Earth was already constituted in body and soul in the way it is today. The mythical story of Genesis concerning the Fall does make Adam and Eve appear as if they resembled humans of today. It must be borne in mind, however, that a myth sees and describes, in imaginative pictures originating from later eras of humanity's evolution, soul processes that occurred totally in the supersensible realm. The myth leaves it open what sort of earthly, historical figures and events may be concealed behind the veil of images.

It goes without saying that in earlier periods of the Earth-aeon the human being could not have resembled its present bodily shape even remotely when, repeating the results of preceding aeons, it began to clothe itself in earthly substance. In a state of sleep, the being of man still rested in the bosom of the higher beings and worlds that supported it. Germinating in the earth element, which was not solidly crystallized but still formless and fluid, the physical body as yet was not the actual dwelling place of the human being who hovered almost completely above it. In the beginning, the physical body was merely like a mirror which reflected back to the human being the first distant presentiment of itself and the world. As anthroposophy makes clear, the natural scientific hypothesis that the human form did not emerge until late from the sequence of the lower and higher animal forms, is not incorrect. It is only wrong and completely misleading to understand this to mean that man descended from the animal. It was always man who passed through the various stages of evolution. After having passed through forms resembling those of animals and having drawn near the actual human form, he could enter the latter more completely and incarnate in it.

Let us try — if only hypothetically — to form a conception of the first emergence of earthly sense organs. The sense of sight, the clearly perceiving eye, presupposes an advanced condition of the planet Earth on which the elements have already become differentiated from each other. From the primordial sea, the solid mineral element has crystallized in a downward direction; in an upward direction, the mists, in which water and air had still been intimately united, have been freed. The free, light-filled, transparent atmosphere has come about. At the same stage of evolution in which the human being arises in the upright form, man opens his eyes with which he now beholds the earth and the sun, the moon and the stars.

The first of the earthly senses was that of hearing. It was formed through the original creative sound of the cosmic word, whose resounding moved the primal waters and brought all development into flow until, finally, the forms of all earthly things emerged. Here we are groping our way to the earliest conditions of the planet Earth, and of the human being. At the beginning of his path of physical incarnation, the human being passed through a form in which a symbolic, cosmic memory has been preserved in the shell. The mysterious sea-like noise which we hear in shells reminds us of the primal sound in which the creative deity spoke its 'Let there be!' We can picture to ourselves an incipient organism in which three of our present organic functions combined: breathing, hearing and speaking. Inhaling is at the same time the beginning of hearing; exhaling is simultaneously the origin of speaking. What is heard? Only the word of God. It is absorbed fully and completely as it is inhaled. Of course, the *Word,* the Logos, is as yet not differentiated for the human being into the *words* which, much later on, are connected with thoughts. It is the primal beginning in which 'the word' is the dominant power in the cosmos. What is expressed? Again, only the word of God. The human being is the ear and the mouth of what the deity speaks. As yet, there is no difference between the divine and the human word. The cosmic word passes through man. In him, it sculpts the nascent world. This initial condition of man could be called the first 'obedience.' The German word for obedience, *gehorsam,* inasmuch as the words 'to hear,' *hören,* and 'hearing,' *Gehör,* are contained in it, points to this connection. To heed the words of God was at the same time to 'hear' them and obey. This is even more clearly expressed in the Greek word, *hypakoē.*

This condition of the human entity must have lasted for long epochs of time, finally arriving at the period indicated by the biblical paradise myth. Then the tragic change occurs. The peace of pure obedience is disturbed. Under the insinuations of the tempter, the Adam-humanity enters the condition of disobedience. Adam's insubordination was no moral misdeed in the ordinary sense. For that, the faculty of freely deciding between good and evil would have been required. This faculty only *originated* through the tragic departure from the cosmic obedience.

'Adam's Fall' occurred with the first beginnings of self-will and sense of self. At some stage, man had to embark upon the path of freedom and egohood. Lucifer's interference, which was not opposed by the higher hierarchies, caused the development of selfhood to begin prematurely. It could only begin with an isolation of the human being, whereby the faculty of hearing and being openly responsive to that first obedience was curtailed. Man's original sense of hearing for God became deaf; what the earthly ear would henceforth hear would no longer be the totality. In the human ear, the world became fragmented. Increasingly, the human being only heard the earthly surface of what was resounding. In the intonations of sacred texts, and in music, a later humanity was to nurture the last remnants of primal hearing, finally forfeiting even these. When, through Adam's lack of hearing, the human being became deaf to God's word, the infinite grace of cosmic guidance did bestow on him the word of differentiated human language. God's word and man's word quickly moved far apart, however, until the arrogant word of man became altogether oblivious to the word of God, even where people constantly made use of the term 'the word of God.'

The genesis and the history of hearing and speaking are at the same time the history of the continuing Fall, of the growing dominion of death in the world.

The obedience of the 'new Adam' is also more than a human, moral virtue. It has cosmic dimensions and effects. Through it, the cosmic word, the Logos, can create the world in man a second time.

Just as hearing was the first of the earthly senses which man developed in the old world creation, so the spirit-hearing, the openness of the soul for 'the Word' in all its levels of being, will be the first of the spiritual organs that are to be awakened in the human being. Through Christ's indwelling, through the activation of the second Adam in us, our deafness and blindness for the world of supersensory reality is overcome. A 'new man' is developing in the sense of a higher anthropology that recognizes the spiritual organs of the soul. These organs atrophied, but through the grace of a higher world they can be reawakened. Thus man can pass beyond the fragmentation of his nature and the grip of death. He can find his true nature. Therefore, just as mankind died through Adam's disobedience, *[un-gehör]*, so they can arise through Christ's obedience *[ge-horsam]*.

The key phrase of the first and second Adam unlocks still another special chamber of secrets in the mystery temple of humanity. There exists a twofold Adam mystery, not only in regard to the relationship between the beginning of humanity's evolution in Adam and the new beginning in Christ but even in regard to the Adamite beginning of the earthly paths of men. And behind the secret of Adam-Christ, there exists an Adam-Jesus mystery.

The ancient secret doctrine of the Hebrews, which in a fragmentary form still emerges in Cabalistic texts as well as Talmudic and Hasidic legends, knew of a merciful action by Providence, carried out for the sake of humanity's future by the higher powers at the moment of the Fall. The Adam soul was superior in power and greatness to all other evolving human souls. Otherwise, it could not have assumed the risk of descending to incarnation in the solidifying earth substance as the forerunner and pioneer of humanity. Its forward urge was utilized by the Luciferic power; as a consequence, the descent became a decline. It was then, however, that those hierarchical powers charged with the guidance and protection of the human being, rescued a part of the Adam entity from the threatening Fall, thus detaining one 'celestial Adam soul' in the spiritual worlds. The terrestrial Adam, becoming increasingly earthly, passed as the first and oldest soul of humanity through many earthly lives. The celestial Adam did not enter into an earthly incarnation, not even when those souls who had hesitated for long epochs of time finally entered the stream of humanity, incarnating on earth as 'young' and 'youngest' souls. A heavenly reserve was retained for a human destiny that was becoming more and more tragic. One day, when a divine being came to redeem earthly humanity, the celestial Adam soul would perhaps be able to serve as a human soul-sheath, thereby building a bridge for it.

To earth, paradise with its pure light had been lost. Yet, in the higher Adam being, held back in the heavens, this light was still alive in all its purity and brightness. And it did not remain totally separated from the darkness through which people on earth had to find their way. At important moments, rays of this pure light fell inspiringly into the earth's darkness when great initiated leaders of humanity had made their souls capable of receiving them. The apocryphal, esoteric traditions, existing side by side with the Old Testament, and retaining ancient secret knowledge, describe Enoch in particular, the great sage of the Atlantean age, as overshadowed and inspired by the 'celestial Adam.'

> The light of the loftiest soul, which flew away from Adam when he was driven from the garden of Eden, ascended again and was preserved in a treasure chamber until the time when Enoch was to come. Then this highest light of the holy soul came into Enoch, and Enoch attained to the same greatness that Adam possessed before the Fall.[51]

Even prior to the Christ event, a story of salvation existed. Invisible to earthly senses, it took place in light-filled heights high above humanity. Paradise, the state of being an image of God, had not solely become a subject of nostalgic, painful memory. In its radiant fullness, it remained present in one human entity. In the pure, celestial soul, the actual archetype of man, his true, living image, held sway over the happenings on earth.

Anthroposophical research describes three fundamental events of the higher story of salvation. Such research makes clear what had been hidden in the old Hebrew legends. On the path of the continuing Fall and the ever increasing bondage to the powers of the depths, humankind faced acute crises and dangers of degeneration on three occasions. Three times, the higher entity, who would later enter into human incarnation in order to bring salvation, intervened in a healing manner. Just as Christ, humanity's 'I,' would become man in the incarnated human being, Jesus, he became human in three pre-Christian Christ events by making use of the celestial Adam being as a sheath. Through the archetype which the grace of Providence had preserved for humanity in the spheres of the spirit, Christ aided human beings who had become estranged from their archetype. He approached humanity in the life-sheath of the higher Adam, bringing to life the image of what the human being is intended to be according to the original will of God, in order to hold the balance against the gravitational powers of the depths.

When the 'higher Adam soul' served Christ as a sheath and organ, it was as the archetypal *Man* rather than as an individual man. It did not possess an earthly sheath and an experience of the ego in the way that earthly men did. But this higher Adam soul was able to develop an etheric body that could have been described as *the* light and *the* life. Innocent and open in devotion to the 'life-giving spirit,' it remained far from the effects of death which on earth penetrated the soul and life bodies, darkening them as a result of their attachment to matter. Rudolf Steiner describes[52] the two later events in the story of salvation, which occurred in the Atlantean age, by saying that it was language, above all, that was bestowed on humanity in order to save men from the imminent danger of bestiality. The 'Word,' which earlier had belonged to the gods, passed on to men. In order to rescue them from descending too deeply, the higher powers gave humanity a share in their own being. Although the human being on earth had long since passed from obedience, listening to God, to disobedience, not listening to him, yet it was granted a share in the divine word; this occurred in anticipation of the fact that one day the descending development of humanity would be turned around by means of the 'Word' into a new ascent. The apocryphal legends point to these mysteries when they relate that as *Metatron,* namely the one filled and inspired by the celestial Adam soul, Enoch is supposed to have been the great teacher who taught human beings to speak.

According to anthroposophy, the celestial Adam soul once drew quite close to earthly humanity during historical time. It did not enter into a complete incarnation then either; but it filled the soul of the great Indian teacher, Krishna, in order to bestow light and wisdom on post-Atlantean humanity.

Then, when 'the time was fulfilled,' the heavenly soul entered into an earthly incarnation for the first time. At Christmas, in the stable at Bethlehem, it was born as the child of heaven to the unassuming Nazarene parents, as related by the Gospel of Luke. In an earthly body, having been permeated with the glow of the fire from Christ's indwelling since ancient times, this soul was now to offer to the Christ the soul-sheath and bodily garment in which he could bring salvation, *the light* and *the life* to humanity.

Our present age must find its way anew to the Christ mystery by learning to distinguish the higher Christ entity from the man, Jesus, who became the *Christophorus*, the Christ bearer. Beyond that, it has to rediscover a higher secret which, in earlier times, was well known to many on a level of feeling: the special mystery of Luke's Jesus child. The Jesus child whose birth is described by the Gospel of Matthew is *a* human being, one who had been a great teacher of humanity in earlier lives. The child of Luke's Christmas, on the other hand, is *the* human being: in it, the pure archetype of man, preserved in the heavens, enters the realm of earthly humanity. This child is the second Adam; he brings to the Christ the pure, light- and life-filled soul and life-sheath that make it possible for Christ to begin the new creation in man.[53] The mystery of the two Jesus children is not mentioned directly in the New Testament. Nevertheless, the Evangelist Luke makes it evident in wondrously artistic manner by aligning his Gospel with that of Matthew. Once we have become familiar with this higher secret, we discern more and more clearly that the Gospel of Luke could not have been formulated the way it was if, in the background, there were not a profound heart-knowledge of this secret, a close acquaintance with the heavenly Adam soul. And by what means did Luke become so intimately aware of the special Jesus mystery? He learned about it by becoming Paul's disciple. Paul's teaching of the first and second Adam is, after all, another way of expressing the same mystery. Thus, in addition to the duality of the first and third Gospels, the providential mystery of the two Jesus children is also mentioned in an indirect way in Paul's letters. In the Acts of the Apostles, Luke's discipleship becomes externally visible. In his Gospel, Luke allows this discipleship to become evident at its deepest root.

How was Paul initiated into the secret of the two Jesus children? We have shown that the Damascus experience was the source from which Paul acquired his insight into the old and the new Adam. From it, he also gained knowledge of the secret which can be termed that of the two Jesus children. It was the resurrected Christ who revealed himself to Paul before Damascus. But the light sheath in which he showed himself to Paul, which Paul became conscious of as being effective in his own soul and body, was the paradisal life- and soul-body of the heavenly

Adam, shining forth in pure light. Because of his earthly deed, the sheath in which the Christ had carried out his heavenly deeds on earthly humanity was now permeated completely with the power of resurrection, with a spiritually transformed physical body. Rudolf Steiner expresses this quite candidly in his lectures, *The Bhagavad Gita and the Epistles of Paul;* the only difference being that in accordance with the specific theme of the lecture series, the celestial Adam soul is here called Krishna, the one through whom, filled with wisdom, it had prepared its earthly service of Christ.

> When Paul had his vision before Damascus, it was the Christ who appeared to him. The flood of light in which he clothed himself was Krishna. Because Christ took Krishna as his own soul sheath, through which he then continued to work, in what shone forth there everything was contained ... [that had once flowed as wisdom through Krishna into mankind.][54]

A marvellous stream flows through the writings of Luke and then ends in the letters of Paul. At the beginning of the Gospel of Luke, in the fields of Bethlehem, the shepherds behold the radiant, paradisal glory that appears over the site of the manger. In the Acts of the Apostles, Paul beholds the Resurrected One in the same glory which has now received into itself the whole content of Easter. And in his letters, Paul translates this light into thought by speaking of the first and the second Adam.

14. Sin and Salvation

The very foundation of Protestant faith and theology has been determined by the doctrine of 'justification through faith,' as interpreted by Luther from the Letter to the Romans. In the last two centuries, the voices have become more numerous and audible of those leading theologians who view Luther's interpretation of Paul as one-sided. Such voices would have the cosmic note and supra-personal greatness in the Pauline proclamation come into their own, thereby counteracting the danger of a too personal egoism regarding salvation.[55]

Still it would not matter too much if, in place of the themes in the Letter to the Romans, those of the Letters to the Corinthians or Ephesians, for example, were moved to the foreground. Luther certainly directed his attention to the Letter to the Romans where the heart of the Pauline perception regarding sin and salvation exists. The tragedy is not that Luther selected one specific view from the wealth of the Pauline vistas and emphasized it one-sidedly; but rather that, since the supra-personal cosmic element was foreign to his religion, he also misunderstood what Paul had to say concerning sin and salvation. Luther could never free himself completely from a purely soul-related, moral and juridical conception of God as contained in the Old Testament. Therefore, the one who has drawn the dividing line most radically between the Old and the New Testament was in many places interpreted by Luther in the spirit of the Old Testament.

Paul will not be understood correctly until the step from the Old to the New Testament is perceived, with all it implies, as the replacement of an old world condition by the beginning of a new one. A new religious proclamation of the relationship between God and man was not the main point. A new cosmic impulse placed not only the human being but all earthly creatures, indeed even the planet Earth itself, at the beginning of a completely new evolution. As conceived by Paul, sin as well as redemption is not a merely human but a cosmic fact.

Remaining under the spell of the Old Testament, Luther could not picture the relationship of man to God other than in a 'forensic' manner: Man stands before the bar of the court of justice; he is the guilty one, the accused, and God presides as the judge. Man would have to be pronounced guilty were it not for the fact that there exists the possibility — perceived by 'faith' — of clemency on account of the surrogate, expiatory sacrifice on Golgotha. The fact that the word usually translated as 'justice,' figures so largely in Paul's vocabulary when he refers to sin and redemption seems to support this basic legalistic principle.

It becomes evident in the tenor of his translation to what extent this basic view predominated in Luther. Thus, he consistently translated *dikaiosynē theou,* which literally means, 'the justice of God,' by the phrase 'the justice that holds good before God.' It is completely alien to Luther's feeling that 'justice' could refer to one of God's characteristics, a spiritual attribute in which man, too, might participate. He can only conceive of it as the standard of justice pertaining to God that, as divine judge, he administers across the abyss. Similarly, he places the related concept, *doxa theou,* [in Latin, *gloria dei,*] 'the glory of God,' into the forensic situation: 'the renown [glory] that we should have from God' (Rom.3:23*B*). The glory of God is to Luther nothing but the praising, honouring judgment of the one whom it befits to pronounce judgment.*

For a long time, there has been an instinctive aversion in Protestant thinking from the appearance of cosmic dimensions in the religious sphere. Today it is likely that none but theologians react like this. It would be beneficial to realize how much this attitude participates in the tragic divergence between nature and morality, which, long ago, became necessary in the cultural stream of the Old Testament. While the latter thereby distinguished itself from the pagan nature religions, today, in the era of natural science,

* Luther also diluted the meaning of the angelic choir at Bethlehem that sings of the shining forth of the divine glory, the light of his Being, with his translation: 'Glory to God in the highest.'

this split has long since caused modern scientific thought to avoid the religious domain altogether, while the religious life has become caught up in an unworldly attitude devoid of influence.

It is even considered a threat to the moral earnestness in religious life, for example, when the term 'sickness of sin' is used on occasion instead of 'sin.' Sickness is a natural process, so it is thought, that runs its course and is to be treated according to unalterable laws of nature distinct from the moral sphere. 'Sin,' on the other hand, is to be understood first and foremost in a moral sense. There is concern, therefore, about the profundity of the sense of guilt that is supposed to cause man to be aware of his misdeeds.

Nevertheless, it is clear that just as in the case of the whole New Testament, so, in Paul's case too, the use of the term 'sin' cannot refer merely to personal 'sins,' to the transgressions of the moral code. 'Sin' does not merely prevail where 'evil deeds' are done; 'good works' fall far short of liberating man from the spell of sin. The Pauline radicalism with regard to the Mosaic Law would contradict itself if the sin from which Christ saves the human being referred to nothing more than transgressions against this Law. In many instances, traditional Lutheran theology recognized this and therefore distinguished the 'sins' perpetrated by the individual from 'original sin,' under whose spell and curse humanity stands, good and evil alike. Yet this distinction remained unclear, for without realizing it people nevertheless persevered in the customary thoughts and emotions of the Old Testament. The term, 'original sin,' is probing towards 'sin as a condition' as well as 'sin as cosmic fact.' Through the Fall, which in itself was a cosmic event, humanity along with all other earthly kingdoms entered the condition of sin, of separation from the original, divine creative powers.

With full justification, this condition can be designated as a sickness of a higher form. The mystery of sin has to do with the 'natural' contrast of death and life much more than with the 'moral' contrast of good and evil. The saying, 'The wages of sin is death,' signifies that sin is a sickness, the consequence of which is death. Death is ordained for all human beings, both evil and good; it is natural, therefore, that all human beings find themselves in the condition of sin. A deficiency affecting all humanity is concealed behind even the most morally proper surface.

The concept of redemption as healing corresponds to that of sin as a sickness. Thus, people at all times have known of the concept, 'sickness of sin,' and made use of it indirectly when they designated Christ as 'Healer.'

To Paul's Damascus-sight, creator and creation, spirit and matter, morality and nature are no longer split apart. The creator has shown mercy on the fallen creation and has moved into it by imposing the yoke of death on himself. The spirit intervenes in dead matter, transforming and infusing it with life; nature, the cosmos, can once again be viewed and comprehended in a moral way. When Paul's letters become instrumental as an impetus and support in striving for a new, exact world conception instead of merely as sources for religious feelings or guiding principles for confessional and theological formulations, then a danger will be averted. The moral element need not be disparaged through knowledge of the natural processes connected with it. On the contrary, the way will at last be open to recognize in nature not merely mechanical processes and laws but the reign of higher moral, angelic powers. To speak then of the sickness of sin will not convey a naturalistic sense. In the highest degree, it will address this illness in a completely moral and religious sense. Sickness is a consequence of sin on every level of existence. Even today, the cause of sickness is in most instances less a bodily than a soul and spiritual one, hence a religious-moral deficiency. Sickness is always an insufficiency of some kind, for the function of this or that organ is impaired or fails because of it. As the bodily reserves of civilized humanity are increasingly exhausted, the fundamental incompleteness of the human being affects the states of health and illness to an unprecedented degree. The inadequacy inheres in the fact that in the soul, life and body, only the lower I — the apparent, illusory I, instead of the true self, the spiritual part of man — is effective. This, however, is only an aspect applicable to practical life, of what we term 'sin as a condition' or 'original sin.' The word which the Greeks — hence also the scriptures of the New Testament — used for sickness, was *astheneia.* We find it in the word 'neurasthenia.' It always indicates weakness, weakness of soul. It therefore presupposes that the human being falls ill not because the body is weak, but rather the soul.

We approach the secret of redemption when we understand it as a healing through the Holy Spirit that becomes active in man. The fundamental lack, the existential incompleteness in man whereby the powers of evil and death gain admission, can be healed when his true self — that merely hovers over him as long as 'sin' hardens him — incarnates in him through the indwelling of Christ and turns into the effective subject of his life.

Many passages of Paul's letters contain sequences of words reminiscent of charts. Almost all of them possess anthropological character directly or indirectly; at the same time, they make it possible to probe deeply into Providence's intention of salvation and redemption. One such chart that surveys mankind's path in immense steps is found in the eighth chapter of the Letter to the Romans. It says there: 'We know that in everything God works for good with those who love him, who are called according to his purpose. For those whom he *foreknew*

he also *predestined* ...; and those whom he predestined
he also *called;* and those whom he called
he also *justified;* those whom he justified
he also *glorified'* (Rom.8:28-30).

So long as theology fails to free itself of the preconceptions arising from the assumption of a merely personal striving for salvation, and does not rise to the broad vistas of a new, objectively spiritual world view, it will attempt in vain to interpret these mystery statements, expressed in this passage by Paul with particular matter-of-factness. Here, his thinking and language refer to mighty cycles involving the whole of humanity. The law of great and small cycles prevails, according to which the great cycles follow one upon the other but, likewise, the smaller evolutionary phases emerge one out of another within a larger cyclical pattern, repeating the past and preparing the future. Since the archetypal nature of the above five stages is the easiest to survey, we shall interpret them in the light of these great cycles in humanity's development.

On the first level, the human being is 'foreknown' by God. The deity's knowing-thinking creatively bestows existence on what it has earlier thought. Humanity comes into existence because God thinks it. The seed condition of an evolution develops where the light-filled glance of God's thought turns. God bestows *existence* on man.

In Greek, the verb of the second stage [English: predestined] is of a wondrous pictorial quality: *pro-hōrizō,* literally, 'to border beforehand.' The actual verb is contained in our word, 'horizon.' Where this celestial line runs its course, the world is demarcated. Limitation, formation enters the still unformed and limitless elements. During the first stage, human beings rested in humanity like single drops in the ocean. For them, the eye of consciousness was not yet opened to the nascent earth; they lay in fertile developmental sleep. Higher hierarchies, who protectively bore the human seed, kept vigil over men as does a mother over her sleeping child. On the second level, the individual beings start to delimit themselves. The very first beginnings of an earthly physicality emerge and bring about the fruitful blossoming of a multitude within the great unity. God bestows *form* on man.

This word for the original limitation, which in Greek shines forth with such atmospheric lightness, becomes *praedestinatio* in Latin. From this, the sombre concept of predestination or predetermination haunts the history of dogma and the churches, a history that is clouded by fanaticism and distortion on this issue more than any other. In the age of Augustine and the other Church fathers when people began to argue about predestination, the differentiating view of the human being which, at least on the emotional level, had still been present in early Christianity was already extinct. Thus arose the terrifying and depressing concept that predestination applied to the whole person including the immortal essence of his being, hence, that from the beginning of creation each man was subject to a preconceived divine judgment, one leading to redemption, the other to damnation.

It is obvious, however, that this primal delimitation and structuring only took place in and through the body. All human beings are subject to a 'predestination' inasmuch as they have had to enter earthly bodies. Originally, no burden would have been implied by this, for bestowing a form on the developing human being was in any case a necessary stage on the path to future independence and freedom of the individual. It was only through the Fall that a tragic burden entered evolution; this, however, affected all men in like manner.

The third, middle level of the five stages is designated by Paul as the 'calling' of man. Within the whole cosmic course of events, we thus come to the mission of our actual earth-aeon: within the rounds of the earth-cycle, man is to become an 'I-man.' Man receives his *name,* inasmuch as the deity calls out, but in such a manner that the one who is being called can also realize that the call is addressed to him.

Natural evolution that concerns all men in equal measure extends to this point, even though, now, the principle of individualization begins that distinguishes one person from another. Now however, the ship of humanity is steering towards rocks. Henceforth things can no longer proceed positively for everybody. The tempting Luciferic powers intervene to disturb the gradual organic process of an ego-development that is nothing less than the divine bestowing of a name. The Luciferic powers induce an impatience that causes acceleration and untimeliness. An ego-impulse emerges that cannot wait. Therefore, instead of the spiritual ego growing quietly into the threefold sheath of body, life and soul and taking up its abode in them, the development of an ego which is mere form and semblance comes about in the soul of man. This 'lower I' has a contracting, hardening and isolating effect on the human being. For this very reason, the true self remains barred and does not find the means fully to enter its sheaths.

The people of the Old Testament were the vanguard of humanity on the way to earthly ego development. Their mission was the execution of the task contained already in the name of the tribal father, Shem. 'Shem' means, 'the name.' The Semites, specifically the Israelites and later on the Jewish nation, had to represent for all humanity the stage of the 'calling,' hence the 'giving of a name.' This brought it about that here, on the racial level, through the greatest possible permeation of the physical sheath, especially the brain, there resulted a kind of secondary predestination. The body permeated the soul more than was the case in other branches of humanity but enclosed it more than was the norm. There arose the danger of a physical predestination in the sense of fixation.

By the time our age arrived, the one-sidedness of incarnation in a body manifest among the people of the Old Testament had long since extended to the whole of civilized humanity, even including those racial groups that originally availed themselves of a more pliant and open physicality. Thus, all humanity confronts the alarming question of whether they will be able to break through the barrier in order to find the fitting, broader paths, or whether the stage of the calling will turn into a dead-end for them.

In the Pauline description of the five stages, the boundary line that must be passed from the third to the next two stages is not indicated. The words of the Gospel, however: 'Many are called but few are chosen,' urgently focusses the mind on this parting of the ways.

It is not as if Paul knew nothing about this. He takes it for granted that it is known. He constantly expresses grave concern for all who, along with him, belong to the people of the calling. In moving words, he will speak of this in the following chapters (Rom.9-11). What would he rather do than help those who were the custodians of the Old Covenant to cross over the dividing line to the New Covenant!

The stage of calling is followed by the next two stages where the human being will partake of 'justice' and 'glory' — employing the traditional expressions. Just as the two levels of 'foreknowing' and 'bestowing of form' point back to an ancient past, thus those of 'justice' and 'glory' point to a far-off future. At the same time, they announce the developments brought about by Christ as 'salvation.' In the sense of Jesus' words in the Gospels, they indicate the 'choosing' that can follow the 'calling';

the further step, made accessible through Christ, but not carried out by all human beings.

1. *proegnō*	*praescivit*	existence	
2. *proōrisen*	*praedestinavit*	form	Calling
3. *ekalesen*	*vocavit*	name	
4. *edikaiōsen*	*justificavit*	justice	Choosing
5. *edoxasen*	*glorificavit*	glory	

It becomes clear from a deeper understanding of Paul's text that it is quite erroneous to interpret 'choosing' in the sense of predestination. The concept of predestination, which is alien to the Greek New Testament and could only become current through the juristic language of the Latin Bible, belongs — if it is to be retained at all — to the natural evolution of body and soul common to all humanity. The concept of 'choosing' only becomes applicable where the spirit already intervenes through Christ's redemption. 'Choosing' does not occur through an external power that proclaims this blessing over the human being. Man decisively cooperates in this. He himself must take the step to cross over the barrier. Only thereby can he be given a share in the two provinces of existence through which he develops beyond the 'man of the calling': 'the justice of God,' and the 'glory of God.'

What spiritual reality is referred to at the fourth and fifth level?

In particular, the word *dikaiosynē* must be removed from the juridical connotation to which it has become attached in the Latin terms *justitia* and *justificatio.* Although they can denote a purely human virtue as well, the English 'justice' and the German *Gerechtigkeit* [literally 'rightfulness'] are so closely connected with the legalistic realm that it is difficult to keep a juridical nuance from entering in. We noted, however, that Luther considered it necessary to emphasize this nuance by saying: 'the justice that holds good before God.'

The Greek word is completely free of any juridical connotation. It tends towards describing the state of something that has become true and genuine only after passing through a fire of purification. In German or English we use such plain words for what is meant here that one hesitates at first to employ them where the Greek language adopts such a solemn, mysterious tone. In order to describe a person who is true to his self, a German says that the person is *recht* or *richtig* — we say 'real' or 'genuine' in English. It would not be impossible to say 'the realness of God' instead of 'the justice of God.' Yet the simplistic, almost trivial sound that this word possesses leaves us dissatisfied. In modern languages, indeed even in Latin, the words that we require here are missing.

This is what is meant: when earth-creation, the human being and the three other kingdoms of nature blossomed forth from the thought and word of God, everything created was identical to its celestial archetypes. All was true and genuine. No semblance was as yet introduced into being. Subsequently, however, especially through the Luciferic temptation and the Fall, creation dropped away from the pure sphere of the creator. Everything acquired an external surface, a facade that concealed and covered up the true nature of things rather than revealing it. A principle of deception and mere semblance moved into the world. The Indian Orient calls this *Maya,* the veil that spreads over the true nature of things in regard to earthly sense perception.

Man, created in the image of God, has become distorted and unlike his archetypal appearance because 'sin' has moved his hardened sheath-nature to the fore at the expense of his spiritual nature. The true being of man is not contained in the physically perceptible human form. The redeeming effect of the deed of Christ is to undertake the rectification, the 'correction' of earth-creation which has fallen victim to mere semblance. Salvation is also a 'solving' or 'dissolving': the hard crust that distorts and suffocates the true being is beginning to melt through the fiery effect of the spirit. The new, ascending evolution must commence within man; from him, it will then radiate upon all creation. Through the indwelling of Christ, the human being can allow his true self fully to enter into his being, thereby truly coming into his own. Then the sun of 'divine rightfulness,' the original truth of the sphere of archetypes, will dawn once more in humanity and in the world.

We shall speak later of the term *dikaiosynē* from other aspects, but here only in its most general aspect. The 'justice of God' is 'the true being,' reconstituted and freed of the spell of distortion brought about by sin. The 'glory of God' additionally enters in when the 'true being,' the 'presence of the good,' radiantly reveals its bright light to the outside. Then, the extinguished light of the original state of paradise is rekindled. The new creation began through Christ's death and Resurrection: now, in a world-transforming manner, the seed of true being and glory, of emanation of the spiritual being, is at work.

Paul's text in Romans, discussed above, proclaims in its last two parts that the true being and the spiritual power of emanation which belong to God, not man, can fall to man's share when he takes the step from the 'being called' to 'being chosen.' To say man 'becomes justified' means that his 'real' being, his lost archetype, becomes present and effective once more in him. Man is 'made glorious' means that he begins to shine because the spirit in him transforms matter.

What part does man play in lifting the spell and stepping across the threshold? Luther read the answer in the Letter to the Romans (3:28) which, in the form he gave to it, turned into the classic watchword of Protestantism: 'Therefore we hold that a man becomes justified by faith alone without the works of law'(*B*). This Pauline passage does indeed contain the answer to our question. Luther has often been reproached for the fact that he added the word, 'alone,' to the Greek text for the sake of emphasis but he certainly emphasized the main point. If anything, a misunderstanding can arise because, in compliance with the Latin Bible, he says: '*without* the works of law.' Here is where the theological antithesis, 'justice through works' or 'justice through faith,' originated. Luther himself valiantly fought for this 'either-or,' and it was this that caused him to say: 'by faith *alone.*' The Greek word, *chōris,* actually does not mean 'without' but 'outside of' or 'apart from.' Paul meant to say that in man 'salvation' does not have its beginning on the moral level of action, hence on the level of personal transgressions, but on the religious level of existence where 'sin' has taken hold of the human being. The damage done to Paul's words by Luther's text lies in the merely moralistic and legalistic connotation of the words, 'become justified.' This sentence could be rendered as: 'We have realized that the true being of man is set right through faith apart from the works of law.'

But what, indeed, is *faith?* In Paul's case as well as in all the other texts of the New Testament, it is out of the question that this word could possibly refer to the attitude of holding certain dogmas to be absolute truth. An organ is addressed that belongs to a deeper level of human nature, the fundamental level of being where death as 'the wages of sin' is effective but where the longed-for 'new life' can also vanquish death.

Two factors come together in the act of faith whereby man united his being with Christ. The first and more negative one relates to the awareness that man has of himself; it is an important prerequisite and preparation for the more positive process.

When a person visits a doctor, the very action implies that he is conscious of an illness of which he longs to be cured. He has confidence in the doctor but not like he has confidence in his fellow man. He trusts in him as a *doctor.*

In the New Testament, the word for 'faith,' *pistis,* first and foremost refers to 'confidence.' One trusts in a person in whom one can 'have faith.' Faith in Christ is therefore a special relationship of trust in him. The question is whether it remains on the surface, or whether, through greater depth of conviction, it assumes clarity and finality. If the latter, then — although in a higher form — the trust must contain the qualities of confidence that a patient exhibits toward his doctor. Christ is the doctor for the fundamental sickness of all earthly and human existence. He who is not aware of this fundamental sickness and impotence of the human being, who, filled with longing for the restoration of the true being in man and the world, does not grieve over this, cannot as yet have the necessary depth of confidence in Christ. Where acknowledgement of the necessity of the event of Golgotha is not intrinsic to one's fundamental feeling towards life, the human being cannot be open and receptive to the healing effects proceeding from Golgotha.

Awareness of sin as the condition of man can also denote the primal sense of guilt. A personal sense of guilt in regard to various moral aberrations and faults, which all too easily inclines towards egotism, must not interfere and falsify this suprapersonal feeling of guilt. Personal guilt can represent a point of departure towards the latter; man, however, must not remain caught up in it. He has to expand the personal conscience that is accusing him into a world conscience. This is what Paul meant when he said that faith is effective in another domain and on a deeper level than the sphere of good or bad deeds — 'apart from the works of law.' Man *should* suffer under the consequences of his moral errors and aberrations — if not, the voice of conscience would already be extinguished in him. Yet he should not wish to be relieved of these consequences, not even by Christ. He has to demand of himself the strength to make amends on his own for the damage he has done, be it in this life or a future one. It is the total and fundamental shortcoming, the tragic incompleteness of his earthly human state, which permits him to turn to Christ as the cosmic healer.

In a lecture referred to above, 'Where do I find the Christ?' Rudolf Steiner points out:

> A person finds the Christ ... when he realizes: ... I lag behind what I am striving for in my capacity of comprehension; I sense my impotence in regard to my goals ... This sense of impotence is a healthy one for it is nothing else but the awareness of the illness, and one is truly sick when one has an illness and does not sense it. Inasmuch as one senses the incapability to rise to the divine ... one senses in one's being the illness that has been implanted in us ... When a person senses this impotence sufficiently and strongly enough, the reversal sets in ... We can sense the illness in our impotence, and we can sense the one who heals, the healing power ... Inasmuch as we sense the Healing One, we feel that we carry something within our soul that can ... arise ... from death ...[56]

Certain Protestants habitually place the greatest emphasis not only on the theme 'sin and mercy' as the fundamental principle but on it representing the substance of all Christian proclamations and confessions. If others are less vocal regarding the mystery of sin and salvation, it is easily possible for a judgment of heresy to be pronounced on them, even denying them any Christian spirit at all. Nothing, however, has robbed the Christian impulse of as much impetus as the constant misuse of something that in the deepest level of man's life represents the prerequisite for the miracle of faith.

In his Letter to the Romans, Paul put into words the objective feeling of sin and impotence in a variety of ways, but the solemn majesty which infuses his language demonstrates that silence itself speaks here; all formula-like echoing of the words is impure and inauthentic. We have already mentioned one of these passages: 'For there is no distinction; since all have sinned and fall short of the glory of God' (Rom.3:23). The original Greek text offers the classic wording: 'All are sinful; they have lost the *gloria* of God, the divinely radiating light-form.' The curse of sin lies in the fact that the paradisal light which shone around the still dreaming and sleeping human being prior to the Fall has been extinguished. Man has become darkly nocturnal as he awakened in the earthly sense. On a new level, however, as awake and free beings, humanity can attain once more to their true nature through Christ, the cosmic healer, and they can begin to shine in the *gloria* of God.

The whole seventh chapter of the Letter to the Romans is a hymn of pain, a Song of Songs of the consciousness of primal guilt:

> Made of earth substance am I, enslaved to the power of sin ...
> I do not do what I want; what I hate is what I have to bring about.
> It is not I that is the subject of my actions but the sin that dwells in my being.
> In me, in my earthly body, the good does not dwell.
> It is given to me to will the good but not to carry it out.
> The good that I will I do not bring about but the evil that I do not will.
> Now if I do what I do not want, I am no longer the subject of my actions but the sin that dwells in my being.

Subjugated am I under the duress of a law, for I who will the good must yet do the evil.
How I love the law of God in my inmost self, but in my limbs I come upon another law that wars against the law which my mind agrees with.
It enslaves me under the law of sin that is active in my limbs.
Wretched man that I am! Who delivers me from the death-grip of this earthly body! (Rom.7:14-24*B*)

We should not misunderstand these words by imagining that they were uttered by a person whose moral will failed again and again in the face of good intentions and who engaged in acts of unruliness and malice instead of the good actions he meant to do. Paul speaks on the deeper level, 'apart' from the domain of the works of the law, the evil and good deeds. In order correctly to understand this dirge over the primal tragedy of human nature, we have to think of it as resounding from human beings who certainly follow their moral intentions, who therefore do 'good deeds' in the sense of the moral law. Nevertheless, the deeper level of impotence and the sickness of sin remains below the 'good will.' Even the good deeds do not measure up to what is truly good. The power of death poisons everything. Moral weakness is simply added to the fundamental weakness of human nature. It can be instrumental in bringing about or increasing the basic feeling of impotence. Yet to remain in the domain of moral weakness would have to signify missing altogether the deeper level where the redeeming power of the Resurrected One can permeate the human being.

The fundamental awareness of sin represents the fulcrum for the positive factor in the act of faith. This consists in the paradox of *active receptivity* which is actually *the* basis for any genuine inner activity. As outer civilization progressed, the preponderance of external activities, which are imposed on man and which because of inner restlessness he believes he has to engage in, has become so oppressive that the faculty for inner activity generally has virtually disappeared. Souls are becoming weaker and weaker;

and the sum of the causes of spiritual sickness is increasing immeasurably. In a sense, one has to start from the very beginning with structuring a religious life that corresponds to modern humanity, a religious life which in faithfully practised concentration and devotion of the soul, in prayer and meditation, makes room once again for genuine inner activity. Everything that thereby comes into being in the soul is concentrated in the act of faith. Man's active share in this consists of bringing about inner tranquillity, of opening the door. In view of the isolation into which the soul of modern man has fallen, it really takes a refining fire to allow entry to the force that wishes to dwell within the human heart. The more conscious the surrender becomes, the more one turns with longing and confidence to the cosmic healer, the more one approaches what Paul understood by 'faith.' If faith is truly present, it is the beginning of Christ's indwelling in the soul of man. In the central Pauline sentence, 'Not I but Christ in me,' the first two words express the awareness of the sickness; the rest stand for the activation of the Healer's influence that brings healing for the deeper level in man where life and death struggle with one another.

It has probably never yet been pointed out with full clarity that in the Christian sphere a new world principle is denoted by the word, 'faith,' which could never have existed in this form prior to the event of Golgotha. In the context of the Pauline perception of Christ, this fact becomes eminently clear.

Faith did exist earlier, and the further back our glance penetrates into the historical and prehistorical past, the more a devout humanity emerges for us. It was, however, always a matter of faith *in* something. The deities who were the objects of religious veneration by the people of antiquity were pictured as existing outside and beyond humanity. Thus, the faith of people in their gods was also transferred to those who had to lead and teach in the name of the gods. The faith in authorities and dogmas to which a man deferred was the principle of the ancient world.

A fundamental change occurred after the death and Resurrection of Christ which remains veiled, however, to the general Christian consciousness so long as people do not yet fully participate in the Pauline advance from the Old to the New Testament.

The more faith in the Resurrected One grows genuine and strong, the less it is a faith *in* something that the human being confronts, something he may perhaps even be separated from by an unbridgeable chasm. When the human heart is seized completely by the Christ-faith, it is really no longer merely man who believes — Christ himself becomes the subject of faith; in man, *he* believes along with man. For this very reason, faith turns into a superhuman power in man by means of which he becomes capable of doing what he could not do through his own strength. This is the Christian magic of the faith that moves mountains; all earthly hindrances that could obstruct the vision of man's soul have to disappear and free vistas open up before him.

Perhaps the most important interpretation that we are allowed to make of the basic Pauline sentence: 'Not I but Christ in me' would be that we learn to say: 'I believe, but it is no longer I who believes but Christ believes in me.' Through the mystery of faith, Christ turns into the god who is inwardly present in man. And the ancient faith *in* something is replaced by the *new faith* as the new world principle: *the faith in and for itself,* the sovereignty bestowed on the human being through Christ's indwelling in his soul.

To the extent that this is the case, faith takes the place of the Law. Hence, it replaces the principle of authority prevalent in antiquity. The prophecies of the Old Testament, the document of the cultural stream of the Law that drew a dividing line between God and man, were fulfilled when Christ was born in an earthly human body. The prophecies of the European pagan nations which were part of the cultural stream of conscience were fulfilled in *faith,* the higher meaning of which is Christ's birth and his indwelling in the human soul that bestows true freedom on humanity.

In the Pauline sense, therefore, sin is lack of freedom, is bondage and serfdom; salvation is the loosening of the chains and fetters, liberation from the yoke of slavery. In his studies dealing with the terminology and semantics of the Greek New Testament, Adolf Deissmann tried to show that the word, *apolytrōsis,* the term for 'salvation,' appears in the same sense as it did in the context of the rituals and traditions of the sacred freeing of slaves. A slave could gain freedom when he was able to save up a certain sum of money; however, he could not personally buy his freedom with the 'redeeming money'; only a god could do that, on whose altar the amount had previously been placed as a consecrated offering. Following this act of buying himself off, the slave was free in regard to men; now however, he was a slave or servant of the deity that had given the redeeming money for him.

Slavery was a picture for the condition in which man finds himself through original sin and guilt. And it is always this meaning that is referred to when the words, 'servant,' or 'servitude' appear. When Paul designated himself as a 'servant,' a slave, a prisoner or one in chains, he may even have been referring in a few instances to the actual state of a prisoner in which he found himself as he wrote the letter in question. What is important, however, is that Paul no longer felt himself to be the slave of sin and death but the slave of Christ, hence, free.

The classic Messianic prophecy of the passion in the solemn hymn of the 'servant of Yahweh' in Chapter 53 of the Book of Isaiah must be understood in this sense: When the Messiah comes he will assume the shape of a servant. He too will enter the state of slavery to which man has succumbed, in order to bring about a liberation for all humanity:

> He was of all men the most despised and rejected,
> filled with pain and sickness.
> He was so despised that men hid their countenances
> from him ...
> Truly, he has borne our sickness and taken the load of
> our sufferings upon himself ... (53:3f*B*).

The Letter to the Philippians contains the Pauline text corresponding to this servant's hymn of the Old Testament. Now what had only been longing and prophecy has been fulfilled:

> Let each of you imbue himself with the attitude that was present in Jesus Christ. He possessed divine being and form, yet he did not claim for himself the likeness with God but made himself an empty vessel, taking the form of a servant. Thus, he entered human existence and in no

wise differed from other men. He humbled and lowered himself under the yoke even unto death on the cross ... (Phil.2:5-8*B*).

Paul speaks of the *kenōsis* of Christ, of his 'becoming empty,' his relinquishing of the divine content, because only by becoming fully man could he enter that domain in which the spell of serfdom to sin and death had to be broken.

By appealing to the inner courage of soul, Paul proclaimed the triumphant freedom that follows from the transition from slavery under sin to servitude under Christ. Truly, no servitude exists any longer in Christ. Had he not said to his disciples when he departed from them: 'You are no longer servants but friends'? What really was meant by this was that they had become brothers of Christ. The men who belong to him are sons of the Father, as he is. The freedom of those liberated from serfdom unfolds to sonship. This must not merely be interpreted in a human sense. The 'brothers of Christ' being *also* sons, do not merely stand *by his side*. He himself, *the son*, is within them. In the cosmic sense, the 'Son' is the creative principle of the universe. Out of the eternal *being* of the Father, the *becoming* once emerged when the world came into existence through the Logos, the *Word of the World*. Must creative sovereignty not shine forth from those men who rightfully can say: 'Christ in me'? Faith is not only a power that moves mountains but one that creates worlds.

Therefore, one of the most important principles of the Pauline proclamation is the concept of 'becoming a son.' The Greek word, *huiothesia*, literally, 'setting up as son,' is translated in most instances, following the Latin, 'adoption' with the words, 'acceptance in place of the son.' More than one realizes, this juridically experienced concept dampens the vitality of what Paul expressed. The original word contains a jubilant call like a fanfare which denotes an inner process of liberation, not a lame, legal declaration of freedom.

There is hardly any subject where the Greek and the Latin Bibles exhibit a more gaping difference. At the beginning of the Letter to the Ephesians, the whole of which is a solemn cosmic hymn of praise, the human word arises in adulation and gratitude to Christ, 'who from the beginning of creation has formed and predisposed us for the sonship that we experience through him and for the union with him': *prohorisas hēmas eis huiothesian dia Iēsou Christou eis auton.* By comparison, the Latin version with its concepts of predestination and adoption sounds dry and prosaic: *qui praedestinavit nos in adoptionem filiorum per Jesum Christum in ipsum,* 'he who predestines us to be adopted as sons ...' (Eph.1:5).

Confronting this motif, even Luther's tempestuous, reformatory courage was unable to keep in step with the daring of the Pauline insight and language. When Paul marked human beings in whom salvation was becoming effective as 'sons of God,' such passages were high-points of his jubilant perception of Christ and freedom. This was too daring for Luther and he therefore translated it as 'children of God,' even though Paul, who was also familiar with the state of being God's child, was referring to something inalienable when he spoke of the 'sonship.' Hence the translation by Luther in the eighth chapter of the Letter to the Romans reads: 'For all who are led by the Spirit of God are children of God' (Rom.8:14). How completely different it sounds in Paul's words: 'In whom the Spirit of God is active as an impulse of life: Sons of God are they!' (*B*).

A few verses later, Paul speaks of the fact that a fulfilment is intended not merely for humanity's longing for salvation but also for that of the remaining kingdoms of created beings. It must proceed from man, just as the cosmic tragedy of the Fall proceeded from humanity. Man dragged all creatures with him into the depths when, following the insinuation of the tempter, he reached for the 'I' too soon. The rapid hardening process which thereby occurred in the human being spread to all earth existence. When the illusory 'I' ceases to be mere empty form, however, and receives into itself the true spiritual 'I' that is united with Christ, then the life-giving spirit, which loosens all that has hardened, rays forth from man onto all creation. The dynamic force whereby salvation is raised from the level of man's soul to the cosmic level can become conceivable in terms of the sonship, the Son's creativity that becomes active in man. In Luther's translation, profound emotions are evoked : 'For the anxious expectation of all creatures awaits the revelation of the children of God' (Rom.8:19). Here was the window through which was glimpsed not only the suffering but the future redemption of creation. The original Pauline text conveys more. It has a kindling quality, and the spark of the courage of faith turns into cosmic confidence:

> For you were not placed under a spirit of slavery that would drive you from one fear to the next; you have received the spirit of sonship ... I consider that all difficulties and sufferings of this present age are irrelevant as compared to the Spirit's radiant power of light [glory] that is to be revealed to us. All around us, every creature waits with great longing for the sons of God to begin to shine among men ... For the breath of freedom shall pass through the kingdoms of creation, too, like a tempest. The tyranny of transitoriness will come to an end. As the spirit-sphere turns light, bondage will be replaced by the freedom which goes forth from the children of God (Rom.8:15-21*B*).

15. Resurrection and Transformation

For Paul, the message of Easter was the very essence of Christianity: 'If Christ has not risen, then our preaching is in vain and your faith is without content.' 'If Christ has not risen, your faith is a delusion and you are still under the spell of sin' (1Cor.15:14 and 17*B*). Did the development of Christian life and thinking follow this basic orientation? Did the concept of resurrection become the leading thought for ritual and theology?

In fact Protestantism, the Christian stream that appealed to Paul most emphatically, believing it was taking an important step towards the future in his name, has been so negligent in the development of an Easter attitude and mood that from its own ranks it has to tolerate the reproach of being a mere Good Friday Christianity.[57] Admittedly, in its one-sided focus on the cross and blood of Christ as the source of all salvation, the theology of Protestantism could appeal to Paul. For at the beginning of the same letter that culminates in the mighty Easter hymn, Paul coins the formula, 'the word of the cross,' *ho logos tou staurou,* (1Cor. 1:18) and he does attribute man's salvation ('justification,' setting right) to the power that proceeds from Christ's blood (Rom.3:25 and 5:9).

The question of the relationship between Good Friday and Easter, between Christ's death and Resurrection, must therefore be particularly well suited to lead us into the very heart of Paulinism. Through Paul, we should find an answer to the question that Protestantism in fact cannot truly answer. If redemption was brought about through the cross and the blood of Golgotha, why did the Easter event have to follow?

Whether we stop at the Good Friday mystery or, proceeding from there, find the way to the Easter fact and hence, as Paul said, discover the decisive central truth, depends on whether or not we can free ourselves from Old Testament thought in trying to comprehend the riddle of Golgotha.

In the final analysis, there are two different ways of picturing the redemptive effect of Christ's blood spilled on Golgotha. One proceeds from the Old Testament concept of the judgmental deity: in order to cancel the immeasurably great debt that humanity has incurred but cannot settle, Christ sacrificed himself and died the death of atonement. With regard to Christ's blood, the very fact that it has been spilled is significant. This manner of interpreting the event of Golgotha has dominated ecclesiastical theology so strongly that the only remaining viewpoint of Christ's resurrection has been to see it as a divine affirmation of what had preceded it, but not as a separate, new, and certainly not *the* fact of salvation. In Protestantism particularly, owing to its inability to free itself of the juridical morality of the Old Testament Law, the facts of Easter have become overshadowed by Good Friday.

The second view was cultivated less in the official theology of the churches but in those groups accused of heresy by the Church, in esoteric Christianity's quiet circles. This view considered the special quality of the blood that streamed on Golgotha from the wounds of the Crucified One. Borrowing the well-known words from Goethe's Faust, 'Blood is a very special fluid,' their attitude could be expressed by saying, 'The blood of Golgotha is a very special, sacred thing.' This, however, is not meant in the sense of the medieval adoration of relics. In contrast to the first, juridical concept, this second view could be termed an 'alchemical' one. Because the sacred blood flowed from the wounds of the Crucified One, a fountainhead has sprung forth in the world from which a formerly nonexistent power can be drawn. And there is room for the concept that through the event of Easter — this time not in the blood but in the body of Christ — a new substance, a cosmic and curative medication has been incorporated into earth existence. What Paul stated concerning the redeeming effect proceeding from the death and Resurrection of Christ can be comprehended simply and solely from this second viewpoint.

In order to advance further, we have to develop what has already been broadly outlined concerning a Pauline anthropology. Paul was far from seeing in the Christ-event a miracle that enters, as it were, from outside into humanity for their salvation. Christ is not a stranger. Even earlier, through all the aeons of creation, he has been closely connected with the being of man. He was and is the 'god of man,' meaning, the genius, the higher individuality, the spiritual ego of humanity as a whole. In his human incarnation, he turns into the 'new Adam' by making use of that human being as his soul-sheath in whom the heavenly archetype of man has been preserved. In his earthly embodiment, Christ involves himself, however, in the full tragedy of humanity's earth-evolution since the Fall. On the one side, we must not see in Christ an alien, divine being who comes to the aid of humanity out of a form of divine arbitrariness. On the other side, Christ Jesus is not simply *a* man. He is *the* man. Among all human beings who are mere fragments because of the sickness of sin, he is the complete man. In him, the being of man as originally conceived by the creative powers makes its earthly appearance. Here, no being walks on earth, enclosed within itself and incapable of allowing the spiritual, overshadowing 'I' to enter in. The I of Christ, which encompasses the 'I' of all humanity, has crossed the barrier and has fully entered into incarnation. Humanity on earth was facing the danger of being cut off from future evolution. Now, through an act of salvation, an act of infinite divine love, it comes about that humanity's own future approaches in pure and undiminished form and becomes present.

The incompleteness of man's being is not only due to the fact that, initially, in place of the true I, merely an I-form could develop in man. If the true I, the spiritual part of man, could enter fully into earthly existence, it would not simply dwell in the sheaths, in body, life and soul; instead, since it is fire-related spirit, it would spiritualize them. In the process, the three lower bodies would become receptive to a higher, spiritual trinity that would permeate and fill them.

Through the work of the I on the soul-body (astral body), spirit-permeated soul develops which in anthroposophy is called 'spirit-self' (ancient name: Manas). Similarly, spirit-permeated life, 'life-spirit' (Buddhi) germinates in the life-body (etheric body). Spirit-corporeality, 'spirit-man' (Atma), develops in the physical body.

It is through this sevenfold configuration that we can begin to survey and perceive the total human image.*

I

soul-body	spirit-self
life-body	life-spirit
physical-body	spirit-man

Now, it would be incorrect to say that because of the influence of original sin no genuine effects of the I exist in man as yet. In prehistoric times, the tragic attachment to mortality came about through the premature Luciferic impulse to egohood, but evolution did not simply stop because of this. The time arrived when, in the further course of creation, the ego should have been born in man in a proper and organic manner. Indeed, that came to pass. The human being began to turn into an I-being, not only possessing a lower, egotistical I, but also in such a way that, henceforth, individual, ego-imbued work by man on himself became possible. This occurred during the first centuries of the Christian era.† Still, the normal I-impulse encountered tragically disturbed conditions and therefore had to make its appearance in a dangerous, double-edged way. The infinite wisdom of Providence therefore saw to it that when the ego began to move into the human being in the course of natural evolution, the helping and healing power was already present on earth through the Christ-event. This is why it is possible, even at our stage of evolution, for man to perform certain activities of spiritualization by exercising his own faculties. He can affect his soul-body in a regulating, disciplining and ennobling manner and therefore bear within his being embryonic beginnings of the 'spirit-self.' It is then,

* Anthroposophy also describes man as a ninefold being inasmuch as it distinguishes an additional three soul members between the three sheaths and the upper spiritual trinity.

† More accurately, around the year 333, the median of the central or fourth post-Atlantean epoch which lasted approximately from 747 BC until AD 1413.

however, that he encounters the tragic shortcoming. As long as he is dependent merely on his own, human competence he has no influence on his etheric and physical bodies. This is not only the case because the full development of 'life-spirit' and 'spirit-man' is a concern of future stages of evolution. In the condition in which the two lowest members of the human being have been since the Fall, the human I encounters an adversary for which it is no match — death!

So far as the physical body is concerned we are constantly made aware of our impotence by ageing, illness and death. As a perishable corpse, we return our physical body to the earth. It is no different in the case of our ether-body; but owing to the materialistic dulling of our thoughts this process eludes our consciousness to a large extent. Anthroposophy describes how in death, three days after discarding the physical body, we have to give up our life-body as well, which then dissolves into the general universal ether. Following ancient convictions of faith, we frequently do speak of 'life after death' in a matter-of-fact way. But what sort of reality is that if the life-forces which were available to us during our earthly sojourn do not endure after death? This is one of the questions which show that, by adding the supersensory to our world view, the riddles do not become less profound; they become greater.

It is only to the extent that we penetrate and spiritualize our etheric body with our I during our earthly life, only to the extent that 'higher life' and 'life-spirit' have blossomed in our life-body, that we have the right to speak of 'living after death.' Our human life-bodies are as perishable and mortal as our physical bodies. 'Eternal life' germinates only in the life-forces that have been transformed by the spirit into 'life-spirit.' We can therefore sense that if it were possible for us to reach our physical body as well with the spirit-power of the true 'I' — even slightly — then something imperishable could begin to wrest itself from the perishable.

Where our own power reaches its limits, is there a power that can help us and can carry us upward to the sphere of eternal life and imperishability, to the realm of life-spirit and spirit-man which, after all, are members of our own higher being?

We have to enlarge our anthropological orientation still further to begin to comprehend the mystery of Christ's blood. The fourfold structure of man's being incarnated in us today, namely physical body, life-body, soul-body and I, is mirrored in the share that the four elements, earth, water, air and fire, have in our physical body. In reality, only the solid components of our physicality, the earth element in us, are our physical body. The fluid element, which is many times greater in us than the solid, represents the physical basis for the activity of our etheric body; the fluid element is the bearer of life. We have to count as part of our body the rhythmically expanding and contracting air-being in us. The air we breathe is not an alien element that merely touches our nature as it passes through. It serves us as the foundation and bearer of our soul element; our astral body weaves in it. Finally, the warmth element is part of our body as long as we breathe and live. It is not merely a condition measurable by degrees of temperature; it permeates us in an essential manner. The warmth-being that we bear in ourselves is the element of our I.

In passing, we should mention that a completely new physiology and medicine must emerge from this extremely simple observation of human life as compared with the view prevalent today which mistakenly sees as the body of man only what lies ultimately on the dissecting-table after the removal of warmth and air and the larger part of the fluid content.[58]

When we view the structure of the human being in this manner, the effect of the inner on the outer nature, of the soul-spiritual on the substance of the body, is not as impossible as materialistic thinking would have us believe. It is, of course, out of the question that we could have a direct, transforming influence with our thoughts and emotions, not to mention our will, on the solid components of our body, for example, our skeleton. But does our warmth-organism, which we bear within as the blood-heat, not react to what occurs in our soul? Do we not blush or turn pale along with a momentary increase or decrease of temperature when certain feelings of shame or fright move through our soul?

The I, destined to work on our sheaths, has as its physical element the warmth-body. If it could learn consciously to affect this in a transforming manner, that would be a starting point to influence indirectly the whole nature of the physical body. In addition, when we consider that the warmth-basis of the I-organization manifests in the blood-heat, a mental image can be projected that reveals something of the wisdom and benevolence of Providence. In the human blood, water and fire, life and spirit encounter each other. The fire-effects that the spiritual 'I' would be capable of exercising on the world of the earth elements would be transferred in the blood directly to the life forces, that is, to the etheric body. Thereby, the blood would become the bearer not merely of the life-body but also of the budding life-spirit. In the blood, the transformation of mortal life into immortal life would take place. Here we catch a glimpse of man's primal outline in its completeness as conceived and intended by the creative powers. The secret of the blood begins to be unveiled to us; in it, temporality and eternity, death and life, matter and spirit reach out to each other. Yet the spell of impotence, of sin and death, hold sway most obviously in the blood. It is here that man encounters the limits of what he is capable of, confined to his own strength.

It is from here that we may dare direct our glance toward Christ as *the* man. He who spoke the words, 'I came to cast a fire over the earth!' was himself a fire. The I of all egos flamed in him. The inner, human aspect of the 'three years' consisted in the fact that the threefold sheath of body, life and soul was spiritualized through and through by the burning fire of his compassionate love so that, here, whole aeons of humanity's future were condensed into one brief space of present time. On earth, even that part of the human being became directly present which otherwise would still hover over the incarnated human being in the heaven of the future. The revealed soul-element was human and yet more than human: pure spirit-self streamed out when Christ spoke to human beings or laid his hand on a sick person. The life forces that stream along in the blood, but here were exposed to the sacred fire of God, ceased to be subjugated to the death forces. Life-spirit moved into them. The miracle of transformation even took hold of the physical body and, in it, brought about the quiet growing of the 'spiritual body' of spirit-man.

Christ's victory over death was not attained in one moment.

The struggle of transformation filled the three years. When spirit-alienated humanity nailed the unrecognized Christ to the cross, there streamed from the wounds no mortal life but higher, immortal life, life-spirit. Henceforth, 'immortal life' existed for humanity. Beginning at Easter morning, the Resurrected One could reveal himself in the form of spirit-man. From the perishable body, the redeemed, imperishable nature had been wrested in the struggle with the power of death. In the 'spiritual body' of the Resurrected One, the seed of a new earth was germinating. Victory over death was now attained on all levels of human existence; the dual fountainhead of new life and new existential substance sprang forth from the hard rock-formation of the earth. Because of Good Friday and Easter, a healing element exists in the mystery of the blood and the body of Christ whereby humanity's future has been redeemed.

The human being can now receive the healing medicine even into his body and blood. It is the mystery of faith that man can be seized with love for Christ in the warmth of his heart and blood. Through this confidence in the healer, Christ himself can turn into the remedy. Christ is present in the soul of the person who opens his being to him in this manner. In man's blood-heat, also, burns the fire of Christ; in man's blood, the blood of Christ flows along. Thus, the higher life that transcends death originates in man, too. And through the seedling of an imperishable new body, a coming transfiguration arises.

The inconspicuous groups of esoteric Christendom primarily nurtured and venerated the profound mysteries of human blood and Christ's blood in the sign of the Grail. The ancient, sacred vessel in which Joseph of Arimathea caught the flowing blood under the cross was the symbol and image of the human heart in which the blood of man receives into itself the blood of Christ. When, in the gathering of the Grail companions, the raised chalice began to take on a rosy hue and the dove of the Spirit descended upon it so that healing and nourishing effects went out from the Holy Grail, this reflected symbolically what took place in the heart through the act of faith.

The Grail theology becomes discernible in Paul's letters if we have the courage to understand the basic Pauline concepts in an anthropological sense and to relate them to the corresponding concepts of modern anthroposophy. The vocabulary that Paul utilizes does not consist of such nebulous, imprecise concepts as could be implied following the traditional interpretation. A magnificent spiritual exactness and concreteness is apparent everywhere in Paul's words.

The term in the New Testament which gives the most appropriate interpretation of the sphere of the 'spirit-self,' the higher, spirit-permeated soul, is 'peace'; for inner tranquillity and harmony fill the soul when the spirit-self germinates in it.

The essence of Paulinism can be surmised from the fact that the conceptual formulation used to indicate the 'life-spirit,' stands fully in the centre. Here, we are dealing with the key word for the redemptive effects that proceed from Christ's death and Resurrection. It is the concept of *dikaiosynē,* the true existence that has been set right, for which the misleading word 'justice' is customarily used. The lowly sphere between body and soul, the life streaming in and through the blood, is the arena of decision. The blood and the life-body of man were distorted by the Luciferic temptation and Fall. When the soul began to be linked too closely to the physical body, 'death became the wages of sin.' Life's adversary rose up and caused the human being to be mortal. Yet where death has gained entry into the being of man, there the battle against death is waged as well and the victory over it won. Here, the Lord of Life himself intervenes. When, encouraged by his power, the soul now links up with the spirit rather than the body, true immortal life can stream once again into the restricted vestige of life which has remained to man. He then no longer descends merely from the old Adam. He descends from the new Adam as a spirit being that brings forth life ('living soul — life-giving spirit,' 1Cor.15:45).

Finally, when Paul turns to the mystery of the 'spirit-man,' the 'spiritual body' that is gaining a share in Christ's Resurrection, he makes use of the light-filled term, *doxa, (gloria* in Latin), glory, transfiguration. Where this mystery is blossoming, the spell of darkness which death exercises on the earthly nature of man is broken. The human being begins to shine; on a new level, he reattains the radiating light-nature which was Adam's nature prior to the Fall. The 'glory of God' that was lost long ago is granted anew. Just as the natural, mortal etheric body forms and induces growth in the physical body during the early years, and later maintains and supports it, so the life-spirit forms and builds a radiant light-form into the earthly body which is becoming infused with spirit.

Thus, the two words in the New Testament, *dikaiosynē* and *doxa,* as well as the corresponding anthroposophical terms, 'life-spirit' and 'spirit-man,' designate the spheres of higher human existence from which natural man is separated to such an extent that through his own resources he is unable to aspire to them. Humbly, however, he may grow into them through the grace of the deity, when, through faith, he merits the right to say: 'Not I but Christ in me.' Here, we grope our way towards the redeeming effects that can become available to man through Christ's death and Resurrection from the dual source of the blood on Golgotha and the new Easter body.

In the eighteenth century, motivated by his alchemical search for traces of spirit in earthly substance, Friedrich Christoph Oetinger, the theosophical prelate from the province of Swabia, dared write a *Theologia ex idea vitae,* a 'Theology Based on the Idea of Life.' Paul's proclamation in fact was already such a doctrine of life and we can discover it afresh in our age for a renewal not only of theology, but of our world view in general.

The term, 'life,' plays a more significant role in the whole of the New Testament than is commonly realized. The reason this is not given much attention is in no small measure due to the fact that in modern natural science, even in biology, the concept of life is referred to only incidentally and prosaically. We do not grasp it exactly, for, on the one hand, we are incapable of defining life on the basis of inanimate matter; on the other hand, we do not work up to a recognition of life as the sphere of the super-sensory which most closely adjoins the realm of sense perception.

In regard to the books of the New Testament, people are even less inclined to interpret the concept of life in an exact sense. They think they understand it in a religious sense but do not realize that thereby they deprive it of all reality, leaving merely an indistinct symbolism. In some passages, solemn resonances have at least endured which deeply touch the soul, for example, in the Gospel of John: 'He who believes in me ... from his body shall flow rivers of the water of life' (7:38*B*), or when John's Revelation refers to the 'tree of life' and the 'stream of life.' In countless passages however, the term, 'life,' generally falls through a mesh of thoughts like a rhetorical embellishment. Who even notices, for instance, that this word occurs with great emphasis four times in the seven Johannine 'I-am words': 'the bread of life'; 'the light of life'; 'the resurrection and life' and 'the way, the truth and the life'? In addition, other most significant Johannine passages are: 'In him was life ...' (John 1:4); 'because I live, you will live also' (14:19); 'the word of life' (1John 1).

In reading Paul's letters, this word is passed over even more readily. It is precisely here that everything depends on whether we can begin, once again, to interpret it in its exact meaning. It is that term which is quite closely related and connected with the Pauline keyword, *dikaiosynē,* the true existence that has been set right. When Paul refers to 'life,' it is almost always the 'higher life,' the 'life-spirit,' the life of Christ in which the life of man can recover from the sickness of sin and death.

> Since, therefore, we have now received true existence through his *blood* (have been restored again, made right again [in RSV version 'justified']) ... we shall be saved by his *life'* (Rom.5:9f*B*).
>
> If, because of the Fall of one man, the reign of *death* has been established, will those who receive the abundance of grace and the gift of true existence (of justification or 'righteousness') not share that much more in the rule of *life* through the one man, Jesus Christ?' (Rom.5:17*B*).

The verse directly following can be particularly illuminating for us. In Luther's translation it sounds somewhat like this: 'For as by the sin of one, condemnation came over all men, so, through the justice of one, the justification of life has come over all men' (Rom.5:18; [RSV: 'For as by one man's disobedience many were made sinners, so by one man's obedience many will be made righteous'].) In the formulation, 'justification of life' or *justificatio vitae,* the juridical element proves itself to be absurd. Here we have clear confirmation that it is more a matter of life processes than a judicial criminal proceeding. *Dikaiōsis zōēs* means 'adjustment of life forces,' 'restoration of the true life' which has been distorted through sin and death. 'For as through the Fall of the one, all men have been drawn into the descending direction, so the lighting up of higher existence in the one will bring to all men the restoration of true life' (Rom.5:18*B*).

The word 'life' moves through Paul's letters like a firm, golden thread. Even the passage in his letter to the Galatians, which contains the basic Pauline formulation of Christ's indwelling, holds such a reference to life: 'It is no longer I who live but Christ who lives in me' ['I live, but in reality I no longer live; the Christ lives in me' *B*] (Gal.2:20). In this context belongs the quotation from the Book of Habakkuk (2:4) which Paul refers to in several passages in order to show that he stands with the ancient prophetic vision in regard to the most central of his insights. Luther who, above all, appealed to this sentence again and again, formulated it in this fashion: 'The righteous one shall live because of his faith' [RSV version: 'He who through faith is righteous shall live'] (Rom.1:17). This is what is meant: Faith is an inexhaustible fountain of the new, true life for the one who has found the way from the world of semblance into that of true being.

It is important to see how the term, 'life-spirit,' coined by modern anthroposophy for the spirit-permeated etheric body, occurs in an exact sense in Paul's texts:

> For the law of the *Spirit of life,* which has taken on form in Christ Jesus, sets you free from the law of sin and death ... If Christ is in you, although death dwells in your bodies because of sin ... the Spirit will ... cause a new fountain of life to spring forth from you which proceeds from true being *(dikaiosynē)* (Rom.8:2, 10*B*).

Finally, we could actually convey Paul's jubilant exclamation in the letter to the Philippians, 'Christ is my life' (Phil.1:21*B*) [RSV: 'For me to live is Christ ...'], in the following words: 'With Christ, my true higher self has moved into me and with it the imperishable life that is liberated from death.'

The essence of Christianity is illuminated by the fact that through genuine, faithfully cultivated Christian religious life, effects of permeation and transformation by the spirit are called forth not merely in man's soul but more especially in his *life forces.* General religious feelings remain in the soul and do not penetrate into the regions of life and body which are particularly in need of salvation. The ego-force of Christ, the mystery of the sonship, breaks the spell and bears man from the sphere of the merely personal to the supra-personal dimension. In order to emphasize this, we shall quote a paragraph from Rudolf Steiner's book, *Occult Science: an Outline.* What is said there concerning the educating and transforming power of religious life does not specifically refer only to the domain of Christianity. It is clear, nevertheless, that it applies mainly to this. The fact that the element of rhythmic repetition is emphasized shows that reference is made to the regular cultivation of a religious life founded on ritual and prayer.

In the specifically anthropological chapter, 'The Essential Nature of Mankind,' a description is given of the way in which the three higher spiritual members of man's being start to come alive through the efforts of the 'I' in the three sheaths, soul-body, life-body and physical body. Dominion over the astral body is attained by the 'I' to the extent that it is successful in exercising a regulating, ordering influence upon lust and desires, joy and pain. If the seed of the life-spirit is to germinate in the etheric body, this transforming influence must be broadened to include character and temperament, hence, something that to a much greater measure is of a permanent nature in the human being.

> Indeed, this change is slow when compared with the change in the qualities described above. The relationship between the two kinds of changes may be compared with the advancing of the hour hand of a clock in relation to the minute hand ... The 'I' is not working upon the astral body if the human being simply gives himself up to pleasure and pain, but if the peculiarities of these soul qualities change. Likewise, the work extends to the ether body if the ego applies its activity to the changing of its traits of character, of its temperament, and so forth. Also

> on this latter change every human being is working, whether he is conscious of it or not.
>
> The strongest impulses producing this change in ordinary life are the religious ones. When the I allows the impulses that flow from religion to act upon it again and again, they form within a power that works right into the ether body and transforms it in much the same way that lesser incentives of life cause a transformation of the astral body. These lesser impulses of life, which come to man through study, contemplation, ennobling of the feelings, and so forth, are subject to the manifold changes of existence; religious experiences, however, imprint upon all thinking, feeling, and willing a uniform character. They shed, as it were, a common, uniform light over the entire soul-life ... Religious faith, therefore, has a far-reaching effect upon the whole soul-life; its influence becomes ever stronger in the course of time, because it works by means of constant repetition. It therefore acquires the power of working upon the ether body. The influence of true art has a similar effect upon the human being ... From this it is evident that hidden within man there is another member of his being that the I gradually develops. This member may be called the second spiritual member, the *life spirit.*[59]

Even before the hour of Damascus when he was still a Pharisee, Paul had emphasised the idea of the resurrection. Spell-bound by his orientation toward a 'judgment day,' he still considered the resurrection of the dead an act in the future drama of the cosmic judgment that would break in upon the earth along with the coming of the Messiah. Subsequently, he was impelled to realize that what he was seeking in the future had already taken place. Now however, he also understood that it was not merely a single, completed historical event. For him, the mystery of resurrection moved, not into the past, but from the future of 'judgment day' into the constantly alive present.

The event of Good Friday and Easter was not merely a divine miracle through which the believer's relationship to God was changed. It was primarily a human event. It was a miracle of grace in so far as a highest, sacred goal of human evolution, fully realized in the present, turned into an earthly fact. Above all, it was a miracle of the divine will of love, considering that humanity had not only lagged far behind on its path but in a tragic sense had strayed from it. Henceforth, the right direction had once again been made available to humanity and with it the full certainty concerning the attainability of the goal. In man, the event of Golgotha and Easter was continued. Along with the mystery of the body and blood of Christ, the secret of the new blood and the new life, of the life-spirit and the spirit-man, flowed as a stream of life through the course of time.

Paul wanted human souls to place themselves in this stream when he said that we must learn 'to suffer with Christ, to die with Christ and to be resurrected with Christ.' He did not merely suggest that we should devoutly contemplate the passion, dying and arising of Christ in the way it is reported by the Gospels as historical fact, in order to produce vivid images and reflections of these events in our soul. We can and should make room for Christ himself in our soul, so that he, and with him our true I, can cause the stages of salvation to come true in the soul over and over again, thus allowing the trinity of the higher human being to germinate and develop: 'peace,' 'justice,' 'glory'; namely, the 'spirit-self' in our soul; the 'life-spirit,' the 'eternal life,' in our blood and life; the transfigured light-body, the 'spirit-man,' in our body.

The Resurrection of Christ as an ever-present, developing life process is nothing else but the mystery of transubstantiation. In bread and wine it radiates forth onto the waiting natural elements. The secret of the chalice and wine in the sacrament consists in the fact that the 'blood of Christ,' the life-spirit, becomes effective not merely through the devout faith of the Christ-filled 'I' in the blood and heart of man but also in the wine and chalice on the altar. And in the bread, the 'glory of God,' the sun-radiant power of spirit-man shines forth just as it can shine forth from the redeemed human being. On the one hand, by the power of the Resurrected One, transubstantiation or transformation is the constant spiritualization of earthly substance, bringing about now what is to come to pass in the future. On the other hand, on the new level, it is the restoration in man and creation of the paradisal archetype which still shone in the glory of God. Therefore, the word that Paul used for 'transformation,' *katallagē,* became unrecognizable because, beginning with the Latin Bible, people saw it as expressing a return to origins. Here too, the juridical nuance of the Old Testament entered in. Hence, the Latin word is *reconciliato,* which Luther consequently translated as 'reconciliation' since it also corresponded to his idea of God as the angry judge.

In the classic paragraph in Second Letter to the Corinthians (5:18-20), Luther's Bible says:

> ... from God, who through Christ reconciled us to himself and gave us the office that preaches the reconciliation. For God was in Christ and reconciled the world with himself, and reckoned not their trespasses against them, and has established among us the message of reconciliation ... So we beseech you in Christ's place: Be reconciled to God ...

Such verses have doubtless evoked worthy religious feelings in the sense of personal consolation and encouragement. Nevertheless, it must be recognized today that this occurred at the expense of the cosmic and supra-personal vista contained in the original text of this passage.

In the preceding part of the same chapter, Paul speaks of the new spiritual body and his utterances rise to hymn-like greatness, culminating in the sentence which cannot be diminished by any sort of translation: 'Therefore, if any one is in Christ, he is a new creature; the old has passed away, behold, the new has come' (2Cor.5:17*B*). The emphasis is not merely placed on the word, 'new,' but above all on the word, 'creature.' It is not just man who becomes new. Inasmuch as the renewal takes hold of man and extends even into the physical body — this has just been the theme earlier — a new, overall creation begins in him. The new earth, the new cosmos, has found its germinal beginning in man who has absorbed into himself the secret of the body of Christ, the Resurrection.

'Transformation' is not such an emotive word as 'reconciliation.' Above all, in an era where the most progressive Christians have eliminated ritual and sacramental life and neither want to know nor understand any longer anything of the secret of 'transubstantiation,' the word has become unpopular if not unknown. It is a term, however, designating a most important spiritual fact and it will bring unselfish, objective breadth of vision into the religious life once our age becomes acquainted with it again.

The words that Luther translates as: '... and gave us the office that preaches the reconciliation,' sound completely different in the original text. What Paul said here has been adjusted by Luther to the conventions of Protestant preaching. Literally, it reads, 'the office of transformation.' Even the Latin Bible says nothing of 'preaching'; it has *ministerium reconciliationis.* Even if we were to retain the word, reconciliation, in accordance with the Latin, it would be clear that what this word stands for should not be preached but performed and carried out. The character of 'office' is unmistakable. We are dealing with the priestly office which in Greek is termed, *diakonia.* The very essence of priestly activity is the carrying out of the transubstantiation. And it is just this that is meant: 'and entrusted us with the ministry of the transformation.' Correspondingly, where Luther translates: '... and has established among us the message of reconciliation,' we are not dealing with a theme concerning a proclamation and a sermon. 'Word' here refers to 'Logos,' hence it is not merely the word by means of which we communicate something to each other, but the Word through the utterance of which something happens, just as the world came into being at creation's beginning.

The chapter in which this passage is contained could be called the Song of Songs of the sacramental continuation of the Easter mystery. Some of it is presented below in a rough attempt at translation:

> We know that when the dwelling shatters in which we live on earth as in a tent, we nevertheless have a building out of God, a house not made with hands, eternal in the heavens. It is to this that our longing and our desire is directed: to be covered over with this hut that is bestowed on us from the spiritual worlds so that, at the moment of death, we stand before the eye of the deity clothed and not naked. For as long as we live in the earthly tent, we have to struggle hard: we do not want to be unclothed but

be covered over so that the mortal in us may be completely received into the true life. The deity who has created us for this goal has bestowed on us the gift of the firstborn, the spirit (which transforms matter) ...

The love of Christ obliges us that we adhere to the guideline: If the one has died for all, all have therewith died. He died for all, that the living henceforth might live no longer for themselves. In future time, their life is a component of the life of him who has died and risen for them.

Therefore, in time to come our knowledge of man is no longer based on the physical. And even if we had known Christ himself in physical form, this knowledge would now no longer be decisive. Who therefore is in Christ: the new creation begins in him. The old has passed away, the new has come. All this the Father God brought about who, in Christ, transforms us back to him and has charged us with the priestly ministry of the transformation. God worked through Christ and, transforming the world, raised it back to himself. He no longer looked upon the fact that humanity and the world had fallen, and in our midst he inaugurated the Creative Word of transformation ...

Therefore, we beseech you in Christ's place: Strive toward God by means of the transformation. For our sake God has made him whose consciousness was not darkened by sin into a component of the world of sin, so that in him we might become members in the world of true being, in God. (2Cor.5:1-5, 14-21*B*).

16. Second Coming: Apocalyptic Elements

As a Pharisee, Paul had been an eschatologist. In a fervently impatient state of soul, he had been looking forward to the future event which he viewed as the last decision over all earthly and human existence: the 'last judgment' on 'the day of reckoning.' The light of Damascus had drawn away the curtain which had veiled for him the secret of his own lifetime. What he had partially longed for and partially dreaded as a future happening was already present. And how different it was from what he had pictured! The light broke in upon him not as a world-destroying flash of lightning; to his opened eye it streamed forth from the whole earthly environment as a wholly new but gentle radiance. Yet it had not ceased being of the future because it had entered the present. It could not be more than a faint budding of future possibilities. It now became important whether human beings would be available as planters and nurturers of this seedling of light; whether they would offer their souls as the fertile ground in which the young crop could grow and bear fruit. For then it would be possible for humanity to journey towards an era of a new Christ fulfilment, a new approach by Christ. And in the active acquisition of the Christ-seed, or in its soulless disregard, world history would turn at last into the cosmic judgment, the final differentiation between good and evil.

As the 'untimely birth' of humanity, Paul was predisposed even in his physical and soul constitution for a future epoch rather than the condition of consciousness prevalent in his age. This was why he had rushed forward so impetuously beyond the present into a dramatic future as early as in the period preceding the Damascus event. Now it became evident what a wonderful potentiality Providence had thereby implanted in his soul. Whereas the first Apostles had been contemporaries of the three years in which the Christ-being had shown himself in physical incarnation, Paul, prepared by destiny, was the contemporary of the new condition into which all earth-existence had been transported by the Easter event. This was the case because, prophetically and ahead of time, Paul even then actualized in his nature that future age when the Christ-seed will have come to full fruition.

The word in the Greek Bible to which reference is made when 'Christ's return' is mentioned, does not mean, 'return,' strictly speaking. There is no reference anywhere in the New Testament to a return in the sense of a 'second coming.' Much misunderstanding has come about because people have nevertheless made use of this word and concept. The Greek word, *parousia* means 'presence' in the sense of a powerful state of being present. It does not simply refer to an unarrived future, for which mankind can only wait. Rather, this word is dynamic; it refers to something which, while it already exists, is in the full sense yet to come — in that, although now present, it is still veiled. After all, it can be veiled because men are blind to it; but then it can find its *parousia* as the scales fall from their eyes and the blind see.*

Owing to his nature and destiny, Paul was predisposed and prepared to experience and proclaim Christ's *parousia.* He was thus its first witness. At the hour of Damascus, the curtain was torn away from him and he was endowed with sight; he beheld the new, Easter-like condition of earth-existence. Yet he saw not only the first rudiments of transformation and the radiance of transfiguration; there appeared to him also the bright sun as it would shine forth in the future of humanity. To open the eyes of others to the light that actually surrounded them even then, had henceforth to be the substance of his whole life and activity. He could do that, however, only by leading them on to the path where, in their inner being, they would discover the strength to pierce the scales that kept their eyes from seeing.

* The concept of a 'return' became popular in times when people no longer adhered to the original Greek text but followed the Latin Bible. It translates *parousia* with *adventus* or 'arrival.' In regard to the new Christ-revelation, the word *advent* strongly appealed, for it reawakened the ancient advent-expectation that imbued humanity when they had looked forward to the first coming of Christ. This was the reason, however, that the knowledge that Christ cannot be lost and remains present because of the event of Golgotha, receded into the background. Instead of 'arrival,' Luther here said, 'future of the Lord.' The word, 'future,' was for him not yet an abstract concept of time, however. For him, it was still pictorially perceptual and referred to something that is coming. He therefore occasionally translated the word *parousia* verbally with, 'when he comes.'

Owing to the lead he had gained over humanity through his destiny, Paul was a fundamental prophecy become living fact. The truth he uttered in the present was at the same time an unveiling of the future. Therefore, all genuine Christian experience would be of a prophetic nature from now on. To be a Christian signified to develop future states of human existence and consciousness ahead of time. This was why it was Paul's fervent concern that the prophetic gift be cultivated first and foremost of the special talents blossoming in the congregations under the powerful presence of the Spirit. This gift contained no vestiges of ancient, ecstatic mediumship; it was of a purely future nature. It awakened in those persons who enkindled the spark of Damascus; who experienced the indwelling of the Christ-ego in their human ego and were thus transported into a future state of humanity's evolution. If they succeeded in awakening in themselves the future condition of humanity they could view the present from the perspectives of the future and were able to decipher 'the signs of the times.' The gift of prophecy, recommended so emphatically by Paul as something to be cultivated, was an apocalyptic talent that proceeded not from a diminution but from an intensification of awakened consciousness.

This is why the word, 'apocalypse,' which in the canon of the New Testament scriptures indicates the step beyond the Pauline letters to the Johannine revelation, belongs to the preferred vocabulary of Paul. This word vividly depicts the 'unveiling' in the most exact sense of the word. The future element is ever-present here, no longer in a spiritual world separated from the sense world. Now its transfiguring radiance of life germinates in all earthly things. Heaven begins to permeate the earth anew. Yet the coarse semblance which is but the surface conceals the sphere where true being approaches. Therefore Paul also calls the *parousia* of Christ, Christ's dawning revelation in the earthly domain, an 'apocalypse.' The longing of those who know of the indwelling of Christ in the human soul is no passive waiting for something that comes from outside and without our having a hand in the matter. It is the inner activity which in itself contributes to the 'apocalypse,' to the 'unveiling of the Lord.' It is nothing less than a struggling for one's own inner awakening. Thus, Paul turns to the Corinthians as to those who in active longing 'await the apocalypse of the Lord' (1Cor.1:7*B*).

In the end, the visionary encounter with the newly revealed Christ will lose the character of an isolated, supersensory experience completely, and will make possible and to some extent cause an inner awakening and intensification of consciousness. This supersensory perception will no longer merely belong to isolated individuals, but will be widespread among humanity. The sun then arising will illuminate many worlds. The revelation of the Christ-being signifies the illumination of the whole spiritual sphere. This was what Paul meant when he announced to the Thessalonians, for example, that divine peace would pervade their souls when the 'apocalypse,' the 'unveiling of the Kyrios together with the angelic kingdoms serving him,' takes place (2Thess.1:7*B*).

With the death and Resurrection of Christ, a new ascending development was introduced not merely for humanity but for all earth existence. Even so, the continuing Fall and descent has by no means been checked. Only those elements of earth-creation will be snatched from the abyss which can be included in the Christianization that begins in the individual person. Thus, ever since the Easter-victory by Christ, the battle rages on. The wider the circle of light grows, the more powerfully the forces of darkness appear on the scene. Since the event of Golgotha, the history of humanity and the earth is inwardly determined by the increasing tension between the coming of Christ, the *parousia,* and the coming of the Antichrist, the 'apostasy' (2Thess.2:3), the maelstrom of the abyss. Ultimately, this battle will continue until the end of the earth-aeon. Then the differences between good and evil human beings will culminate in a cosmic event of the greatest magnitude. The 'new earth,' the part of earth-existence that is united with Christ and transformed through him, will rise like a phoenix from the ashes of cosmic conflagration. Wresting itself free of the weight and power of death, it will develop into the new form of our planet that will shine like a sun. All that has remained unchanged shall be eliminated like a lunar dross and will stay under the law of weight and death.

Paul refers to this in the mighty resurrection-chapter of the First Letter to the Corinthians (1Cor.15). At Easter, a trend has begun that henceforth streams through all future development. With the mystery of transformation a power has entered earthly evolution that causes imperishable life to germinate. Just as a mortal generation of men descended from the first Adam that increasingly came under the spell of death, so the new Adam turns into the ancestor of a humanity that is moving toward resurrection. Through the sovereignty of spirit over matter, this future generation will bring the seed of a new, indestructible life to ever greater unfolding. Finally, the time will come when Christ's Easter-victory over death is repeated on a telluric, cosmic level that includes all humanity. Death as the last enemy, in so far as it is a cosmic power, will be overcome (1Cor.15:26).

On the path leading from Golgotha to the end of the world, there will be an evolutionary stage on which the decisions of the 'last days' will even then cast their reflections. Thus, the age when this occurs will assume a decidedly eschatological, apocalyptic mode and a character of preliminary decision. To a special degree, this phase of evolution will be under the sign of the *parousia,* the 'Second Coming' of Christ. Paul must have felt more at home in that future age than in his own. Being a contemporary of this future, namely the era of the consciousness soul, Paul became the admonishing herald of the *parousia.*

Eventually a critical culmination of the mighty battle will take place. On the one side, the secret of 'the Day of the Lord' will become powerfully manifest. Yet this will not be a matter of an outwardly visible, datable day. There will be 'daylight' in the supersensory realm, the etheric domain, the sphere of the life and formative forces. An era is drawing to a close in which the nocturnal powers, the forces of darkness, had the upper hand. A break of day is approaching; a higher daylight begins its reign. It will be around the time indicated by ancient Asian prophecies that speak of the transition of a 'dark age' lasting five thousand years, the Kali Yuga (3101 BC until AD 1899), to a 'light age.' The hostile forces that employ the cold skills of human cleverness in order to make the dark wall of the material world, with its fascinating riches and technological possibilities, even more dense and impenetrable, will then also reach a climax. Initially, the Antichrist will have the advantage. Though he and his hosts are not of 'flesh and blood' (Eph.6:12) but of supersensory nature, the Antichrist will carry out his magic in the sense-realm, thus bringing humanity under his spell of deception and delusion. The developments and deeds of Christ, on the other hand, occur in the etheric realm and can pass mankind by unnoticed. Fascinated by what will ultimately bring calamity after calamity, destruction upon destruction, men are in danger of sleeping through the unique event that is taking place for their sake in the spiritual domain.

This is already indicated by the ancient prophecies which state that the coming of the Antichrist will precede that of Christ. Paul follows up on this. In the etheric realm, Christ with his sunrise is already present. Among the human beings incarnated on earth, however, the adversary attempts to pre-empt Christ by doing everything to divert souls from the sphere in which the decisive miracle takes place. Paul touches upon profound riddles of destiny when he says that it corresponds to the will of Providence that humanity would pass through an era in which the tendency towards deceit would reach the heights of its activity and power: 'God sends upon them the fully unfolded power of deception' (*B*), or as it drastically says in Luther's translation: 'Therefore God will send upon them *powerful errors* to make them believe in falsehood' (2Thess.2:11). In human striving for knowledge, as well as in cultural and social practices, the magic of delusion brings it about that people consider as truth merely the material surface of the world and humanity. Along with the world of the supersensory, they deny the reality of the sphere that is the stage of the *parousia*.

The Antichrist, the Satanic-Ahrimanic power of the lie that appears with the pretension of truth, does not itself enter the realm of physical visibility. Yet where it gains influence over human souls, it finds expression in a certain type of man. Paul calls him 'the man who brings about the chaos' *(ho anthrōpos tēs anomias,* RSV: 'man of lawlessness'); through such a man, the 'magic of chaos' *(to mystērion tēs anomias,* RSV: 'mystery of lawlessness') finds expression. Its last subject is the 'chaos in person' *(ho anomos,* RSV: 'the lawless one'), 'the spirit of chaos' itself (2Thess.2:3, 7f). Here, Luther's Bible fails to reach the spiritual terseness of the Pauline text. Proceeding from the Latin wording, it equates the concept, *anomia,* with 'sin' and 'wickedness': namely, 'the man of sin,' 'the secret of wickedness' and 'the wicked one.' Yet, here we are by no means dealing with the 'moral evil' which these terms designate. The reference here is to the 'objective evil' which comes to expression as the power of the 'intellectual Fall'* in thinking, when man's thought no longer follows anything but the laws of icy cleverness. Has this one-sidedness not penetrated on a broad basis the development of science in the last centuries? And from the domain of thinking, objective evil has taken hold of all areas of modern civilization and turned into 'social evil.'†

Literally, the Greek word, *anomia,* means 'lawlessness.' Yet how this word resounded from the lips of Paul, the opponent of the law! Paul made an assault against the autocracy of the Mosaic Law because it holds man back in an immature, unfree state. He did so with greater vehemence because he was aware of the law of the Spirit and of freedom which in constant creative vigour originates from the 'inner giver of the law,' the 'Christ in us.' Therefore, more than against the Law of Moses, Paul fought against the power that aims for the abolition of all manner of lawfulness. Indeed, he fought for just this reason against the external law because he prophetically foresaw how it prepares the way for the disintegration of all laws and the spirit of chaos.

What Paul referred to has become almost tangible in our age. Today, the stream of the external law has reached, on the one side, modern political and social legislation; on the other, the scientific and technological utilization of natural laws. Does it not become more and more evident day by day that an unceasing

* Title of a lecture series by Rudolf Steiner.

† The difference between evil in a personal, moral sense and a cultural, social sense was clearly pointed out, for instance, by the Russian philosopher, Vladimir Solovyov.

process of dissolution and confusion is taking place in regard to all traditional order in those areas where the law we wish to work with is on everyone's lips? People try to bestow order on modern life by constantly enacting new laws but are forced to experience how the binding force of the law is lost by reason of the countless laws enacted which in the end are no longer observable. And where we believe we have arrived at special triumphs of the human spirit in the discovery and technical utilization of laws operating in material existence, we are even now working with forces of destruction that really elude our grasp.

In our age, the stream of the external law is turning upside down. From behind the mask of all the talk of law, the countenance of the one whom Paul declared the spirit of dissolution of all laws, the lord of chaos, leers at us. The Antichrist camouflages his intention for absolute disintegration by leading humankind to the point where, the more noticeably the foundation of all traditional order is shaking, the more they will talk of law and order. Is not the disappearance of respect in human souls an evident effect of modern civilization? 'The adversary exalts himself against all that is known as divine and worthy of adoration, and in actuality *he* takes his seat in the temple of God' (2Thess.2:4*B*). The various church denominations have long since been on the defensive. They do not realize that all attempts at merely preserving the old are in the long run hopeless, the more they leave intellectual investigation and social development to the secular world. Thus, instead of doing battle for human thinking and the scientific world conception against the Ahrimanic power, they themselves allow the achievements of the anti-Christian intelligence to gain entry even into their own domain.

The epoch for which Paul, as herald and precursor, proclaimed the first culmination of the battle between Christ and the Antichrist, must be characterized by mighty catastrophes through which an old world falls into ruin. It is not true, however, that the mighty destroyer, the lord of chaos, will be at work in this solely against the will of the benevolent powers. His activity is tolerated by God just as shadow is admitted by light. The ultimate cause of such catastrophes is to be found in what is occurring in the spiritual realm, extending even into the etheric realm of the earth's circumference. Behind the walls of the senses' semblance, above humanity, Christ's *parousia* is attaining a new degree of powerful reality. Something is happening that can be illustrated allegorically by what holds sway between earth and clouds. The humidity arising from the ground remains invisible until the air is saturated with it to a certain degree. Then it becomes visible in the developing cloud formations. When it increases even more it condenses still further and falls as rain back to the earth.

Likewise, the advance of the *parousia* continues quietly for a long time. Eventually, however, it begins to make itself felt even in the earthly realm owing to its dynamism. Much that was thought to be unshakeably established becomes unsettled; nations experience internal and external turmoil. The light itself is not revealed as yet; still, in the shadows it casts out of the clouds on to the earth, the changes and movements it undergoes can be deciphered even now. In the foreground on earth, at the sense-periphery of the world, ample latitude is given the destroyer, the sinister powers of chaos. The Antichrist is permitted to show his arts and, in the fullness of time, to come to grief. He makes use especially of the opportunity he has been given to spread the veil of illusion over everything. Men's thinking and perception is led astray; he uses the fear and cowardice of souls to tie them to the sensory world. He knows that his power is curtailed and broken wherever human beings penetrate to a true insight of what is taking place. Christ's *parousia* can nullify the *parousia* and magic of the Satanic power; like a mist, the Kyrios can disperse the spirit of chaos with the 'breath of his mouth,' with the spirit of his word, 'by his appearing and his coming' (2Thess.2:8). This, however, does not happen without the cooperation of human beings. When men make their souls the stage of Christ's *parousia,* thereby not only transforming their being but also their consciousness, then, through them, Christ is victorious over Ahriman.

The apocalyptic imagery with which Paul speaks prophetically of the Christ-event behind the veil of the sense-world suggests, in some passages, that in a single, outwardly datable, future moment the decisive conjunction of events will occur. When he was still involved in the eschatology of the Pharisees, even Paul himself had the idea that the coming of the cosmic judge on Doomsday would have to break upon the world as a tremendous, external catastrophe in which the graves would open and the dead would come forth for the Last Judgment. The words he now uses may in some ways resemble those customary in Pharisaic circles; yet he now tears away the curtain and reveals processes of development and decision in the midst of which we find ourselves even today. They are filled with dramatic tension and move towards decisive culminations. As they did for Paul at the noon-hour of Damascus, they will issue like lightning and be fulfilled in the future first for individual human beings, later on for whole groups. They will continue until the end of the earth.

In particular, the words from the fifteenth chapter of the First Letter to the Corinthians suggest the misleading conception of an instantaneous world-event to those who picture what is said in an outward, physical sense: 'Lo! I tell you a mystery. We shall not all succumb to the sleep of death, but we shall experience the mighty change in ourselves' (*B*). '... and this, suddenly, in a moment, at the time of the last trumpet' (1Cor.15:51f). This is what is meant: the mighty transformation, whereby a person who is united with Christ attains a share in Christ's Resurrection and the mystery of 'spirit-man,' powerfully comes over individuals, whether they are in their earthly body or in the kingdom of the departed. The essential power of the *parousia* then grips them in such a way that they are lifted beyond space and time. In the Greek version, the words that Luther translates as, 'suddenly, in a moment,' are both not concepts of time. The first one, *en atomō,* ('in the atom') is a concept of space; it refers to space that has shrunk down to a final, no longer divisible measure. Likewise, the word, 'moment' is meant to indicate a seeing in the final, smallest span of the course of time. Man's being is lifted out of physical existence into what transcends space; in his consciousness, he arises into what transcends time. Thus, as it emerges from space and time, man's nature is taken hold of by the transforming power of Christ's *parousia.*

If anything, an indication of a certain phase of future evolution is implied in the words, 'at the sound of the last trumpet.' Paul makes use of the same pictorial concepts here that form the substance of John's Apocalypse. But this accord with the last book of the Bible demonstrates that the resounding of the last, seventh trumpet by no means signifies 'the last day' in the sense of a final, decisive end. In the first place, the sound of the seventh trumpet accompanies the unfolding apocalyptic drama of a whole world-epoch. (In Revelation, the descriptions of the spiritual events that call forth the sounding of the seventh trumpet extend from the middle of the eleventh chapter to the first part of the fourteenth chapter.) In the second place, the sounds of the seven trumpets are followed by the outpouring of the seven golden bowls from the temple of heaven, lasting through seven cycles of time.

As in the Apocalypse, where the seventh trumpet is mentioned, Paul also points to a definite future period. It is the age that Paul experienced in advance through his nature, namely, our present age of the consciousness soul in which the battle between Christ and the Antichrist is entering upon its culmination. The First Letter to the Thessalonians contains an apocalyptic date similar to the one in the First Letter to the Corinthians which leads us further: 'For the Lord will reveal himself from the spheres of heaven: when the watchword sounds, when the archangel raises his voice and the trumpet of the spirit resounds' (1Thess.4:16*B*). Here Paul refers to *Michael.* The figure of this archangel likewise appears in John's Apocalypse when the seventh trumpet resounds. There, the battle reaches a climax: Michael fights against the dragon for Christ, the spiritual sun; he attains victory in heaven. On earth, the dethroned adversary separates into the twofold beast that arises from sea and land. It is the task of those who are united with Christ to continue Michael's celestial struggle on earth and particularly to withstand the attacks and misdirections of the cold, Satanic-Ahrimanic power, the 'objective evil.'[60] If, therefore, we try to relate the apocalyptic dates of Paul's letters to a definite historical epoch, we arrive at the Michael-age that began in the last third of the nineteenth century. We are now approaching its decisive culmination.[61] The need for a 'watchword' in our time was something that Goethe already proclaimed meaningfully in his apocalyptic *Fairy Tale of the*

Green Snake and the Beautiful Lily. When the words, 'The time has come,' sound for the third time, the great sacrifice is due and the transformation begins.

Paul himself never tired of proclaiming his awakening call to human souls. He let it resound in the most trumpet-like manner in the Letter to the Ephesians (5:14) by making use of an ancient mystery-call and relating it to Christ:

Awake, O sleeper!
Arise from the dead!
Christ shall illumine you!

With these words, the hierophant roused the disciple in the mystery temples of antiquity from the deathlike temple-sleep which had lasted for three days. Transformed in being and consciousness, the initiated person then rose from the tomb. Now, however, what a transition has occurred in humanity's inner history! No longer aloof from life nor subjected to authoritative, hypnotic soul-guidance, the disciple finds illumination. In the midst of life, without any forceful interruption of normal consciousness, as his own hierophant, the seeker has to discover the path to Christ. The waking call is not meant to awaken him from a temple-sleep but from the sleep of the senses. Without relinquishing his normal consciousness — which in regard to the higher world is a form of sleep — the human being must awaken to higher consciousness. It is both wrong and lazy-minded, indeed even a form of cowardice towards the supersensory world, to interpret Paul's apocalyptic calls merely in an emotional sense, as an appeal addressed to men's good will. The awakening is not meant simply as a symbol. Having been illuminated by the light of Damascus, Paul struggled with all his might to call to life in his listeners an ordered training and elevation of the cognitive consciousness. He wanted to be humanity's guide and herald on the path from mere sense perception and intellectual insight to the perception of the supersensory and the recognition of the spirit. It was his wish that spirit man would awaken and open his eyes in earthly man.

Following the Ephesian verse of awakening, when he invited those whom he was addressing to put on spiritual armour for the

Michaelic battle — waged not against flesh and blood but against the demonic powers and forces of darkness — more than a sum of good and devout intentions was meant by the words, 'girdle of truth,' 'breastplate of righteousness' and 'helmet of salvation.' Through inner activity, through faithful, transforming work on his will, emotions and thinking, the human being can and should do his part so that the Christ-I works alongside his true self, clothing him as in a coat of armour with an invulnerable body that consists of his own higher members of being. Here, the word translated as 'breastplate of righteousness' by Luther is of prime importance. The true, spirit-permeated life forces that have been wrested from death — the life-spirit that causes the lost, divine archetype to shine forth once again in the human being — are what cause man to become invulnerable even beyond death. The life-spirit encompasses not merely a higher existence; it is the bearer of an illumined consciousness. By means of it, the human being becomes integrated, not only unconsciously but with full consciousness, in that ether-sphere, woven of higher light and life, where the *parousia* of Christ takes place.

Paul makes the song of spiritual awakening, in which he addresses the Thessalonians as 'sons of light and sons of the day' (1Thess.5:5), culminate in the assurance that the grace from above will come to aid their striving and will bestow on their being, on spirit, soul and body, the higher integrity, the purified archetype, whereby they can be true witnesses of the coming of Christ (5:23).

The words of Paul's call sound as if they had been addressed to our age:

> You know the urgent secret of the age,
> how the hour calls us even now to awaken from
> sleep.
> For salvation is come nearer to us now
> than it was in the beginnings of our faith.
> The night is far gone, the day is at hand!
> Let us then cast off the works of darkness
> and put on the armour of light.
> Woe to us if we do not measure up to the new day!
> (Rom.13:11-13*B*).

When Paul had to defend himself in the initial stage of his 'trial' in Jerusalem before the Sanhedrin, he turned the fanatical argument, prevailing between the Pharisees and Sadducees, to his advantage. When he announced that, like the Pharisees, he believed in the 'resurrection of the dead,' the feuding parties among his accusers attacked each other instead of jointly pronouncing the sentence of condemnation on him. In reality, however, the view of the Pharisees who saw the resurrection of the dead as an important act in the Messianic drama of the end of days, was not too different from that of their opponents who, as politicizing materialists, disavowed such a resurrection. After all, the idea that the tombs will open and the dead will come forth awakened to new life, when the Messiah appears to carry out the Last Judgment, could only become current in an age when, along with the final perception of the supersensory, sympathetic understanding for the further destinies of the departed was extinguished. The materialistic idea had come about that the dead dwelt in the graves and could emerge from them again at a given time. Long since, an impenetrable veil had been woven before the spheres of the supersensory world in which human souls actually sojourn after death and continue on their way. His Damascus experience, in refutation of his earlier Pharisaic eschatology, had also taught Paul a different view of the 'resurrection of the dead.' Henceforth, he knew through his own experience that man need not wait until he dies in order to gain a share in the Resurrection of Christ. Indeed, Paul learned that if the human being does not attain to at least a germinal share of this during life on earth, it will not be bestowed on him after death. Because the veil concealing the world of the departed became increasingly dense with the approaching materialistic world view, the conception of the 'resurrection of the dead' and the 'resurrection of the flesh' in particular, which was derived from Pharisaic eschatology, was retained as a concept far into the history of Christianity. For Paul, on the other hand, this view was thoroughly outdated — though he appeared to agree with it before the Sanhedrin — for, brilliantly illumined, the spheres of the spiritual world had opened wide to his soul.

Paul's living knowledge concerning the paths of the departed becomes evident in a special way when he refers to the continuing passion of Christ. He revealed to the congregation of Thessalonica as an important secret that those who experience the growing light-presence of the Resurrected One while dwelling in the earthly body have no advantage thereby over the departed. The souls of the dead who are united with Christ need not await a distant future resurrection in order to behold the radiant figure and sphere of Christ. To them, the sunrise in the spiritual sphere is made known perhaps more readily than to earthly men because they themselves are in this sphere.

A similar mystery had taken place earlier when, at the hour of Golgotha, the sun had turned dark on earth. When Christ died on the cross, his followers had been cast into the dark abyss of sorrow. He, on the other hand, entered the realm of the departed as a bright light. The secret of 'Christ's descent to hell' lies in the fact that while earthly humanity still sorrowfully awaited the dawn of Easter, the Easter-sun was even then rising in the sombre realm of the shades. The human souls who had passed through death prior to Christ's incarnation, but due to their Messianic longing and presentiment harboured within themselves the seed of a future connection with Christ, were thus able to become witnesses of Easter earlier than the women at the tomb and the Apostles in the Cenacle.

Thus, the dawn of Christ's second coming is already made known to the departed souls who are prepared for Christ and united with him, while the scales still cover the inner eyes of Christians on earth. And when the culmination of the new Christ-presence approaches; when, in the midst of collapsing old world orders, the Antichrist exercises his suggestive art on earth and human beings begin to decipher the approach of the light at most from the dramatically revolving shadows, then many souls who have passed through death are gathered devoutly and expectantly around the Christ-sun in the spheres of the spirit. Likewise, many unborn souls who are on the verge of descending to earthly incarnation bring along in the inmost core of their being an afterglow of this celestial witnessing of Christ.

> For this we have to say to you as a word of the Lord himself, that we who still live in an earthly body shall

> have no advantage over those who have died when the *parousia* of Christ emerges more clearly. When the watchword and the cry of the archangel and the trumpet of the Spirit resound, he, the Lord, will reveal himself from the spheres of heaven. Then the dead who are united with Christ will attain the first share in the resurrection; after that, we who dwell on the earth shall be caught up in our souls with them into the etheric world, freed of the spell of the earth's weight, to meet the Christ, and we shall remain inseparably united with him. (1Thess.4:15-17*B*).

Paul himself who had been sent forth by the light of Damascus to cast 'the day of reckoning' and with it the future of the Christ-humanity into a permanent present, lived in a world that had begun gently to radiate under and behind the external light of day and night. This radiance shines through all the words of his letters, be they gentle or stern, loving, threatening or admonishing. The earth appeared transformed to him; through what had occurred on Golgotha it had quietly begun to turn into a sun.

We can gain an understanding for the hidden dimension of this golden radiance when we pay heed to the word, *doxa* or *gloria,* which refers to glory in the sense of the radiance of transfiguration, and at other times to the soft, solemn sounding of a bell.

As if it were a fifth element that is added to earth, water, air and warmth, Paul teaches us to experience all around us the sphere of *doxa,* the spirit's traces of transformation shining forth in matter. This glory is more of the future than of the present, but our future-orientated spiritual will turns into the organ with which we behold it even now. We can learn to breathe in this wafted auric light of transformation. In the same chapter of the First Letter to the Corinthians, where Paul calls the Resurrection the alpha and omega of the Christian faith, he pictures a person who asks, 'How are the dead raised? With what kind of body do they come?' (1Cor.15:35). The answer is not imparted in conclusive concepts. Our glance is directed outward to nature. In each and every thing, nature is an allegory. How wonderful it is when the plant receives a new physical form from the seed; in what infinitely rich and varied manner the miracle stands before us in all the kingdoms of creation! Would this abundance be so eloquent, so like a teaching of revelation, if there were only physical bodies? 'There are terrestrial, physically visible bodies, and there are celestial, supersensory bodies' (1Cor.15:40*B*). And it is only the influence of the celestial bodies, brought into play on the terrestrial bodies, that makes the wealth of forms in nature so transparent for the deepest cosmic secrets. What our eyes behold is not yet the sphere of existence where the resurrection takes place. That is only seen by eyes able to perceive in the present what lights up of the future. Along with the etheric realm, the sphere of the *doxa,* the gently glowing light-seeds and light-forms, opens to such eyes.

> The light form of the celestial bodies is one, and the glory of the terrestrial bodies is another. There is one glory of the sun, and another glory of the moon, and another glory of the stars; for star differs from star in its glory. In this realm, the resurrection of the dead takes place (1Cor.15:40-42*B*).

Hidden from physical senses, the Easter-garden, the new earth, grows and blossoms in and between the things of the old creation.

However, the transfiguring radiance neither takes hold of earth existence from outside nor by itself. Even through the mystery of Golgotha, the new earth is not simply present here and now. Nevertheless, it has come into the world as an inspiring possibility.

In man alone, the miracle of resurrection and transformation can begin. The hearts of those who permit Christ to dwell within them are the centres of radiation for the light that is able to turn the earth into a sun. This is why creation so anxiously waits for the transfiguring light to begin to shine forth from those human beings who have turned into Sons of God (Rom.8:19ff).

Through the light of Christ's *doxa,* Paul's eyes had been opened before Damascus. Yet this had not come to him from outside. 'It pleased God to reveal his son *in* me' (Gal.1:15f*B*). He thus realized that it is the mystery of Christ's indwelling of the human being that is the source of the transfiguration and transformation of the world.

> The mystery hidden for ages and generations has now been made manifest to those who sanctify themselves to it. To them God chose to make known what infinite riches of glory, of transfigured light, can go forth from this mystery among the nations of the world. It is the 'Christ in you,' the transforming glory's fountain of hope' (Col.1:26f*B*).
>
> We speak of the wisdom of God* that rested hidden in the mystery. Before the aeons of our world, this wisdom was already formulated by God as the seed of the spirit-light that is meant for us eventually. None of the mighty ones of this world have ever known it. For if they had, they would not have nailed the Lord of the spirit-light *(doxa, gloria,* glory) to the cross (1Cor.2:7f).

Along with the approach of Christ's *parousia* to humanity's level, those who are united with Christ draw near the secret of life-spirit and spirit-man, hence near the sphere of the *doxa,* the radiance of transformation. After all, the glory of Christ can become effective in the world only when it finds its centre of emanation in man. We must understand the mystery of the 'inner second coming of Christ.' Human beings either begin spiritually to radiate light or they bypass the miracle of light that is present and growing in the etheric surroundings. Then they are at the mercy of the shadows of decline which themselves are intended as admonishing signs to perceive the light.

> We feel ourselves to be citizens of the heavenly spheres from whence we await the coming of our Lord Jesus Christ. He will transform our degraded corporeality and will implant in it the body that is like his glory, his light-form (Phil.3:20f*B*).
>
> For you have died, and your life, your true self, is yet hidden, united with Christ, in the spiritual worlds. But when Christ who bears your life, your true self, in him, is revealed, then you also will be revealed with him and will begin to shine in the spirit-light (Col.3:3f*B*).

* Here, the exact word used by Paul is *theosophy.*

One of the most beautiful passages in Bible translation belongs here. Although he only proceeded from the Latin text, the magic power, which like an atmospheric element rays forth from the word *doxa* in Paul's letters, induced Luther here to leave aside all his concepts reminiscent of the Old Testament, and to interpret Paul's words in a genuinely Pauline manner — with the poetic nuance which pervades Paul's letters in all those passages where reference is made to the light-body of Easter:

> And now, with unveiled countenance, the Lord's clarity is
> mirrored in all of us, and we are transfigured into the
> same likeness from one clarity to another (2Cor.3:18).

17. Congregation

The period when Paul and the other Apostles were active fell at the beginning of the first three centuries of early Christian life — a specially blessed time. During those three hundred years humanity passed through an exceptional state similar to that which had held sway, in surpassing greatness, during the three years between the Baptism in the Jordan and Golgotha.

The miracle of the three years did not consist so much in the effects on the small group of people surrounding it; but in a single human figure as divine embodiment and realization of the total human condition. Something was present on the earth that had never existed before and will never exist again in the same way. The miracle of the early Christian centuries was a metamorphosis in the growth of this special new beginning. The divine being, who at the same time is the I of all humanity, grew beyond the boundaries of a single incarnation tied to space and time, pouring himself into the development of a new human community. He sought for a larger body, in which individuals and groups of people were the limbs and organs, intimately formed into a unity through a higher, common bloodstream.

The miracle of becoming a congregation in which a higher, invisible factor intervened so tangibly was felt with a special, elemental force in the age of Paul and the Apostles. This was not merely because they had shared in person in the events of the three years, and therefore enjoyed special esteem and authority. A momentum and vigour was developed by the accompanying supersensory event in its nascent state. Wherever the Apostles went, particularly Paul, a higher entity went along. They could have been compared with people who walk with powerful magnets across fields containing a number of metals, so that everywhere the iron is sorted out as if by itself. There were people everywhere, ready and filled with expectation, who relinquished their former ties in favour of the new community in order to become limbs of the developing body. Christ's earthly biography continued beyond the life of Jesus in the origination of the first Christian congregations and in the special blessings and gifts bestowed on early Christian life.

This grace-filled growth nevertheless had to confront a painful limitation that nobody suffered under more than Paul himself. The ancient principle of community which had been linked to the physical kinship of blood obstructed the new communal development; particular among those who came from Judaism it proved to be a nearly insurmountable obstacle. How valiantly Paul struggled to win from among his own race a multitude of people for the step that he himself had taken! After all, this was a nation that was in possession of the most sacred promises, and like no other could look back on a divinely guided history. In Chapters 9 and 11 of the Letter to the Romans, he joined issue with the tormenting riddle of destiny inherent in the failure of this, his particular concern and wish. The difficulty was not just that those Jews who adhered to the Messianic faith were blind and obdurate in regard to the fulfilment of their own longing. Rather, the problem was that these people were bonded to their ethnic group by the closest of blood relationships. Only with the greatest strength of mind were they able to be receptive to the miracle of the new process of communal development.

The Israelite-Jewish stream had been the nation of the 'calling.' As the representative and vanguard of all humanity, they had led the way for an ego-form to come to birth, which, upon Christ's arrival, would be capable of receiving into itself the higher content of the I. For this, it had been necessary for the whole folk group to undergo the evolution toward earthly egoity. By means of the strictly enforced law of intermarriage with near relations, which among culturally advanced nations elsewhere had long since ceased to be a matter of concern, a racial community came into being that was so tightly segregated as to be unique in the human race of that time. This caused the physical bodies to be formed and patterned through and through for egoity. Out of these particular blood relationships, the physical form required for his human incarnation could be made available to the Christ-being who was moving towards embodiment. Then, however, the tragedy became evident that was the shadow side to the development of the chosen people. Owing to the rigid, formative force indwelling them, the souls incarnated at that time as Jews lived in bodies which made it infinitely more difficult for the soul to open itself to the higher content that had now appeared. It was even harder for these people to become receptive to the early Christian miracle of community. As a result many of these souls were pushed back even further into themselves and imbued with hate. The higher substance that was shaping a body for itself in the development of the community was, indeed, the very entity that for three years had constituted the divine I in the bodily sheath of Jesus of Nazareth.

The Jewish people then living were not socially minded in the sense of the newly appearing principle of spiritual kinship or relations by choice. The special structure of their bodies predestined them to the ties of blood relationship. When they came together either within the family or the sternly segregated ethnic group, they were a unity; as such they even arrived at significant, inspired thoughts. Among strangers, on the other hand, each one of them was cast as if by a spell into his own egoity. And even though many in time found individual contact with the Christ mystery, the communal miracle of the early Christian era was hardly ever more than a slight intimation in the Jewish Christian congregations.

When Paul was made the Apostle of the non-Jewish, 'heathen' nations by the power that was developing its community from above, this coincided with the possibilities existing among the people then incarnated. In Asia Minor as well as in the flourishing, younger European nations, the people, devoted to the deities of nature, had more porous bodies and therefore more childlike, open souls than the members of the cultural stream of the Old Testament which had become alienated from nature. Here, the receptivity and sensitivity existed for a possible indwelling of a higher spiritual power in both the individual and the community. Yet here a different one-sidedness and danger had to be reckoned with which was the direct opposite of the one in Judaism. The souls bore less of the stamp of the ego-nature, and therefore were more susceptible to a chaotic activity of atavistic, ecstatic forces.

The purely doctrinal, moral piety of the Jews, which lacked nearly all ritual, caused too much formalism; the abundant ritual life of the pagan nations, on the other hand, had in some areas brought about too little structure. On the one side, strong repression held sway because of a gloomy sternness which in many cases appeared fanatical and assumed an Ahrimanic nuance; and on the other, there was a danger reaching into the Luciferic extreme. In so far as it was a matter of inaugurating and cultivating congregations, this was the situation Paul encountered in his apostolic work. By and large, only the non-Jewish world offered open doors to him. Yet, for some time, world Jewry had no longer been composed exclusively of people of Jewish descent. Usage of the Greek language extended to the wording of the scriptures of the Old Testament and their synagogal application. Even among those born as Jews, this had brought about a lessening of the bodily and mental rigidity and a closer resemblance to the cultural attitude of the nations inhabiting the northern coastline of the Mediterranean. Paul's never-faltering hope of finding an audience in the synagogues was therefore to some extent justified by the prevailing situation. After all, Paul, too, had emerged from Hellenistic Jewry.

In one regard however, Paul's struggle for those of Old Testament background found fulfilment in much greater measure than has commonly been realized. When studying the Pauline journeys, we noted the great importance of the Essene communities as points of contact and departure for the origin of early Christian congregations in all the lands to which Christianity had initially spread. Although the religious attitude of the Essene circles differed fundamentally from that of Orthodox Jewry, and particularly from the beliefs cultivated among the Pharisees and Sadducees in Jerusalem, the Essenes were nevertheless important representatives of world Jewry at that period. They were open to the miracle of early Christian congregational developments, for they had always avoided the deliberate cultivation of the blood community.

The miracle of early Christendom — that the body of Christ was beginning to embrace all humanity — did not simply descend by itself as a gift from heaven into human relationships. It was by no means enough for the Apostles to find open hearts for their proclamation. Something special, a transforming process, had to occur if souls wished to make a connection with the exceptional state existing at that time. It was the 'baptism with fire and the Holy Spirit,' prophesied by John the Baptist and promised to the disciples by the Resurrected One, which in each case allowed the spark to ignite, and incorporated the individual soul into the newly developing community. The result of going through this inner sacrament was that the wondrous possibility of a community-building closeness to Christ became an earthly and social reality.

Through the baptism by the Spirit, the mysteries of the Holy Grail, the Christ-permeated blood, were included in the historical development of Christendom. When describing the relationship between Paul and Apollos,[62] we spoke of the manner in which the practice of baptism by water, alongside that by fire, was effective in the first Christian congregations. The baptism by water lost the magical quality which it had possessed in pre-Christian life and during the baptisms performed by John the Baptist. There, through the total immersion of the one to be baptized, it had caused a state of excarnation not unlike the condition the hierophant brought about in the pre-Christian mystery centres when he placed the neophytes in a hypnotic temple-sleep. In the Christian realm, this baptism was merely the sacramental conclusion of the long process of cleansing and purification, through which the neophytes prepared themselves for acceptance in the congregation. The actual process of transformation, during which the purified vessel accepted the mercifully bestowed higher content into its being, only followed afterwards. It started with speaking about Christ to the one who had received the baptism with water in a way which made it possible for him to place Christ's image over and over again in a new, life-imbued way before his soul. This was not done for the purpose of enriching his conceptual life but in order to produce a direct heart-relationship. In time, the fire of a loving and devotional confidence was enkindled in his heart and blood. As a result, such a person finally beheld Christ instead of merely picturing him mentally.

Nowadays, in regard to such events, people are apt to speak of over-active fantasy, imagination and auto-suggestion. In reality, an awakening to supersensory perception occurred as if, through the inner fire, the scales over the eyes of the soul had been burned away. More easily than in later times, souls attained to translucency and perviousness; the wall between the sense world and the sphere of the supersensory was more tenuous. From the other side, as a close after-effect of the Easter event, a loving readiness to be revealed and known came to meet the soul with all directness.

The spiritual baptism established a new consciousness and a new existence. In it, a perception emerged whereby all distance between the perceiver and the object of perception vanished. On a higher level, this state resembled the condition referred to by the Old Testament in such words as Adam 'knew' his wife. A flash of lightning passed through the soul of the perceiver during this act of knowledge enabling him to say, 'Do I know or am I known?' What Paul had predicted as a future event, 'Then I shall understand fully, even as I have been fully understood' (1Cor. 13:12), became present experience. When this happened, one who received the spiritual baptism was able to say with justification: 'Christ in me.' For perception was the portal through which the I of Christ gained entry into the soul in order to indwell it.

The light of a delicate clairvoyance of the heart was enkindled in those who had thus been made ready to receive the higher content into themselves. When they had been privileged to behold the Christ as the spiritual sun, even if only as a faintly sensed shimmer of light, at the same time they became gifted with sight for the world that was being illumined by it.

We could also describe the transformation which then occurred in the following way. The true self, the spiritual ego of man, which in the merely natural life is separated from man and unable to gain entry into him, could now begin to be active owing to the fact that the Christ-ego had opened the path for it. Its element is the blood's warmth; this was intensified by the ardent love for Christ. In this sacred fire the ego entered effectively into the earthly sheaths. From the direction of the warmth element, the I of Christ aided the spiritual ego of man to influence and transform the three sheaths of soul, life and body. The Christ particularly encountered the life forces of the etheric body, since the element of warmth which belongs to the I meets in the blood the fluid element in which stream the life and formative forces. In man's blood, Christ's blood streams. In this way, the baptized person became incorporated into the communal circulation of the blood which, together with the blood of Christ filled with life-spirit, pulsed in all people who were united with Christ. This was the secret of the early Christian congregational developments. Through the baptism by water, one who approached the community was permitted to enter its domain; through the baptism by the Spirit or fire he became a member of it in the exact sense of the word. He became a limb on the body of Christ, pervaded by the pulse of Christ's blood.

Earlier, we spoke of the inaccuracy of the prevailing opinion that the transforming effect of the baptism of the Spirit was brought about by the laying on of hands. The essential point — in contrast to the baptism by John, the last magical form of baptism by water — was that the baptism of the Spirit depended primarily on man's own inner activity, the power of faith, and that it was not brought about from outside. The laying on of hands merely concluded the drama of transformation which had occurred in the soul. It blessed this process and bestowed on it steadfastness and stability. From this derives the name confirmation, 'affirmation,' which was given to this sacrament. In addition, the laying on of hands was connected with the transference of the initially intimate and individual process into the communal relationship. In it the share in the apostolic succession was sensed and enjoyed not only by those who exercised the priestly functions but by all Christ-permeated Christians. During the three years, the Apostles had come into physical contact with Christ. Through the laying on of hands, they passed on something of this to the priests and, through them, to the future generations of priests; in a different way, however, they also passed something of this on to every person who received the baptism by the Spirit. It was by these means that a continuous transition took place from the body of Christ, as it had been present during the three years, to the congregation as his newly developing body.

In his lecture cycle in Kassel dealing with the Gospel of St John, Rudolf Steiner described the nature of the baptism by the Spirit in its relationship with the Christian mysteries of the blood:

> The procedure of the old initiation ... was directed to a certain culmination which was achieved by having the candidate lie in a grave for three and a half days, as though dead ... In order that in the sphere of his etheric forces he might behold the spiritual world ... it was necessary at that time to withdraw the etheric body. Formerly these forces were not available in the normal state of waking consciousness. The neophyte had to be brought into an abnormal condition.
>
> Christ brought this force (of renewal) to the earth for initiation also; for today, it is possible for man to become clairvoyant without the withdrawal of the etheric body. When a person attains the maturity to receive so strong an impulse from the Christ, even for a short time, as to affect the circulation of his blood — this Christ influence expressing itself in a special form of circulation, an influence penetrating even the physical principle — then he is in a position to be initiated within the physical body ... Anyone who can become so profoundly absorbed in what occurred as a result of the Event of Palestine and the Mystery of Golgotha as to live completely in it and to see it objectively, see it so spiritually alive that it acts as a force communicating itself even to his circulation, such a man achieves through this experience the same result that was formerly brought about by the withdrawal of the etheric body ...
>
> What is active here is no abnormal event, no submersion in water, but solely the mighty influence of the Christ-Individuality. No physical substance is involved in this baptism — nothing but a spiritual influence; and the ordinary, everyday consciousness undergoes no change. Through the spirit that streams forth as the Christ impulse something flows into the body, something that can otherwise be induced only by way of psycho-physiological development through fire — an inner fire

> expressing itself in the circulation of the blood. John still baptized by submersion with the result that the etheric body withdrew and man could see into the spiritual world. But if man opens his soul to the Christ impulse, this impulse acts in such a way that the experiences of the astral body flow over into the etheric body, and clairvoyance results. There you have the explanation of the phrase, 'to baptize with the spirit and with fire,' and those are the facts concerning the difference between the John baptism and the Christ baptism.[63]

In the present-day state of mind it is not easy to form an idea of the tension and excitement of the first congregations. The coarse caricatures of this existing in some religious sects as supposed imitations of early Christendom considerably increase this difficulty. A powerful spiritual vibration must have passed through the congregations, since all their members had been placed in a special condition of openness and proximity to the Spirit by virtue of the baptism by fire and Spirit. Simply coming together may often have sufficed to evoke a stirring of the Spirit and an intensification of the state of perception. Then, when words were read or spoken, people heard the speaking of a higher world through human speech. The level on which reason seeks to grasp and retain the thought content of words was not thereby absent. From the very first, however, it was exalted because of a clairvoyant seeing and hearing in images and a transmission of energy that connected the soul with the supersensory essence of what the words had expressed. This was true even more of the usually quite unassuming ritual proceedings that were carried out. A higher element ensouled the human community, establishing it as such over and over again by entering into it as its body.

From the very beginning, however, the congregations must have differed from each other in this regard as much as individuals differ from one another. If a congregation had a predominantly Jewish Christian character, the supersensory occurrence retained an element of restraint and distance. By contrast, where ancient, ecstatic religious inclinations had prevailed, frenzied mental states may frequently have occurred that could be transformed into harmony only with difficulty. Paul's letters reflect much of the specific attitudes existing in the congregations to which they were addressed. The congregation at Philippi may have been one in which a lovely balance, a golden mean between extremes, held sway. Where such a balance existed or was attained, the element of 'spirit-self,' the substance of peace, moved through the room and everything that was said and done evoked an inner uplifting as of the rushing of angels' wings. In conformity with the beatitude promising the pure heart that it will behold God, the warmed heart and blood of those present became aware of the presence of the Resurrected One.

The Letters to the Corinthians are an invaluable, instructive document because there the life of a congregation is shown in which the exceptional state, whereby the Christian sphere distinguished itself from the surrounding world, vibrated with particular intensity and complexity. Here almost an extreme gift for ecstasy and openness of soul held sway. An abundance of special talents had been conjured forth among the individual members of the congregation through the spiritual baptism. Yet it was just this wealth of such individual potential that brought with it severe obstacles for the higher ensouling of the community. We see how Paul strove with greatest tolerance and wisdom but also with penetrating force and certainty to bring into being the shape of a higher, harmonious order from the threatening chaos.

It is understandable that for many centuries theology faced numerous difficulties and nearly insoluble riddles on account of Paul's letters concerning the special charismatic talents in the early congregations. What is one to make of all this in an age in which such soul phenomena do not appear at all or at most in abnormal form? Those who were motivated by fundamentalism to affirm unquestioningly the 'spiritual' gifts as they did the 'miracles' of the Gospel, which implied comprehending them in an external, superficial sense, inadvertently permitted the rise of two unproven presuppositions which made the tangle of riddles even worse. First of all, it was assumed that these phenomena appeared in all congregations in the same way and to the same extent. Secondly, it was believed that these had to be viewed as completely new soul potentials come to the fore as first fruits of the Christian faith, whose arousal ought to be part even today of the ideals and goals of Christian life.

We can and must understand these special spiritual talents historically. In those days, the times were not yet far gone when humanity had enjoyed a living interchange with the forces and beings of a supersensory world. It was only in the course of time and due to the accelerating hardening of the body that human souls lost the faculty of perceiving and working with supersensory powers. This loss had not moved at the same speed among all nations and in all climates. It was the more complete, the more the earthly I-impulse had gained strength in particular regions and hereditary relationships.

The exceptional conditions of the first Christian centuries in those places where the Christian proclamation penetrated, caused a new awareness of the Spirit to be called forth in each individual through the spiritual baptism. This was not comparable to the nearness to the supersensible realm that souls had naturally enjoyed in former times. Yet this new closeness was not brought about by man's slowly progressing work on himself but through special grace and benevolence of destiny. Owing to this, it was inevitable that remnants of atavistic soul faculties also reawakened in one locality or another where souls had remained more porous than was normal. This must have been particularly the case in Corinth.

There were, however, variations between the special soul faculties. Some of them reappeared exactly as they had existed in the past in a far more general manner, when a dimming of consciousness was one of the conditions of their appearing. A notable example of this was speaking in tongues. It took place in a state of ecstasy. Therefore, the individual practising it did not himself understand what he was saying. On the other side, there was the activation of more ancient capabilities which now appeared in a new ego-imbued manner, and therefore contained the seed of future spiritual faculties. Among them must be counted, for example, the 'prophetic gift' and the 'faculty to discern the spirits.' In between were those special capabilities which, as yet, had not been extinguished in that age and could be considered normal.

Among them, above all, belonged the faculty of healing through strength of soul, something that was still practised far and wide as the popular art of medicine; for instance, by the 'Therapeutae' among the travelling Essene brothers. This gift of healing particularly makes it possible for us to form vivid conceptions concerning the way in which a number of spiritual talents appeared with a new I-impulse in the Christian congregations. When the one gifted in healing laid his hands on the sick, was it not inevitable that the patient was reminded in the most vivid manner of his own baptism and the laying on of hands connected with it, and was thus spontaneously transported into the condition of spiritual fulfilment? Then, suddenly, it was no longer a healing from outside as in the case of the healers of antiquity; instead, the fire of one's own spiritual I repelled from within that aspect of the illness which had to be healed. The healed person could be told: 'Your faith has cured you.'

In the twelfth chapter of the First Letter to the Corinthians, Paul lists a great variety of special talents: 'The utterance of wisdom; the utterance of knowledge (gnosis); faith (pistis); the grace-filled gift of healing; utilization of supernatural powers; the gift of the prophetic sense; the ability to distinguish between spirits; the gift of speaking in tongues; the faculty of interpreting the speaking in tongues' (1Cor.12:8-10*B*). It would probably be wrong, however, to view this list and also the partially related reference to a number of offices as an exact system. Against this stands the fact that 'faith,' which would actually be presupposed in every member of the congregation, is counted here among the special talents. Paul had in mind the special condition of the Corinthian congregation. Here he wished to give as much room as possible to the individual gifts which were astir in such conspicuous abundance. He was concerned, however, that disturbances might be created by them, obstructing the descent of the community spirit whose body the congregation was meant to be. There was not only the threat of a split into various factions, one wanting to listen more to Paul, another more to Apollos. There also existed a danger in the very wealth of disparate individual talents which, by their nature, would come to expression with ecstatic vigour.

The uniqueness of Paul's genius is evident in the manner in which he tried to bring about a balance between the whole and its individual parts. Spiritual and evolutionary processes had begun, the likes of which had not previously existed anywhere. Already equipped with the future light of the consciousness soul, Paul could illuminate what was supersensibly coming into being above and in the nascent congregations, and coin the necessary concepts for it. He did not do this in a theoretical, theological manner but by wisely guiding and directing what was taking place. Under his careful grooming and leadership, the earthly, human community became adjusted to the miracle of grace that approached in the sphere of archetypes and strove to incarnate. Thus he gave to the Corinthians the classic teaching concerning the true congregation as the body of Christ, and the individually gifted human beings as the limbs of this body. Community building through obedient inclusion of the single person had always existed, but guided by the principles of blood relationship and authority. What was new was the communal, blood circulation which was activated only when, in full accordance with their own different backgrounds and individuality, individuals became integrated in it. In Corinth, particularly tolerant generosity had to be practised in regard to accommodating the individual element. For here not only the natural individual differences, but the special gifts imbued with supersensory intensity had to be brought into harmony with each other. The instruction which Paul gave is of classic terseness, and in a restrained manner bears within the music of a solemn hymn:

> For just as the body is one and has many members, and all the members of the body, though many, are *one* body, so it is with Christ. For by *one* Spirit we were all baptized and united into *one* body — regardless of whether we were Jews or Greeks, slaves or free — and we all drank the drink of *one* Spirit.
>
> For the body does not consist of one member but of many. If the foot should say, 'Because I am not a hand, I do not belong to the body,' that would not make it any less a part of the body. And if the ear should say, 'Because I am not an eye, I do not belong to the body,' that would not make it any less a part of the body. If the

> whole body were an eye, where would be the hearing? If the whole body were an ear, where would be the sense of smell? But as it is, God has assigned to the organs, to each one of them, the place in the body that is meant for it. If all were a single organ, where would the body be? As it is, there are many parts, yet one body. The eye cannot say to the hand, 'I have no need of you,' nor again the head to the feet, 'I have no need of you.' On the contrary, often the most unassuming parts are the most indispensable ... There may be no discord in the body and the members must all care for one another in the same manner. If one member suffers, all suffer together; if one member is illumined in the Spirit, all rejoice together. Now you are the body of Christ and individual members of it (1Cor.12:12-27*B*).

In reference to some of the special spiritual talents, Paul was faced with a difficult task. For he was a devotee of the clearest state of wakefulness and alertness, possessing a state of mind and perceptual faculties for the supersensory sphere towards which humanity can only develop in the future. He discerned that ancient, atrophied and atavistic soul forces were stirring once again in these special gifts. Above all, he could not help viewing the gift of 'speaking in tongues' as an atavism. Despite the religious ecstasy, and even though one or the other manifestation of the spiritual world emerged through this gift, it could well signify in the one practising it an inner, possibly harmful, regression. Should he have recommended that no use be made of this late mediumistic afterglow of the ancient word-magic that was timely once in Egypt? Paul was far from being doctrinaire and intolerant. He adhered to the words of Christ that 'every teacher who has passed through the discipleship in the kingdom of the heavens is like a householder who alternately brings out of his treasure chest what is new and what is old' (Matt.13:52*B*).

Nevertheless, Paul felt obliged to state clearly what he thought. Discreetly pointing to his personal intercourse with the higher world, he said that if he were so inclined he would certainly be in a position to employ the gift of speaking in tongues, probably even surpassing all the others in it. 'Nevertheless, in the congregation I would rather speak five words with my intellect in order to instruct others, than ten thousand words in a tongue' (1Cor.14:19*B*).

He gave twofold advice to counter the dangers of mediumistically subdued consciousness. He counselled those who practised the speaking in tongues to become their own interpreters. For as a rule those who employed this talent first placed themselves in a sort of trance. By doing this, they drew their own 'I' out of the process of speech so that other entities could speak through them in a sort of gibberish. When such individuals returned to their normal consciousness, they no longer knew anything of what had been spoken through them. Therefore they were dependent on another person who possessed the necessary special faculty to translate the babbling. Now, according to Paul's advice, they were to pose the task to themselves of training and strengthening the inner I-force to such an extent that they could maintain sufficient consciousness during the speaking in tongues to retain what had been said and be able, afterwards, to interpret it. Most of those who set themselves this task as recommended by Paul probably discovered that the gift of speaking in tongues was soon inhibited in them since it presupposed a certain instability of the I-force. Paul himself certainly would not have considered such repression a loss.

The other counsel that the Apostle gave was addressed to the congregations as a whole. It was his wish that the gift of prophecy be given preference in all instances over that of speaking in tongues. 'Strive for the spiritual gifts but most of all cultivate the prophetic-apocalyptic sense' (1Cor.14:1*B*). The gift of prophecy surely did not refer to a mediumistic or atavistically clairvoyant deciphering of future events. Otherwise it would not have been contrasted so starkly with the mediumistic speaking in tongues. After all, the point was to free the souls from the spell of the past which held sway in all those instances where the intellectual wakefulness of normal consciousness was abandoned. It would have been self-contradictory to pursue glimpses of the future with methods of the past. What Paul understood as the prophetic faculty lay in the direction of a thinking that is further developed and intensified through a process of inner strengthening. To recognize the seeds of future happenings in present conditions, be it in the individual person or in contemporary events and constellations of destiny, or — to put it differently — to behold the spiritual and supersensory in the physically perceptible, in what has come into existence — this is what is meant here. It is the art of reading the signs of the times; it is acquired through training one's apocalyptic sight. Where this gift was utilized appropriately, a person neither could nor was supposed to foresee the earthly events that would occur in the future, only what would be possible. Otherwise, the higher soul force born out of freedom would immediately have crushed this very freedom. There must have been gatherings in the first congregations in which, following the soul's awakening in the baptism by the Spirit, people strove eagerly for the cultivation of such an enlightened power of judgment. This is what Paul was concerned about; he wanted to see to it that special emphasis was placed on such efforts and that it would help play a major part in determining the inner attitude of the congregational life. He was hoping for the wind of the future to fill the sails of the ship that he was steering.

Everything that Paul told the Corinthians of the charismatic spiritual gifts, and also of the mystery of the body of Christ, was woven into a grandly conceived instruction concerning the *sacrament.* The Christian ritual, above all the sacrament of bread and wine, receives its meaning first and foremost by serving the process of spiritual incarnation which represents the secret of forming congregations. After the sacramental transformation, when we call the bread the 'body of Christ' we confess to the fact that the same grace-filled occurrence by which a group of people turns into a congregation, the 'body of Christ' can grow and stream out beyond the human sphere until it also embraces that of the earthly creatures and elements. And when we receive the wine as 'Christ's blood,' we partake of the sacrament's blessing for the inner transformative process through which, alongside our blood filled with faith and love, Christ's blood begins to stream. The secret of the chalice is the affirmation of the new blood circulation that pulses through the congregation as the body of Christ, for it establishes a new kind of blood relationship. 'The blessed cup, does it not establish the community of the blood of Christ?' (1Cor.10:16*B*).

In view of the newly inaugurated ritual in which such a unique renewal of creation took place, inherent above all in the act of transubstantiation, the advance in consciousness that Paul embodied signified a favour of Providence that could not be valued highly enough. All the congregations lived in and through the stream of energy and new life that had begun to flow for humanity because of the Easter event. It was Paul who permeated this new form of existence with consciousness; through concepts that did not possess anything however of the pallid abstraction of later intellectualism, he was able to make it surveyable and accessible to a comprehending perception.

This was all the more necessary since a number of earlier tendencies affected the initially quite simple pattern of the early Christian ritual depending on the religious background of the congregation. A great variety of such tendencies must have flowed together in the community at Corinth, just as the spiritual gifts appeared there in particular diversity. Here, Paul had to calm the storm of constantly threatening chaos. In his efforts for a higher order and harmony — since he did not simply wish nor could decree a ready form of ritual — it was an advantage that he had direct access to the spiritual sphere whence the ritual derives. He made that evident when he, who after all had not been present on Maundy Thursday in the Cenacle, took the sacramental words that had accompanied the original Last Supper and, as something received from the Resurrected One himself, secured them for the sacramental act (1Cor.11:23-25).

Much of what Paul said to the Corinthians regarding the form of Christian ritual has been thoroughly misunderstood in Luther's Bible and subsequent theology. Instead of beginning from the religious and cultural background as it was in Corinth and elsewhere, theologians proceeded from the bourgeois conditions of early Protestantism which were estranged from ritual. It was therefore thought that it was above all moral and social abuses in the manner of conducting Holy Communion which Paul chastised in the following words:

For when the Lord's Supper is to be held, each one goes

> ahead with his own meal, and one is hungry and another is drunk. What! Do you not have houses to eat and drink in? Or do you despise the congregation of God and humiliate those who have nothing? (1Cor.11:21f*B*).

Certainly, in one area of early Christian life, the sacrament was initially carried out in the form of a communal meal. This took place in memory of the sacred round table on the eve before Good Friday. Such a practice derived from the congregational life of the Essenes. It implies a total misconception of the spirit of early Christianity, however, to believe that people simply partook of communal meals and that in the course of these not only a difference between immoderation and moderation was unpleasantly felt but also a distinction between the rich who could eat and drink plenty, and the poor who would have liked to eat and drink more if it had been available to them. In Corinth, however, it was not a matter of differing moral and social attitudes but of contrasting cultural principles that collided with each other. Some of the Corinthian congregation came from religious streams that cultivated a 'rich' ritual life; others came from a 'poor' one. Alongside the Greeks who came from Dionysian customs tending towards ecstasy and intoxication, there were former Essenes for whom an ascetic element had become second nature. In addition, there were those who, coming from Judaism, brought along a minimum of ritual; for this reason, the genuinely Jewish Christian congregations called themselves Ebionites, from 'ebyon,' meaning 'poor.' Differences, such as threatened to drive Corinth into chaos, exist to this day between Catholicism and Protestantism, particularly in its extreme Calvinistic form.

Finally, the Apostle uttered the magic word which alone could truly calm the storm and bring the chaos into order. This word swelled into the mighty hymn that crowns all of Paul's utterances: 'If I speak in the tongues of men and of angels, but have no *love* ...'

The word, 'love,' *agapē,* is ambiguous in this passage and yet it has but one meaning. In the life of the congregation, it is the name by which the celebration of the sacrament of bread and wine is denoted. Yet it is also used outside this specific context.

Then, however, it does not designate the natural love of man for man. It indicates an objective, higher force which like a sacred stream emanating from God himself, is present in the world. Human beings can make themselves into its instrument when they are completely unselfish. The sacred meal is a 'love feast' not simply in the sense that the participants thereby draw closer to each other in love, but because it offers a channel on earth for God's objective love. The sacrament is an earthly manifestation of God's divine love. It opens a door to the loving surrender and incarnation of the Resurrected One in the human community which thus turns into his body. A community of love thereby comes into being among humans also, not primarily because they love one another, but because, together, they are loved out of higher worlds. The consequence of being loved like this is also the indwelling of divine love in the single human being, and in this higher love, the true selves of the individuals are united in an intimate community. Out of the love for God, which is nothing else but man's sensing that he is being loved by God, blossoms the true love for his fellow men.

Paul adds his praise of *agapē* to what he has told the Corinthians in an affirmative and yet also regulatory manner concerning the charismatic spiritual gifts. He makes it clear that he now leaves the level of these special forces behind and is entering a higher stage: 'Strive for the better, higher spiritual gifts. I will show you a way that leads far beyond all this' (1Cor.12:31*B*). *Agapē,* the divine love, is the true gift; without it, all others are without value and empty. Beginning with the very first sentence, that is the meaning of this great hymn. Without love, the speaking in tongues is nothing but 'a noisy gong or a clanging cymbal.' And will he who treads the path of love still be able and want to practise the speaking in tongues? Even 'faith,' which Paul counts among the special soul faculties, threatens to remain in a vacuum unless 'love,' the indwelling higher being, becomes the subject of faith: '... and if I have all faith, so as to remove mountains, but have not love, I am nothing.' Faith can bring about the indwelling of the higher element; love, however, *is* already this indwelling and arranges all single parts into the whole.

This hymn of love spreads out what is condensed into one

sentence in the Letter to the Colossians. In Luther's translation, it says, 'Love is the bond of perfection' (Col.3:14; RSV: 'And above all these put on love, which binds everything together in perfect harmony'). These words presuppose the inner path which in the ancient mysteries led through strictly arranged stages to initiation. 'Love' is the guideline along which the Christian finds the way to his spiritual goals. The hymn of love in the letters to the Corinthians raises the curtain before the wondrous world of this path which is no longer merely the path of the individual, but signifies at the same time the development of the community as the larger body of Christ. Here it is not a matter of appealing in a moral sense to the will for love that man brings to life in himself again and again by means of good resolutions. *Agapē* is the element of true life flowing all around us. If we proceed on our path, placing ourselves into this element again and again with an open heart through faithful discipline, then the future works on us as a force of the present. In the sacrament of bread and wine, even in outward forms, the element of *agapē* can surround us as the sphere of devotion. Yet we also enter this temple through the quiet personal cultivation of prayer and meditation. Faith, hope and love represent the three higher charismatic spiritual gifts. 'But the greatest of these is love' (1Cor.13:13).

18. Pistis and Gnosis: Faith and Knowledge

When Albert Schweitzer called Paul 'Christianity's patron saint of thinking,' it was his intention to clear away from the text of the letters the dust of a centuries-old dislike of knowledge. The original Greek is illumined by the light of a new courage of thought and enthusiasm for knowledge. We need only become aware of the wealth of exact, differentiated concepts that were available to Paul to describe the various ways of gaining knowledge. Here, we shall cite at least two examples. When Paul tried to clarify the questionable nature of speaking in tongues to the Corinthians, he said:

> Imagine that I were to come to you and amongst you should speak in tongues; would I do you a service with that? I would truly do you a service only if I spoke to you either in the form of revelation *(apocalypse),* or from an intellectual viewpoint *(gnosis),* or through the prophetic sense, or in the manner of a teaching *(didache)* (1Cor. 14:6*B*).

We also discover in this passage how clearly Paul distinguished between the various forms and sources of knowledge.

To the congregation in Colossae he writes how much he longs to be present again among them and the neighbouring congregation of Laodicea. He would like to console their hearts so that they might gather courage and assurance from the divine love *(agapē)* 'to have all the riches of assured understanding *(synesis)* and the knowledge *(epignōsis)* of God's mystery of Christ, in whom are hid all the treasures of wisdom *(sophia)* and knowledge *(gnōsis)*' (Col.2:2f*B*). Is it permissible for Christians in our days to feel that they are excused from the tasks of knowledge posed by Paul to the congregations, and to assume that the Apostle merely meant to edify his followers with such learned language?

In modern times, people have been unable and unwilling to interpret the term, 'knowledge,' in any way other than as the activity of the brain-bound intellect, experienced as contradicting and impairing the ardour of religious feelings. The varied terminology used by Paul for the modes of knowledge are considered more or less as synonyms.

We have to say that it is a profoundly tragic circumstance of fate that a large part of modern humanity has become acquainted with Paul only through Luther's mediation. Owing to decisive experiences evoked by the Letter to the Romans, Luther was drawn to Paul with elemental force and sensed a kinship with him. Yet in their epistemological attitudes, no greater contrast could have existed than between Paul and himself. Luther envisioned the dawning era of the intellect as a terrifying and oppressive spectre. During the translation of the Bible in the Wartburg, Luther beheld the Ahrimanic power approaching, confident of victory, in the form of the devil peering over his shoulder and causing him to throw the ink-well at him. This apparition was a shadow of the power of icy cleverness, which would bring about the increasing alienation of humanity from God through the achievements of the scientific, technological age. Only by drawing a dividing line between faith and thinking, by dismissing the 'Whore Intellect' and the Satan of head-thinking from the domain of holiness, could he maintain the hope of saving access to God through faith. If Luther nevertheless invoked Paul — a man who already spoke with a Christian, hence a redeemed, thinking and knowing — in his fundamental religious experience, then this could only be a misunderstood Paul. His translation of Paul's letters therefore was unlike Paul and devoid of the radiant joy of knowledge. It will be some time before people fully understand how much trivialization and mediocrity infiltrated particularly those passages of Paul's letters which contain new insight for thinking and knowledge.

We shall cite an example of the distortion that Luther placed on the Pauline words concerning questions of consciousness and knowledge. In the eighth chapter of the Letter to the Romans, both Luther and the Revised Standard Version have:

> For those who live according to the flesh set their minds on the things of the flesh, but those who live according the Spirit set their minds on the things of the Spirit. To

> set the mind on the flesh is death, but to set the mind on the Spirit is life and peace (Rom.8:5f).

You cannot interpret this other than as contrasting two moral attitudes. One is determined by sensuous desires, the other by an idealistic state of mind; the first penalizes itself by leading to death, the other is rewarded with peace and life. On the other hand, where this text speaks of 'setting one's mind,' the Pauline text unmistakably makes use of expressions which designate the direction of thinking, the manner of thought. This is also true of the Latin text. Because of his negative outlook on the thinking process, Luther gave the wording here a moralistic connotation which it did not contain. The Latin Bible even translated the Greek, *phronēma,* quite radically as *prudentia* or 'cleverness.' Hence it says, *prudentia carnis* or 'cleverness of matter' and *prudentia spiritus* or 'cleverness of spirit.'

The passage should be translated as follows:

> Those who dwell completely in the physical possess a form of thinking that comprehends only the material element; those who dwell in the spiritual can understand the spiritual as well. The form of thought concerned with the physical produces death; the form directed to the Spirit brings forth life and peace.

It goes without saying that Paul was far from giving epistemological descriptions and definitions. As always, even though he spoke with an intimate, discerning awareness of the various kinds and nuances of thinking, perception and knowledge, he assumed without more ado that people would understand him. Indeed, to a much higher degree than we could possibly imagine today, he was able to count on a form of thinking and comprehension which, although not yet so intellectually honed, was instead permeated by a half visionary, clearly sensing instinct. Not until later did thought become intellectual, fully alert and contoured in the modern sense. This, however, meant that thinking became blind to the deeper and truer levels of existence.

The main point is that the form of reflective perception prevalent in Paul's day — and this is true especially of a mind as highly trained as his — was felt as but a stage of metamorphosis in a great evolutionary process. The present-day blindness of intellectualism is held to be the only possible form of consciousness and perception and thus it projects itself into the past and forward into the future. It holds that in the past the intellectual consciousness was more primitive and less developed; in the future it will evolve to still greater precision and skill. In principle, however, it was and is always the same. The truth is that in the era of late antiquity which includes the early Christian centuries, the ongoing change of awareness in humankind was an aspect of vital human consciousness and sense of self. This very change was linked to the feeling of a progressive twilight of the gods, which arose in the mythological images of some civilizations. People were far from arrogantly believing that their present consciousness was superior to that of former times. On the contrary, filled with nostalgia, they looked back to a golden age when gods were still guests in the homes of men and the light of vision still burned in their souls.

Paul knew and expressed in his own manner that, through the central event of humanity's history which had taken place on Golgotha, a decisive turning point had likewise occurred in the development of human consciousness and perception. The descending stream of evolution could now be followed by an ascending one.

Paul called the insight attained by thinking in his age, *gnōsis.* He knew that it was a kind of ending. Once, during a primordial age, the earth had been as large as the heavens, not yet contracted into the hard structure that it later became. As yet, possessing no clearly contoured form and poured out into the world, the human entity reflected the consciousness and thoughts of higher divine beings. It was still far removed from a centred consciousness of its own. When man, tempted by the Luciferic power, had 'eaten of the Tree of Knowledge,' earth and humanity plunged into the hardness of matter and external form. An awakening, earthly self-awareness gradually replaced the celestial consciousness which, for man, had remained half asleep and dreamy.

Nevertheless, for a long time, images in which supersensory elements were reflected into the soul persevered within the flow of consciousness. For the supersensible part of the human being remained larger — to use a spatial comparison — than the gradually developing physical body, and flowed over and around it. A vestige of the ancient condition of human nature and consciousness continued even into early historical times, as referred to by the Old Testament prior to the stories of the Patriarchs. Especially in regard to the head's configuration, the corresponding part of the astral and etheric body continued to extend beyond the physical head. In this way, the ancient visionary consciousness endured at the expense of the sense organs which, still undifferentiated, did not cognize in a clearly contoured manner. Yet the more the etheric head became adjusted to the physical head, contracting to the point of congruence with it, the more the old clairvoyant awareness attenuated into a thinking consciousness. The wealth of supersensory perception was extinguished; instead, the world of the earthly senses spread out clearly in forms and colours. With Moses, humanity took the step from vision to thinking. The cultural stream of the Old Testament preceded the rest of humanity in the development of abstract thought bound to the physical brain. This civilization scorned all imagery so as to extinguish the ancient dream as thoroughly as possible.[64] Likewise, in Greece thought was born on the forehead of man. Here, however, thinking as well as sense perception survived longer in the proximity of imagery and therefore continued for a while to be imbued with poetry and inclined towards beauty.

The evolution of human consciousness could be called a journey to Golgotha, a development towards an ever closer tie with the human 'place of the skull,' finally with the brain. Here thinking reaches the stage of death. Less and less of the etheric body's life forces flows into the process of thinking; because of this fact, man can only eventually perceive the inanimate. The cross on the hill of Golgotha in Jerusalem was a sign not just for the fact that Christ was assuming humanity's fate of death, but also its nadir of consciousness. It also signified that the 'intellectual Fall,' introduced by 'eating from the Tree of Knowledge,' had now come close to the point of nothingness and death. Of course, the empty tomb of the Resurrection was no less a sign. Not merely for man's existence but equally for his consciousness, there exists henceforth the possibility of re-ascent and resurrection to new life.

Since then, in its evolution of consciousness, the human race has only continued its descent into death, the 'intellectual Fall.' Even though Paul had made himself the herald for the resurrection of consciousness and the Christ's redemption of thinking, Christendom preferred to march along the general path of secularization. Christians believed they could be excused from the responsibility towards thinking by virtue of separating faith from knowledge. After the first Christian centuries had passed, the result has been that through the exertion of immense forces of intelligence a civilization has come into being which, proceeding from dead thoughts, is filled with tendencies towards death and threats of destruction. And in an age when the sunrise of a new nearness of Christ is proclaimed in the spiritual sphere, a wide path is cleared initially for the Ahrimanic power, the anti-Christian forces, and everything they require plays into their hands for them to exercise the magic of the great illusion. Will it not be possible, even in the eleventh hour, to develop from the rudiments of a Pauline Christianity of consciousness a spiritual counterbalance, so that the power that wills evil will nevertheless have to help create the good?

The form of insight termed *gnōsis* by Paul was at an end; and yet, paradoxically, the final extinction of this stream of knowledge had not yet occurred. Borne by the still radiant lightness of the Greek language, it was the form of thinking that dominated the Hellenistic world of that time. Although the degree of abstraction in thought had already become much greater than in the golden age of Pericles and Plato, a last vestige of the clairvoyant and colourful vision of long ago still breathed in the language. The letters of Paul are themselves the noblest proof of how this form of thought could blossom once more through the Christian impulse, so that a dawning radiance blended even then with the after-glow of this thinking. Originating with Paul, there existed a 'Christian Gnosis' until the third century, represented in particular by the theologians Clement and Origen, of the Alexandrian school. As soon as the Greek language was pushed into the background in Christianity, however, religious tendencies opposed to thinking appeared on the scene. Eventually they were the reason that Origen was declared a heretic and his writings prohibited.

Independently of Paul or, indeed, of any link with the developing Christian congregations, a special Gnostic stream emerged in the second century. The incipient church was justified in its resistance to and disavowal of this movement, although it is regrettable and tragic that, in the end, fanatical persecution and total destruction of its literature was instigated by the Church. It is predominantly this stream that is referred to when people speak of 'Gnosis' in the sense of ecumenical history. This Gnosticism originated from various declining Greek mystery schools, some of which practised an ascetic, monastic life-style. The form of thinking nurtured in this Gnostic stream was not the same as the *gnōsis* of Paul. Instead, it was one which artificially had been held back at an earlier stage of imaginative consciousness. In it, a pictorial element that could not be clearly controlled predominated over that of logical concepts. It was therefore able to turn to the supersensory aspect in the nature, life and destiny of Christ but in doing so remained detached from the earth. It did not arrive at the level where the incarnation and death of Christ had taken place as a physical event, thus at the level where the Resurrection can be fully affirmed and understood as an actual transubstantiation. By pointing to this heretical Gnosis, theology believed it had an excuse for not taking the Pauline *gnōsis* seriously, and thus for leaving undone the task that results from it, namely, introducing the Christ impulse into the evolution of thinking. Those who frequently and rather indiscriminately attack 'Gnosticism' today should realize that the modern intellectualism in which they themselves are caught up is the last, withered form of this gnosis. Today, however, it is truly the corpse of what appeared even then as something that was drawing to a close but which, in the Pauline *gnōsis,* had received a seed leading to resurrection.

Whereas *gnōsis* was an end, *pistis,* faith, was a new beginning. It was tragic that the history of Christian theology and the church placed the two in opposition to each other. As a result 'faith' could not be what it was supposed to have become according to Paul, namely the seed of a new Christian perception. What dies at the 'place of the skull,' in the human head, can arise from the human heart. Luther felt this when he coined the sentence: 'Faith is another sense, far beyond the five senses.' Yet in his distaste for thinking he would naturally have denied that a renewal of thinking could come from faith. Intellectual thinking is pale, cold and dead, for it has turned into a one-sided affair of the head. Without becoming caught up in fantastic and uncontrollable elements, could there not be a way to involve the *whole* human being, hence also feeling and will, in the act of cognition? The problem today is that through the coldness of head-reasoning the heart, too, has turned cold and stony, and the will is paralysed. If we can speak of Christ's indwelling not in empty phraseology but with real meaning, could not the spiritual fire in the blood and heart help the head to think better and more truly? To involve feeling and will in the act of thinking does not mean that sentimental emotions should become mixed up in intellectual thought. An intellectualism that is coated with feelings and stirred by impure instincts of the will is far more dangerous and damaging than one that merely remains in clever abstractions. In a strictly epistemological sense, it should be possible to speak of a thinking encompassing all of human nature. Directions could then be indicated that would lead to a new form of pedagogy and discipline of thinking.

What is said here concerning faith as the seed of a new cognition becomes more comprehensible when comprehended by an anthroposophical outlook, which, while referring to later centuries of Christian development, nevertheless encompasses Paul's spiritual intentions.

The 'filioque' controversy, which in the ninth century led to the split of Christianity into the Byzantine Eastern church and the Roman Western church, resulted from uncertainty in regard to the nature of the Holy Spirit and spirit in general — an uncertainty already noticeable for centuries. The ancient confessions of faith had stated that the Holy Spirit proceeds from the Father. The East unyieldingly clung to this formulation, even when, in the West, the opinion became increasingly prevalent that the Spirit must be pictured as proceeding from the Father *and from the Son* — a view finally included in the Credo as: *qui ex patre filioque procedit* (who proceeds from the Father and the Son). Though even then lacking clarity of thought, the Western Church was groping for a truth that the early Christian age in its imagery had certainly been familiar with. This truth was presupposed everywhere by Paul. In creation's primal beginning, the Father bestowed on mankind a spirituality that was sacred because it was still divine, not yet human. After the Fall, humanity increasingly obscured and used up this sustenance, and by the time of Christ clear signals of its exhaustion had become evident. It was then that the Father, who in the beginning had sent the Spirit, sent the Son. And when Pentecost followed upon Good Friday and Easter, a new fountainhead of the Spirit sprang forth. It was not as if the ancient Holy Spirit had simply been renewed. Fifty days after Easter, the disciples looked with prescience into the development of a new spirituality which would heal and sanctify the fallen consciousness and being of humanity, for it poured into the stream of transformation proceeding from Christ's death and Resurrection.

As a result now the Father alone did not send the Spirit; the Son sent the Father's new Spirit. When western Christianity sensed that this should be expressed in the text of the Credo, people vaguely felt that in this way they would comply with the step taken out of the collective, group-soul element into the individual realm, something that had long since been embarked upon by the more progressive among humanity, and for which they had even then received a sanctifying content in the Christian experience of faith. After all, the principle of the Son was the ego element in the higher sense. One must remember, however, that as soon as western theologians had carried through the *filioque* issue, they made the individual character of the new Christian Holy Spirit illusory again through the dogma of 869 AD which attributed merely body and soul to man but no individual spirit.

On the other hand, why did the Eastern church reject the *filioque* so vehemently? In the East, the ancient sustenance of God-given spirituality was not as exhausted as it was in the West. As ardently as the eastern Christians loved the Resurrected One, so they correspondingly failed to sense the necessity for a new wellspring of spirituality, since they were still rich. The more they were disquieted and revolted by the tendencies towards secularization and individualization emerging in the West, the more they clung to the ancient spirituality.

Despite the commitment to the *filioque* formula, the West did not truly utilize the new spiritual source. This would have had to be done by overcoming the chasm between faith and knowledge, through the development of a new thinking and perceiving based on faith. Thus dogma would have to be renounced. This is why the Holy Spirit was henceforth mentioned only outside the general developments of consciousness and, later on, of science. In the East as well as in the West, the history of thinking continued on the descending path, the direction leading to the 'place of the skull.' The spiritual potential naturally bestowed on the human being by the Father in the beginning, evolved further in increasing confinement to body and brain. Especially after the Islamic influence with its singular Father-spirituality poured into Europe from the East — 'God is God and has *no* Son!'* — this spiritual potential shrank into the modern intellectualism which now dominates the sciences, technology and human life.

How would consciousness have developed if the specifically Christian spirituality proceeding from the Son had been made fruitful for thinking? We must not believe that thinking would have undergone a dubious religious embellishment. This is exactly what happened in all those instances where Christian devotion went its way *apart* from the development of thought, *out of the way* of the so-called triumphs of the human spirit in civilization and technology.

In the Pauline sense, the Son-principle exerts its influence not from outside but from within. Through the indwelling of the Son, the sonship comes about in man as an intensified and fulfilled egoity. Man himself turns into 'the Son of God.' Therefore, a Son-imbued spirituality is of a kind that creatively originates in the human being through the fact that the higher 'I,' the Christ-filled spiritual ego, turns into the subject who perceives and thinks. Then the blossom of faith flowers into knowledge; in it,

* This principle of Islam is proclaimed today in large letters from the cupola of the Dome of the Rock in Jerusalem which stands on the site of the former Temple of Solomon.

the heart helps the head to attain to a better, truer thinking and perceiving.

The tragedy of the whole modern machinery of civilization lies in the unrecognized fact that man in his true nature is not fully within his thinking. The brain thinks, not the spirit. The content of consciousness, assimilated through sense perceptions and absorbed intellectually, is brought increasingly closer to the ideal of the machine. Is it any wonder that man's perception penetrates only to the external phenomena? Not until man in his true nature, his spiritual self, becomes the subject of thinking, can he expect the true spiritual essence of the world to become apparent to his perception. Man presumes to think; in reality an It is thinking through him, but a cold, impersonal It, not a higher, divine one. The unavoidable consequence of this is that like his thoughts man finally no longer has any control over things. With apocalyptic intensity, our age is teaching us what has become of the ancient Holy Spirit: an unholy, soulless spirit, a demon.

Eventually, the fruit of the Christian impulse will have to be that people become creative in thinking and perceiving by courageously learning to draw from the spring of the new Holy Spirit, not merely in regard to their existence but also their consciousness. Then, permeated with true Spirit from within, he will find the way to sanctify what he had desecrated and profaned.

Pistis (faith) can also be translated as 'courage.' The modern spirit of research considers itself to be courageous and daring. Yet it is actually being driven — often with manic recklessness — by the lure of ultimate mechanical perfection. But 'faith in the machine' in any form is only a camouflage for the lack of faith in an inwardly creative thinking. This has made human souls cowardly and weak. Through intensifying their outer activity, people conceal from themselves the paralysis and failure of inner activity. They are not even willing to notice the frightening loss of inner tranquillity and ability to concentrate which, after all, are the precondition for inner freedom and creativity, be it ever so humble. The deluded belief that intellectual industry is inner activity is especially fatal. It is merely the I-form tied to the physical body, particularly the brain which engages in such industry. The proper self of man, the spiritual I, is not involved.

In 1886, Rudolf Steiner, in his preface to the second volume of Goethe's scientific writings edited by him in the *Deutsche National-Literatur,* called attention to the extinction of courage and inner freedom in modern scientific thinking. Here he saw the origin of a new dogmatism added to that of the church. The 'dogma of experience' joined the 'dogma of revelation.' He said:

> It is true, we are able to list advances in all areas of culture. Yet it can hardly be claimed that these are advances *in depth.* And for the substance of an era, only the advances *in depth* are essential. One could characterize our age, however, by saying: it generally rejects advances in depth as inaccessible to the human being. We have become discouraged in all areas, particularly that of thinking and the will. In regard to thinking, we make endless observations, store them and lack the courage to shape them into a scientific conception of the whole of reality. German idealistic philosophy, on the other hand, is accused of being unscientific, for it has this courage. Today, people only want to see,* not think. All confidence in thinking has been lost. It is not considered sufficient to penetrate into the secrets of the world and life; one even foregoes any solution of the great riddles of existence. The only thing that is considered feasible is to bring the statements of experience into a system. People forget one thing, however: that this is to approach a standpoint long since held to be outmoded. In a deeper sense, the rejection of thinking and the insistence on experience is really nothing but the blind belief in revelations as held by religions. And that is simply based on the Church's delivering ready-made truths which people have to believe. Thinking may struggle to penetrate their deeper meaning but it is prohibited from *testing* the truth *on its own,* to penetrate the depths of the world through its own strength. And what does empirical

* What is meant here is to perceive physically.

> science demand of thinking? That it should listen to what the facts state and then interpret these statements, to bring them into order, and so on. Naturally, empirical science, too, forbids thinking to penetrate the core of the world. On one side, theology insists on the blind surrender of thinking to the demands of the church; on the other, science insists on blind surrender to the demands of sense observations. In neither instance does independent thinking that probes the depths count for anything.[65]

To have faith *in* thinking is the prerequisite for faith *within* thinking. And this 'faith within thinking,' which intensifies the power of thought through animating and training the soul — and extends knowledge to the point of awakening a new supersensory process of perceiving and knowing — this is what produces a Christian thinking in the first place. Speaking in Pauline terminology, it signifies the entrance of the Christ-impulse into man's thinking and insight.

Once we leave behind the old prejudices of carrying into all Bible reading the customary attitude of the contrast between faith and knowledge, of distrust towards thinking, we find that, everywhere, Paul's letters begin to speak joyfully and prophetically of the disenchantment, redemption and elevation that thinking can experience through the indwelling of the Resurrected One in the human soul:

> Take off the old nature with all its activities ... and put on the new nature, which, through the inner renewal, is growing into a knowledge that is in accordance with the archetypal world of its creator (Col.3:9f*B*).

The most solemn passage are sentences in which the great Hymn to Love culminates:

> Our knowledge is still a fragment and so is our prophetic sense; but when we come closer to the goal the fragment ceases to be ... For now we see in a mirror dimly ... But then we shall see face to face. Now my knowledge is patchwork; then I shall attain to true insight where perceiving and being perceived are one (1Cor.13:9-12*B*).

Their hymnal greatness notwithstanding, the words are meant to be understood in an exact, epistemological sense. The prevailing sensory and intellectual knowledge does not convey the object of perception in its true form. It merely transmits the external side — darkened replicas instead of the archetypes woven of light. This is why Plato compared our sense perceptions with the shadows cast by the actual objects against the wall of the cave in which we dwell. Not until the spirit-man awakens in us shall we begin to confront the world of true reality in our perception and knowledge. The tapestry of the senses, which is like a projection screen, becomes transparent. Then we shall be beings among beings, and no longer will what we have perceived be merely an object; simultaneously, it will be a subject of which we sense that it recognizes us. Instead of being confronted merely by the world's obscure shadow-images and reflections, we ourselves become the mirror in which the light-forms of the world of truth can reflect themselves as living beings. Perceiving turns into communion with the perceived.

The goal of humanity's evolution of consciousness ensouled and enthused Paul so completely that, again and again, we encounter the motif of the eventual unity between perceiver and perceived:

> If any one imagines that he knows something, he has not yet realized how true knowledge comes about. But if one loves God, one is known by him (1Cor.8:2f*B*).

And this extends to the words:

> But now the light-form *[gloria, doxa]* of the Lord is reflected in all of us with unveiled countenance, and we are all changed and become one with his likeness from one degree of illumined being to another (2Cor.3:18*B*).

It is not that there have never been any efforts made in the spiritual history of humanity for overcoming the chasm between faith and knowledge and the Christianization of thinking. Since the extinction of early Christian wisdom however — in particular the theological direction which could be called 'Pauline gnosticism' — it has no longer been the theologians but the outsiders and children of this world who struggled for a new ensouling and spiritualization of human insight. There were many during the era of Goethe who pointed with great emphasis to this goal and the necessities resulting from it. And Goethe himself was destined to take effective steps in this direction. Without employing Christian terminology, he aimed for and utilized, with marvellous results, a form of thinking and perception extending even into the field of natural science, in which we can recognize the beginnings of an actual Christ-permeation in the Pauline sense. He observed the organic world, before which mere reason has to fall short, for since it only comprehends the inorganic the secret of life eludes it. Mobilizing the inner creative power of the human spirit, Goethe developed *living* thoughts by bringing percept and concept so close to each other that he was able to say that if the archetypal plant or *Urpflanze,* which he beheld with his 'perceptive power of judgment' in all individual plants, were an 'idea,' then he indeed beheld this idea with his eyes.

Goethe's concepts sprang not from intellectual thinking but from a thinking originating from the whole human nature, something that was of importance particularly in his scientific work. It can be seen, particularly in this example, that proper participation of feeling and will in the act of thinking does not add anything arbitrary or wilful to knowledge. On the contrary, whereas intellectualism only too frequently contains rapier-like sharpness, here complete relaxation and harmony hold sway, since the thoughts themselves assume the character of perceptions. A 'pure,' 'living' thinking contains the concurrence of life and consciousness. The human being is so totally involved in this thinking that it can be said: his true genius thinks in his thinking. But here, the component of grace by far outweighs the component of achievement and the character of the act. The creative element in the act of thinking turns completely into *charis.* An artistic element works alongside thinking not infringing upon the results but elevating them. Something of the world's true essence becomes evident that is not found on the level of what can be measured or dissected. Indeed, as if from a concealed background, even a religious element enters the union of science and art, emerging clearly out of man's true ego-centre which, according to Paul, is the germinal nucleus of inner sonship. The reality of the encounter between subject and object is contained in it. Does a form of cognition which sees the archetypal plant in a plant and the eternal entity in earthly, physical man, not clear the way a little towards a truly Christian perception which would recognize the Christ in Jesus?

Following Goethe, Rudolf Steiner placed his whole life's work in the service of a rebirth of human knowledge. Through his epistemological writings (until 1900), he newly established *faith in thinking* by defining the true nature of thinking. In the abundance of what he subsequently gave to humanity as a researcher of the spirit (until 1925), either as direction for souls, as perception of the supersensory, or as realizations of cultural and social impulses, the concept of 'faith in thinking' came to fruition. A vista opened towards an unlimited elevation and expansion of human perception in the light of Christ.

The essential breakthrough, like a modern Paulinism, came early on in the philosophical writings of the years between 1880 and 1890, which — like Goethe's scientific writings — still abstained from the use of Christian terminology and a direct discussion of religious problems. Thinking was being rehabilitated. The senses merely perceive one half of the world, as it were, the half that is turned to the outside. In thinking lies the seed for a cognition of the other, spiritual half of reality. Even thinking as it exists today is more than a faculty for arranging sense perceptions and drawing conclusions from them. But it is demeaned when man no longer believes in it. Thinking therefore has forfeited awareness of itself. A thought conceived in awareness, hence 'with faith in it,' completes the world which, by itself, is unreal or at most half real, and makes it into total reality. Although initially shadowy, such a thought adds the spiritual half of the world which has slipped away from man to the sensory half which is, after all, merely the surface.

In the preface of 1886, quoted earlier, Rudolf Steiner writes:

> One who acknowledges that thinking possesses a perceptual ability extending beyond mere sensory perception is also forced to admit to objects lying beyond the reality accessible merely to the senses. These objects of thinking, however, are the *ideas*. As thinking takes hold of the idea, it fuses with the fundamental existence of the world. The element that is active outside enters the spirit of man. Man's spirit becomes *one* with objective reality in its

> highest potency. *Becoming aware of the idea in reality is the true communion of man.* In relation to the idea, thinking has the same significance as the eye has for light, the ear for sound. It is the organ of perception.[66]

The epistemology broached here in its beginnings is presented in detailed expositions in the books, *A Theory of Knowledge Based on Goethe's World Conception* (1886), *Truth and Science* (1892) and *The Philosophy of Freedom* (1894).

Much would be gained if it were recognized that the dividing line between faith and knowledge negates for a significant area of human life the redemptive effects that can proceed from the deed of Christ. People close their eyes to the fact that, in the age of the consciousness soul, human existence is determined more and more exclusively through consciousness. It lies in the nature of things that science, born of unbelief, claims to be able 'scientifically' to prove this unbelief. And so it comes about that in the domain of consciousness and perception, the 'scientifically proven' unbelief is in the end declared to be Christian.

Just as we fail to recognize the hidden Christian element of Goethe's form of perception, so the fundamentally unchristian element of Kant's philosophy is still not recognized. It is unbelief masked as science. The *Critique of Pure Reason* is correct in so far as it determines the relativity and narrowness of our sensory knowledge. By establishing the limits of knowledge for all time, however, from which follows the essential unknowableness of the 'thing in itself,' this work is blind to the creative ability of the liberated human ego, of the 'faith that can move mountains' and can grow and blossom in thinking.

Kantianism perpetuates pre-Christian conceptions developed in the Orient in times preceding the emergence of the ego, according to which the world spread out before our senses is the realm of *Maya,* the great illusion, through which the cognizing human spirit may not penetrate to reality. The old eastern spirituality which descends from the 'ancient Holy Spirit' of the paradisal period, but owing to the Fall is a darkened variation of it, could not know anything of the Christian impulse that theologians later groped for when they formulated the concept, *filioque,* ('and of the Son'). The tragedy, however, is that following the Christ-event, the evolution of consciousness and thinking within Christianity has still not assimilated this impulse. Where the separation of faith and knowledge is maintained as a matter of principle, as in Kant's case, the pre-Christian condition of human consciousness essentially continues unchanged. That Kant was designated 'the philosopher of Protestantism' marked the tragic alienation from Paul's thinking which, beginning with Luther, has clung to the Reformation. Luther, believing that he could cope with the devil of the approaching age of intellectualism age by chasing him away, turned it into a principle.

What the Orient tried to express when it declared the sensory world to be *Maya* is closely related to what the Bible calls 'sin.' Sin is not merely a power at work in man which drags him down morally. It has become objective following from the fact that when man 'ate of the Tree of Knowledge' he was also expelled from the paradise of truth. Sin drew an obscuring veil for him over the world's true nature when his outer eyes were opened. *Maya* is the objective consequence of the Fall. To believe, however, that through sin's obfuscation of his spiritual consciousness, man is finally and irrevocably placed before the curtain of illusion, would mean to deny the redemption that has come into the world through Christ. To be a Christian means to enkindle the heart's courage in thinking, the spark of faith which ignites to become the flame that burns away the curtain. By every word he spoke to the congregations, Paul tried to awaken this courage. 'For as through man death came into the world and into knowledge, so, by a man — if he but fills himself with the power of the *man* — the new life will be borne into the world and into knowledge' (in pursuance of 1Cor.15:21ff).

On many occasions, Rudolf Steiner described his work for the renewal and rebirth of man's perceptual life as the metamorphosis and continuation of Paulinism, suited for our time. Since we are dealing here with future tasks and perspectives of great import, we may refer to several relevant passages from his lectures:

> In all Eastern religions including Buddhism, you find the doctrine that proclaims the outer world to be Maya. So it

is, and in the East that is established as absolute truth. Paul knows of the same truth; he certainly asserts it emphatically. At the same time, however, Paul emphasizes that man does not see ... reality when he looks at what is outside him. Why is this? Because in his descent into matter he himself recast external reality into illusion. It is man himself, through his own act, who has made the outer world an illusion. Whether you call this the Fall, as the Bible does, or give it another name matters not. It is man's own fault that the outer world now appears as illusion. Eastern religions blame the gods for this. 'Beat your breast,' says Paul, 'for you have descended and thus so dimmed your vision that colour and sound no longer appear spiritual. Do you believe that colour and sound are materially existent? They are Maya! ... (But) what you have reduced to Maya, that you must restore within yourself. This you can do by taking into yourself the Christ force, which will show you the outer world in its reality.'

Here lies a great impulse for the life of western countries, a new impulse, which as yet is far from having been fully disseminated. What does the world know today of the fact that in one part of it an endeavour is actually being made to create a modern Pauline theory of knowledge? Such a theory could not affirm as Kant does that the thing-in-itself is incomprehensible. It must say: 'It lies within you, O man. Through what you now are, you are bringing about an untrue reality. You must yourself go through an inner process. Then will Maya be transformed into truth, into spiritual reality.'

The task of my books, *Truth and Knowledge* and *The Philosophy of Freedom,* was to put a theory of knowledge on a Pauline basis. Both these books are focused on what is the great achievement of the Pauline conception of man in the Western world.[67]

It is not the sense world that is incorrect but human perception which has been obscured by the Luciferic influence ... This is why Paul says, 'Do not stifle the joy in existence (as Buddha taught) but purify it ... This can be done by receiving the power of Christ into one's being which, when it penetrates the soul, takes away the darkness of soul ... Pass through your incarnation but pervade yourselves with the Christ, and in a distant future all illusions that man has brought about will have vanished ... Despite the nearly 2000 years that have passed since the Mystery of Golgotha, people today are only at the very beginning of receiving the Christ-impulse. Large areas of life are as yet not permeated by it, for example science and philosophy. It was much easier for Buddha to give his teachings for he based it on an ancient wisdom which was still sensed in his days. The Christ-impulse can only penetrate gradually. A theory of knowledge which is based on these facts sharply contrasts with that of Kant who is not at all aware that it is specifically our perception which must be purified.[68]

Kant said that the world is our mental picture, for the mental pictures we make of the world are formed according to the way we are organized ... This Kantianism is completely refuted in my books, *Truth and Knowledge* and *The Philosophy of Freedom* ... What is disclosed to us through our senses is not full reality, it is only *half* reality ... In the activity of forming mental pictures of the world we add, by means of thoughts, that which we suppressed through the body (thus completing reality for ourselves) ... The task of real knowledge and therefore real science is to turn half reality, i.e., semblance, into the complete reality. The world, as it first appears through our senses, is for us incomplete. This incompleteness is not due to the world *but to us,* and we, through our mental activity, restore it to full reality. These thoughts I venture to call *Pauline thoughts in the realm of epistemology.* For it is truly nothing else than Pauline epistemology, carried

> over into the realm of philosophical epistemology, that man, when he came into the world through the first Adam, beheld an inferior aspect of the world; its true form he would experience only in what he will become through Christ. Christianity can wait in philosophy, in epistemology. But the introduction of theological formulas into epistemology is not the point; what matters is the *kind* of thinking employed. I venture to say that, though my *Truth and Knowledge* and *The Philosophy of Freedom* are philosophic works, the Pauline spirit lives in them. A bridge can be built from this philosophy to the Christ Spirit ... As long as Kantianism prevails in philosophy, representing as it does a viewpoint that belongs to *pre*-Christian times, philosophy will continue to cloud the issue of Christianity.[69]

Paulinism is not a self-contained system but a living seed, a ferment of consciousness for the future of Christianity. It must begin to come forth in the age which Paul, as humanity's premature birth, represented ahead of time in the days of the Apostles. This age is the age of the consciousness soul, in the midst of which we find ourselves today. Where Paulinism is understood, taken in hand and developed further, it will essentially affect the spiritual awakening of a humanity sunk in the sleep of materialism. A mighty transformation of consciousness will also come to meet the growing and blossoming of this Paulinism. It is making itself felt today in its first, still tumultuous beginnings.

A new clairvoyance of the etheric world, the supersensory sphere closest to us, is trying to awaken in man so that it will be as if scales were falling from his eyes. As yet, the Ahrimanic spell of cold, illusory cleverness oppresses the soul. Then, however, a light similar to that which suddenly shone forth from within as Paul approached Damascus, will here and there free a number of people from darkness. With painful throes of destiny, the new consciousness will be born. Two thingswill then help humanity to discern what is going on around and in them. The first will be the properly understood message of Paul from the days of early Christianity. The second will be the anthroposophical life-work of Rudolf Steiner — the new, modern gift of the spiritual worlds and, at the same time, an advanced Paulinism.

We spoke of the fact that instead of referring to the stream of the Law proceeding from Moses, Paul linked up with the stream of consciousness flowing across from northern and western Europe into the Graeco-Roman culture. The higher voice speaking from the centre of man's inner being was a worldwide preparation for what Paul proclaimed from his Damascus experience, namely, that faith was to become the human force of courage facilitating Christ's indwelling in the human soul.

The new consciousness that is awakening to the spirit grows out of the intimate cooperation and unity between conscience and faith. Conscience turns into knowledge when the former has been fructified through faith in Christ.* In the lectures referred to above, dealing with 'The Origin of Conscience' and 'The Further Development of Conscience,' Rudolf Steiner reveals this future perspective of Paulinism:

> When we recall what has often been emphasized, that now, after the conclusion of Kali Yuga (the dark age), we are going through a transition in which new forces will have to be developed, we shall easily understand that we are moving toward [a new condition in the] development of conscience ... We have strongly and clearly emphasized the fact that we are advancing toward a new Christ event; the soul will become capable of perceiving the Christ by means of a certain etheric clairvoyance, and of re-experiencing in itself the event of Damascus ... What will happen regarding the experience of the development of consciousness in future epochs?[70]
>
> At a particular time conscience arose; before that it was altogether a different thing. It will be different again after man's soul has developed for some time in the light of conscience ... Paralleling the appearance of the Event of

* According to their root, the words for 'seeing' and 'knowing' are both contained in the Greek word for 'conscience' *syneidēsis:* 'knowing seeing,' 'seeing knowing.'

> Damascus, a great many people will experience something like the following in the course of the twentieth century. As soon as they have acted in some way, they will learn to contemplate their deed. They will become more thoughtful and will have an inner picture of the deed. Only a few will experience this at first but the numbers will increase during the next two or three thousand years. As soon as they have done something, a picture will be there. At first they will not know what it means, but those who have studied spiritual science will know: Here I have an image! It is not a dream ... it is a picture showing the karmic fulfilment of the act. One day what is pictured will take place as the fulfilment, the karmic balancing of what I have now done. This experience will begin in the twentieth century. Men will begin to develop the faculty of seeing before them pictures of far distant acts still to be accomplished ... Such faculties as this will become more frequent ...
>
> [This will come about] as the result of the soul having stood for some time in the light of conscience.[71]

The older form of conscience, which was a *reflecting* conscience, still tied to concepts of law and habits of duty, will change into a *previewing* one, a seed of a prophetic ability which in time will be able to decipher the etheric world which is illuminated by the light of the new closeness of Christ, just as we today decipher the world of sense perceptions.[72]

Rudolf Steiner gave many personal directions in order to point the way to Damascus for the consciousness soul which, at this point, is still unyielding and cool because of the one-sidedness of the head. In conclusion I shall speak of one of these directions which reduces the basic principle of Paulinism to a quite simple formula. In the lecture, 'The Mission of Devotion,'[73] devotion is described as the school in which the consciousness soul comes fully into its own. Thinking, which should evolve out of the consciousness soul from its one-sided characteristics to its full power and dignity, ready for an expansion of consciousness beyond the realm of sense perceptions, requires the proper cooperation of feeling and will. Love is the crowning of feeling, submission that of the will. Devotion is the confluence of love and submission. When, through genuinely and faithfully practised devotion, thinking can be aided to assume perceptual character so that it turns into vision, the redemption of thinking can take place. And the consciousness soul loses all cramped elements; thinking becomes devotion, and devotion, thinking; and perceiving, grace.

References

1 Steiner, 'Kunstgeschichte als Abbild innerer geistiger Impulse' (Oct 5, 1917).
2 William Wrede, *Paulus.*
3 Otto Etzold, *Die Botschaft des Römerbriefes.*
4 Bock, *Cäsaren und Apostel,* Chapter 1.
5 Steiner, *The Gospel of St Mark* (Sep 16, 1912). See also the corresponding chapters in *Kings and Prophets.*
6 Steiner, 'Jeshu ben Pandira' (Nov 5, 1911).
7 Bock, *The Three Years:* 'The Raising of Lazarus.'
8 Steiner, 'Easter: The Festival of Warning' (April 2, 1920).
9 Steiner, 'Whitsun: The Festival of the Free Individuality' (May 15, 1910).
10 Steiner, 'Easter: The Festival of Warning' (April 2, 1920).
11 Bock, *Kindheit und Jugend Jesu:* 'Nazareth and Nazarene Life.'
12 Bock, *Cäsaren und Apostel:* 'The Pharisees and Jewish Hellenism.'
13 Bock, *The Three Years:* 'Apollonius of Tyana.'
14 Steiner: *The Gospel of St John and its Relation* (July 7, 1909).
15 Steiner, *The Gospel of St Luke* (Sep 15, 1909).
16 Beheim-Schwarzbach, *Paulus* p.30f.
17 Deissmann, *Paulus,* first edition, p.148.
18 Concerning the passage from the fourth chapter of the Letter to the Galatians here discussed, see Steiner, *Deeper Secrets of Human History* (Nov 23, 1909).
19 Bock, *Genesis,* p. 135ff and *Moses,* 'The Mystery Centre of Jethro.'
20 Frieling, *Von Bäumen, Brunnen und Steinen.*
21 Steiner, *The Principle of Spiritual Economy* (April 11, 1909).
22 Detailed descriptions concerning this scene as well as the interconnections of Moses' mission, which are only alluded to here, are contained in *Moses.*
23 See Chapter 10, 'Trial and Martyrdom.'
24 Steiner, *Christ and the Spiritual World* (Dec 31, 1913).
25 Bock, *Kings and Prophets,* Chapter 28.
26 See, for example, Friedrich Zucker, *Syneidesis — Conscientia,* Jena 1928.
27 Steiner, *The Christ-Impulse* (May 2, 1910).
28 Steiner, *Metamorphoses of the Soul* (May 5, 1910).

29 Steiner, *The Christ-Impulse* (May 2, 1910).
30 Steiner, *The Christ-Impulse* (May 8, 1910).
31 Steiner, *Metamorphoses of the Soul* (May 5, 1910).
32 Bock, *Cäsaren und Apostel,* 'The Easter-Experience of James.'
33 Bock, *Cäsaren und Apostel,* 'The Cenacle.'
34 Deissmann, *Paulus,* second edition, p. 174 ff.
35 Beheim-Schwarzbach, *Paulus,* p. 55.
36 Bock, *The Three Years,* 'The Miracles of Apollonius.'
37 See Chapter 18, 'Pistis and Gnosis: Faith and Knowledge.'
38 Steiner, *Theosophy of the Rosicrucians* (June 6, 1907).
39 Steiner, *Ursprungsimpulse der Geisteswissenschaft* (March 25, 1907).
40 Bock, *Cäsaren und Apostel.*
41 Bock, *Cäsaren und Apostel,* the chapters on Sadducees and Pharisees.
42 *Epistolae Senecae ad Paulum et Pauli ad Senecam.*
43 Steiner, *The Bhagavad Gita* (Dec 30, 1912).
44 Deissmann, *Paulus* second edition, p.5 and 9ff.
45 Bock, *Cäsaren und Apostel,* 'Griechentum.'
46 Steiner, 'Where do I find the Christ?' (Oct 16, 1918).
47 Steiner, *From Jesus to Christ* (Oct 9, 1911).
48 Steiner, *From Jesus to Christ* (Oct 10, 1911).
49 Steiner, *From Jesus to Christ* (Oct 12, 1911).
50 Bock, *Genesis,* page 16ff.
51 Gorion, *Sagen der Juden* I, and *Genesis,* p. 66.
52 Steiner, *Christ and the Spiritual World* (March 5, 1914); *Vorstufen zum Mysterium von Golgatha* (March 5, 7, 30, and June 1, 1914); Bock, *Kindheit und Jugend Jesu,* 'Three pre-earthly Christ-events.'
53 Details in Bock, *Kindheit und Jugend Jesu.*
54 Steiner, *The Bhagavad Gita* (Jan 1, 1913).
55 A spirited compilation of the more important theologians who have interceded for a more comprehensive understanding of Paul is given by the Protestant theologian, Dilschneider, in his booklet, *Die gefesselte Kirche.*
56 Steiner, 'Where do I find the Christ?' (Oct 16, 1918).
57 Dilschneider, *Die gefesselte Kirche.*
58 Steiner, *The Bridge between Universal Spirituality* (Dec 17–19, 1920).
59 Steiner, *Occult Science, an Outline,* p. 40–42.
60 Bock, *The Apocalypse of Saint John,* Chapter 7.
61 Bock, *Michaelisches Zeitalter.*
62 See Chapter 9, p. 174f.
63 Steiner, *The Gospel of St John and its Relation* (June 30, 1909).
64 Bock, *Moses.*

65 Steiner, Preface to Volume 2 of Goethe's natural-scientific works.
66 Steiner, Preface to Volume 2 of Goethe's natural-scientific works.
67 Steiner, *The Christ Impulse* (May 8, 1910).
68 Steiner, 'The Event of the Christ-Appearance in the Etheric World' (Feb 27, 1910).
69 Steiner, *The Karma of Materialism* (Sep 4, 1917).
70 Steiner, *The Christ Impulse* (May 2, 1910).
71 Steiner, *The Christ Impulse* (May 8, 1910).
72 Hiebel, *Paulus und die Erkenntnislehre der Freiheit,* p. 88f.
73 Steiner, *Metamorphoses of the Soul* (Oct 28, 1909).

Bibliography

Beheim-Schwarzbach, Martin, *Paulus. Der Weg des Apostles,* 2 ed Hamburg 1947.

Bock, Emil, *The Apocalypse of Saint John,* Floris, Edinburgh 1986.

——, *Cäsaren und Apostel,* Urachhaus, Stuttgart 1978.

——, *Genesis,* Floris Books, Edinburgh 1983.

——, *Kindheit und Jugend Jesu,* Urachhaus, Stuttgart 1988.

——, *Kings and Prophets,* Floris Books, Edinburgh 1989.

——, *Michaelisches Zeitalter,* Urachhaus, Stuttgart 1979.

——, *Moses,* Floris Books, Edinburgh 1986.

——, *The Three Years,* Floris Books, Edinburgh 1987.

Deissmann, Adolf, *Licht vom Osten. Das Neue Testament und die neuentdeckten Texte der hellenistisch-römischen Welt,* 4 ed Tübingen 1923. (Tr: *Light from the ancient East,* London 1910.)

——, *Paulus, eine kultur- und reisegeschichtliche Skizze,* Tübingen 1911. (Tr: *St Paul. A Study in Social and Religious History,* London 1912.)

——, *Paulus,* 2 ed Tübingen 1925.

Dilschneider, Otto, *Die gefesselte Kirche,* Stuttgart 1953.

Epistolae Senecae ad Paulum et Pauli ad Senecam (quae vocantur) ed. Claude W. Barlow, American Academy in Rome, 1938.

Etzold, Otto, *Gehorsam des Glaubens, die Botschaft des Römerbriefes an die heutige Christenheit,* Gütersloh 1947.

Frieling, Rudolf, *Von Bäumen, Brunnen und Steinen in den Erzväter-geschichten,* reprinted in *Studien zum alten Testament,* Urachhaus, Stuttgart 1983. (Tr: *Old Testament Studies,* Floris, Edinburgh 1987.)

Goethe, Johann Wolfgang, natural scientific works in *Deutsche National-Literatur,* published by Joseph Kürschner.

Gorion, Josef ben *Die Sagen der Juden,* Frankfurt a.M. 1913–27.

Hiebel, Friedrich, *Paulus und die Erkenntnislehre der Freiheit.*

Steiner, Rudolf, *The Bhagavad Gita and the Epistles of Paul,* Anthroposophic, New York 1971.

——, *The Bridge Between Universal Spirituality and the Physical Constitution of Man,* Anthroposophic, New York 1958.

——, *Christ and the Spiritual World – The Search for the Holy Grail,* Steiner Press, London 1983.

——, *Christianity as Mystical Fact,* Steiner Press, London 1972.

——, *The Christ-Impulse and the Development of Ego-Consciousness,* Anthroposophic, New York 1976.
——, *Deeper Secrets of Human History in the light of the Gospel of St Matthew,* Steiner Press, London 1985.
——, 'Easter: The Festival of Warning' in *The Festivals and their Meaning,* Steiner Press, Bristol 1992.
——, 'The Event of the Christ-Appearance in the Etheric World' in *The Reappearance of Christ in the Etheric,* Anthroposophic, New York 1983.
——, *From Jesus to Christ,* Steiner Press, Sussex 1991.
——, *Goethes Naturwissenschaftlichen Schriften (Einleitungen),* Steiner Verlag, Dornach 1987.
——, *The Gospel of St John and Its Relation to the Other Three Gospels,* Anthroposophic, New York 1982.
——, *The Gospel of St Luke,* Steiner Press, London 1988.
——, *The Gospel of St Mark,* Anthroposophic, New York 1986.
——, 'Jeshu ben Pandira' in *Esoteric Christianity and the Mission of Christian Rosenkreutz,* Steiner Press, London 1984.
——, *The Karma of Materialism,* Anthroposophic, New York 1985.
——, *Kunstgeschichte als Abbild innerer geistiger Impulse,* Steiner Verlag, Dornach 1981.
——, *Metamorphoses of the Soul,* Steiner Press, London 1983.
——, *Occult Science an Outline,* Anthroposophic, New York 1985.
——, *The Philosophy of Spiritual Activity: A Philosophy of Freedom,* Steiner Press, Bristol 1992.
——, *The Principle of Spiritual Economy,* Anthroposophic, New York 1986.
——, 'Spiritual Bells of Easter II' in *The Festivals and their Meaning,* Steiner Press, London 1981.
——, *A Theory of Knowledge Based on Goethe's World Conception,* Anthroposophic, New York 1968.
——, *Theosophy of the Rosicrucians,* Steiner Press, London 1981.
——, *Truth and Knowledge,* Steinerbooks, New York 1981.
——, *Ursprungsimpulse der Geisteswissenschaft,* Steiner Verlag, Dornach 1989.
——, *Vorstufen zum Mysterium von Golgatha,* Steiner Verlag, Dornach 1990.
——, 'Where do I find the Christ?' in *Der Tod als Lebenswandlung,* Steiner Verlag, Dornach 1986.
——, 'Whitsun: The Festival of the Free Individuality' in *The Festivals and their Meaning,* Steiner Press, Bristol 1992.
Werfel, Franz, *Paulus unter den Juden,* Berlin 1926. (Tr: *Paul among the Jews. A tragedy,* London 1928.)
Wrede, William, *Paulus,* Halle 1904.
Zucker, Friedrich, *Syneidesis – Conscientia,* Jena 1928.

Index of biblical references

Index

GENERAL THEOLOGICAL SEMINARY
NEW YORK